The Last
Pioneer

The Last

Pioneer

John Taylor,

a Mormon Prophet

by Samuel W. Taylor

SIGNATURE BOOKS ❧ SALT LAKE CITY

LIBRARY OF CONGRESS CATALOGING-IN-PUBLICATION DATA
Taylor, Samuel Woolley
[Kingdom or nothing]
The last pioneer : John Taylor, a Mormon prophet / by Samuel W. Taylor.
p.   cm.
Originally published: The kingdom or nothing. New York : Macmillan, c1976.
Includes bibliographical references and index.
ISBN 1-56085-115-5 (pbk.)
1. Taylor, John, 1808-1887.   2. Mormon Church—Presidents—Biography.
3. Church of Jesus Christ of Latter-day Saints—Presidents—Biography.
4. Mormon Church—History—19th century.   5. Church of Jesus Christ of
Latter-day Saints—History—19th century.   I. Title.
BX8695.T3T39   1998
289.3'092—dc21
[B]   98-4090
CIP

To my collaborator,
Raymond W. Taylor

Contents

Introduction

THE STORY of the Great Basin is a vital segment of western Americana; yet it has never been told. The Great Basin is, of course, Mormon country. Rather amazingly, despite all that has been published about the Latter-day Saints, the complete saga of their pioneer period simply hasn't been put between the covers of any one book.[1] Works on the subject seem either to fragment the story or to mire it in the proselyting effort. As a result, we have three distinct concepts of pioneer Mormonism, none complete.

To the outside world, the pioneer story means Brigham Young, polygamy, and colonization of the Great Basin. To Mormons, the vital story is of Joseph Smith, founder and prophet of the faith (and the less said about polygamy the better).[2] The third version is the proselyting concept so vigorously presented by the far-flung missionary system; it is a mixture of doctrine and mythology, only incidentally historical.

Unfortunately for biographers, neither the life of Joseph Smith nor Brigham Young spans the pioneer period. Joseph was killed when the Saints were still in Illinois. Brigham brought the faithful to Utah and for thirty years carried on the long war between the Mormons and the Gentile world. He died, however, on the very eve of the climactic struggle, which lasted another decade.

---

[1] I am speaking of trade books for general circulation in the "Gentile" world. Such works as Orson F. Whitney's *History of Utah*, and B. H. Roberts' *Comprehensive History of the Church*, are faith-promoting works for internal readership.

[2] Mormon apologists have gone to astounding lengths to sweep plural marriage under the historical rug. Preston Nibley, for example, wrote a 552-page biography of Brigham Young without mentioning that the man had more than one wife.

John Taylor, a contemporary of both Joseph and Brigham, played a leading role during fifty-one violent years of pioneer history. He became leader of the Saints upon Brigham's death and was in command during the final decade of the long war. Taylor's death marked the end of the original concept of Mormonism, the grand plan for the impossible ideal. Modern Mormonism began under new leadership. He was, quite literally, the last pioneer, the final man in authority to represent the old era.

I would like to acknowledge the contribution of my collaborator, brother, and best friend, Raymond W. Taylor. This really should be his book, not mine. He had a lifelong ambition to write the biography of John Taylor. I agreed to act in an advisory capacity. Raymond's literary style, however, was what he himself called "reformed Egyptian" (the language of the golden plates from which the Book of Mormon was translated). Since I didn't have Joseph Smith's gift of translation, we decided on a collaboration, he to do the research, me to write. He certainly did his end of the bargain, flooding me with twice the material that was possible to use.

This, then, is not my book. It is our book. Except for circumstance, it would have been Raymond's book.

SAMUEL W. TAYLOR
Redwood City, California

I

The Strange Death
of Brigham Young

A BLUE-BOTTLE FLY buzzed in the muggy heat of the Church Office
building as John Taylor worked at the pile of old ledgers. A fastidious
man, Taylor had removed his Prince Albert coat and white vest and
turned back the stiff cuffs to dig through musty financial records dating
back thirty years. Though windows were open, the curtains hung limp;
no breath of air stirred in Salt Lake City this blisteringly hot Wednesday
afternoon of August 29, 1877. In the oppressive heat there was a muted
air of apprehensive expectancy.

Through the curtains Taylor could see the guards stationed within the
nine-foot cobblestone wall enclosing Brigham Young's estate. From beyond the wall came the hushed murmur of the crowd that filled South
Temple Street. Thousands were gathered for the news that might come
at any moment. He could see rows of faces pressed at the gaps of the
heavy picket gates leading to the Lion House, Church Office, and Beehive
House, eyes peering through, waiting.

Brigham Young was dying. For a period of seven days the Lion of the
Lord had fought his last great battle. He lay now in the Lion House,
attended by four doctors and intimates of his family. As President Young
sank, there was intense interest in Utah Territory, and, in fact, speculation throughout the world as to his successor. Who would fill the shoes
of the man who had led his people to the Great Basin, built a desert
empire, and ruled it with an iron hand for three decades? Who *could*?
Brigham's successor would face formidable problems. The church was

drained white by the long war between the Mormons and the United States government. Except in Utah, where the Saints clutched at the desperate faith that God would somehow save them, their defeat was considered inevitable. A Gentile minority had for years blocked the Mormon attempt to gain statehood for Utah, and the Territory was ruled by political hacks from Washington. Internally, the church was being torn apart by the struggle over polygamy, tenaciously fostered by the leadership but repugnant to the great body of the Saints. It was freely predicted that Brigham Young's death would mean disintegration of the church.

There were several rival claims to succession, but John Taylor, president of the Quorum of the Twelve Apostles, believed that he should emerge the new leader. For thirty-three years he had lived in Brigham's shadow, obedient to counsel from a man he despised and who heartily detested him in return. Now he was determined that no pretender should usurp his rightful place in the sun—particularly since this was, he believed, the Lord's will.

During the past week, as he worked on the ledgers, Taylor had received periodic reports of Young's condition. The end could come at any time.

Though to the outside world the image of Brigham Young had remained that of the hearty leader in his prime, the faithful flock had been aware, over the past decade, that his vitality had dwindled. His cane was no longer an article of dress, but an aid to a gait that had become progressively unsteady; he used both cane and crutch during rheumatic attacks. Photographers had learned the best camera angle—three-quarter left profile, lens low to emphasize the firm mouth and jaw—and their work of recent years displayed careful retouching; a recent picture at seventy-six showed firmer skin tone and fewer lines about the eyes than photographs of twenty years previously. The resonant voice, which he formerly had projected without effort to outdoor audiences of thousands at the old Bowery, had become reedy, and, when he was over-tired, so thin that the audience within the acoustic marvel of the New Tabernacle strained to catch his words.

Brigham hadn't really been well since his sudden and violent sickness four months earlier when he attended the dedication of the St. George Temple in southern Utah. Taylor and other church officials were also felled with acute attacks of vomiting and purging. There were whispers of possible poisoning in connection with the Mountain Meadows affair. John D. Lee had been executed on the site nearby just the previous month. Emotions were high. Publication of Lee's *Confessions* had inflamed the nation.[1]

---

[1] Twenty years previously, Mormons and Indians massacred more than a hundred members of a California-bound wagon company, slaughtering everyone except young children, while the party was camped at Mountain Meadows. The event took place

During the summer Brigham refused to allow his physical debility to interfere with church and business interests. Then on Thursday afternoon, August 23, he began vomiting. He attended a meeting in the early evening, but on returning home was seized with an attack of what his physicians termed cholera morbus. While some attributed this to overindulgence in a supper of green corn and peaches, Taylor again wondered if there had been foul play.[2]

Brigham was wracked by vomiting and purging throughout the night.

---

during the hysteria of the Utah War. Brigham Young tried to keep the lid on, blaming the event entirely on Indians; but the truth seeped out—Indians wouldn't have spared the children.

After two decades the Gentile clamor for justice finally had to be satisfied, and John D. Lee became the scapegoat—although he wasn't the leader and was no more guilty than some fifty-five other Mormons involved. After two trials, Lee was convicted; he was executed on the site of the massacre.

See Juanita Brooks, The *Mountain Meadows Massacre*; also her *John Doyle Lee— Pioneer—Builder—Scapegoat.* Her work did much to aid the century-long struggle of the Lee family to clear his name. On April 20, 1961, the Mormon Church officially authorized "the re-instatement to membership and former blessings of John D. Lee."

[2] Ninety-three years after Brigham Young's death, the author submitted the report of the physicians attending Brigham's last sickness to a prominent Sacramento, California physician, Dr. Max L. Dimick, asking him to comment on the possibility that Young was poisoned. After studying the report and consulting with pathologists, Dr. Dimick replied:

"What you would like to know is who had access to his lunch that day. It must have been arsenic and it had to be acute rather than chronic poisoning."

He enclosed an article, "Inorganic Arsenic" (from The *Pharmacological Basis of Therapeutics* by Louis S. Goodman and Alfred Gilman), saying, "Read the enclosed on arsenic poisoning and I'm sure you will agree the picture fits." A few infections, such as "typhoid fever, paratyphoid, or bacillary dysentery," could "produce a profound and devastating enteritis" such as Brigham had; however, he said, "in such case he should have been ill over a prolonged period of time."

As for cholera—"forget it."

The article points out that arsenic was the "popular poisoning agent of the Middle Ages and remained in favor with criminals until early in the twentieth century. Many factors combined to give rise to this popularity. Arsenic was easy to obtain. The symptoms could be made to develop insidiously and to simulate disease. Arsenic compounds have little taste and, consequently, could easily be administered in food without detection."

Its use declined following discovery of improved methods of detecting its presence in the victim.

Although an arsenic compound was popularly used as an embalming fluid at the time of Brigham's death, Dr. Dimick suggested, "If there was a fragment of bone or a hank of hair to check for arsenic it might be revealing." He quoted pathologists to the effect that as a poison arsenic would be carried into the bones and hair of the living organism, but that after death embalming fluid wouldn't be.

Previous attempts on Brigham's life were mentioned in his obituary in the *Deseret News*: "Like all great men, he has had bitter enemies. . . . His life has been frequently sought. The bullet and the knife of the assassin have been prepared to shed his heart's blood. . . ."

At five the next morning the doctors injected opiates to relieve muscle spasms in his legs. During the day and most of Friday night he was in continuous pain, though he bore it stoically, and even made light of the concern of his family with "humorous remarks." Toward morning the symptoms eased, and Brigham enjoyed the first sleep since the onset of his illness.

If he realized the end was near, he was unperturbed. Brigham Young had unshaken faith in the hereafter and in his own position in the celestial glory. He had previously prepared detailed instructions for his funeral, noting everything from the type of casket ("I want my coffin made of plump 1¼ inch redwood boards, not scrimped in length") to the attire of family mourners ("I wish . . . the male members to wear no crape . . . the females to buy no black bonnets, nor black dresses, nor black veils . . .").

On Saturday morning Brigham's pain went away, and for about twelve hours he seemed to be convalescing. But by mid-afternoon his abdomen began to swell. This was diagnosed as the dreaded "inflamation of the bowels," almost invariably fatal. The four doctors reported that the condition gave rise to "a poisoning of the blood, from the pressure of the swelled bowels, causing a prevention of return currents of the circulation to the heart and lungs." To ease the suffering, the doctors gave Young opium. During Sunday and Monday he also received a mixture of milk and brandy, a spoonful every half hour, and a teaspoon of ice water between times. In addition to medication, various brethren frequently administered faith healing.

Although he sank into a semi-comatose condition Monday evening, he rallied during the night, and, enlisting help from attendants, got out of bed twice. Then he had a relapse and sank down, apparently lifeless. Doctors kept the vital processes functioning by artificial respiration, coupled with hot poultices over the heart, for nine hours.

A telegram went out to presidents of stakes, advising them that President Young's condition was very low. This was the first public acknowledgement of Brigham's sickness, and all of Utah was stunned. Soon there was another wire:

HAVE ALL THE PRAYER CIRCLES IN YOUR STAKES MEET AS OFTEN AS THEY CAN AND PRAY FOR PRESIDENT YOUNG UNTIL OTHERWISE ADVISED.

John W. Young administered the ordinances for the sick, calling upon the Almighty to restore his father, and Brigham revived sufficiently to say, "Amen." When the young man asked hopefully, "Do you know me, Father?" Brigham's lips formed the shadow of a wry smile as he replied tartly, "I should think I ought to." Then he declared that he felt better and wished to rest.

The doctors reported:

This condition remained until about eight in the evening, when partial prostration again ensued and his case was considered exceedingly critical by the attending physicians, Drs. S. B. Young, W. F. Anderson, J. M. Benedict, and F. D. Benedict. After consultations an entire filling up of the lower part of the bowels by injection was determined upon, for the purpose of creating an action through the alimentary canal, but was not persevered in, on account of fainting symptoms, and the patient objecting to the treatment, which caused him to cry out with pain. He passed the night in a semi-comatose state.

On Wednesday morning symptoms of approaching dissolution were plainly evident.

That afternoon as John Taylor worked on the old ledgers in the Church Office building adjoining the Lion House, the clock began to strike. Four P.M. He shut the books with a sigh. From rough calculation, he had estimated that approximately a million dollars credited to Brigham Young's estate actually belonged to the church. The person who undertook to straighten out the tangled affairs of the last thirty years would be in for a sticky wicket.

He arose, stretching to his full height, a fraction under six feet, and shrugged the kinks from his shoulders. He had gone gray early, and now, at sixty-eight, his wavy thatch was gleaming white, as was the short beard beneath his chin—a vivid contrast to his deep tan. Work on his farm, brisk daily walks, upkeep of his wives' homes on Taylor Row had kept him trim and muscular, in better shape than most men half his age.

At the commode he rinsed the grime of the old books from his hands and was fastening the heavy gold cuff links when George Q. Cannon came in. His stricken eyes told Taylor the news before his fellow apostle spoke: Brigham Young was dead. In a hushed voice Cannon said that Brother Brigham's spirit had departed at one minute past four o'clock; his last intelligible words being of the prophet, Joseph Smith, "Joseph . . . Joseph . . . Joseph."

Taylor had a strange sense of loss, as if a sturdy prop had been kicked from under him. He felt scant grief at Brigham's death—he had clashed with him for forty years—yet they had worked together in the Lord's vineyard, each respecting the other's abilities while disliking his personality. Brigham had valued the potency of Taylor's pen in the long war against the world, calling him "the strongest editor who ever wrote," while Taylor had vast respect for Brigham's ability as an administrator. Now there was a void. During four decades Taylor hadn't been nearly so concerned with accounting to his Maker as of meriting the hard-won approval of the man who disliked him. Now Brigham was gone; Taylor had lost a valiant *confrère* whose frank antagonism had always been a spur.

While discussing funeral arrangements with Cannon, Taylor reminded him that any rumor of foul play in Brigham's death must be refuted. Cannon agreed; to squelch whispers that were going around he would publish the report of the attending physicians in the *Deseret News*. Taylor suggested that the report should also state that Brigham was entirely free of narcotics at the end. It shouldn't appear that the church president died full of dope.

Cannon hurried out. Taylor took hat and stick (his "rascal-beater") and left the office, pausing at the guardhouse while two burly sentries swung the gate open to admit newspapermen. To their questions he said he would make no comment beyond the account in the *Deseret News*.

As he passed out the heavy gate and through the dazed crowd in the street toward Elizabeth Kaighin's home, he was aware of being followed. Elizabeth, his first plural, had been his "official" wife since the death of his first wife, Leonora Cannon, nine years ago. Deputy U.S. Marshal Samuel H. Gilson considered John Taylor a widower with no wives at all, and, while Gilson couldn't prove that Taylor wasn't "legally" married to Elizabeth, he did his level best to make sure that Taylor didn't visit his five other wives for so much as a matter of minutes. This would be *prima facie* evidence of unlawful cohabitation, an offense in Utah Territory for which the United States Congress had passed increasingly stringent penalties. His six living wives were respectable women with families, all past childbearing age except the youngest, Margaret. To be deprived of the company of his families was a galling and almost intolerable situation for Taylor.

But, as he glanced back at the two deputies shadowing him, a pixie smile twisted the corners of his lips. What Sam Gilson didn't know was that in addition to his six known wives he had at least nine others unsuspected by Gilson and unknown even in church circles (in fact, the exact number of women he had married was a secret between himself and God).[3]

On Friday evening Taylor attended a private viewing of the remains at the Lion House, the residence of about a dozen of Brigham's families (the number fluctuated). The dining hall in the basement normally seated about fifty for each meal. There were twenty bedrooms on the upper floor for older children and childless wives; the main floor had apartments for wives with youngsters. Other wives had homes at various locations. The legal wife, Mary Ann Angell, called "Mother Young," lived east of Eagle Gate in the White House. She had presented Brigham with his three favorite sons: Joseph, Young Briggie, and John W. The spirited beauty Harriet Amelia Folsom, the infatuation of the prophet's old age,

---

[3] See list of John Taylor's wives and notes relating to the "lesser-known" ones. Brigham Young University, Special Collections.

planned to live across the street from the Beehive House in the ornate mansion under construction dubbed "Amelia's Palace." The rebellious Ann Eliza Webb had divorced him, written a book about polygamy called *Wife No. 19*, and was now traveling about the country lecturing on the secrets and horrors of Mormonism.

The casket, banked high with flowers, was on view in the large parlor on the main floor. The wives and families were stationed beside it in patriarchal order. Mother Young was on its right with her family; Lucy Decker, the first plural, was on the left; the remainder of the family took places in strict order of seniority.

Taylor knew Lucy Decker better than many of the others because she was mistress of the structural complex, connected by hallways, comprising the Lion House, President's Office, and the Beehive House (which was Brigham's residence). At fifty-five she was a handsome woman with clear white skin, large brown eyes, and a melting smile that revealed two delicate dimples. As her husband's official hostess she had radiated warmth and charm befitting her station.

Taylor shook hands and offered a quiet word of condolence to the family members and to a number of black-clad women who had no place in the family grouping. These were wives of the dead church president, whose existence was unknown and unsuspected among the Saints, and, in fact, among the other wives. Ann Eliza Webb had called herself "wife number 19" yet her book would have been more accurate had she known enough about her husband's family—she was number 51.[4]

In shaking hands with the male members of the Young family, Taylor's manner was marked by reserve, particularly in the cases of John W. and Young Briggie. His long-standing feud with their father had rubbed off on them, and their resemblance to Brigham, in looks and manner, would have alienated Taylor even without the rivalry for succession. Both were big men; Young Briggie, at forty, bore a striking resemblance to his father as Taylor remembered him at Nauvoo, though much heavier than Brigham had been at that age. John W., though only thirty-two, appeared middle-aged because of his girth.

Eliza R. Snow sat a bit apart, a slight and fragile figure resembling a piece of Dresden china in the black silk dress with lace trim. Taylor greeted her with genuine warmth. She was the widow of both Joseph Smith and Brigham Young, venerated as the first lady of Mormondom. As president of the Relief Society she held the highest office open to women; she had written some of the church's most-loved hymns and was considered its poet laureate. Taylor had known her during forty violent years as the Saints were driven from place to place—Kirtland, Far West,

---

[4] John J. Stewart published a list of fifty-three wives of Brigham Young in *The Glory of Mormonism*. Stewart's material was based on research by Stanley S. Ivins.

Nauvoo, Winter Quarters, the Great Basin—and they shared literary interests; as editor of the Nauvoo *Neighbor* and *Times and Seasons*, he had published some of Eliza R. Snow's best poems.

Most of Taylor's wives, both known and secret, arrived for the viewing. His greeting to them was formal, no word or gesture that might provide gossip or offer testimony in a court of law; one never knew who might be a traitor, spy, or informer, even in a group like this.

It was a frustrating situation, because in order to live the Principle correctly he should have been able to bring his wives together in harmony as sisters in the great patriarchal family. But that fond dream would have to await the hereafter.

Railroads ran special excursions from all over Mormon country. The city by the Great Salt Lake was jam-packed with more people than had ever assembled before, and every train disgorged more.

Taylor was occupied with preparations for the funeral until after ten the next day. When he left the tabernacle the waiting queue stretched across Temple Square, out the south gate, and alongside the wall almost to Main Street. The tabernacle would remain open throughout the day and night until an hour before the funeral to give some 25,000 souls the opportunity to have a last glimpse at their beloved leader.

He returned to the Church Office with the *Tribune* under his arm. While many Saints refused to read this scurrilous rag, Taylor recognized that it was well-written; he also felt that it was a mistake to ignore what the enemy said. He was at his desk scanning the paper when Lucy Decker came in and invited him out to the courtyard for composition tea.

As he stirred cream and sugar into the weird brew,[5] she asked if he'd seen the *Trib*'s front-page story: "JOHN W. YOUNG"? Taylor admitted that it made highly interesting reading.

The story said that instructions left by Brigham would be read at the funeral services, and that

> among those instructions will be the election of First Counselor John W. Young to the prophetic throne. . . . The Young dynasty is to be continued, and the Twelve, who are assigned to be head of the church after the death of their inspired founder, will again be relegated to a subordinate position.

Taylor assured her that no such action would take place. No such instructions would be read. John W. Young would not speak at the funeral. He himself would be the last speaker and in a position to rebuke any attempts to discuss succession until the proper time. Talks would be

---

[5] The concoction was composed of various leaves and spices. See *Brigham Young at Home*, by Clarissa Young Spencer and Mabel Harmer.

short; the speakers had been counseled to emphasize that this was the Lord's church, not the church of any one man or faction. Every effort would be made to prevent the scattering of the people among various self-proclaimed prophets, as had occurred at Nauvoo upon the death of Joseph Smith.

That night, Taylor lay awake in the muggy heat. He was president of the Quorum of Twelve Apostles, the same office occupied by Brigham Young when Joseph Smith died. Therefore . . . but . . . on the other hand . . .

Suddenly, about midnight, there was the flash of lightning, then a tremendous clap of thunder. This was followed by pelting rain that rattled the shingles. He thought of the thousands of people, in the queue to view the remains, scattering for shelter. The air turned chilly; the storm had broken the heat wave and settled his anxiety. This was the Lord's church, and He would guide it. John Taylor went to sleep amid the violence of the thunderstorm.

Morning broke bright and cool; the rain had settled the dust. A better day couldn't have been arranged for laying Brigham Young to rest. When Taylor passed through the fortress gate at ten-thirty he found the sidewalks roped off along the route of the funeral procession, and the crowd was already pressed against the ropes. They would have to wait another two hours, if there was no delay in schedule.

Temple Square was packed. Recognizing him, the crowd made way. Entering the tabernacle, he took his seat on the rostrum behind the lectern, the area reserved for general authorities. The balcony, open to the general public, had been full since dawn; in fact, many had been there all night to be sure of a seat.

Behind him were the reserved seats of the choir; to his right the front platform was reserved for the city council, the glee club, and the band, behind them the high council of Salt Lake Stake and visiting high councils; on his left were seated bishops and counselors. The first rows of the main floor were reserved for the family of the deceased. Various sections behind the family seated the seventies, high priests, elders, and lesser priesthoods.

The main floor filled slowly, as those authorized to enter struggled through the crowd outside. During the delay, the orchestra and organ provided prelude music, George Careless conducting. As a special feature, Joseph Daynes played his own composition, *Brigham Young's Funeral March*, on the great pipe organ.

The ceiling of the dome was looped with strands of flowers, a massive center piece depending from their midst. The columns supporting the balcony were covered with wreaths, festooned from column to column, and pendant basket bouquets. Decorations embellished the organ, the stand, and the entire front of the platform. The casket itself was surrounded by an impressive floral display. Nothing had been spared to make this the grandest and most memorable funeral the Territory had ever seen.

At noon, an hour behind schedule, the casket was closed and services began with a song by the choir. As planned, speakers were brief. They confined their remarks to eulogizing the departed, with no mention of the big question in every mind—succession.

At the conclusion of the services, the procession formed outside. The Tenth Ward Band led the way, followed by the Union Glee Club, Tabernacle Choir, Salt Lake City Council, employees of Brigham Young, and Young's four living brothers: Phineas, Lorenzo, Joseph, and Edward.

Clerks and workmen of the prophet carried the bier. Taylor was one of nine apostles following as honorary pallbearers. Next in order came the counselors of Brigham's presidency, the family and relatives; then the church patriarch, the first seven presidents of seventy, the presidency and high council of the Salt Lake Stake, visiting stake presidencies, bishops and counselors, elders, and the lesser priesthood. As the procession slowly passed east along South Temple Street, the vast crowd ducked under the sidewalk ropes and fell in behind.

Near Eagle Gate, the horse of a man named Miles became excited and plunged over the rope, throwing its rider. Except for this incident, everything went smoothly as the procession turned through Eagle Gate toward the summit of the hill on which the vault had been prepared according to Brigham's specifications.

"Thus was concluded the grandest and most impressive funeral it was ever our lot to witness," the *Deseret News* declared.

"Thus closed the most eventful day in the annals of the Territory," the *Tribune* said.

> The Mormon church was stronger at four o'clock Sunday afternoon than it ever will again become; the remarkable will and organizing force of the dead leader departed with him, and have been transmitted to none other in his church; and we may now watch with complacency, if not with joy, the gradual disintegration of the whole Mormon fabric.

Would the church again be fragmented by the death of its leader? Much depended upon the man selected Tuesday to succeed Brigham.

Utah and the world awaited the outcome of the meeting of the Quorum of the Twelve. "The success of Mormonism will depend much on the man who shall become Young's successor," the San Francisco *Chronicle* predicted. Speculation regarding succession had been a popular guessing game both inside and outside Utah for several years. The San Jose *Mercury* listed Brigham's legacy as

> nineteen widows, forty-five living children, several millions in money that he couldn't take with him, a few mourners, and a quarrel before he is in the grave over the apostolic succession to the Mormon Church.

Under the title of "The Successorship," the Salt Lake *Tribune* said:

Three distinct and widely diverse parties or interests claim our attention as the probable future governing power of Mormonism. First is the Smith family. . . . Second is the Young dynasty represented by Brigham, Jr., and John W. Young. Thirdly are the Twelve Apostles of the church of whom John Taylor is the nominal president. The question is which of these parties, or interests, will obtain the control of the church?

The paper noted a "powerful undercurrent" in favor of the Smith family:

The name of Smith has a charm for all the old Mormons; and Brigham's exacting avarice, tyranny, and worldliness have caused thousands to look back with fondness to [the prophet Joseph] Smith's more generous rule . . .

Now was the opportunity for the prophet's nephew, Apostle Joseph F. Smith. "Will he avail himself of it?" the *Tribune* asked.
As for Brigham's family, the paper declared:

There can scarcely be any doubt but the Youngs, notwithstanding the Apostles have a clear right to control, will endeavor to obtain their father's place. John W. will no doubt assume that his counselorship to his father entitles him to a place in the new presidency; and Brigham, Jr., will probably assert his right to first place by virtue of his heirship to the deceased prophet, seer, and president.[6]

Though members of the Quorom of the Twelve remained silent regarding succession, rumors and speculations continued throughout Utah and the world. If the president of the Twelve became the new leader, as had Brigham in that office, several members of the Quorum could challenge John Taylor's position as senior apostle. Wilford Woodruff was older than Taylor and hadn't forgotten that, originally, ranking in the Twelve was by age, not seniority; but, in fact, Brigham had become president of the Quorum because of age. Orson Hyde and Orson Pratt had both been ordained to the Twelve before Taylor; but their seniority was debatable because they had been cast out, then forgiven and reinstated. The ques-

---

[6] For several years this newspaper had charged Brigham with planning a family dynasty. T. B. H. Stenhouse in his *Rocky Mountain Saints* said that "Several years ago, Brigham secretly ordained his three sons apostles—Joseph A., Brigham, and John W.—with the intention that Brigham Junior should subsequently be president of the Church, and his two brothers counselors." See also Reed C. Durham and Steven H. Heath, *Succession in the Church Presidency*: "John Willard Young (October 1, 1844) was ordained by his father, Brigham Young, February 22, 1855." Thus John W. Young became an apostle while a child of ten. His ordination might well have outraged the quorum of the twelve when the secret leaked out. Of the three sons so ordained, only Young Briggie was accepted into the twelve.

tion was whether they lost their seniority upon being dropped or whether the forgiveness restored it.

On Tuesday the Quorum met to make a decision; an *Epistle of the Twelve Apostles and Counselors to the Church of Jesus Christ of Latter-day Saints in All the World* annouced the result:

> Beloved Saints:
>
> . . . on Tuesday last, September 4th, the two counselors of President Young and ten of the Twelve Apostles [two being absent on missions] . . . held a meeting, and waited upon the Lord . . . the Lord blessed us with a spirit of union and condescended to reveal to us what steps we should take. Elder John Taylor, the senior Apostle, and who has acted as the President of the Twelve, was unanimously sustained in that position. With the same unanimity it was voted that the Quorum of the Twelve Apostles is the presiding quorum and authority in the church.

John Taylor was sustained to this position by the people at October conference; his counselors were John W. Young, Daniel H. Wells, and George Q. Cannon. The following morning's *Tribune* reported that "John Taylor feels as big over his elevation to the throne as a little boy with a pair of red top boots."[7]

The Gentile press freely predicted the decline of the church under the new leadership. The Indianapolis *Sentinel* said that "though it would be rash to assume that Mormonism is dead, it would be equally rash to believe it can survive, for any extended period, the death of its great leader." The Omaha *Republican* believed that the Saints would melt into the general populace, "and probably long ere Brigham's successor shall have gone to his fathers, there will remain little in Utah . . . to impress the traveler that he is 'a stranger in a strange land.' "

On the other hand, Stenhouse, in his *Rocky Mountain Saints*, had said of John Taylor: "There are few more powerful men than this apostle, and, had not Brigham made it a point to hedge him round, and arrest his development, he would have been a great man in Zion." Writing before Brigham's death, Stenhouse had said that Taylor was a "manacled giant," waiting to "burst forth into freedom."

Brigham Young had put the imprint of his powerful personality so firmly on the church that to the public mind he personified Mormonism. Yet to a handful of insiders who realized the radical difference in personality and philosophy between Brigham and his successor, deep and lasting changes of policy seemed inevitable. What would this do to the

---

[7] At this time Taylor was church leader in his position as president of the Twelve. He occupied this office for three years, as had Brigham after Joseph's death, then became president of the church. In modern times a new president is named within a matter of hours.

church? Those who feared change quaked in apprehension. Those to whom Brigham's every word had been inspired of the Lord might be shattered as the church changed policy on matters long held sacred.

Who knew John Taylor? What could he do? There was a rush to reread his talks, as printed in the *Journal of Discourses*. In particular came renewed interest in the *Autobiography* of Parley P. Pratt. A great friend and fellow apostle, Parley had known John Taylor as no one else. After Parley's death, Taylor had helped edit the *Autobiography*; it was a prime source for those who hoped to project the future from guideposts of the past.

2

"Where is our Philip?"

DURING THE EVENINGS as he worked on the Pratt manuscript, a torrent of memories flooded over John Taylor. He and Parley Pratt had shared twenty-one years of friendship and adventure during the violent early Mormon history. And so, some fifteen years after Parley's murder, when his son had asked Taylor's help in collating and editing the materials for Pratt's *Autobiography*, Taylor was glad to assist. He believed the work would be one of the finest personal narratives of the church's literature.[1] Yet more than this, Taylor had always had a particular regard for Parley Pratt. His first meeting with this salesman of salvation had changed the entire course of John Taylor's life.

He was at work in his shop, turning a chair leg on the lathe, when Leonora came in from the house with the baby, Mary Ann, in her arms and two-year-old George tagging along to announce the visit of a Mormon missionary. She handed her husband a letter of introduction from a merchant friend, Moses Nickerson.

Taylor was a bit nettled by the interruption, feeling that his friend was imposing on him. The Nickerson family had joined the Mormon faith, and, while the family was composed of good people, it was common knowledge that when members of this sect gathered together they became trouble-makers and were driven out by their neighbors. Taylor told Leonora to send the fellow away.

---

[1] The book was published in 1874, and is still in print a century later. Though the style is a bit purple by modern standards, the narrative is exciting and moving, filled with miracles, faith-healing, casting-out of devils, high adventure, fervent faith, and robust humor.

Leonora replied that at least he could show the courtesy of having a cup of tea with Pratt, and, anyhow, it was time to quit for the day. She was always after him about working too late in the shop.

Taylor reluctantly put away his chisels, brushed the wood shavings from the lathe, and swept the floor of his turning shop. He'd heard enough about Mormonism to want nothing to do with it. Though Joseph Smith had convinced his credulous followers that an angel had led him to buried plates of gold, from which he translated the Book of Mormon, fifty-one residents of Palmyra, New York, who had known the Smiths signed a statement that Joseph and his entire family were preoccupied with seeking buried Spanish treasure and that they spent much of their time in digging for money which they pretended was hid in the earth. They were also particularly famous for visionary projects.

Joseph's father-in-law, Isaac Hale of Harmony, Pennsylvania, claimed that young Smith had "carried off my daughter, into the State of New York, where they were married without my approbation or consent," and said that when he first became acquainted with Joseph the young man was

> in the employ of a set of men who were called "money diggers"; and his occupation was that of seeing or pretending to see by means of a stone placed in his hat and his hat closed over his face. In this way he pretended to discover minerals and hidden treasure.[2]

A year after the marriage, when Joseph brought his wife to Harmony to visit her father, "Smith stated to me, that he had given up what he called 'glass-looking,' and that he expected to work hard for a living," Hale said. However, when Joseph and Emma Smith moved from Palmyra to Harmony, "I was informed that they had brought a wonderful box of Plates down with them." Hale was allowed to heft the box, but not to look inside. A family argument resulted. Hale

> informed him that if there was anything in my house of that description, which I could not be allowed to see, he must take it away; if he did not, I was determined to see it. After that, the Plates were said to be hid in the woods. . . .
>
> The manner in which he pretended to read and interpret was the same as when he looked for the money-diggers, with the stone in his hat and his hat over his face while the Book of Plates were at the same time hid in the woods![3]

The young prophet's father-in-law became convinced that "the whole 'Book of Mormon' (so called) is a silly fabrication of falsehood and wickedness, got up for speculation, and with a design to dupe the credu-

---

[2] Affidavit in Eber D. Howe's *Mormonism Unvailed*, Painesville, Ohio, 1834, pp. 262–6.
[3] Ibid.

lous and unwary—and in order that its fabricators may live upon the spoils of those who swallow the deception."

In addition to such stories, Taylor had heard horrid whispers that Joseph was secretly fostering the abomination of polygamy. At Hiram, Ohio, the prophet had been tarred and feathered by neighbors incensed at stories that he'd made improper advances to a girl.

As Taylor took off his shop apron, ran a comb through his heavy thatch of wavy hair, put on his coat, and went into see his visitor, he was definitely not in the mood to be receptive to Mormonism. However, he already had made a reputation as a defender of individual liberty; he believed that every man had the right to his own faith and the right to be heard. He'd see what this fellow, Pratt, had to say.

As Pratt arose from the rocker in the sitting room to greet him, Taylor was surprised to find not a hollow-eyed fanatic, but a husky fellow of twenty-nine, barrel-chested and bull-necked, exuding vitality, and a heavily handsome face framed by curling black hair. Despite Taylor's bias against Mormonism, he felt an instant rapport with Parley Pratt. It soon developed that the two had much in common; both were writers and students of the scriptures; both were mystics and seekers after eternal truth. Taylor admired Parley's courage in traveling as a missionary for so unpopular and derided a faith. So that, while he considered Pratt mistaken in his beliefs, he couldn't help liking him as a person. Could he perhaps bring Parley to the truth? As a lay preacher, Taylor had made many converts to Methodism. A person with Parley Pratt's gifts could contribute much to the faith.

In turn, Parley was appraising his host. John Taylor was tall and powerfully built, with the hands of a craftsman and the eyes of a scholar. Though not yet thirty, his wavy hair was sprinkled with gray. An outdoorsman, obviously; he was deeply tanned. The massive head, strong nose, and iron jaw suggested to Pratt that here was as stubborn a man as ever was born; yet the quirk at the corners of the lips and the leavening of wit in his talk showed that he wasn't a bigot. Could he bring Taylor to the truth? He would be a person difficult to convert. He wouldn't be overwhelmed with emotionalism. If he became interested in Mormonism he would examine the seams. But if Taylor made up his mind to accept the gospel, nothing on earth would shake his decision. The young church needed Taylor's erudition and intellectual depth as well as his combative temperament and quick wit. If only . . .

Leonora served tea, then sat by with the children while the two men talked. Parley presented an entirely different picture of Joseph Smith from the one Taylor had conceived. He told of a teenage boy wrestling with corruption of the flesh, having visions and being derided by his neighbors because of them. He quoted Joseph,

. . . being of very tender years, and persecuted by those who ought to have been my friends, I was left to all kinds of temptations, and mingling with all kinds of society, I frequently fell into many foolish errors, and displayed the weakness of youth, and the corruption of human nature, which I am sorry to say led me into divers temptations, to the gratification of many appetites offensive in the sight of God.[4]

From his own struggles to conquer himself, Taylor could understand and sympathize with Joseph. This youth was in the pattern of holy men of all ages, who felt corrupted by the flesh and engaged in titantic struggles to subdue it in order to gain the kingdom of heaven. "In consequence of these things I often felt condemned for my weakness and imperfections," Joseph recorded. On the evening of September 21, 1823, at age seventeen,

I betook myself to prayer and supplication to Almighty God, for forgiveness of all my sins and follies, and also for a manifestation to me, that I might know of my state and standing before him. . . .[5]

And it was "while I was thus in the act of calling upon God" that a light appeared in the bedroom "which continued to increase until the room was lighter than at noonday" and a personage appeared "standing in the air" wearing "a loose robe of most exquisite whiteness." On the following night this personage showed him the golden plates hidden in a hill, but did not allow him to take them. For the next four years, on that same date, the angel showed Joseph the plates, until, when he fully realized the responsibility of the trust and had grown into a man worthy of it, he was allowed to take them.

Taylor was conscious of Parley's close scrutiny during this part of the story, for skeptics found it easy to ridicule. Taylor, however, had no difficulty accepting the visitation by an angel. As a child he himself had had a similar experience. He had seen an angel in the heavens with a trumpet heralding a message to all nations. The essential difference between his experience and Joseph's was that Smith had been apprised of its purpose; Taylor had been left to wonder at the meaning of the visitation.

Parley said that on the night that Joseph was visited by the angel there were wondrous manifestations. Heber C. Kimball, with his good friend, Brigham Young, and their families, had seen what appeared to be a great battle in the heavens between the hosts of good and evil. Years later, upon first hearing the Joseph Smith story, they had remembered it.

Taylor, thinking back, could not pinpoint his own mystic experience so exactly. He was three years younger than Joseph and had been four-

---

[4] Joseph Smith, *The Pearl of Great Price.*
[5] Ibid.

teen, apprenticed to a cooper at Liverpool, at the time Smith was first shown the plates. The apprenticeship had lasted only a year, but coming as it did during his early adolescence it had had a profound influence on his character.

Big for his age and looking older than his fourteen years, Taylor roamed the docks with the swagger of a man, talking to sailors who had been to the ends of the earth, striking acquaintance with rough water-front characters, eyeing painted street women, frequenting pubs with men of the world and drinking shoulder to shoulder with them.

Though his wages were small they were free and clear; his keep came with the job, as well as a ration of grog. He came to look forward to splicing the main brace; before long every farthing of his wages, plus what he could pick up with odd jobs on the waterfront Sundays and evenings, went over the bar at the Lion and Crown, where he was a man among men. He was particularly flattered to be accepted at the table where Mr. Winters presided. Mr. Winters, who had once been a gentleman of some substance, still maintained a degree of gentility, with the manners of one born well and the vocabulary of a former university professor. He was widely read, urbane, and possessed a good sense of humor and a broad outlook. Here, thought young John Taylor, was the sort of person he'd like to become, except for one thing. The one flaw in Mr. Winter's character was that every night he had just a drop too much and had to be helped home.

One night John Tayor had the privilege of supporting the swaying man through the foggy streets to his residence, enjoying the erudition and wit of his remarks. Then, at the door of the hovel, came the shock of seeing the haggard wife, the hollow eyes of the ragged children. This was how Mr. Winters returned home every night to loved ones destitute because of his weakness. He woke up every morning filled with remorse that his life, and that of his wife and children, had been poured into the bottle, that this was why he no longer was a professor at the university. And yet, by evening, he was driven by something stronger than self respect and family ties to the Lion and Crown, to repeat the daily nightmare.

"I'll take care of him, lad, and thank you for bringing him." The wife's quiet acceptance of the situation, her hopeless resignation, put a cold knot inside the youth. She helped her husband inside, and then, as she closed the door, paused to look straight inside John Taylor. "You're too young for this sort of thing, lad. Don't let it get hold of you."

He never entered the Lion and Crown again.

During the period that Joseph Smith was growing into the stature of a prophet, John Taylor experienced questing years of development; he, too, was a seeker. The cooperage went bankrupt; he returned home to Hale, in the Cumberland Lake district near his birthplace at Milnthorpe, and was apprenticed to a wood turner at Penrith. Here, England's highest mountains and most beautiful scenery had inspired some of its finest writers; William Wordsworth, Robert Southey, Samuel Taylor Coleridge, and Thomas De Quincey were near by, while across the Scottish border Sir Walter Scott was pouring forth his prodigious literary output. It was a time of creativity, imagination, an awakening to truer relations with Nature, a revolt against artificial restraints of stylized tradition, and John Taylor came to manhood in the middle of it.

At Penrith he devoured the classic tales of Robin Hood and the Knights of the Round Table; he read Fielding, Milton, Shakespeare, Scott, Spenser, Goldsmith, along with the Lake poets. He discovered *Don Quixote, Gulliver's Travels*, and that the Bible was good literature as well as scripture.

He prowled the dense forests of the mountains, once stumbling upon the bones of two bogus coiners, hanged in chains with the bodies left dangling as a warning. He swam the lakes, explored castle ruins, walked the roads bordered by hedgerows in the valley called the "Vale of Eden." And always he had the feeling that he wasn't alone. Not wanting to be branded one of the wild-eyed insane who roamed at will, he said nothing of the melodious music that came sweet and soft to him in this enchanted land. The feeling grew that he was set apart. The music played for him alone. But for what purpose? Toward what unknown sea did the river of life flow?

He probed at the pattern of the universe, the plan of salvation. His early upbringing in the Church of England, its doctrine permeated with the sense of sin and unworthiness, didn't fit his surging and optimistic vitality. He began attending the local Methodist services and joined that faith. His missionary zeal was such, that, at the age of seventeen, he was commissioned a Methodist exhorter.

His first appointment as a local preacher was in a little town some seven miles from Penrith. As he and a companion walked to it one Sunday morning, he stopped suddenly, transfixed, as a voice sounded. After a few moments he said, "I have a strong impression that I have to go to America to preach the gospel!"

Now he knew his destiny; but there was a persistent doubt that kept nagging at him: Did he yet have the gospel he was to preach?

Now, ten years later, as he listened to Parley Pratt in the sitting room of his Toronto home, John Taylor was impressed by the missionary's faith and zeal; but that didn't mean the man's message was right. When he asked what sort of man this Joseph Smith was, Parley Pratt's objectivity vanished; the missionary had obviously attached his love of the gospel to its prophet. Taylor was amused at Pratt's description. Joseph Smith seemed to possess every virtue and no faults. No one, it seemed, was neutral about the Mormon prophet; he was either idolized or passionately hated.

Taylor soon terminated the discussion and Parley left, crestfallen; he'd felt divinely guided to the address. Taylor sighed, then turned to Leonora, saying he'd have two words with Moses Nickerson for sending the zealot here.

"But he may be a man of God," Leonora said.

He was in enough trouble with the church already, Taylor pointed out, without getting mixed up with Mormonism. He'd recently lost his license to preach because of his activities in a Bible study group. What he didn't need, right now, was Mormonism to complicate the situation.

The next afternoon Leonora brought Parley Pratt into the shop. The missionary was disappointed, dejected, and shaken; he'd come to say goodbye. Fresh in his mind was the memory of that evening at Kirtland, Ohio, when Heber C. Kimball called him to the mission in Canada. Parley had been reluctant to accept the call; having lost everything when the Saints were expelled from Jackson County, Missouri, he was now deeply in debt. His wife, Thankful, was very ill, ravaged by a disease that had ridden her for six years.

"Brother Parley, thy wife shall be healed from this hour," Kimball had promised, "and shall bear a son, and his name shall be Parley, and he shall be a chosen instrument in the hands of the Lord."[6]

"This prophecy was the more marvelous," Parley told Taylor, "because, being married ten years, we had never had any children."

Having made these promises, Kimball had exhorted Parley to "Arise, therefore, and go forth in the ministry, nothing doubting. Take no thoughts for your debts, nor the necessities of life, for the Lord will supply you with abundant means for all things." At Toronto, Kimball predicted, "thou shall find a people prepared for the fulness of the gospel, and they shall receive thee." Many would be brought to the true faith, Kimball had promised.

However, after bumping against reality, Parley was ready to quit. He'd spent all day in a fruitless search for a place to preach. The clergy had closed the doors of their churches to him. The sheriff had refused permission to use the court house for a meeting. He'd been unable to find a public hall that could be hired.

"Rather an unpromising beginning," Parley admitted wryly, "considering the prophecies on my head concerning Toronto." Under the circumstances, he had decided to leave town. Perhaps Toronto would be opened to the gospel at some later date.

---

[6] Parley P. Pratt, *Autobiography*.

The sound of the front doorbell came, and Leonora went into the house to answer it. Taylor, intrigued with mystic experiences, asked about the other part of Kimball's prophecy—was Pratt's wife pregnant?

Too soon to tell, Parley said; he'd left within a few days after being called on the mission. But he was convinced she *would* be.

Taylor coughed to repress a laugh. Pratt's faith-promoting story suddenly was complete nonsense. No part of it had transpired.

Parley Pratt picked up his valise, saying he'd say good-bye to Mrs. Taylor. They turned to the door leading to the house, then paused; the voices in the sitting room beyond were talking about the missionary. Leonora was telling another woman (whose voice Taylor recognized as that of Isabella Walton, a widow, who with her son John, belonged to the Bible study group) of Pratt's failure to find a place to preach. "I am sorry to have him depart," Leonora said. "He may be a man of God."

"Tell the stranger he is welcome to my house," the widow said. "I have a spare room and bed and food in plenty. And there are two large rooms to preach in."

That evening, John and Leonora Taylor were among a dozen people around the large table in the Walton parlor as Parley Pratt told the story of Mormonism. The widow and several of her friends were so overwhelmed that they requested baptism. The whole thing, Taylor felt, was sheer emotionalism. How could these silly women make up their minds on so vital an issue with so little discussion and investigation? He suspected that it was the handsome missionary's vitality and magnetism, more than his message, that warped their judgment.

Next day, Leonora came in the shop with a wondrous tale. Parley Pratt had performed a miracle; he had caused the blind to see. At Mrs. Walton's urging he'd visited Emily Herrick, a young widow with four small children, who had gone blind from an eye infection several months before. Since the onset of her affliction, she'd been unable to continue teaching the Methodist school and had been living on the charity of the church society. When Parley Pratt arrived, Leonora said, Emily Herrick's eyes were inflamed, heavily bandaged, and she was in great pain. Pratt put his hands on her head and when she removed the bandages she was instantly healed, her sight restored.

He'd have to see this to believe it, Taylor said.

Emily would be at the Walton home for the meeting that night, Leonora declared, and he could see for himself.

Taylor looked at Leonora's shining face with a nagging worry. Was she being infected by Mormonism? His wife certainly wasn't an emotional, unstable type of person. He'd met her through the church, when she arrived from the Isle of Man as companion to the wife of the private secretary of Lord Aylmer, Governor General of Canada. As her class leader, Taylor was immediately attracted to the slender and dark-haired Leonora Cannon, who, at thirty-six, was mature, accomplished, charming, witty, and possessed all the attainments of a lady of culture. Taylor immediately became a suitor, but Leonora gave him scant encouragement. She thought him handsome but unpolished; he hadn't been to the right schools nor attended a university; his intellectualism was flawed by gaps of the self-educated. Beneath the charm and humor crouched the tiger. He was a man who would always be involved in battles for principle. Would she want such a life? When he proposed, she rejected him. She said no perhaps a dozen times before finally accepting for a reason valid in religious circles: a dream, accepted as guidance.

The Walton parlor and sitting room wouldn't hold all who came to the next meeting; some stood in the yard by the doors and windows. Emily Herrick was radiant, her eyes sparkling bright. As people badgered her, she repeated her story: "He laid hands upon my head in the name of Jesus Christ and commanded my eyes to be made whole and restored to sight; and it was instantly done."

"Then give God the glory. This man is an imposter, a follower of Joseph Smith, the false prophet."

"But I can *see!*"

"It is Satan's counterfeit, to lure you from the true faith. If you join these fools, the Mormons—remember, you won't have any more support from our society, you won't teach school for us. How will your children live?"

Emily Herrick rejected Mormonism. John Taylor decided to investigate further.

A clergyman invited Parley to meet with the Bible group at the home of a wealthy man named Patrick.

After the meeting was opened, John Taylor arose and read the New Testament account of Philip preaching at Samaria. There was great joy as the people heard the word and witnessed the casting out of devils, the healing of the sick and the lame, the conversion of the bewitched; many were baptized into the faith. When the apostles at Jerusalem heard that Samaria had accepted the gospel, they sent Peter and John to lay hands on believers that they might receive the Holy Ghost. "Now, where is our Philip?" John Taylor asked. "Where are the signs and the miracles? Where is our Peter and John? Where are our apostles? Where is our Holy Ghost by the laying on of hands?" If the present pattern of belief differed from that of the New Testament, "What claim have we to be considered the Church of Christ?"

Nothing definite was concluded on when the old preacher who invited me arose and said: "There is a stranger present who, perhaps, might wish to speak."

... I arose, and observed that I was a stranger from the United States;

but not a stranger to the great principles under investigation at this meeting.[7]

Parley preached for three nights at the Patrick home, while crowds increased. The excitement concerning his claim that the primitive Church of Christ had been restored caused the minister to fear for his flock, and Parley found the door of the Patrick home closed to further meetings. He simply returned to the Walton residence and continued preaching, the house and yard crowded by his audience.

> The truth was now plainly before this people, who had been in so wonderful a manner prepared for its reception, as predicted by Brother Kimball on my head before leaving home.

John Taylor was both excited and shaken by these meetings. He took detailed notes of eight sermons by Pratt and compared them with scripture. He studied the Book of Mormon and the *Doctrine and Covenants*. "I made a regular business of it for three weeks," he wrote, "and followed Brother Parley from place to place."

When he made his decision, he found that Leonora, too, was ready. Now he knew the meaning of the angel with the trumpet; he understood the celestial music, and he was certain of the mission in America of which the voice had told him. On May 9, 1836, John and Leonora Taylor were baptized.

Parley made a trip back to Kirtland to bring Thankful to Canada.

> I found my wife had been healed of her seven years' illness from the time Brother Kimball had ministered unto her, and I began to realize more fully that every word of his blessing and prophecy upon my head would surely come to pass. After a pleasant visit with the Saints, I took my wife with me and returned again to Toronto, in June 1836.

The Pratts lodged at the home of Taylor's friend, Joseph Fielding, a member of the study group who, along with the families of John Goodson, Isaac Russell, John Snyder, and others, had accepted the faith.

When Taylor and Leonora called at the Fielding home to meet Thankful, the first sight of Parley's wife gave him an eerie feeling—a tall and emaciated woman with great black eyes and silky jet hair contrasting transparently pale skin with veins showing through, a hacking cough, and feverish pink spots on the hollow cheeks. The onset of Thankful's illness, he realized, had coincided with Parley's call to the ministry. Dedication to the gospel always required a sacrifice. Was this what was required of Parley P. Pratt?

The summer at Toronto was a time of wondrous events. Parley wrote of a night at Joseph Fielding's home, when

---

[7] Ibid.

the voice of the Lord came unto me in a dream, saying: "Parley!" And I answered: "Here I am." . . . And he said: "When did I ever reveal anything unto you in a dream and it failed to pass?" And I answered: "Never, Lord." "Well, then," he continued, "go unto this people and cry unto them with a mighty voice that they repent. . . ."

Two apostles, Orson Hyde and Parley's brother, Orson Pratt, arrived to help with the work in Canada. Taylor joined them on preaching tours that brought many to baptism.

After a highly successful summer the apostles returned to Kirtland in October; they appointed John Taylor presiding elder of the Canadian district. He and Leonora accompanied the party to the dock, waving good-bye as the boat moved out into Lake Ontario. Taylor turned away haunted by the huge eyes and pallid face of the frail woman at the rail.

Leonora, however, was radiant. "John, you'll never guess what Thankful told me," she confided. *"She's going to have a baby!"*

Except for an occasional stifled moan from the bedroom, Parley Pratt's house was quiet. John Taylor sat with Parley in the front room, occasionally shuddering with the chill that had crept into his bones during the long vigil. He'd been there all night, waiting with Parley, while in the bedroom Patty Sessions, the midwife, attended Thankful. Whether the chill in his bones came from the night air, Thankful's condition, or the chaos in his soul, Taylor didn't know. He was too completely shattered to analyze his reactions to the shock that came upon visiting Kirtland, Ohio.

Taylor had arrived in the spring with the zeal of a convert; expecting a veritable Garden of Eden he found Kirtland torn by dissention. A wild fever of speculation in city lots had collapsed and many—including those high in the church and close to Joseph—were accusing the prophet of fraud. The gathering of the Saints at Kirtland was being denounced as a mere scheme to sell real estate to arriving converts at inflated prices. The bank started by Joseph and church associates was on the verge of disaster; in fact, the prophet and his first counselor, Sidney Rigdon, had been arrested in connection with their handling of the bank's affairs, and the case was awaiting trial. Some were accusing Joseph of being a false prophet.

It was enough to sicken the soul of a man, and John Taylor sat through the night of March 24 with his heart like stone.

It was almost dawn when suddenly there was a scream from the bedroom. Parley started up, then sank back into his chair. There was nothing a man could do at a time like this. It was the lot of women to bring forth children in sorrow. Even male doctors weren't allowed to violate the modesty of a woman in labor, except through subterfuge in cases of extreme emergency.

The rattle of the door latch came loud in the stillness. Patty Sessions, angular and lantern-jawed, emerged from the bedroom. She met Parley's beseeching eyes and made a helpless shrug.

"We must have a doctor."

Parley sprang up and hurried outside. Taylor asked the midwife if there was anything he could do. No, Patty said, nothing. Then in a whisper she said she'd have to arrange the bedclothes so that Thankful wouldn't know a man was present when the doctor came. She returned to the bedroom.

Presently Parley returned with Dr. Williams, a compact, efficient man of fifty. Frederick G. Williams was second counselor to Joseph in the church presidency, but was among those charging the prophet with fraud and deceit. He had come in a hurry, hair disheveled from the pillow, nightshirt tucked into trousers, his medical bag clutched in one hand. The doctor rapped lightly at the bedroom door. It opened a crack, and from within Patty Sessions made a gesture for him to get down. Williams got on hands and knees, then as the door opened crawled inside. Patty reached through the doorway for his bag then closed the door.

Thankful would never know a man was present at her childbed.

Through the window the wooded hills of Ohio showed in purple silhouette with the false dawn when from the bedroom came a gasp, then a wail. Parley's heavy face bloomed. A baby was crying!

The door opened. Dr. Williams crawled out, followed by Patty Sessions with the infant. The doctor got to his feet, brushed the dust from his knees, and went to the commode in the corner to wash up. Patty brought the baby, tiny, wizened, and red, to the father.

"You have a son, Brother Pratt."

"Thankful . . . ?"

She turned away, saying she had to wash and dress the baby. Parley crossed to the commode. How was Thankful? Dr. Williams continued washing his hands. He shook his head and quietly said there was nothing he could do.

John Taylor went in the bedroom with Parley. Thankful lay frail and exhausted, the death rattle in her throat. They lay hands on her head and administered a blessing. Presently Patty brought the baby in. Thankful reached for it, and her great eyes were filled with the joy of completion as she took it in her arms.

She died in peace.

Taylor followed along as Parley walked for hours through the wooded hills, half-crazed with grief and disillusionment. It was all a fraud, Parley cried. Heber C. Kimball had promised that Thankful would be cured. Joseph had declared the church bank would become the greatest institution in the world, and it was on the brink of collapse. Parley had bought three lots for two thousand dollars that hadn't cost the prophet a hundred, and he couldn't get his money back.

"Joseph and Sidney have led the people astray!" Parley shouted. "False prophesying and preaching! They'll lead the church and themselves down to hell!"[8]

Taylor didn't try to reason or argue, not then. He followed the grief-crazed man only to make sure Parley wouldn't try to destroy himself.

---

[8] See letter, P. P. Pratt to Joseph Smith, Jr., May 23, 1837, printed at the time in the newspaper, *Zion's Watchman*, and quoted by Max H. Parkin, *Conflict at Kirtland*.

3

Crisis in Kirtland

IT WAS LATE AFTERNOON, and a chill was in the air, as Taylor walked up the hill toward the temple. It sparkled in the sunlight from the crockery crushed into the stucco—the women had donated their dishes for it.

He paused, looking over toward Parley's house. In need of a wife to care for his baby, Parley had married an attractive widow, Mary Ann Frost Stearns, six weeks after Thankful's death. Then, facing financial disaster because of speculation, he wrote a bitter letter to Joseph, accusing the prophet of swindling him in the name of religion.

Since then, Parley had kept to himself, staying away from church, avoiding former friends. He was now preparing to go on a mission to New York; he still believed in the true church. "It is because of my belief," he told Taylor, "that it hurts me to see the Lord's prophets guilty of covetousness, extortion, and taking advantage of a brother in the gospel by undue religious influence."[1]

After prayerful consideration, Taylor had told Parley that he couldn't hold the Lord to a human scale of values, nor judge His prophets. God chooses whom He will. Prophets of ancient times—Abraham, Moses, David, Solomon—were guilty of sins and misdeeds, yet were divinely selected. Regardless of all accusations against Joseph, he remained the chosen instrument of God, and no aspersions on his character could cast a shadow on his position as the Lord's mouthpiece.

---

[1] See Pratt's letter to Joseph, May 23, 1837; also his *Autobiography*, and B. H. Roberts, *The Life of John Taylor*. Parley's "period of darkness" kept him in turmoil for more than a year.

Taylor continued toward the temple. He was sure Pratt would emerge from the dark cloud strengthened by adversity.

Only a few early arrivals were present in the temple. Taylor paused to warm his back at the stove; the heat was welcome in the chill of early evening. A man moved along with a taper, lighting the lamps, as darkness began closing in. Taylor slipped into a seat, allowing the feeling of reverence inspired by this house of the Lord to suffuse him with a warmth as tangible as that from the stove. This was the first temple of the dispensation. Here, under the hands of the prophet himself, John Taylor had received endowments that could be obtained nowhere else on earth. He was a member of the holy order, invested with blessings from on high. Upon him had been bestowed charisma that he might go forth from this house armed with the Lord's power, his welfare in the charge of angels. No weapon would be effective against him, and whosoever should dig a pit for him should fall into it himself. No combination of wickedness should prevail over him, for the Lord would smite those who smote him and would deliver him from the hands of all enemies. He cherished this endowment of power and invulnerability; this endowment which would enable the Saints to gather for the redemption of Zion, to throw down the towers of their enemies so that the Kingdom of God might roll forth and overwhelm the entire world. Parley Pratt had been so confident following his own endowment that he had said, "I will state as a prophecy that there will not be an unbelieving Gentile upon this continent fifty years hence."

The main assembly hall was a large rectangular room with a tier of four pulpits rising at each end—those at the west end being for the Melchizedek (higher priesthood) and at the east end for the Aaronic (the lower priesthood). Flanking the pulpits were elevated pews for the choir. The congregation sat in stalls with movable pews, so that people could turn in either direction to face the pulpits. Curtains on rollers attached to the ceiling could be lowered to enclose each tier of the pulpits and also to divide the room itself into four compartments for various services.

The main hall was designed for meetings of the entire membership. Directly above it was a room of identical size used for meetings of adult males—the priesthood—and an attic story which provided five rooms for school instruction and meetings by various priesthood quorums.

Taylor regretted that he hadn't been present at the awe-inspiring manifestations accompanying the temple dedication. Angels had appeared during the ceremony to accept the dedication. The next evening, George A. Smith testified,

> hundreds of the brethren received the ministering of angels, saw the light and personages of angels, and bore testimony of it. They spake in new

tongues, and had a greater manifestation of the power of God than that described by Luke on the day of the Pentecost.[2]

To Taylor, the most impressive of all the remarkable events was an incident told him by Eliza R. Snow. A woman arrived for the dedication with her baby. On learning that children in arms weren't admitted for the ceremony, she appealed to the church patriarch, Joseph's father; she had come from afar and couldn't bear to miss the event. The patriarch waived the rules, personally escorting her to a seat. Then a most wonderful thing happened. At the climax of the ceremony, when the congregation gave the sacred shout, this baby, only six weeks old, joined in, crying, "Hosanna! Hosanna! Hosanna! To God and the Lamb forever and ever, amen, and amen!"

Yes, it was a time when the heavens were opened. "Every man's mouth was full of prophesying," Heber C. Kimball said. "During this time many great and marvelous visions were seen."

Yet despite the miraculous signs and the visitation by heavenly beings, in just one short year the spiritual ecstacy had curdled to dissension and apostasy. It was, Taylor was sure, Satan's work. Inasmuch as the restoration of the true church would usher in the millennium, during which Satan would be in chains, he was desperately at work to block its progress and seduce its officials. The tool of the adversary was simple and effective—money. Men would fight and die for their faith; they would starve and endure torture for it; they would let themselves be thrown to wild lions or boiled in oil rather than renounce it; but they would sell it for a few pieces of silver.[3]

Hectored by lawsuits and deeply in debt as a result of the bursting of the frenzied boom of land speculation and the impending collapse of the church bank, Joseph had gone to Cleveland in an attempt to raise money. Brigham Young and Williard Richards were in New York on the same mission.

Yet in the middle of chaos, the prophet's faith had never faltered. At this darkest period he conceived the grand plan of taking the gospel to England, and John Taylor had paved the way with letters to British ministers. He now was packing for the return trip to Canada, where he would help with preparations for the mission.

The hall was filling. Emma Smith, the prophet's wife, came in with her three children, accompanied by Eliza R. Snow. Emma was tall, dark,

---

[2] JD, 2:214.

[3] "Apostates and corrupt men were prowling about like so many wolves," Taylor said. "Fraud, false accusation, and false swearing, vexatious lawsuits, personal violence, and bare-faced robbery abounded." Heber C. Kimball declared that in these dark days not more than twenty people remained on earth who would support Joseph Smith as the prophet of God.

and angular compared to the petite poetess. The group joined Taylor in his stall. He'd stayed at the prophet's house while in Kirtland, becoming friends of the family and of Eliza, a spinster who resided there.

A group of militant apostates filled stalls near the Melchizedek pulpit. Warren Parrish, Joseph's former secretary, together with John F. Boynton, moved from stall to stall among the group for whispered consultations. Parrish was enraged that the bank failure should be blamed on his defalcations, while Boynton's mind had darkened when he and a fellow apostle, Lyman E. Johnson, failed in their mercantile enterprise, promoted on a grand scale on credit.

The prophet's father presided at the services. Tall and ramrod-straight at sixty-six, the gray-haired patriarch talked of the troubles afflicting the Saints. These were, he declared, a direct result of weakness and lack of faith. Then as he began chastizing various members, the accused began shouting back, not only from the audience but from seats in the pulpit.

Taylor was appalled that open bickering should break out in the Lord's house. Eliza Snow's face was white, while Emma, fearful of the effect on the children, whispered that she shouldn't have come. Perhaps, Taylor thought, Parley was right in staying away.

From their seats in the pulpit, David Whitmer and Oliver Cowdery were excoriating the prophet. David cried out that Joseph had revised the revelations from the Lord and was now purporting to receive the revelations without use of the seer stone; he was tampering with the Lord's word. Oliver spoke up bitterly against the prophet's affair with his servant girl, Fannie Alger. At this a voice from the audience cried out warning Oliver to keep silent about sacred matters, while another from the rear shouted that Oliver himself had taken a plural.

Satan had bent every effort to lure the three witnesses away, and, as David and Oliver ranted from the stand, Taylor was afraid that the Devil was chuckling.

Who, Warren Parrish yelled, could believe in Joseph's later revelations? The one stating that the Kirtland bank would swallow up all other banks, and never would fail, made either Joseph or the Lord out a liar. At this, Father Smith accused Parrish of having precipitated the bank's downfall by embezzling its funds. "Liar!" yelled Parrish. He leaped up, charged to the pulpit, and began wrestling with the patriarch. As a young man, Smith was known for his prowess in physical combat; but now Parrish had the advantage of youth and agility. The patriarch called to Oliver Cowdery for help, but Oliver ignored the plea. Then William Smith sprang to the defense of his father. As he grappled with Parrish, John F. Boynton leaped into the scuffle, unsheathing his sword cane and threatening to run William through. Men were springing up and rushing to the pulpit to join the fray. One leaped upon Boynton from behind, wresting the sword away. Apostates with pistols and bowie knives tried to gain command, but a concerted rush by other men overwhelmed them.

Taylor helped Emma and Eliza gather the wraps of the children. Women were screaming, escaping by doors and windows. Taylor ushered Eliza and the prophet's family through the milling throng and to the door, then turned back just as a fighting group of men bumped the stove. The long pipe toppled over, billowing soot and smoke. Taylor found himself in the thick of the fray. He kicked a pistol from a man's hand and grabbed the arm of another which held an upraised bowie knife. He had a sense of fantasy, as if this were a nightmare, as he found himself fighting men he had revered as the Lord's prophets, and doing it here, in the first temple of the Lord of this dispensation.

The struggle was violent but brief. The dissidents were cast out of the hall, the stovepipe put in place, doors opened to get rid of the smoke, and the meeing resumed.

Taylor found himself on the rostrum, defending the prophet. Though dismayed at the brawl, he took satisfaction in the fact that the open conflict had brought the majority of the Saints to the prophet's defense. When the chips were down, they supported Joseph and his gospel. Taylor reminded the Saints that it was Joseph who was chosen to restore the true church, and that they must look to him for further guidance. Just as the children of Israel fell into rebellion and idolatry, even after seeing the power of God manifested in their midst, just so were the Latter-day Saints in danger of losing the faith.

Taylor left for Canada the next morning unaware that his support of the prophet would be a turning point of his life. He was given a glimpse of the future while en route. His party stopped over at Queenstown for Sunday and held services in the lee of a cliff below Niagara Falls. Here, in the awesome grandeur of the setting, Taylor experienced a religious exaltation, and spoke in tongues as the spirit whispered a tremendous secret. As he went into Queenstown to find a hall and preach, he was filled to bursting with the burning knowledge that he would be called to the position of one of the Twelve Apostles of the restored church.

Leonora wasn't too sure she entirely liked what had happened to her husband. Since his conversion, he had neglected his business for his church work; and now, after returning from Kirtland, he was almost constantly out working in the branches under his supervision. The Canadian mission was proving a phenomenal success, as predicted by Heber C. Kimball. Two hundred wagons headed south toward Kirtland, filled with converts dedicated to the gathering of Zion. During the summer, John organized other groups which would follow.

He was away when Sampson Avard arrived at Toronto. Avard,

smiling and glib, informed Leonora that he had been appointed to preside over the Canadian Saints in place of John Taylor. Leonora knew that it would be a blow to John, being replaced, but she felt it was for the best. Now he could spend more time in the shop and less in the pulpit. As the lathe stood silent and customers went elsewhere, she didn't fully share his abiding faith that the Lord would provide. With two small children, and pregnant again, she worried more about security than salvation. She would rather have cash in the bank than depend upon ravens to be fed. Why couldn't John be like other men—spend Sunday with affairs of the spirit and the remainder of the week providing for his family? With Avard now in charge north of the border, John could get busy in the shop, catch up on back orders, and meet bills falling due.

Upon returning home, however, John was delighted to learn that Avard had been sent to preside in Canada. Now that he was released from the position, he could plan on gathering with the Saints at Kirtland.

Leonora was appalled. They were settled at Toronto, established in business, among their own people. She was dubious about moving to the States, particularly to Kirtland, a hotbed of apostasy and dissent.

All the more reason for the faithful to gather, he pointed out. And, besides, the collapse of land values had made investment in Kirtland property a rare bargain. He and a friend, Henry Humphrey, had planned on opening a furniture-making shop at Kirtland. Humphrey had located a five-acre farm for them, with good house and barn, at a bargain price.

Nothing could stop John; his mind was made up. Leonora could only wonder at his complete faith as he liquidated his Toronto assets to put everything, including their savings, into Kirtland property.

Taylor was thrilled when Joseph Smith arrived at Toronto in August, together with the first counselor to the church presidency, Sidney Rigdon, and Thomas B. Marsh, president of the Twelve, to tour the Canadian branches. Again, as on his first meeting with the prophet, an electric current seemed to vibrate Taylor's arm as he clasped Joseph's hand. He felt a kinship with this big and vital man, full of the joy of life and full of the spirit, who bore the weight of a desperate crisis in the new church without losing his optimism or sense of humor.

Leonora served supper, chicken and dumplings, which Joseph attacked with gusto, bringing a beaming smile to the cook with his compliments. Marsh also did full justice to the meal; but Sidney, Leonora declared, didn't eat enough to keep a bird alive. Rigdon explained that he was very tired; it had been a hard trip and a long day.

Taylor learned that since he'd left Kirtland, apostates had started a rival church there, rejecting Joseph and claiming authority. Various prophets had sprung up like weeds. One, a young woman who received revelations by means of a black seer stone, had made a considerable number of disciples. Frederick G. Williams of the first presidency now was her scribe, and the three witnesses had been led astray by the seeress, who held meetings each Thursday at which her followers danced, shouted, spoke in tongues, leaped about, quivered, quaked, jerked, barked while working themselves into a fever pitch of mass hysteria.

Sidney Rigdon declared that this was Satan's counterfeit at work. Such apostates must be lopped off, root and branch. Joseph was more tolerant of human frailty. Financial setbacks had plunged many into darkness, and they blamed the church for their own avarice. Mistakes had been made, he said, and he was not prepared to censure anyone. Banking was as much a science as the legal profession. A man might be a celebrated divine while knowing nothing of medicine or finance; he would be as liable to fail in the management of a bank as in the constructing of a balloon or in the making of a watch.[4]

Marsh had said very little. Now he spoke up, saying it was too bad that Joseph hadn't told the people this when they were speculating in real estate and buying stock in the bank.

Taylor was surprised at the bitter tone of the apostle's comment. For a moment he wondered if there would be a scene over his dinner table. But Joseph threw back his head for a hearty laugh, reminding Brother Thomas that it was much easier to have hindsight than foresight, even for a prophet. Taylor's great laugh boomed, Sidney joined in, and Marsh forced a smile. The incident was over.

Instead of brooding over past mistakes, Joseph was looking forward confidently to the future. He was sure that the mission to England would infuse the church with fresh blood, and would be a greater success, even, than the work in Canada.

After supper, Rigdon and Marsh went to bed early. Joseph, however, suggested a walk. Taylor set a moderate pace, because of Joseph's limp; but the old injury, botched by a frontier doctor, hadn't impaired the prophet's strength, and soon Taylor was hard-pressed to match him stride for stride. When they returned home, Taylor was tingling from the workout, ready to relax at the hearth.

Leonora served tea and biscuits. As she poured, Joseph asked about affairs in the Canadian mission. Surprised at the question, Taylor said that Brother Sampson Avard would be the one to make such a report, inasmuch as he was in charge. Joseph regarded him curiously, saying that he knew nothing about Sampson Avard being appointed head of the church in Canada. This evidently had been done by the apostate group.

Taylor was dismayed. If he hadn't been so sure that Avard's appoint-

---

[4] For Joseph's attitude, see *Messenger and Advocate*, July 1837.

ment was a prelude to his own call to the apostleship, he might have checked Avard's authority more closely. He went to bed wondering if he had shattered Joseph's confidence in him by the mistake.

The next day Taylor took the party to nearby Scarborough, where they found Avard presiding at a church conference. When confronted by Joseph, the man's servile attitude was in marked contrast to his arrogance in taking authority from Taylor. Avard claimed that he had been misled into believing his authority had come from the prophet, and he begged forgiveness for any mistake. Here, Taylor decided, was a cunning and ambitious sycophant who would always abuse power.

Except for this confrontation, the tour of the Canadian branches was a spiritual feast for Taylor, who reveled in the opportunity to be associated with the prophet of God whose every word, to him, was inspired.

Before returning to Kirtland, Joseph ordained Taylor a high priest. Then, late in the fall, a letter from Joseph informed John Taylor that he had been chosen to fill a vacancy in the Quorum of the Twelve.[5]

After closing out his affairs at Toronto, Taylor was solvent, but just barely. Time spent in church work during the past two years had cut heavily into his income, while his surplus had gone into the property at Kirtland. As he set about preparing for the move to Zion he had no team, no wagon, no provisions, and no money. But he had an abundance of confidence that the Lord would open the way.

Winter swept down from the north. Leonora, her belly swollen with child, took a more practical attitude toward the move. A number of families were planning on going together, and John had set the date for departure. Yet, as he went about bidding farewell to the Saints in the various branches, as he helped attend to the affairs of everyone except himself, she couldn't help worry about how he expected the Lord to provide.

John returned home four days before the scheduled departure beaming with good news. He'd called on John Mills, a well-to-do convert, to say good-bye. Mills had planned on going with the group, but then had changed his mind. Now he changed it again, John said, and, what's more, he'd invited the Taylors to go along with his wagons.

Leonora heaved a great sigh of relief. Now they had transportation, at least. But what about provisions? Was the leader of the expedition required to beg his breakfast every morning?

Don't worry, he told her—the Lord would provide. There were still three more days before departure.

Then, during those three days, gifts showered down from the branches

---

[5] However, he was not officially ordained to the position until the following winter.

—flour, ham, bacon, cakes, roasted geese and ducks, even clothing and money.

The morning of departure was clear and cold. John Taylor was at the reins of the leading sleigh. Leonora tucked the buffalo robe about the children, George and Mary Ann, seated snugly between the parents. The Mills family sat in the rear, bundled against the cold. Behind in a long line were sleighs of other families, while strung out in file were baggage wagons containing furniture, supplies, tents, provisions, hay and grain for the teams, household utensils, farm implements, chickens, and pigs. Bringing up the rear were the herders with the livestock: horses, cattle, and sheep. In the company were men who could repair a broken axle or set a broken bone, there was a midwife; the company could be self-sustaining enroute, and it carried everything necessary to exist from scratch in a new land.

John Taylor slapped the rumps of the team and the journey began.

Spring was in the air and the roads were turning to slush when the party reached Kirtland. But this place was no longer Zion. Joseph and Sidney, hectored by writs, judgments, warrants, and lawsuits, had fled Kirtland in January, pursued more than two hundred miles by enemies, "armed with pistols and guns," the prophet reported, "seeking our lives." The church printing office had been attached by the sheriff, but before he could take possession someone put the torch to it. To meet a legal judgment, the temple on which the Saints had lavished such sacrifice and hard work was auctioned off for $150.[6] The apostates who remained, and the sharpers who'd come in to take possession of property, reminded Taylor of wolves prowling a deserted city.

The new place of gathering unto Zion was some eight hundred miles away at Far West, Missouri, a Mormon town not yet a year old; it was in Caldwell County, which had been expressly created for occupancy by the Saints after they had been expelled from Jackson and Clay counties. Some of the faithful at Kirtland had followed Joseph to Zion. Taylor found the remainder, some five hundred strong, organizing into Kirtland Camp, which planned to travel in a body to Far West.

His plan of setting up a business at Kirtland was, of course, up the spout. He got rid of the property for what it would bring at a forced sale, then, after exchanging sled runners for wheels, led his party toward Zion.

---

6 The building subsequently was used as a recreation hall, while the basement served as a cattle barn. Some forty years after the Mormons left Kirtland, the Reorganized LDS Church obtained title to the temple and rehabilitated it. It is still maintained by this sect.

4

Expel or Exterminate

WITH THE SPRING THAW, the roads were quagmires. Wagon wheels became huge balls of mud; on really bad stretches two and even three teams had to be put on every wagon while men got behind to push. After three days of this, Taylor called a halt until the roads hardened.

The respite gave the women a chance to boil clothes and bedding for the first time since they'd left Canada. Men repaired harness and wagons, sought work in a nearby village. The teams had a chance to rest up from the long trip.

Skilled furniture makers were scarce on the frontier, and Taylor had no trouble locating a job in a cabinet shop. In the evenings he used the place as a meeting hall to preach to the Gentiles. When the roads hardened, he led the group toward the gathering in Zion, preaching along the way to anyone who would listen.

At a town near Columbus, a large group gathered at an open-air meeting to hear him. He was pleased at the turnout until he was tipped off that it consisted of a mob intent upon giving the Mormon preacher a coat of tar and feathers. The advice was terse: "Git."

Instead of slipping away, Taylor mounted a stump and surveyed the sea of hostile faces, admitting that he was filled with peculiar emotions. He was recently from Canada, under monarchical rule; now he stood upon the soil of the republic, among free men whose fathers fought for the right of free speech, freedom of the press, freedom of religious belief, the right to life, liberty, and the pursuit of happiness. Could the sons of the patriots plan to tar and feather a man for his religious convictions? "If so," Taylor said, "here I am."

The crowd listened with respect while he preached for three hours.

In May, Taylor stopped near Indianapolis; Leonora's time was near. While the remainder of the train went ahead, he worked in a cabinet shop, went into the city at night to preach, and in his spare time began building a carriage. On June 8 Leonora presented him with his third child, a boy he blessed and christened Joseph James.

During his two months at Indianapolis, other Mormon groups passed through, the most memorable being the one led by his old friend, Isaac Russell. Taylor and Leonora visited the camp, having supper with a number of Toronto Saints. Russell had married Mary Walton, daughter of Isabella, the widow who by opening her house to Parley Pratt had been instrumental in the phenomenal success of the Canadian mission. Isabella was there at the camp, as was her son John, John Goodson, and other old friends.

Isaac Russell was just a year older than Taylor and like him had been born in the English lakes country; he shared Taylor's fondness for literature, had been a Methodist class leader at Toronto, and a member of the study group to which Taylor belonged. When he heard Parley Pratt's first sermon in his mother-in-law's home, he had arisen to declare, "This is the gospel that I wish to live and die by."

Russell was among the handful of missionaries who revitalized the church with the first foreign mission, to England, where he had a remarkable record of conversions. His stories of the English mission provided a spiritual feast for Taylor and Leonora during supper.

Later, when Russell preached to the camp, Taylor and Leonora exchanged disturbed glances. For one thing, he worked his listeners into an emotional frenzy; they began leaping up at the campfire, shouting, dancing, speaking in tongues, screaming in ecstasy. Worse, Russell claimed he was the chosen of the Lord to lead the people to this land, which "will be redeemed by the hands of the Lamanites," the Mormons joining Indians to vanquish their enemies.

When Taylor spoke, he reminded the people that Joseph disapproved of mass emotionalism. He also rebuked Russell for arrogating leadership. But the faces of the group were like stone. On leaving, Taylor felt a lead weight in his belly, and Leonora was crying quietly. These friends and associates had been particularly dear, sharing in the great discovery of the gospel; now they were following a new prophet.

After two months at Indianapolis, where he'd raised up a branch of the church, Taylor again headed west with his family for Zion, driving the new carriage he'd made.

On an afternoon in September he reined the team on the crest of a hill. Below, on the bottomlands of the Grand River near its junction with the Missouri, was a little town; a number of covered wagons were camped about. This was the settlement of DeWitt, Missouri, some fifty miles from Far West. It was the first Mormon town he'd seen since leaving Kirtland in early spring.

The heavy wagons of the emigrants had cut the road to pieces. With his foot on the brake, Taylor eased the team down the steep slope toward the bottomlands. Leonora clutched the baby, warning George and Mary Ann to hold on, as the carriage lurched over ruts and chuckholes. As a wheel struck a rock Taylor was jolted almost off the seat. His foot slipped off the brake, and he plunged over the dash. His first thought as he fell was of Leonora and the children. Then came the crushing impact of the front wheel, numbing his arm. He tried to roll out of the way of the rear wheel but couldn't move, and the iron tire crushed across the arm. He lay helpless as the carriage clattered down the hill, the horses running away.

He was struggling to arise, green sick, when Leonora ran into view up the hill. Was he all right? His arm! Everyone was safe; she'd seized the reins and got the team under control; George was tending the horses, and Mary Ann had the baby. She insisted that he lie down, while with his penknife she slit his sleeve, examining the arm. It was severely bruised, but no bones broken.

His friend, Henry Humphrey, welcomed him at DeWitt, inviting him to stay until recovered from the accident. How long this might be, Taylor didn't know. The arm was badly swollen, turning black and blue. Leonora bandaged it and made a sling from a diaper. At bedtime Henry asked him if he'd like a stiff shot of whiskey to deaden the pain. Taylor declined. He would have taken one, earlier, as a social lubricant, but he didn't use liquor as a crutch. He got little sleep that night, and by morning the arm was throbbing like a toothache.

During breakfast Henry said that trouble with the Missourians was again brewing. Most of the Saints at DeWitt were refugees from Jackson and Clay counties; now, here in Carroll County and also at Far West in Caldwell County, mobs were in action. As if confirming the fact, a rider galloped into town, while they were still at breakfast, with the news that two preachers, Sashiel Woods and Abbot Hancock, were leading a mob to drive the Saints from DeWitt.

Leonora protested as Taylor took his injured arm out of the sling and began unwrapping the bandage. No time now for being an invalid, he told her. He borrowed a rifle from Humphrey, then went out and bought a brace of pistols. When the mob arrived, he was among the armed force waiting to repel it. Finding the Mormons ready to defend the settlement, the mob leaders reconsidered. They dispersed after warning that all Mormons must leave DeWitt within ten days, or every man, woman, and child would be killed.

Next morning Taylor headed north toward Far West, rifle across his knees as he drove the team, pistols in his waistband, alert for ambush. A new and strange emotion possessed him, until he paid scant attention to his throbbing arm; his senses were quickened as he watched for signs of the enemy at every thicket and bend of the road.

When he reached Far West, three days later, he met the church leaders —Joseph, Sidney, Brigham Young, Heber C. Kimball, Thomas B. Marsh, Orson Hyde, Parley Pratt, Lyman Wight, Hyrum Smith—and they, also, had changed. They were all armed now, and the talk was of strategy, plans for defense and attack.

Taylor had always considered himself a minister of the gospel, carrying God's word to the unsaved. Now he realized that he also was a soldier. A war was on. With an enemy to fight, Parley Pratt had forgotten his bickering at Kirtland. It was all for one and one for all, to present a solid front against the enemy. These men were spiritual leaders, but they also had become military commanders, directing the forces of the Kingdom of God against the mobbers.

Joseph, speaking to the group, said, "O ye Twelve, and all Saints, profit by this important key, that in all your trials, troubles, and temptations, afflictions, bonds, imprisonment, and death, see to it that you do not betray heaven, that you do not betray Jesus Christ, that you do not betray your brethren." And, summing it up, he emphasized, "Whatever you do, do not betray your friends."

This became Taylor's creed. Until the end of his life he was to be at war, fighting one battle after another for the faith. There could be no compromise, no quarter; for him it would be the Kingdom of God, or nothing; all or none. The greatest crimes of war were treason, betrayal, and giving aid and comfort to the enemy. Truth was a relative thing. A basic rule of war was to confuse and mislead the enemy; any device to this end was justified. Apostates—traitors—were to be rejected utterly, denounced as complete liars, their characters destroyed. Treason was the greatest crime, not because the traitor lied, but because he revealed war secrets, the truth.

John Taylor would never again from this moment admit to any fact, regardless of the evidence, that involved violation of this creed.[1]

John Taylor found that he had arrived in Zion at the climactic battle of the war in Missouri. His part in it, however, was to fight with his pen rather than his gun. Joseph, who had had atrocious luck with his scribes and historians falling from the faith, welcomed him with open arms and gave him a most important assignment: He was appointed to a committee

---

[1] An understanding of this attitude is vital to gaining an appreciation of the people and events of the Mormon story. Official church history is, actually, war propaganda, with the viewpoint of the other side of the conflict completely discarded. John Taylor was a product of this war. He never in his life gave the enemy—which was the entire outside world—any more than the equivalent of his name, rank, and serial number.

which would draft a report to the Missouri state legislature on the persecution of the Mormons. The committee consisted of nine men, including
the presiding bishop of the church, Edward Partridge, and two apostles,
Brigham Young and Heber C. Kimball. While the committee as a whole
would conceive and shape the report, the nitty-gritty of getting it down
on paper would largely be a collaboration of Taylor and Partridge.

While Taylor was without personal experience of the violent events
during the past seven years in Missouri, resulting from the Mormon
attempt to settle Zion, eye-witnesses abounded; settlements of the society
in Far West, DeWitt, and Adam-ondi-Ahman were full of families who
had been expelled from Jackson County, "invited" to leave Clay County,
and now were under seige in Caldwell, Carroll, and Daviess counties. As
for the Gentile viewpoint, he had personally parleyed with leaders of
the mob at DeWitt; he knew the rabid anti-Mormon bias of the two
ministers, Abbot Hancock and Sashiel Woods, who rode at its head and
the uncompromising hatred of such men as Col. William Peniston, the
leader of the state militia. A visit to any tavern or grocery where Gentiles gathered was sufficient to encounter first-hand hostility. The experience of Bishop Partridge, who had been president of the church in Zion
and a recipient of mob violence, was of particular value in framing the
report; a balanced Gentile viewpoint was available from Joseph's lawyer,
Alexander Doniphan, who also was a general of the state militia.

After three months the report "To the Honorable Legislature of the
State of Missouri" was presented to that body by a Mormon member
of it, John Corrill:

> We, the undersigned petitioners and inhabitants of Caldwell County,
> Missouri, in consequence of the late calamity that has come upon us taken
> in connection with former afflictions, feel it a duty we owe to ourselves
> and our country to lay our case before your honorable body for consid-
> eration. It is a well known fact, that a society of our people commenced
> settling in Jackson County, Missouri. . . .
> Soon after the settlement began, persecution commenced. . . .

Though well aware of underlying motivations, Taylor added no other
explanation of the violence than the single word "persecution." He wasn't
writing history; his pen was a weapon, a cannon blasting at the enemy's
position.

In traveling through the state, he had found Missouri sparsely settled
by frontier people living in log cabins, eating a diet of corn pone and
wild game cooked over a fireplace with mud-plastered chimney. The
people wore deerskin, a few with homespun and gingham for Sunday
best. They cleared timberland for their corn patches, avoiding the rich
prairies because they didn't have plows capable of breaking the tough sod.
Independence, county seat of Jackson County, consisted of a brick courthouse, three stores, and not more than twenty houses, mostly log. And

here, in the spring of 1831, had come what seemed an endless stream of Mormon wagons as the Saints invaded a county whose total population was less than 3,000.

The frontiersmen had distrusted the Mormons from their first contact with advance missionaries, who had largely ignored the whites to prose-lyte among the Indians. As Mormon numbers increased, Missourians feared an alliance between them and the redskins. Also, the Saints were primarily northerners, moving into a slave state, and were, it was charged, abolitionists.

When the prophet arrived at Independence, he declared it the land of promise for the building of the city of Zion. He dedicated a lot near the courthouse as the site for the temple, laying the cornerstone by rolling a rock into place.

Missourians heard Mormons talk of the grandeur and glory that would come upon Zion, with the wicked destroyed and the land prepared for the return of the lost tribes of Israel. The Kingdom of God in these last days would roll forth like the little stone the prophet Daniel saw cut from the mountain without hands, until it should fill up the whole earth. The Latter-day Saints were the people chosen to establish the kingdom as a prerequisite of the millennium. Some Mormon settlers went about attempting to buy property at bargain prices, with the frank warning that the offer had better be taken, for the time had come when the riches of the Gentiles were to be consecrated to Israel.

In just two years there were more than 1,200 Saints in Jackson County —about one-third of the total population—and more pouring in. They worked together, shared the wealth, pooled labor, broke the sod, built houses, performed miracles by their cooperative industry. They thought alike, and they voted as a unit at the direction of their leaders.

"It requires no gift of prophecy to tell that the day is not far distant when the civil government of the county will be in their hands," a mass meeting of old settlers declared. The county historian noted that, "They had nearly taken possession of Independence, and were rapidly extending their settlements," by the spring of 1833.[2]

The sparks that ignited the powder keg came from W. W. Phelps' printing office. Phelps was preparing a compilation of Joseph's revelations in a book called the *Book of Commandments*. Advance copies confirmed the worst fears of the old settlers, who were frankly referred to as "your enemies," living in "the land of your inheritance." One revelation stated that "it is the Lord's business to provide for his Saints in these last days, that they may obtain an inheritance in the land of Zion." And the Lord himself promised that "I will consecrate the riches of the Gentiles unto my people."

---

[2] *History of Jackson County, Missouri*; Kansas City: Union Historical Co., 1881.

Coincidental with this bombshell, Phelps, in the July issue of the church newspaper, *The Evening and the Morning Star*, printed advice to a handful of free Negro converts who wanted to come to Zion. Missouri law required that before entry they must have a certificate of citizenship from another state. Phelps reprinted this statute, "To prevent any misunderstanding . . . respecting free people of color, who may think of coming to . . . Missouri, as members of the church."

To the old settlers, this was an invitation for free Negroes to flood the state. In addition, said the county historian,

> [The Mormons] grew bolder as they grew stronger, and daily proclaimed to the older settlers that the Lord had given them the whole land of Missouri; that bloody wars would extirpate all other sects from the country; that it would be "one gore of blood from the Mississippi to the border," and that the few who were left unslain would be the servants of the Saints, who would own all the property in the county.

Sporadic mobs began stoning Mormon houses, burning haystacks, and shooting livestock. On July 20, 1833, several hundred Missourians gathered at the courthouse in Independence, and warned that "the society must leave the county immediately."

> Being in a defenseless situation, to save a general massacre it was agreed that one half of the society should leave the county by the first of next January, and the remainder by the first of the following April.[3]

The exodus was too slow. In October

> the wrath of the mob again began to be kindled, insomuch that they shot at some of our people, whipped others, and threw down their houses, and committed many other depredations; indeed the society of Saints were harassed for some time both day and night; their houses were brick-batted and broken open and women and children insulted. The store-house of A. S. Gilbert and Company was broken open, ransacked, and some of the goods strewed in the streets.

When the Mormons captured one of the mob, Richard McCarty, in the act of looting the store, a Gentile justice of the peace refused to issue a warrant for McCarty's arrest; instead, he jailed the Mormons for false arrest. The futility of appealing to the law was self-evident; the Saints organized for defense.

Parley Pratt became leader of an armed force of some sixty men, David Whitmer of another. Whitmer's forces clashed with marauders, and in the fight two Missourians and one Mormon were killed. Inflamatory reports of the affray terrorized the country. The old settlers called upon Lieutenant-governor Lilburn Boggs to muster the state militia for protec-

---

3 Report to legislature.

tion from the Mormons. Boggs, a resident of Independence and one of the largest landowners of western Missouri, was apprehensive of the influx. He called up the militia, putting it under command of Col. Thomas Pitcher, who had been a signer of the manifesto that the Saints must leave Jackson County.

Pitcher immediately demanded that the Mormon troops surrender their arms. The apprehensive Saints obeyed only after Boggs personally guaranteed that the militia would also disarm the mob. Pitcher, however, had absolutely no intention of honoring Boggs' promise. After collecting the Mormon guns, he and his troops either looked the other way or actually joined the mob which sprang into action with news that the Mormons had been disarmed.

> The next day, parties of the mob, from fifty to seventy, headed by priests, went from house to house, threatening women and children with death if they were not gone before they returned. This so alarmed our people that they fled in different directions; some took shelter in the woods, while others wandered in the prairies till their feet bled; and the weather being very cold, their sufferings in other respects were great.[4]

Some 1,500 Mormons were driven from Jackson County. One party of six men and about a hundred and fifty women and children wandered over the prairie in a bone-chilling November rain for several days, without shelter or sufficient food. The main camp waited on the banks of the Missouri to be ferried across, a few in tents, the majority with makeshift shelters of wagon covers, horse blankets, or quilts propped on sticks; their household goods were piled about in the mud. As the driving rain continued the sick lay in wet beds and women gave birth to babies. At the height of their misery, as the refugees huddled in the wet during a long night, "we were called up by the cry of signs in the heavens" at about 2 A.M., Parley Pratt related.

> We arose, and to our great astonishment all the firmament seemed enveloped in splendid fireworks, as if every star in the broad expanse had been hurled from its course, and sent lawless through the wilds of ether. Thousands of bright meteors were shooting through space in every direction, with long trains of light following in their courses. This lasted several hours, and was only closed by the dawn of the rising sun. Every heart was filled with joy at this majestic display of signs and wonders, showing the near approach of the coming of the Son of God.

Other signs and miracles reinforced the faith of the Saints during their travail. In the battle between David Whitmer's band of guerrillas and the Gentiles, a Mormon named Philo Dibble was shot "in the body through his waistband; the ball remained in him," Parley said.

---

[4] Committee report.

He bled inwardly, and, in a day or two his bowels were so filled with blood and so inflamed that he was about to die. . . . The smell of himself had become intolerable to him and those about him. At length Elder Newell Knight administered to him, by the laying on of hands. . . . He immediately discharged several quarts of blood and corruption, among which was the ball with which he had been wounded. He was instantly healed, and went to work chopping wood.

The ferocity of the Jackson County mob brought a wave of public sympathy throughout the remainder of the state. Clay County, directly north, received the Saints as persecuted refugees.

After the society had left Jackson County, their buildings, amounting to about two hundred, were either burned or otherwise destroyed, and much of their crops, as well as furniture and stock . . . for the loss of which they have not as yet received any remuneration.

There had been growing dissention among the Saints in Zion, Taylor learned, because the prophet seemed to neglect them in favor of Kirtland —building the temple there instead of at Independence, the land of their inheritance, and favoring Kirtland residents with important church office, while Joseph himself lived there. Then, when news of the expulsion from Jackson County reached Kirtland, the prophet's reaction sent a chill through many victims of mob violence. Instead of offering sympathy, Joseph announced that the Lord had caused affliction to come upon the chosen people in Missouri "in consequence of their transgressions, envying and strifes, and lustful and covetous desires." Furthermore, the disorganized and destitute refugees were exhorted to march back to Zion and vanquish the enemy:

And go ye straightway into the land of my vineyard . . . break down the walls of mine enemies; throw down their tower and scatter their watchmen; and inasmuch as they gather together against you, avenge me of mine enemies, that by and by I may come with the residue of mine house and possess the land.

Bishop Partridge confided to Taylor that this commandment caused consternation among some of the dispossessed and poverty-stricken society, licking their wounds as they tried to find new homes and some means of making a livelihood among strangers. And, Partridge said, Gentiles hooted at the revelation, considering it so choice a bit of heretical bombast that copies sold for a dollar apiece.

By revelation, Joseph promised the outpouring of God's wrath upon the mobbers. The prophet would raise up an army at Kirtland for the redemption of Zion and would "lead them as Moses led the children of Israel" back to the promised land. About two hundred men joined the army, called Zion's Camp, which marched out of Kirtland to redeem Zion. But Jackson County was eight hundred long and dusty miles away.

En route, the weary troops became torn by bickering and dissention. Then cholera struck the camp, thirteen died. The prophet disbanded the army, announcing that its purpose was not "to fight the battles of Zion," but instead was "a trial of their faith." A goodly number didn't survive the trial.[5] The breach widened between Joseph and some of the men who had been his closest associates.

With the Saints resettled in Clay County, the tension between them and their neighbors had steadily increased, until, three years later, they were "invited" to leave or, as a citizen's committee advised, "a civil war is inevitable." Once more the Mormons picked up and moved, this time north to the prairielands, where Caldwell and Daviess counties were created for their occupancy.

This exodus took place at the time the financial bubble burst at Kirtland. The strain of the double blow was too much for the faith of many; a wave of apostasy decimated the society in Missouri and Ohio.

The smooth-talking and ambitious Sampson Avard—the same man who had usurped Taylor's authority in Canada—seized the opportunity, presented by the dissention within the society and the desire to protect itself against aggression, to form a secret band of armed guerrillas. Its members

> entered into a covenant, that the word of the presidency should be obeyed, and . . . all things must be in submission to them, and moreover all tattling, lying, and backbiting, must be put down, and he that would not submit willingly should be forced to it, or leave the county. . . . Many were opposed to this society, but such was their determination and also their threatenings against them, that those opposed dare not speak their minds on the subject. They said they meant to cleanse their own members first, and then the church. In order to carry on their operations, they organized themselves into companies of fifties and tens, with a captain to each company, that they might be ready to act in concert on any occasion.[6]

This secret band of zealots had various names. One was the "Big Fan," in reference to the blowing of chaff from the wheat at threshing time; others, "Daughters of Zion" and "Avenging Angels," from the occasional practice of disguising members in women's clothing on their disciplinary forays. But the name that stuck was "Sons of Dan," shortened to

---

[5] In Mormon lore, Zion's Camp is looked upon as invaluable in winnowing out the chaff, leaving men who were destined for church leadership. A few months after the expedition the Quorum of the Twelve Apostles and the first Quorum of Seventies were organized, members of these important groups consisted principally from those who had survived the test of Zion's Camp.

[6] *A Brief History of the Church of Christ of Latter Day Saints (Commonly Called Mormons), Including an Account of Their Doctrine and Discipline, with the Reasons of the Author for Leaving the Church* by John Corrill, a Member of the Legislature of Missouri.

"Danites," which referred to the little stone spoken of by Daniel which would roll forth and fill the world; it also applied to the reference in Genesis: "Dan shall be a serpent by the way, an adder in the path, that biteth the horse's heels, so that his rider shall fall backwards."

The church leadership had at first endorsed this organzation, which was typical of other secret groups formed by zealots dedicated to achieving the Kingdom of God. Sidney Rigdon in particular was obsessed with the necessity of rooting out dissenters. He didn't have Joseph's tolerance nor breadth of vision, and Sidney was frantic in stamping out incipient apostasy.

One of the first Danite acts was to write a letter to Oliver Cowdery, David Whitmer, John Whitmer, William W. Phelps, and Lyman E. Johnson—five prominent and revered Saints—excoriating them for being "united with a gang of counterfeiters, thieves, liars, and blacklegs." They were accused of running a "bogus money business," of "swearing falsely," of "stealing, cheating, lying, instituting vexatious lawsuits," purloining letters from the post office, arson, and swindling. As if counterfeiting wasn't bad enough, they were charged with selling "stones and sand for bogus"—of not even being honest crooks.

Sidney Rigdon and eighty-three Danites signed these charges, not realizing that, in attacking prominent Saints, they were smearing the entire church. The accused fled with their families. They were cut off and delivered to the buffetings of Satan in a purge that included four members of the Twelve; a fifth, William Smith, the prophet's brother, narrowly escaped expulsion.

In purging the church, Avard admitted smugly that the ruthless methods of the Danites "succeeded admirably, and to the satisfaction of those concerned."

When John Taylor arrived at Far West, the city was not quite two years old—yet already it was a thriving metropolis of some three thousand inhabitants, the largest town in the state north of the Missouri River. Joseph had laid out the city on a plat containing four sections—two miles square—with wide streets forming blocks of four acres and each acre divided into four lots. The large public square in the center of the city was atop the highest knoll of the surrounding prairie, and from it Taylor could see for miles in all directions—the cultivated fields of the Saints, the endless sweep of the rolling prairie dotted with Gentile villages, their white church spires gleaming in the sunlight. In the public square was the temple site, an excavation one hundred and ten feet by eighty, marked by large stones rolled into place at each corner. But work on the basement had been suspended due to trouble with mobs, which followed the Saints to their new location.

Local elections had again triggered off violence just a few weeks before

Taylor's arrival. Fearful of Mormon domination at the polls, men at the little town of Gallatin attempted to prevent the Saints from voting. Gentile fears had been aroused when Mormon males of the county held a meeting at Adam-ondi-Ahmen just before election. One of those present, John D. Lee, reported that "At that meeting all the males over eighteen years of age were organized into a military body, according to the law of the priesthood, and called 'The Host of Israel.' "[7]

On election day, Lee was lying on the grass near the polling place at Gallatin when "a drunken brute by the name of Richard Weldon" stepped up to a small Mormon named Brown in the line and provoked a fight.

"Are you a Mormon, sir?" Weldon demanded.

"Yes, sir, I am."

"Do you Mormons believe in healing the sick by laying on of hands, speaking in tongues, and casting out devils?"

"We do."

"You are a damned liar," Weldon declared, "and Joseph Smith is a damned imposter!"

With this, the drunk leaped on Brown and began beating him. When another Mormon tried to pull Weldon off, a half dozen Gentiles pitched in. Close at hand was a pile of oak hearts remaining from a shingle-making operation, handy clubs three inches square and four feet long. Riley Stewart snatched one and leaped in to defend his fellow Saints, fetching Weldon a clout that felled him almost atop Lee, who states that "Immediately, the fight became general."

John L. Butler, one of the captains of the Host of Israel, gave the Danite sign of distress.[8] The Mormons snatched up oak hearts, and "in the battle, which was spirited, nine men had their skulls broken, and many others were seriously injured in other ways. The severe treatment of the mob by the Danites soon ended the battle."

When exaggerated reports of this melee reached Far West, Sampson Avard gathered a force of 150 men and rode into Daviess County, accompanied by Joseph and Sidney, "to view the situation." The alarmed cit-

---

[7] At this same meeting the Danites were organized in Daviess County, the members, according to Lee, "placed under the most sacred obligations that language could invent. They were sworn to stand by and sustain each other. *Sustain, protect, defend,* and *obey* the leaders of the church, *under any and all circumstances unto death*; and to disobey the orders of the leaders of the church, or divulge the name of a Danite to an outsider, or to make public any of the secrets of the order of Danites, was to be punished with death. And I can say of a truth, many have paid the penalty for failing to keep their covenants."

[8] Made "by placing the right hand on the right side of the face, with the points of the fingers upwards, shoving the hand upwards until the ear is snug between the thumb and fore-finger."

izens of Daviess considered this expedition an armed invasion and secured warrants for the arrest of the leaders. Lilburn Boggs, now governor, again called out the militia. The Mormons claimed that this merely gave official sanction to mob action and that officers of the militia units were preachers of rival sects. Civil war had again broken out in Missouri. Col. William P. Peniston of the militia reported to the governor that Mormon forces had collected for the purposes of driving all Gentiles out of the county:

> . . . our worst apprehensions have been fulfilled. They have plundered or robbed and burned every house in Gallatin, our county seat, among the rest our post-office; have driven almost every individual from the county, who are now flying before them with their families, many of whom have been forced out without necessary clothing, their wives and little children wading, in many instances, through snow without a shoe. When the miserable families are thus forced out, their houses are plundered and burned. . . .[9]

Believing themselves invulnerable, fighting God's war, members of Avard's fanatical organization constituted a formidable guerrilla force. Lee said he considered himself "bullet proof, that no Gentile ball could ever harm me. . . . I thought that one Danite could chase a thousand Gentiles, and two could put ten thousand to flight."[10]

As with all wars, there were excesses on both sides, atrocity stories typical of armed conflict. Lee reported an example of war humor: The Danites took prisoner a Gentile named Tarwater, but after talking with him let him go, telling him he was free to return home. As the man turned and ran happily toward freedom, a Saint who was particularly revered by Lee "stepped up to a tree, laid his gun up by the side of the tree, took deliberate aim, and shot Tarwater."

Taylor's committee reported to the legislature that a mob of from two

---

[9] The Mormons blamed the sacking of Gallatin and Millport on the Missourians. Lyman Wight testified that mobbers "entered into one of the most diabolical schemes ever entered into by man: . . . Firstly, by loading their families and goods in covered wagons, setting fire to their houses, moving into the midst of the mob and crying out the Mormons have driven us and burnt our houses." (See *Times and Seasons*, July 15, 1843.) The very extent of this diabolical scheme, the damage to property, the number of people involved, and the suffering of the dispossessed people, causes this claim to fall of its own weight—not to mention the body of testimony to the contrary.

Too many eyewitness accounts survive to doubt that Mormon armed forces under David Patten sacked Gallatin, Lyman Wight with another company attacked Millport, and Seymour Brunson raided Grindstone Fork.

[10] The death of "Captain Fearnot," David W. Patten, leader of the Mormon forces at the battle of Crooked River, was a severe shock to many. When Patten fell, it "spread a mantle of gloom over the entire community," Lee said. "If *Fear Not* could be killed, who could claim immunity from the missiles of death hurled by Gentile weapons?"

to three hundred attacked the little Mormon settlement at Haun's Mill, and that "eighteen were killed and a number more severely wounded." While women and children fled into the brush, Mormon males took shelter in the log blacksmith shop, which proved to be a death trap. Missourians surrounded it and poured bullets through windows and every hole in the chinking, despite the attempt of those inside to surrender. The dead and wounded were thrown into a well thirty feet deep, filling it with bodies to within a yard of the surface. The committee reported that Thomas McBride, an old veteran of the Revolution,

> threw himself into their hands and begged for quarter, when he was instantly shot down; that not killing him, they took an old corn cutter and literally mangled him to pieces. A lad of ten years of age, after being shot down, also begged to be spared, when one of the mob placed the muzzle of his gun to the boy's head and blew out his brains. The slaughter of these not satisfying the mob, they then proceeded to rob and plunder.

On a dank Sunday morning, John Taylor and a dozen church leaders arrived in two carriages at Lyman Wight's ferry at the west fork of the Grand River. It had rained heavily the night before and was still drizzling. A dozen wagons were waiting to be ferried across; Mormon families were fleeing from the mobs and gathering for protection at Adam-ondi-Ahman, which was on the bluff across the river. Wagon wheels were balled with mud. Men were gathering wood from the bottomland thickets; women cooked breakfast over smouldering fires, while kids huddled about for warmth.

Recognizing the importance of the new arrivals—Thomas B. Marsh, president of the Twelve and also president *pro tem* of the Saints in Missouri, apostles Brigham Young, Heber C. Kimball, David Patten, Parley Pratt, Orson Hyde, Bishop Edward Partridge, and other dignitaries—the waiting people invited the brethren to move to the head of the line. They declined and awaited their turn. It was mid-morning when they had crossed the river and were shaking hands with Joseph, Hyrum, and Sidney in the town atop the bluff. From this vantage point the prairie and wooded river bottoms rolled away on all sides in a gorgeous vista. Joseph had designated Independence as the site of the Garden of Eden, and here at Adam-ondi-Ahman, in the valley of God, was where Adam had resided after the fall.

After a meeting with the brethren to discuss strategy, Joseph took them to inspect the army, bivouacked on the prairie. The Host of Israel seemed a bedraggled lot to Taylor—the men shivering around a few smouldering fires in the drizzle, teeth chattering, noses red, indulging in the universal army pastime, griping.

Joseph hurried among them, pulling them to their feet. "Get up! Move! Wrestle, jump, run! Warm yourselves up! Don't mope about!"

At the prophet's direction the men formed a ring, then Joseph stepped into the center, challenging all comers. One by one the strongest among them pitted brawn and skill against the prophet—and ended up with shoulders on the grass. When winded, Joseph relinquished his place to another man who remained until thrown, when his victor in turn held the center of the ring.

The men were warm now, excited, cheering the contestants, gripes and the chill drizzle forgotten. Then, at the height of the fun, Sidney Rigdon arrived. He rushed into the ring with drawn sword and declared that the sport must stop. It was sinful to break the Sabbath in such a manner.

Joseph stepped into the ring. "Brother Sidney, the boys are amusing themselves at my suggestion. You go ahead and get ready for meeting, and leave them alone."

Sidney stiffened, his dignity ruffled by having his order countermanded. Then Joseph, grinning, with a sudden movement grabbed Rigdon's wrist and the sword went spinning to the turf. "Now, old man, either leave or join the fun!" Rigdon tried to struggle, but the husky prophet, chuckling, dragged him from the ring, ripping Rigdon's fine pulpit coat from collar to waist. As the older man gathered his ruffled dignity, Joseph called, "Go to it, boys; have your fun!"

Taylor was appalled by the shattering defection of prominent Saints. Sampson Avard broke with Joseph and turned traitor, revealing details of the Danite organization and activities. Thomas B. Marsh, president of the Twelve, together with apostle Orson Hyde, slipped away in the night. Marsh made affidavit, endorsed by Hyde, of the sacking of Gallatin and Millport by Mormon forces and of Danite looting; he also said that Avard proposed "to start a pestilence among the Gentiles" by poisoning their crops.[11]

George M. Hinkle apostatized, swearing that while troops were at Diahman, he saw "a great deal of plunder" brought into camp and "placed in the hands of the bishop." There was "much mysterious conversation in camp, as to plundering and house-burning." This, Hinkle believed, "would ruin us; that it could not be hid, and would bring the force of the State upon us."

---

[11] Curiously, while the Marsh affidavit, which Hyde corroborated, has been published time and again by Mormon historians as an example of apostate lies, it has always been presented in a bowdlerized version, its most telling points deleted. For the complete affidavit, see *Correspondence, Orders, Etc.* . . .

Although both men repented and returned to the church, Taylor was never able to forgive their betrayal. Though Hyde's defection was brief, and he was received back into the Twelve, four decades later Taylor said that Hyde "told me he would give his life over and over again, if that were possible, to wipe out the recollection of that act." And, Taylor said, "he was not, I think, the man he was before."

Hinkle's apprehensions proved all too true. The Mormon dream of conquest received a rude awakening when Governor Boggs issued an order to the state militia that the Saints must leave Missouri by the following spring:

> The case is now a very plain one; the Mormons must be subdued, and the peace restored to the community. . . . The ringleaders of this rebellion should be made an example of; and, if it should become necessary for the public peace, the Mormons should be exterminated or expelled from the State.

Once more the Saints were disarmed. Joseph, Sidney, Parley Pratt, Lyman Wight, and George Robinson were surrendered by Hinkle as hostages; they were ordered by the commander of the militia to be shot the next morning in the public square at Far West. Gen. Alexander Doniphan, the officer ordered to perform the execution, flatly refused to execute it, "for I consider it cold-blooded murder."[12] His defiance caused reconsideration, and Mormon leaders were jailed to await trial for high treason, murder, burglary, arson, robbery, and larceny.

Edward Partridge was one of the Mormon militia lined up at the public square, where he and fifty-five others had their names read off and were forced to sign deeds of trust forfeiting their property to defray the expenses of the war.

In the pressure to get away, the Mormons "not infrequently traded a valuable farm for an old wagon, a horse, a yoke of oxen, or anything that would furnish them with the means of leaving," historians noted.

> Charles Ross, of Black Oak, bought forty acres of good land, north of Breckenridge, for a blind mare and a clock. Some tracts of good land north of Shoal Creek, in Kidder township, brought only fifty cents an acre. Many of the Mormons had not yet secured the patents to their lands, and though they had regularly entered them, they could not sell them. . . . These kind of lands were abandoned altogether, in most instances, and afterwards settled upon by Gentiles who secured titles by keeping the taxes paid.[13]

Brigham Young was in charge of the exodus of the Mormons from Missouri. The Saints, harassed by mobs, forced to leave behind what

---

[12] It should be remembered that Alexander Doniphan was Joseph's lawyer; thus his refusal to shoot the prophet was motivated by more than a sense of justice—it would have been unthinkable for an attorney to execute his own client without due process of law.

Doniphan's previous work for the Saints had included introducing the bill in the state legislature setting aside Caldwell and Daviess counties for Mormon occupancy. He subsequently did yoeman work in defense of the jailed Mormon leaders.

[13] See *Histories* of Caldwell and Daviess counties, as quoted in B. H. Roberts' *The Missouri Persecutions*, Salt Lake, 1900.

wagons wouldn't carry, were required to travel across the entire width of the state, ill-equipped for winter storms, seeking a new Zion at a place as yet unknown. It was Brigham's first opportunity to exercise his administrative ability, and he displayed a most remarkable talent in organizing a defeated people, infusing courage, making the retreat to Illinois in midwinter a heroic endeavor rather than a rout. Taylor's role was to act as liaison between the Saints and the state militia.

On December 19, 1838, at Far West, John Taylor was ordained an apostle of the church, under the hands of Brigham Young and Heber C. Kimball. At this same meeting, he and Bishop Edward Partridge were appointed a committee to draft a petition of Mormon grievances to be sent to the federal government.[14]

Taylor arrived at Liberty, in Clay County, on a bright winter afternoon. As he drove into the little town, the road was turning to mud and icicles dripped from the eaves of the houses. The warmer weather would be a blessing for the Saints en route across the state toward Illinois. He turned his rig north at the town square and, just beyond it, stopped at a solid stone building having mere slits for windows. This was the Liberty jail, considered escape-proof. The heavy masonry had an inner shell of squared oak logs forming two cells, one atop the other; the lower one, sunk half into the earth, was called the dungeon.

At the house of Samuel Tillery, the jailer, Taylor was refused permission to see the prisoners. The Mormons had tried to escape, and as punishment they'd been put in the dungeon, with no visitors.

Taylor didn't argue the point. He told Tillery he'd just leave the hamper of food Leonora had fixed for the prisoners; she'd also baked an apple pie for the guards, in appreciation of their good care of the brethren. Tillery cut the apple pie into quarters, and Taylor joined him

---

[14] Nothing came of this petition, nor the previous one on which Taylor and Partridge had worked. The petition to the state legislature was presented by John Corrill, and while it caused lively debate, "when the Missouri legislature published . . . what is alleged to be the documents in relation to the disturbances with the 'Mormons,' etc., neither this document nor any account of the debate which followed its introduction . . . appears." (*Documentary History of the Church*, 3:238.)

In Washington, the Senate Committee on the Judiciary reported March 4, 1840 that the case "is not one as will justify or authorize any interposition by this Government. . . . The allegations in the petition relate to the acts of the citizens, and inhabitants, and authorities of the state of Missouri. . . . It can never be presumed that a state either wants the power, or lacks the disposition, to redress the wrongs of its own citizens. . . ."

With fine irony, historian B. H. Roberts notes that the Missouri legislature, "while the petition of the Saints for a redress of their wrongs was lying before it, appropriated two hundred thousand dollars to defray the expenses incurred in driving the 'Mormons' from the State, and dispossessing them of their property!" (*Missouri Persecutions*, 269.)

and the two guards, Jacob High and John Hogarth, in eating it accompanied by a cup of steaming coffee. Presently Tillery wiped his mouth with a bandana and allowed that inasmuch as Taylor was already here, he might as well let him in—but don't go stirring up the prisoners, you hear?

The plump guard, John Hogarth, opened the dungeon door, stepping aside as Taylor entered, then quickly shutting the door to avoid the fetid air that almost made Taylor's stomach turn over. The room was heavy with smoke; the tiny stove, whose flue connected with the one of the cell above, had little draft. Beds were mounds of moldy straw on the floor; sanitary facilities consisted of pitcher, basin, and reeking commode. Confined in this dank room, fourteen feet square, was the presidency of the restored church of Christ, Joseph, Hyrum, and Sidney, together with three stalwarts of the faith, Lyman Wight, Caleb Baldwin, and Alexander McRae.

Sidney Rigdon remained lying on his straw pallet as the others eagerly attacked the hamper of food. Lyman Wight declared that the jail fare was abominable. McRae said it was worse than bad; they were trying to poison the prisoners. Hyrum declared that for a period of five days they were served human flesh.

Taylor took a chicken breast to Rigdon, helping him sit up to eat it. Though only forty-six, Sidney was an old man; and he'd suffered a collapse under the rigors of confinement. Because of the state of his health, he'd been given his freedom by the court, but was staying in jail for protection. The mob was infuriated that charges against him were dropped, and men had sworn that Sidney would never get out of Missouri alive. As Rigdon asked in a quavering voice how much longer he must remain in this hell hole, Taylor advised him to be patient just a little while longer. The attempted jailbreak had delayed things a bit; it was thought best to wait until things settled down.

But the jailbreak *almost* worked, Joseph declared with zest. Watching as the prophet strode back and forth in the confined space, eating a chicken leg as he talked about the escape attempt, Taylor realized the importance of such schemes as a morale factor. Prisoners of war were taught never to cease planning escape; this kept hope alive and spirits bright.

Taylor looked up at the narrow slot of a high window as a voice called his name. Three faces were peering in. Hey, Taylor—had he heard of the Mormon women they'd raped? That one in the church was the best of all. She'd tried to hide in there, but they caught her and tied her on the pulpit, then sixteen of them had at her—and how that bitch did yell!

Sidney rose up, shaking with fury, and in a cracking shriek invoked the wrath of heaven to strike dumb these minions of Satan. The poor woman died, Sidney cried, leaving three small children; and though these sons of perdition laughed now, they would suffer the torments of the damned through eternity.

The men at the window guffawed. More faces crowded other slits. Ol' Sidney sure as hell was in good voice, wasn't he, now? Knowed how to ream a man out without using cuss words; a real art.

Beside himself, Sidney screamed, his voice reaching a high pitch while foam flecked his lips. Then suddenly the voice broke, and Taylor leaped to support him as he fell in convulsions.

The men outside roared. Look at that, would you! Ol' Sidney's having a fit! Guess the Devil snuck up and grabbed him, all right!

Taylor said farewell, not knowing if he'd see the brethren again. As he went out with the guard, he asked about prison fare. Were the men fed human flesh?

"Mormon beef," John Hogarth said with a grin, "horsemeat. Trouble with those guys, they can't take a joke."

Why were people allowed to torment the prisoners?

Just young bucks letting off steam, Hogarth said. Better to be teasing the Mormons than cooking up lynch parties. And if the prisoners didn't rise to it every time, they wouldn't be molested.

As Taylor went toward his carriage, Sheriff Samuel Hadley dropped in alongside. Things ought to be better for the prisoners from now on, the sheriff said; Joseph had gained the respect of the guards and the people as well. Taylor untied the halter ropes at the hitching rack, wondering what else was on the sheriff's mind. Hadley mentioned what Taylor already knew, that Joseph's lawyers were working for a change of venue. Then the sheriff hesitated, glanced about, and in a low voice said the prisoners would never come to trial in Missouri. The governor didn't want the kind of evidence that would be put on the public record. Joseph Smith was an embarrassment to Governor Boggs, and getting more so every day.

The prisoners would be granted a change of venue to another county, the sheriff said—but they'd never get there. There was a plan to assassinate them en route.

Taylor looked at the sheriff steadily. There was only one reason why the man would be telling him this. Hadley rubbed the fingers of his right hand significantly against the thumb. Taylor nodded agreement. It was a matter of money. It might be possible, the sheriff suggested, that the prisoners would escape while being transferred. And if he made a deal with the prophet, he wanted to be sure that somebody would stand behind it.

Taylor gave his personal guarantee that the bribe would be paid, then he climbed into the rig and drove away.

Soon afterwards, Taylor bundled Leonora and the children into the carriage and followed his people across the state and over the Mississippi to Quincy, Illinois. The Missouri era of Mormonism had ended after seven years—the years of the locust.

5

"A Going Among the Mulberry Trees"

A TWIG SNAPPED. John Taylor instantly was awake. Cautiously he raised to an elbow, peering from his bedroll under the wagon. In the purple of the false dawn he could see the other wagon among the trees of the grove where the party had camped. There was no movement, no sound except the heavy breathing of the sleeping men. Then from behind came a muted thump. Taylor turned to see a figure slip between two trees, near where the horses were haltered. He pulled aside the blankets, took the pistol from under the folded coat serving as a pillow, and, moving cautiously from tree to tree, crossed toward the horses.

This camp was in the very heart of enemy country. They were within a day's travel of Far West; the members of the expedition—Brigham Young, Orson Pratt, John E. Page, Wilford Woodruff, George A. Smith, Alpheus Cutler, and John Taylor—were on a mission which the Missouri mobs had sworn to prevent.

A man's figure was huddled near the horses. The hammer of the pistol clicked loudly as Taylor cocked it. "Stand, sir." The figure slowly arose, turning. Taylor lowered the weapon on recognizing the man. It was the driver of his wagon, Alpheus Cutler.

Just graining the teams, Cutler said; it would be a long day's travel to Far West. Taylor helped him put on the nose bags, then returned to the wagons and awakened the other men. They'd need an early start, particularly since they might have to hide out during daylight hours from Bogart's mobbers.

For seven days they had traveled through enemy country, on a mission to vindicate the prophet. The previous July, when the bustling metropolis of Far West had been the gathering place of Zion, the Lord had revealed to Joseph that the apostles should go on a mission to Great Britain:

Let them take their leave of my Saints in the city of Far West, on the twenty-sixth day of April next, on the building spot of my house, saith the Lord.

But now—April 25—the city of Far West was a ghost town. It had been pillaged by the mob, many buildings burned or demolished; grass grew in the streets. The site of the temple was just a hole in the ground. The last remnants of the Mormon population were being driven away by Capt. Samuel Bogart's mob-militia, who swore that this was one of Joe Smith's revelations which they'd damned well make sure would never come true.

At Quincy, Illinois, temporary gathering place for the refugees from Missouri, Taylor had attended a meeting of the brethren to discuss the matter. Should the apostles undertake the long and hazardous journey to fulfill the literal wording of the revelation? Several at the meeting, Joseph's father in particular, spoke strongly against it. Only three of the Twelve Apostles were at the meeting, the patriarch pointed out—Brigham, Orson Pratt, and Taylor. Of the others, Parley Pratt was in jail at Richmond, Missouri; Heber C. Kimball and John E. Page were members of a committee helping the last of the Saints evacuate the state; and the remainder had either fallen away or were in darkness. Governor Boggs' extermination order had been a hunting license for hoodlums and riffraff. Every family arriving at Quincy told new stories of mob outrages. And if the three apostles *did* undertake the expedition, how could they "take leave of my Saints" at Far West when the place was virtually deserted, even the aged and infirm being driven out? Nor could the church presidency bid farewell, for Joseph and Hyrum were still in jail at Liberty, while Sidney had suffered a complete collapse after his release. Under the circumstances, Father Smith counseled, the Lord would take the will for the deed.

However, when Brigham asked opinions of his two fellow apostles at the meeting. Orson and Taylor agreed that the Lord had spoken, and they wouldn't make him out a liar.

At dawn the next Thursday, April 18, Taylor was packed up and ready when the two wagons stopped outside. Taylor drew back the curtain to see Wilford Woodruff at the reins of the lead wagon, Brigham Young and Orson Pratt with him. Alpheus Cutler drove the second outfit, with portly George A. Smith in the seat beside him. All were bundled against the raw morning. As Taylor picked up his luggage, Leonora wrapped the muffler around his neck and tucked the ends in his coat collar.

"John, be careful."

On the fourth day out from Quincy they were rounding a treacherously slippery road on a steep hillside when they came upon an overturned wagon, its load scattered along the slope. The owner and his family were busily scooping up what could be salvaged from an upset barrel of soft soap. The man elbow deep in it was Apostle John E. Page, a member of the committee evacuating the last Saints from Far West and now enroute to Quincy. Taylor and the other men leaped out, got the wagon upright, and the load back on it. Then Brigham told Page it was his duty as a member of the Twelve to go back to Far West with them.

Page hesitated. He had lost his wife and two of his children to the persecution and was on the verge of calling it quits; a man can take only so much. He told Brigham he didn't see how he could do it; he had to take his family to Quincy. Brigham promised that no harm would befall them. Page drew a long breath. "How much time have I got to get ready?"

"Five minutes."

Page drove the wagon down the hill, handed over the reins, walked back up, and climbed into the wagon beside Taylor. As the wagons rumbled along, the two men chatted easily. Taylor felt a particular kinship because Page had made a remarkable record as a missionary in Canada, where he had personally converted more than six hundred souls. Page had brought a company of Canadian Saints to DeWitt during the period of mob violence coinciding with Taylor's arrival there; subsequently, both men had been ordained apostles the same day.

Page was worried about leaving his family in enemy territory. He resented Brigham's arbitrary manner in giving him five minutes to get ready and say his farewells. He wasn't at all sure that Brigham had authority as president of the Twelve, anyhow. Page pointed out that position in the Quorum was determined by age. Thomas B. Marsh had been president of the original Quorum because he was the oldest man in it, even though the other eleven apostles had been ordained to the office several months before Marsh; standing in the Quorum was determined by date of birth. Brigham was third in this order and had become president of the Quorum when the two ahead of him were removed, Marsh by apostasy and David W. Patten through death. But, Page pointed out, he was himself two years older than Brigham—so shouldn't he by rights have become president of the Twelve upon being ordained an apostle?

With a wry grin Taylor told Page it would be a cold day in July when Brigham relinquished his authority.

Throughout the last day's travel to Far West, Taylor felt the Lord was sheltering them, for they were unmolested. En route, they met wagons of Saints heading for Quincy. A number of men left their families camped, to accompany the brethren; when the company arrived late that night it consisted of some thirty men.

There was a bright moon, and Taylor was filled with a consuming rage at the sight of the devastated city; chimneys standing stark among burned ruins, piles of brick and timber marking the sites of demolished business and church buildings, fences down, homes unroofed, weeds tall in the wide streets.

The men put up in vacant houses; the apostles camped in the residence of Morris Phelps, who was in jail at Richmond with Parley Pratt and others. They were making supper when the back door opened and a bald, powerfully built man slipped inside. It was Heber C. Kimball, with news that he had passed the word around the countryside, and the faithful still in the vicinity would gather at the temple site soon after midnight.

Then, eyes sparkling, Heber gave the big news—Joseph and the brethren at Liberty jail had escaped! Even now they were riding on fast horses toward Quincy. Heber had verified this report and had paid $400 to a man who presented an order drawn by the prophet for purchase of the horses used in the escape.[1]

Taylor was filled to bursting with joy as he spread his bedroll on the floor. Through the grace of God the prophet had been spared.

He'd hardly closed his eyes, it seemed, when Father Cutler touched his shoulder. It was midnight. The new day was beginning. Taylor crawled out and, hunched in the raw chill, walked in the moonlight to Samuel Clark's place, where the brethren had a meeting at which thirty-one people were cut from the church. Taylor felt as if a cold ball of lead was in his belly. Included among the outcasts were associates from Canada—Isabella Walton, the widow whose home had been the birthplace of the church there, along with members of her family; her daughter, Mary, was on the list, together with her husband and Taylor's old friend, Isaac Russell. As he left the meeting, Taylor felt a desperate need for a hot cup of tea.

A group of the faithful were huddled in the chill moonlight at the hole in the ground marking the temple site when the apostles arrived. After an opening hymn, the men proceeded to lay the foundation of the temple, in accordance with the prophet's revelation. Under direction of Alpheus Cutler, who was master workman of the building committee, they put their shoulders to a big boulder, rolling it to the approximate southeast corner; this was the official cornerstone of the temple of the Lord, the remainder of the edifice to await more suitable time for construction. Seated upon the rock, Wilford Woodruff and George A. Smith were ordained to the Quorum of Twelve Apostles to replace those who had

---

[1] Part of the bribe was still owing. Subsequently, the Missouri sheriff came to Nauvoo and collected it.

fallen. Services closed with the hymn, "Adam-ondi-Ahman," composed by W. W. Phelps:

> *This earth was once a garden place,*
> *With all her glories common;*
> *And men did live a holy race,*
> *And worship Jesus face to face—*
> *In Adam-ondi-Ahman. . . .*
>
> *Hosanna to such days to come—*
> *The Savior's second coming,*
> *When all the earth in glorious bloom*
> *Affords the Saints a holy home,*
> *Like Adam-ondi-Ahman.*

The apostles then took leave of the Saints to start on their mission beyond the Atlantic.

The route to England was via Nauvoo. Passing back through Quincy, Taylor was dismayed to find that already the attitude toward the Saints in Illinois was hardening. Whereas the dispossessed Mormons had been welcomed as innocent victims of brutal persecution, within a few short months friction was building with their Gentile neighbors—the same antagonism that had snowballed into disaster at Kirtland and at every Mormon location in Missouri. On May 1, the day of his return from Far West, Taylor wrote a letter to the editor of the Quincy *Argus*:

Sir,— We warn the citizens of Quincy against individuals, who may pretend to belong to our community . . . who never did belong to our church, and others who once did but for various reasons have been expelled from our fellowship. . . .

Two days later, Taylor went with the apostles to Judge John Cleveland's farm near Quincy, where Joseph was staying, to greet the prophet and his companions who had been six months in jail. At this time Joseph assigned Taylor to write an account of Mormon difficulties in Missouri, which had been requested by the editor of the St. Louis *Gazette*.

In organizing his material for the *Gazette* article, Taylor realized that it would require a book to do justice to the subject. He decided that for the *Gazette* he would confine his account to a straightforward recital of fact.

However, when he sent in the article, the editor evidently found the facts too strong a dish for the Missouri table and rejected it. Taylor wasn't surprised. He put the article in his luggage as he packed up for England, trusting that the Lord would open the way for its publication.

Leonora and the three children were in bed, racked by chills and fever, as Taylor kissed them good-bye. It was August, the worst period of the sickly season. The marsh miasma was taking a dreadful toll of the Saints; finding enough able-bodied men to dig graves was a problem. Leonora had made a home in a single room of the old log barracks, abandoned by the military, at Montrose, in Iowa Territory, across the Mississippi from Nauvoo. Brigham Young's family occupied another room, as did the families of Wilford Woodruff, Orson Pratt, and other church authorities. Those not so fortunate lived in wagon boxes and tents, while working on their "good" days (the periods between attacks of the ague) clearing land, felling logs, and raising cabins against the approach of winter.

As Taylor turned to start afoot for England without purse or scrip, leaving his wife and children penniless and sick, his spirit faltered. As he paused, and might have turned back, Leonora's voice whispered, "God bless you, John, till we meet again." This gave him strength to walk out.

Taylor crossed the river on the ferry to the lower landing at Nauvoo and walked the short distance to the prophet's log-and-frame house near the shoreline. The earth was spongy underfoot from the many springs oozing from the bluff rising on the east. A few men were digging at a drainage ditch, but progress was slow with so many felled with ague and so much other work to be done. Few had cabins yet; thousands were camped on the marshy flatland. As Taylor picked his way among the tents and wagons, clouds of insects rose up before him, drawn by the fetid stench of diarrhea and vomit.

Taylor made his way among scores of the stricken who lay in the prophet's yard hopeful of a cure by the laying on of hands. Joseph had given over his house to the sick and was living in a tent. Taylor found him and Hyrum administering to the sick. Under their hands some arose and declared themselves cured; but the ague was tenacious, and some of those made whole subsequently relapsed. Daily, wagons moved east along the Carthage road piled high with coffins for the graveyard.

The prophet told him that Wilford Woodruff, who was to be Taylor's missionary companion, was waiting at the stone house near the upper landing. They found Woodruff lying deathly sick upon a side of sole leather in the shade of the building. "Well, Brother Woodruff," Joseph said, "you have started on your mission."

"Yes; but I feel and look more like a subject for the dissecting room," Woodruff admitted.

"What did you say that for?" the prophet demanded. "Get up and go along! All will be right with you," he promised.

As Woodruff struggled to his feet a wagon came along, headed for Carthage. The driver waited while Joseph blessed the missionaries and gave them instructions. Taylor was surprised that Joseph gave them counsel to preach only the first principles of the gospel—faith, repentance, baptism, and the laying on of hands for the gift of the Holy Ghost. They weren't to discuss the restoration of the priesthood to earth by heavenly beings, nor tell of Joseph's vision, when an angel showed him the golden plates of the Book of Mormon;[2] they weren't even to tell about the prophet's revelations from the Lord, collected into the *Doctrine and Covenants*. Joseph told them to avoid the mysteries, keep the message simple; feed the milk of the gospel to infants in the faith until they were strong enough for the meat.

Taylor helped Woodruff into the wagon, and it rattled off toward England.[3]

On the outskirts of the settlement they came upon two other apostles, Parley Pratt and Heber C. Kimball, stripped to the waist and barefoot, hewing logs for cabins. Parley had nothing to offer the departing men except an empty purse, which he gave Woodruff; Heber dug into his pocket and produced a dollar to go with it. So as the wagon continued it no longer was entirely true that Taylor and Woodruff were traveling to foreign shores without purse or scrip.

On the third day they reached Macomb, after "four hours over a very rough road of stones and stumps," Woodruff wrote, "lying on my back in the bottom of the wagon, shaking with the ague, and suffering very much." The prophet's youngest brother, Don Carlos, lived here with three other families on a farm owned by George Miller, who had been very helpful to the Saints. In addition to providing use of the farm, Miller had given 8,000 bushels of grain to the destitute refugees from Missouri. Meanwhile, he was reading the Book of Mormon, and, despite being "somewhat perplexed" by parts of it, was daily "growing in the faith."

The missionaries stayed with Don Carlos and announced an open-air meeting in a nearby grove. Woodruff, who could scarcely stand, made his remarks brief, then Taylor preached to the multitude. At the conclusion of the sermon, George Miller came forward for baptism, becoming the first convert of the mission.[4]

Zebedee Coltrin, an early convert, volunteered to take the missionaries as far as Cleveland in his wagon. The local Saints contributed nine dollars to the travelers, and Miller donated a horse. At Springfield, the two

---

[2] What is now known as the first vision—the appearance of the Father and the Son to the boy—was unknown to the membership at this time. It was not published until some twenty years after the event.

[3] Details of this mission have been most thoroughly documented. The men kept journals, Woodruff's in particular being detailed and complete; they wrote tracts, published a periodical, and exchanged letters in the mission field. Taylor wrote an excellent account of his experiences in *The Latter-day Saints Millennial Star*, May 1841.

[4] After baptism, Miller recorded, his cattle were shot, fences laid down, "flocks and herds of the prairies turned on my grain fields," and was "vexed with petty lawsuits." He moved to Nauvoo to "gather with the Saints," and rose to the office of presiding bishop of the church.

apostles stopped several days to hold meetings. Taylor sold the horse there to finance the printing of 1,500 copies of the article on the Missouri persecutions which the St. Louis *Gazette* had rejected. This was the first published work of John Taylor, an eight-page pamphlet entitled, *A short account of the MURDERS, ROBBERIES, BURNINGS, THEFTS, and other outrages committed by the MOB and MILITIA of the State of Missouri, upon the LATTER-DAY SAINTS. The Persecutions they have endured for their Religion, and their Banishment from that State by the Authorities thereof.*

This pamphlet established Taylor's reputation among his people as a writer in defense of the Society. His "short account" in outline, approach, and manner of presentation, became the pattern for all subsequent Mormon accounts of the Missouri persecutions—the dispassionate piling of fact upon fact, outrage upon injustice; the damning of enemy leaders by their own words. Joseph marked Taylor for the editorship of the church paper at Nauvoo upon his return; Brigham Young, who wasted no love on Taylor personally, was to call him "the strongest editor who ever wrote."

As the missionaries continued the journey, Woodruff remained very sick. They had been on the road twenty days and were near Terre Haute, Indiana, when, he recorded, "Up to this time, Elder John Taylor had appeared to enjoy excellent health, but the destroyer did not intend to make him an exception to the rest of the apostles." Taylor became suddenly and violently sick. Coltrin reined the team to allow him to relieve himself, but as Taylor climbed out he fell as if shot. The other two lifted him into the wagon, and as it rattled along both missionaries lay upon the jostling wagon-bed, Taylor fainting several times. For days Taylor seemed to get sicker by the mile. After spending a bad night with a "bilious fever" at Germantown, he insisted on holding a meeting the next day. It was Sunday, and he was on a mission to carry the gospel to the Gentiles. "He wished me to speak, and I did so," Woodruff recorded, "dwelling upon the first principles of the gospel. He followed me, and spoke until he was exhausted." At the verge of collapse, both men spent another bad night.

The next day Woodruff and Coltrin held a consultation. It was obvious that Taylor's time had come. After "committing Elder Taylor into the hands of the Lord," the other two went on, leaving him to die.

Here, at a tavern owned by Jacob Waltz, "among strangers, a distance of several hundreds of miles from my home," Taylor was "brought down to the gates of death several times."

> The people in this neighborhood treated me with the greatest kindness, and as there was a chapel close to the inn where I stayed, at their request I preached to them, but I was so weak that I had to sit down and preach.

After staying here about five weeks I was so far recovered as to be able to proceed.

Taylor took a coach to Richmond, arriving at five that afternoon. Two hours later he was lecturing to a large audience on "Mormon difficulties in Missouri." Next morning he was en route to Dayton, where he preached the next day, "but the fatigue was too much for me, and I was again taken sick, and lay there for three weeks."

Theodore Turley, George A. Smith, and Reuben Hedlock, missionaries en route to England, found Taylor shaking with chills and fever at a Dayton inn and carried him along in their wagon. At Cleveland they met Brigham Young and Heber C. Kimball, traveling on the same mission. Taylor went with them by stage to Kirtland, where he was again sick for three more weeks, but got out of bed several times to preach in the temple.

The other missionaries were not much better off. "Elder Turley was taken out of his bed and put into a wagon when he started" from Nauvoo, Taylor wrote. Both Turley and George A. Smith were "so blind with disease" that they drove over a stump, "were upset out of the carriage, and were in so helpless a state that they lay in this position until assistance came."

The Saints at Kirtland were for the most part remnants of the faction cool to the faith, without the zeal to gather at Missouri or Illinois. Brigham called a council with local officials, where he proposed that some of the missionaries stay a few weeks and rekindle the fire. John Moreton, the local leader, rejected the suggestion, saying candidly that there were many gifted preachers available in the area, and that men of such mediocre talents as Brigham and his companions "could do no good at Kirtland." "He thought probably Brother John Taylor *might* do," Heber reported, he being the best of a poor lot, "but he was not sure."

When the others were ready to go on, Taylor climbed out of bed and joined them.

> I had been laboring under a very severe fever, but I felt determined, sick or well, to proceed; so I started, and although I traveled a distance of about 600 miles, night and day, with the exception of one night's rest, my fever left me, and I did not experience any return of it after.

Taylor arrived in New York December 13. He had never asked for money or begged a meal, yet hadn't been hungry nor unable to pay hotel and doctor bills en route.

Woodruff had been in New York for some time and was impatient to leave on the *Oxford*, which would sail the following week. Taylor told him to go ahead and book passage. When Woodruff asked about the fare, Taylor said airily, "I have plenty of money."

This was good news to his host, Parley Pratt, who was now in New

York presiding over a branch of the church. Parley drew him aside and said he planned to publish his *Voice of Warning* and *Millennial Poems.* "If you could furnish me with two or three hundred dollars, I should be very much obliged."

"You're entirely welcome to all I have," Taylor said, and brought from his pocket a copper penny.

Parley's jaw dropped. "But—I thought you said you had plenty of money?"

"Yes; and so I have. I am well clothed, you furnish me plenty to eat and good lodging. With all this and a penny over—is that not plenty?"

They laughed together, but Woodruff couldn't see the joke. He came to Taylor later in the evening and pointed out that the ship sailed in six days, and fare must be paid in advance. Taylor told him not to worry about the money. Theodore Turley, meanwhile, had heard about Taylor's financial abundance and had offered to do the cooking aboard if he was furnished passage. "Book passage for myself and Brother Turley," Taylor told Woodruff. "The money will be on hand in time." Woodruff turned away, shaking his head. Taylor went to bed and slept like a baby. The Lord would provide. When the *Oxford* stood out from New York harbor, Woodruff, Taylor, and Turley were aboard, passage paid, though it had literally taken Taylor's last penny.[5]

As the packet ship *Oxford* of the Black Ball Line, Capt. John Rathbone in command, was towed out of New York harbor by a steam tug on the cold and gusty December day, Taylor and his companions stood at the rail watching the city recede. Seventy-nine passengers were aboard, fifteen having paid $140 for cabin passage (including wine; $120 without). The missionaries went by steerage for $15, furnished their own food, bedding, cooking utensils (which had been supplied by women of the New York mission), sleeping two to a berth, eight to a cabin.

Outside the harbor, Taylor watched the twenty sailors swarm into the *Oxford*'s rigging to spread her canvas; as the sails caught the wind and the ship began crashing through heavy seas, Taylor went below, and for the most part stayed there for two weeks as the wind continued to howl at gale force, with "trunks, boxes and parcels tumbling about in the cabin," while at night "it was with much difficulty that we kept our berths." On brief excursions on deck, he returned dripping wet.

For the first week he, and practically everyone else, was seasick, the steerage "crowded and unhealthy," reeking with vomit and overrun with cockroaches and rats; it was not until the fourteenth day that he came out on deck on a calm morning to watch the sun "rise beautiful and clear;

---

[5] B. H. Roberts, *The Life of John Taylor.* . . .

we had not seen it in five days." He sat upon the anchor with Turley and Woodruff. They made a breakfast of butternuts while discussing the plight of the English mission. The great initial success had been followed by wholesale falling away; now the church faced a time of testing.

When the ship landed at Liverpool, Woodruff went to Staffordshire, Turley to Birmingham, while Taylor remained at Liverpool, where he'd lived as a boy. He looked up his wife's brother, George Cannon, at number 43, Norfolk Street, whose invitation to make it his headquarters solved the problem of food and lodging. He returned the favor by promptly baptizing Cannon, his wife, Ann Quayle, and three of their children who were old enough for ordination.[6] When Brigham, Heber, the Pratt brothers, Smith, and Hedlock arrived on the *Patrick Henry* three months later, Taylor had already brought twenty-seven souls to the gospel.

"In regards the work in general, it is prospering here on all hands," he wrote to Joseph Smith at Nauvoo; the gospel was "rolling forth, and, to use a sectarian expression, 'there has been a going among the mulberry trees,' 'a shaking among the dry bones.' "

His proselyting method was simple and direct. Instead of trying to till the stony soil among the fallen—the drunks, prostitutes, and riffraff of the waterfront grog shops—Taylor worked the vineyard among people already interested in religion, at their own churches. On his first Sunday at Liverpool, he and Joseph Fielding, his old friend from Canada, made the rounds of churches, requesting the privilege of speaking. When this was granted, he startled both pastor and flock by informing them they were in darkness, without authority to baptize, bestow the Holy Ghost, or act in the name of God, and warning them to prepare for the great and dreadful day of the Lord's return. During the week, "We visited many of the leading ministers in Liverpool," Taylor reported, "but found them generally so bigoted and wrapped up in sectarianism that there was very little room for the truth in their hearts." They were "too holy to be righteous, too good to be pure, and had too much religion to enter into the kingdom of heaven."

Taylor was so busy going among the mulberry trees during the week that, by the second Sunday, he had hired a hall which a crowd of three hundred filled at the first Mormon meeting at Liverpool. "Many wept under the influence of the spirit," he reported, and "after preaching, ten persons came forward to be baptized."

Taylor thereupon took a year's contract on the Music Hall in Bold

---

[6] One of the children, twelve-year-old George Q., was destined to become closely associated with Taylor through many turbulent years and one of the most influential men in the church.

Street, which, with a capacity of 1,500, was the largest auditorium in Liverpool, and announced a series of lectures.

Brigham Young's group had arrived at Liverpool aboard the *Patrick Henry* on the tenth anniversary of the founding of the church, April 6. They'd had a very rough voyage, which, in addition to the ague, had reduced all except George A. Smith to walking skeletons. Taylor had never seen George A. looking better; an extremely fat man, he'd "puked up his ague" on the voyage, felt fine, and was happy about losing 50 pounds.

Taylor accompanied the group to Preston for conference. When they arrived at Willard Richards' home on Meadow Street, Richards shook hands around in greeting, then with a puzzled expression asked, "Where's President Young?" He hadn't recognized the emaciated figure.

After conference, the twelve met in council at the home of "Mother" Moon, a widow of Penwortham, where Taylor helped bless and drink a bottle of wine she'd made and saved forty years for just such a special occasion. During the evening Wilford Woodruff told of his own remarkable labors in the vineyard. At Ledbury he'd converted John Benbow, a wealthy farmer connected with a group who had broken from the Methodists and taken the name United Brethren. Its members were searching for the truth; Woodruff gave it to them. He made an early convert of Thomas Kington, superintendent of both the ministry and membership of the group, then began converting the ministers with their entire congregations. "The power of God rested upon us," Woodruff said. "The sick were healed, devils cast out, the lame made to walk."[7]

Taylor, who had great respect for the power of the printed word, warmly endorsed the decision of the twelve to issue a monthly magazine, the *Millennial Star*; compile a hymn book; and publish an edition of the Book of Mormon. Taylor was to help with the hymn book and take charge of preparing the Book of Mormon for the press.[8]

During the evening Taylor and Parley got together to discuss publishing plans. Parley said that, inasmuch as he would be serving an extended mission in England as magazine editor, Brigham had agreed that it would

---

[7] "The first thirty days after my arrival at Herefordshire, I had baptized forty-five preachers and one hundred and sixty members of the United Brethren," Woodruff recorded. "This opened a wide field for labor and enabled me to bring into the church, through the blessings of God, over eighteen hundred souls during eight months, including all of the six hundred United Brethren except one person."

It might be interesting to know something of the sturdy individualist who alone refused conversion among his group, but his identity seems lost to history.

[8] The *Latter-day Saints Millennial Star* began publication the following month, and was issued for 131 years, until discontinued with the reorganization of all church publications in 1971.

be all right for Parley's wife and family to be with him; in fact, Parley planned to sail back to New York and return with his family. Immediately, Taylor thought of how wonderful it would be to have Leonora with him, away from the pestilence at Nauvoo. Three days after his return to Liverpool he wrote to Brigham, mentioning the delicate state of Leonora's health and her anxious desire to visit family and friends in her native land. He was planning on taking the gospel to the Isle of Man, where she was born. Her family connections and wide acquaintanceship both there and in Liverpool, where her brother lived, would open many doors to the gospel. And, inasmuch as Leonora had means of her own to pay her way, she would not "be burdensome." She could, he suggested, travel with missionaries en route to England.[9]

This request was denied. Taylor swallowed his gorge when, later that summer, he went to bid farewell to Parley as his fellow missionary set sail to bring his family from New York.

"Perhaps it is all for the best you're not coming," he wrote to Leonora, the letter accompanying presents for her and the children: raisins, tea and coffee, a pair of boots for Leonora, a coat for George, a frock for Mary Ann, and a trinket for the baby. He sent the box by a returning missionary, together with £8. "Do not pinch yourself or family for food or necessity," he wrote, "for when you are contented I am happy."

Leonora acknowledged receipt of the package, but, she wrote, the missionary gave her no money. Taylor sent her £5 by another missionary, which she got.

Leonora wrote of affairs at Nauvoo. The prophet had been to Washington to seek redress for property losses of the Saints in Missouri, but had been rebuffed by the Congress and the president. At conference, church members "declared their determination to appeal to a Higher Tribunal," she wrote. "I cannot describe the sensation caused by three thousand voices crying Amen to this decision—it seemed to rend the heavens."

She subsequently sent a poem written by Eliza R. Snow, indicative of the bitterness of the Saints on the subject, which Parley published in the *Millennial Star*:

ODE
For the Fourth of July

Shall we commemorate the day
Whose genial influence has pass'd o'er?
Shall we our hearts best tribute pay,
Where heart and feeling are no more?

---

[9] Taylor to Brigham, April 19, 1840.

Shall we commemorate the day
  With freedom's ensigns waving high,
Whose blood stain'd banner's furl'd away—
  Whose rights and freedom have gone by?

Should we, when gasping 'neath its wave,
  Extol the beauties of the sea?
Or, lash'd upon fair freedom's grave,
  Proclaim the strength of Liberty? ...

Columbia's glory is a theme
  That with our life's warm pulses grew,
But ah! 'tis fled—and, like a dream
  Its ghost is flutt'ring in our view! ...

PROTECTION faints, and JUSTICE cow'rs—
  REDRESS is slumb'ring on the heath;
And 'tis in vain to lavish flow'rs
  Upon our country's fading wreath!

Better implore His aid divine,
  Whose arm can make his people free;
Than decorate the hollow shrine
  Of our departed liberty!

The heart which could read these beautiful lines "without a deep sensation," Parley noted, "must be void of sentiment and feeling."

Within a few days after being rebuffed regarding Leonora's proposed visit, Taylor was surprised to learn from a letter written by Willard Richards, that Brigham "intends to prepare what hymns he can and forward them to Elder Pratt" for publication in the hymn book. Fuming, Taylor stiffly pointed out to Richards that the hymn book was to be compiled by a committee consisting of himself, Parley, and Brigham, who were to meet together to decide on the final selection after each man had made his own list. "I should feel obliged if Elder Young would favor me with his views on this subject," Taylor wrote Richards, too nettled to write Brigham direct.

Brigham got the message; meetings were held. However, Brigham Young generally had his own way, and the publication of the hymn book under Brigham's direction still rankled two months later when Taylor sent him a sample page proof of the Book of Mormon, prepared for the press. Taylor had employed as proofreader a convert working as compositor for the Liverpool *Mercury*, a person who was, he wrote Brigham, "a very prudent, intelligent man and scholar." It was "necessary to be very particular about the proof," he pointed out, adding that, "I see that there are many typographical errors in the hymn book." He suggested that "this brother might attend to them," if Brigham so desired; "however, in this I shall be guided by what you say."

As Taylor heated red wax over the gas flame to seal the letter, he chuckled aloud. What *could* Brigham say—that he wanted errors to remain in the hymn book?[10]

Taylor and his fellow missionaries attended to an amazingly busy schedule despite being almost constantly afflicted by various undiagnosed ailments they either accepted as part of life or suspected were part of Satan's nefarious attempt to hamper the spread of the gospel. Yet none of them, when sick, thought of going to a doctor. When upset, Taylor might fast, except for tea and a little wine for his stomach's sake; but for healing he relied implicitly on the power of faith, the laying on of hands by authority of God; if the Lord couldn't heal him, what could mere doctors do?

Though feeling only "tolerably well," Taylor decided it was time to take the gospel to Ireland. He called around one evening at the home of Brother Mack, a convivial Irishman he'd converted, to invite him along. He found Brother Mack (whose name was McGuffie) having a drop of Irish dew with a visiting friend from the auld sod, a Lisburn farmer named Thomas Tate. Sure and he was hoping Brother John would happen by, Mack greeted him, to help bring a sinner to the true faith.

Taylor accepted a drop of dew and engaged in a lively discussion that lasted far into the night, he and Tate defending their positions and hurling proof-texts at each other. As Taylor put on his greatcoat to leave, Mack took up a lamp to lead the way down the hallway. On the stoop, Mack observed that to be sure it had been a fine evening, but Tom Tate was stony soil for the gospel.

"Don't worry, Brother Mack," Taylor told him. "I will tell you now that your friend will be the first Saint baptized into the church in Ireland."

Then as he walked home through the foggy night, Taylor wondered what rash impulse had caused him to make so outlandish a statement.

In company with Mack and another missionary, William Black, Taylor crossed the Irish Sea and sailed up Carlingford Lough to Newry, an ancient village in the green Irish hills. McGuffie seemed to know everybody, and through his influence Taylor obtained the County Down sessions house to hold meetings, while Mack dispatched the town bellman through the streets to announce that Mormon elders would preach. Taylor was glad to have Brother Mack along to open the door, for he had no illusions regarding the difficulty of converting the Irish. The Protestants and Catholics had been fighting each other on the Shamrock Isle for a long time; how would they receive the claims of a church just ten years old which declared both of them wrong? There was the tradi-

---

[10] The hymn book was reprinted. The Book of Mormon issued at this time was so highly approved that this edition is still in use.

tion of centuries at Newry; it was here that Maurice M'loughlin, king of Ireland, had established an abbey in 1175.

When he arrived at the sessions house that evening, Taylor was delighted to find that through McGuffie's efforts more than five hundred people were crowded into the hall to hear the Mormons. But Brother Mack himself wasn't there.

Taylor was well into his sermon when the door burst open and Brother Mack came in with a noisy swarm of friends, all happy from the Irish dew. Mack fondly called out a greeting to the speaker, and as his cronies noisily found seats he loudly reminded them that sure and he'd punch the nose of any rascal who didn't pay proper respect to this man of God.

As McGuffie climbed onto the speaker's stand he stumbled and fell flat, to the vast amusement of his cronies. He struggled to his feet and roared for silence. Sure and we're here to pay proper respect to an apostle of God who has come to warn us to prepare for the coming of the Son of Man, he declared. Then Mack slumped into the chair beside William Black and promptly fell asleep.

As Taylor tried to continue the sermon, the audience was filing out. He cut the session short, then helped Black carry the sleeping man to the inn.

Next morning, Brother Mack had an enormous hangover and was abjectly repentant. Truth and he'd give his right arm to undo the mischief, he moaned. Taylor accepted the repentance, and Brother Mack went out to apologize to everyone in town. He did this so handsomely that, as Taylor and Black were getting ready for the evening's meeting, McGuffie's friends carried him through the streets to the inn and put him to bed to sleep it off. When Taylor arrived at the sessions house, only a handful of McGuffie's tittering friends were on hand, there because they'd promised him. Taylor made his remarks extremely brief and adjourned the meeting.

With Brother Mack's conviviality hanging around his neck like an albatross, Taylor decided to cut the Irish mission short, head north for Lisburn and Belfast, and take ship for Glasgow. That night in a vision a prominent citizen of Newry appeared to him, asking him to remain and bring the gospel to the citizens of the town. With morning, Taylor and his companions packed up to travel. As they left the inn, Taylor found himself face to face with the man he'd seen in the vision, and, as in the dream, this man requested that he stay and give his message.

All his life, Taylor had been guided by promptings, impulses, voices, and visions. But he also placed great value upon his own dignity and integrity. Under the circumstances not even a message from heaven could make him stay.

He told the gentleman that he was sorry but urgent appointments made it impossible to stay. However, he said, putting a hand on Mc-Guffie's shoulder, Brother Mack would be returning to Newry in a few days to stay and preach the gospel.

As the man turned away, Mack regarded Taylor with incredulous dismay. With throbbing head, bloodshot eyes, flannel mouth, and stale dew on his breath, he was the very picture of the repentant sinner. Sure and Brother John couldn't be meaning it—after disgracing the gospel, making a fool of himself among his own people—the devil himself couldn't require him to come back to Newry to preach.

Not the devil, Taylor said, but the Lord did.

It was a chastened Brother Mack who traveled through the countryside with his fellow elders. Taylor thoroughly enjoyed the beauty of the landscape, the undulating pattern of small farms cut up by neatly trimmed hedgerows, the green of the Emerald Isle spotted with the whitewashed walls of thatch-roofed cottages.

At the four towns of Bellimacrat a friend of McGuffie's named Willie allowed Taylor to preach in his barn that evening; the message touched no hearts, the audience being largely composed of students of a local college, who came to be entertained. Next morning the three missionaries headed for Lisburn on foot, carrying their luggage. The sun was three hours high when they reached the farm of Mack's old friend, Tom Tate. After giving the visitors a spot of tea, Tate insisted on carrying Taylor's valise awhile on the journey. As they came to the shore of Lough Brickland, Tate spoke in Biblical idiom: "See, here is water; what doth hinder me to be baptized?"

Taylor replied in Philip's words: "If thou believest with all thine heart, thou mayest."

Taylor took him to the water and baptized the first convert on Irish soil.

Subsequently, a humbled Brother Mack reported from Newry that he was making converts there. And thus the gospel was brought to Ireland.

Solomon and Ann Pitchforth agreed that their lodger was altogether as fascinating a young man as they had ever met. And from a woman's point of view, Ann pointed out, it was small wonder that the fair sex thronged to his meetings; she couldn't remember when an evangelist as handsome and charming as John Taylor had visited the Isle of Man. Yes, her husband agreed, and a welcome relief to long-faced sin-stompers. Taylor had the rare combination of deep spirituality with a lively sense of humor. Nobody went to sleep during his sermons.

Being Jewish, the Pitchforths could view Taylor's missionary activities dispassionately, as entertainment; and, they agreed, certainly no theatrical event had aroused more interest nor provided half the show as did John Taylor's introduction of Mormonism to the Isle of Man.

It had indeed been a lucky circumstance that Solomon had paused on a street corner to hear the young apostle preach, during Taylor's first day in Douglas. Solomon invited the interesting chap to dinner, and the meal proved so stimulating to the family that the host urged Taylor to use the home as his headquarters during his stay in Douglas.

For Taylor, hospitality at the luxurious Pitchforth mansion at Hanover Street on the North Quay provided a scale of living such as he'd never before enjoyed. Solomon Pitchforth was a wealthy businessman and patron of the arts. Tapestries and oil paintings covered the walls; the library had hundreds of rare books. Ann, the hostess, was a beautiful woman of forty, of good breeding, cultured, well read, and an accomplished pianist, with a family of four beautiful and talented children. Samuel, the oldest, was a brilliant young man. The three girls had their weekly music and elocution lessons, and gave every promise of developing the grace, charm, and loveliness of their mother. Taylor was completely captivated by this family. It was too bad the Pitchforths weren't Mormons, nor even Christians. Well, perhaps he could bring them to the truth.

Taylor soon made his presence known at Douglas. As he became embroiled with rival ministers, the *Manx Liberal* devoted columns to his sermons. To accommodate the crowd, he hired the Wellington Market Hall, the largest in town, with capacity of one thousand. The Pitchforths made a habit of going early to be sure of a good seat, for the place was well filled for every meeting, and, when he debated with rival ministers, there was standing room only.

"After a long service in preaching to a large congregation I sit down to write you a few lines," Taylor wrote to Brigham after three weeks at the Isle of Man, explaining that he simply was too busy to attend church conference at Preston scheduled for October 6. "A Methodist publication has come out in opposition," he explained, "and the fire is beginning to rage." In the midst of exciting battle he couldn't "leave the field" until the enemy was vanquished.

The *Liberal* reported two days later that Taylor was

interrupted in a very indecorous manner by a party of Primitive Methodist preachers, and a young man by the name of Gill, who is both an itinerant bookseller and a Wesleyan Methodist local preacher.

The hecklers disrupted the meeting, shouting that Taylor was misquoting the word of God, uttering blasphemy and decoying souls to perdition. For a few tense moments Taylor feared a riot was inevitable; the audience shouted at the dissenters either to shut up or get out. Then Taylor got rid of them by agreeing to a public debate the following Monday evening.

The champion for the ministers would be a preacher named Hamilton.

Each party would have an hour to present his case and an additional half hour for rebuttal.

> . . . on Monday evening, at the time appointed, the large room was completely filled by persons anxious to witness the coming conflict betwixt the two champions.
>
> All preliminaries being over and chairmen chosen, Mr. H. was called to defend his charges. He instantly rose and commenced his harangue by shewing what a clever fellow he had been, what he had done, and, by inference, what he was still able to do. He said that he once took part in a similar discussion, and so effectual were the weapons of his oratory that his antagonist died within three days, and that on a subsequent occasion he was equally successful. This, as might be expected, raised some excitement in the meeting, and created some alarm for the safety of his opponent, who seemed doomed to fall before the fatal influence of his death-striking logic. . . . But as he proceeded it soon became apparent that he was a mere braggadocio, possessing no qualifications save ignorance and presumption.

In reply, the *Liberal* reported, Taylor

> did right well, for while poor Mr. Hamilton writhed beneath his heavy flagellation, it was truly heart-rending to witness his [Mr. H.'s] agony. There he sat biting his lips and shaking his head, and every muscle of his distorted countenance seemed to implore the mercy of the meeting. Mr. T. concluded his speech by affectionately exhorting Mr. H. to repent and be baptized for the remission of sins and to enter by the door into the sheep-fold.

As Taylor rode home with the Pitchforths in their carriage, the spirited team driven by a coachman in livery, Ann congratulated him on vanquishing his rival.

"No great honor," Taylor said. "He was a very ignorant man." A more worthy opponent would have provided a better discussion for the audience.

Solomon pointed out that others would rise to the challenge, men better and wiser, with long training in the scriptures. What if Taylor should find himself bested?

Taylor regarded him curiously. Bested? "But the Lord," he said with complete confidence, "is on *my* side."

Ann was amazed at the sheer vitality of the missionary. In addition to a heavy schedule of lectures and debates, he carried on a lively battle with his pen, refuting the attacks of rival ministers with three pamphlets and writing long letters to the *Manx Liberal* and *Manx Sun*.

She had never seen such religious excitement on the Isle of Man. But while crowds flocked to the Market Hall to hear Taylor, the churches of Douglas were virtually empty on Sundays. With glee, Taylor told her that the priests were complaining bitterly. One minister went to the high bailiff and demanded that something be done to put the Mormons down. Last Sunday this man of God had opened services to an empty chapel. No single soul attended. So he went to the New Market where Taylor was preaching, but the hall was so packed he couldn't get in. "My whole congregation was there," he complained. He demanded that the Saints be driven off the island.

The high bailiff, however, pointed out that England provided freedom of worship. And very probably, Ann surmised, he felt that the ministers of established faiths had earned their comeuppance. Taylor had shown her the London *Dispatch* attack on the Mormons, written by Capt. D. L. St. Clair, who claimed that the purpose of the missionaries was to plunder the deluded converts by convincing them to "give away their property to these false apostles . . . in the hope that they shall live with Christ, on the banks of the Mississippi, in glory and happiness for a thousand years!"

Yet even St. Clair pointed out that the clergy had none but itself to blame for the inroads of Mormonism. Some 500 souls had joined the "humbug saints" from parishes within eight miles of the cathedral of Gloucester,

> whose Bishop has now two palaces to reside in, besides a prebendal house at Westminster, in Pear's Yard, and two rectorages, in all about 9,000 pounds a year. Has this Bishop, so well paid for attending to the flock, done anything to abate this ignorance? Is it not the fact that there are not fewer than eighty non-resident clergymen under him . . . that at the Quarter Sessions there are frequently more clergy than laity at the dinner table; and that ignorance is so great, that not one adult in fifty of the rural population can read? Can we wonder that these unfortunate creatures are led away by "every wind of doctrine," and that the gaols and madhouses are filled with the victims of ignorance and superstition? The Mormonites were wise . . . in squatting upon this diocese, and in all probability their next remove will be to the diocese of Canterbury . . . celebrated for the number of clergy, the vast income of its prelate, and the ignorance of its Christian population.

Certainly the Mormon elders were a contrast to the entrenched clergy, Ann concluded, as they went among the poor without purse or script, sometimes sitting down to a meal to share the last loaf of bread.

Two of Ann's friends from the countryside came to Douglas to hear Taylor. They invited him to hold a "chimney corner" meeting at their home. Ann and the children went with him; she marveled at his personal magnetism that evening as he sat talking informally to the group, and before the meeting broke up eight people asked for baptism, six of whom had never seen him before.

Ann found herself particularly interested in the strongly Hebraic aspect of Mormon doctrine. The Book of Mormon people were Jewish emigrants to the new world, who enscribed the golden plates with "reformed

Egyptian" characters. The Latter-day Saints believed in the literal gathering of Israel and in the restoration of the Ten Tribes. Taylor told her that apostles Orson Hyde and John E. Page had been called on a mission to Jerusalem.[11] Joseph had declared that the Jewish people "had been scattered abroad among the Gentiles for a long period; in our estimation, the time for the commencement of their return to the Holy Land has already arrived."

Ann Pitchforth didn't realize what was happening to her until the day John Taylor looked directly into her eyes and asked, "Are you ready for baptism?"

She answered, "Yes."[12]

Ann Pitchforth discovered that she would pay a stiff price for her new faith. Solomon tried hard to reconcile himself to his family becoming Christians and Mormons; but when his only son was called to be a missionary, it was too much. The marriage broke up. Ann moved with the children to the home of her father; Solomon went to Australia.

When John Taylor and fellow apostles sailed on the *Rochester* the next spring, some eight thousand souls in Great Britain had been brought to the faith. An agency was established to help converts gather in Zion, and they were embarking by the shipload (passage, £4—which included food). The Book of Mormon and the hymn book were in print, the *Millennial Star* launched, with Parley Pratt staying in England as editor.

---

[11] Although both Hyde and Page had temporarily been in darkness, they had repented and been restored to fellowship.

[12] "I am no enthusiastic girl in her teens, but have seen a good deal of the world, and am accustomed to be extremely cautious and weigh well all circumstances and things ere I jump to a conclusion," Ann Pitchforth wrote, explaining her decision. "In spite of my Jewish unbelieving heart, I could not deny baptism and at the same time believe the New Testament; however, I was so resolved not to be deluded, that I thought I would just get baptized, and only go so far as I could see was right." (See her "Letter to the Saints in the Isle of Man," written from Nauvoo. *Millennial Star*, July 15, 1846.)

6

The Rise and Fall
of Nauvoo

It had taken only a month for the *Rochester* to cross the Atlantic, Liverpool to New York; but the river boat, *Cicero*, spent nineteen frustrating days on the final leg of the trip, Pittsburgh to Nauvoo. As the craft kept running aground in the low water of the Ohio River—once held on a sand bar for three days in burning heat, many passengers sick with ague and cholera—John Taylor felt like leaping ashore and striking overland afoot.

But this was forgotten as, on July 1, the *Cicero* churned around the great bend of the Mississippi and Nauvoo came into view. After two years in England, he was back home. A crowd was waiting by the stone house of the upper landing—300 people, the prophet tall among them, waving and calling greetings as the *Cicero* nosed in at the dock. Joseph sprang aboard and was first to grasp the hands of the returning apostles: Brigham Young, Heber C. Kimball, and John Taylor. Then came a hectic period of greetings—old friends from Canada, associates from Missouri days, converts from England who'd preceded Taylor to the "gathering" in Zion—yet as he shook hands, exchanged bear hugs, called greetings, his eyes searched the crowd for someone who wasn't there.

Leonora hadn't met the boat.

"Papa."

It took a moment to recognize his son. George, now going on eight, had grown amazingly in the past two years. Taylor caught the boy up.

Had he taken good care of Mama, Mary Ann, and young Joseph James? And where were they?

"Mama's sick."

They crossed the river on the *Maid of Iowa*, little Dan Jones in command. As Taylor walked through the weeds to the decrepit Montrose barrack, roof sagging, log walls rotting at the base, gaps in the chinking, he was overwhelmed by pity and compassion. Poor Leonora. While he'd been traveling over a good share of the world, engrossed in the excitement of battling for the gospel, she'd been cooped up in a single room. He paused in the doorway to allow his eyes to adjust to the gloom. The tiny window was brilliant with the sun, bars of light showing through the gaps of the chinking. Then he was able to see the bed in the corner. Leonora lay pale upon it, wet with cold sweat and racked with ague, as she'd been two years ago when he said good-bye.

With a shock he realized that Leonora was getting old.

He sat beside the bed, holding her hand, while in a weak voice she poured out her travails. The old barrack was so dilapidated that a skunk came in every night. Twice she'd found a huge snake in the room. On a night when the children were sick, drunken Indians had come to the door, trying to get in. And in all the months he'd been away, not a single one of his relatives had put a nose in the door to offer help.

Things would be all right, he soothed. Now he was back home again, and things would be all right.

Presently the elders filed in, twenty of them, crowding the small room. Two of them anointed her head with oil and administered a healing blessing by the laying on of hands; then they formed a prayer circle. When they left a few minutes later Leonora already was feeling better. Next morning she was up and about.

Taylor promised to get her out of the barrack before another winter. Within a short time he was building a nice frame house in Nauvoo at the corner of Parley and Granger streets, his property adjoining Brigham Young's lot at the rear.

Taylor had left a pestilence-ridden camp on a marshland. He returned to the largest city of Illinois. In two years it had boomed to 8,000 souls. Trenches had drained the flat; the health of the people was much better. Typical of boom towns, people flocked to Nauvoo for wealth; however, the riches which drew people to the holy city were not of this earth, but treasures stored in heaven.

During the two years of his absence the same conditions had arisen that had caused trouble at Ohio and Missouri. Just the previous week the Anti-Mormon political party had been formed; the frank purpose was to drive the Mormons from Illinois.

Spearheading the opposition was Thomas Sharp, rabid editor of the

Warsaw *Signal*. Joseph's belligerent younger brother, William, who edited the Nauvoo *Wasp*, hadn't helped matters by carrying on a running feud with Sharp, deriding the length of his nose, accusing him of violating hospitality by eating at Joseph's table and then printing lies about the prophet, referring to him as "Thom-ASS."

Tom Sharp viewed the booming city with alarm. It was evidence of the intended Mormon takeover—the Kingdom of God the Saints boasted about—first Hancock County, then the state, eventually the nation and the whole world. What was the purpose of the Nauvoo Legion, he asked; why should a city have a well-drilled army larger than the state militia? The heavy walls of the temple looked more like a fortress to Sharp than a house of worship.

The two major building projects underway, the temple and a hotel called the Nauvoo House, were being erected by commandment of God; but, aside from this, they were necessary as welfare projects for the converts swarming to Zion. Most of those arriving by the shipload from England were city people—factory workers, miners, pottery makers, shopkeepers, clerks—with trades and skills useless on the frontier. They couldn't harness a team, plow a furrow, use an axe, man a sawpit, shoot a rifle, or split a shake; but they had to eat and they had to be kept busy.

The appearance of prosperity was an illusion. There was no valid reason why the location of Nauvoo should be the site of the largest city of Illinois. The Des Moines rapids effectively stopped river commerce below the city during periods of low water. While the soil was rich, there was almost no market for produce, thus the low prices—ruinous for farmers. There was no mining, no timber, no manufacturing nor trade to attract such a population. The prime industry of Nauvoo was the building of houses for the influx of converts. The life savings of the people streaming in from afar, with stars in their eyes, constituted the financial base of the city.

To Leonora, the rising tide of anti-Mormon sentiment was simply a matter of persecution by pukes and Philistines—Satan once more trying to destroy the restored church. The Gentile newspapers—particularly the Warsaw *Signal*, the *Sangamo Journal*, and Alton *Telegraph*—were edited by demons who delighted in printing vicious lies, that the holy city was a hotbed of vice, crime, and abominations.

As an apostle, member of the city council, and close friend of the prophet, Taylor soon realized that the Gentile accusations had a core of truth. During his absence an organized underworld had developed in the holy city, of a type ordinarily found only in great metropolitan centers such as New York or London. Nauvoo had its night life, including brothels. One bordello, on the hill near the temple, became so notorious that the Gentile press jibed at it, forcing Mayor John C. Bennett—one of its good customers—to have it pushed over the bluff. There were dram shops—"groceries"—at Nauvoo where a man with a parched throat could wet his whistle with bootleg.

At outlying settlements of the Saints things were even worse. Taylor visited the stakes at Ramus and at Crooked Creek at the time both were dissolved because of the "organized band of false brethren" who had infiltrated. Satan, Taylor discovered, had found a way to attack the Saints through their greatest strength, the "gathering."

As the Saints "gathered" at Nauvoo—physically, spiritually, and psychologically—they were on the frontier; the bottomlands of the Mississippi valley were infested with notorious gangs of banditti—knaves, cutthroats, horse thieves, counterfeiters, outlaws of every stripe—organized and so powerful that some settlements and even counties came under their control. Watching the Saints gather, it didn't take long for the banditti to realize the opportunity. What was a more perfect cover for outlaw operations than the Mormon organization—this tightly-knit Society which sprang instantly to the defense of any single member, regardless of circumstance? And so the banditti quietly moved in, got baptized, sang hymns, and prospered mightily. Yes, they had to tithe, but "protection" was always a necessary business expense of organized crime. Ten percent was a bargain.

Joseph was helpless to cope with the situation. He increased the police force. He denounced stealing time and again from the pulpit. However, too many people smiled in their sleeve, discounting what he said. Too often in the past what had been preached from the stand and printed in church publications was not to inform the Saints—who knew better— but to mislead the Gentiles. This had been the case with Danite activities in Missouri. Doubletalk characterized all public discussion of the Kingdom of God—the plan for the Mormon takeover—and a major cause of the growing lack of credence in official statements was the elaborate obfuscation concerning plural marriage. On this subject there had been doubletalk dating back almost to the time of the church's birth—furious repudiation from the pulpit, but secret fostering of the practice within a select circle of the elite.

Soon after his return, Taylor was confronted with the issue. In council with the Twelve, assembled in the upper room of the prophet's store, he listened in disturbed silence as Joseph told the apostles that the practice of plural marriage must be instituted as official church doctrine.[1]

---

[1] John Taylor related: "Joseph Smith told the Twelve that if this law was not practiced, if they would not enter into this covenant, then the Kingdom of God could not go one step further. . . . The revelation says, 'All those who have this law revealed unto them must obey the same.' Now, that is not my word. I did not make it. It was the Prophet of God who revealed that to us in Nauvoo. . . .

Taylor found himself in a strange situation. He was now looking at girls as he had when single, appraising each as a possible wife. However, there was a vital difference. Before taking a second wife, he should get approval of the first. He shrank from confronting Leonora with such a request. She was outraged at whispers of polygamy, denouncing them as vicious gossip. While perhaps in time she might come to accept the Principle as a trial of faith, a sacrifice required of those attaining celestial glory, it didn't have to be right away, did it? She was pregnant again, having a bad time of it at the age of forty-five. So, for the present, until the baby came . . .

It was a hot summer, with numerous interruptions in his work on the new house. Joseph kept him working constantly on official documents—another petition to Congress for redress, refutations of Missouri charges, proclamations. He was a member of the city council, on the board of regents of the University of Nauvoo, judge advocate of the Nauvoo Legion with the rank of colonel. At the height of the sickly season he was felled by the ague for several weeks. Despite all this, he completed the house and on October 2 moved Leonora and the children across the river to their new home.

Several weeks later Taylor saddled a horse and rode east out Parley Street to the Carthage road, then presently turned right across the ravine to the graveyard. There, he met Joseph, visiting the grave of his younger brother, Don Carlos.

Very concerned, the prophet spoke to Taylor with deep solemnity. "Look here, those things that have been spoken of must be fulfilled." Taylor felt a sinking sensation, realizing that matters couldn't be indefinitely postponed. "If they are not entered into right away," Joseph warned, "the keys will be turned."

Taylor drew a deep breath. The keys to the Kingdom depended upon obedience. The Lord had spoken through his prophet.

"Brother Joseph, I will try and carry these things out."[2]

That evening when the children were in bed, he told Leonora that he must discuss a serious matter. She surprised him by saying yes, she already knew—the wives of the Twelve had been talking about it. It was difficult for her to believe that the restoration of the true gospel of ancient times would require the family life of the old prophets—the taking of wives and concubines. Knowing the nature of men, it was much easier to believe that Joseph was rationalizing his own lusts.

"I had always entertained strict ideas of virtue, and I felt as a married man that this was . . . an appalling thing to do. . . . It was a thing calculated to stir up feelings from the innermost depths of the human soul.

"We seemed to put off, as far as we could, what might be termed the evil day."

[2] Taylor related this incident a number of times during the remainder of his life.

To believe that, Taylor said, was to accuse Joseph of being a fallen prophet.

Leonora made a defeated sigh. She realized this, she said, and that is why she must accept the Principle. Joseph had made it an issue on which the entire gospel depended.

Then, turning sharply on him, she asked if he'd picked out his plural? She'd warn him right now that she wouldn't be a sister in the Principle with some baby-faced tease young enough to be her daughter and without a brain in her silly head.

No, that wasn't the type of wife he wanted, Taylor said. He admired women of mature culture and refinement; that's why he'd fallen in love with her at Toronto. During the time since Joseph had spoken, he'd been looking around and had decided there was a young lady at Nauvoo who would make an excellent wife and also could be a sister in the Principle to Leonora.

Leonora asked if she knew the girl.

Taylor nodded. "Your cousin—Elizabeth Kaighin."

Elizabeth Kaighin was from the Isle of Man. As a child there, she knew her cousin Leonora Cannon as a grown-up, Leonora being fifteen years older. Elizabeth emigrated to Toronto as a young woman, where she renewed friendship with Leonora, now the wife of John Taylor. She joined them in the investigation of Mormonism, and the three were baptized by Parley Pratt the same afternoon.

Now that he was free to think of her in that way, Taylor found it easy to fall in love with Elizabeth Kaighin. At thirty she was tall and willowy, with a chiseled face and aristocratic bearing, fastidious in dress and reserved in manner—a true lady of refinement.

Whatever reservations Elizabeth might have had at his proposal were swept away. It was the Lord's command, and she had always admired Leonora's handsome husband. Through fasting and prayer she received a testimony to the Principle; in a private ceremony she was joined to John Taylor in the new and everlasting covenant, her name entered in the Book of the Law of the Lord.

John Taylor subsequently discovered—as did other men to whom the Principle was revealed—that taking the first step was the most difficult. Once the commandment was obeyed, taking additional wives became progressively easier.

As Taylor joined the select circle to whom the Principle had been revealed, he was swept into the policy of secrecy and deception, of double life and doubletalk. In consequence, there were among the Saints two levels of interpretation: the people took great pride in knowing what was meant from what was said—in distinguishing the "true coin" of "*seeming* denials" of plural marriage from "Satan's counterfeit"—and knowing the whispers meant more than the official statement—rumor was believed rather than official policy.

And so it was that there were knowing smiles from the underworld when Joseph exhorted his people to cease thievery and bogus making. More doubletalk, for the benefit of the Gentiles. The Gentiles, meanwhile, contrasted official denial of crime in the city with cases that proved the contrary; they accepted sworn statements of Danite activities; they believed wild tales of the Kingdom of God; and, to cap it all, there was the sensational scandal of polygamy. Small wonder the neighbors surrounding the holy city branded it a hellhole of vice and crime.

The first editor of the monthly *Times and Seasons* had been the prophet's youngest brother, Don Carlos Smith. Since the death of Don Carlos from the ague, Joseph had been dissatisfied with the paper, now a semimonthly. Six months after Taylor's return, the prophet took direct editorial control, with Taylor as his associate. Joseph was also unhappy about the belligerent manner in which another brother, William, edited the weekly Nauvoo *Wasp*; however, William was planning to run for the state legislature. With the Nauvoo vote behind him, his election was assured, after which Taylor would take over the *Wasp*, modify its policy, and change its name.

While Joseph was the designated editor of *Times and Seasons*, he had too many other things occupying his time to give the job the attention it needed. Taylor, in fact, often had to take the galleys in the night to some house where Joseph was hiding. For a good share of the time the prophet was on the dodge, avoiding the never-ending attempts by Governor Boggs to bring Joseph across the river to stand trial in Missouri on the old charges of "treason, murder, arson, burglary, robbery, larceny, and perjury," to which had been added escape.

When Boggs was defeated for office, in reaction for his harsh treatment of the Mormons, his efforts to ensnare Joseph became a mania. Then, on a black and stormy night in May 1842, someone tried to assassinate Boggs. The ex-governor was seated in his study, at Independence, reading a newspaper when an assassin crept up to the window and fired a pepperbox pistol, loaded with buckshot, point-blank at the back of his head. The assassin dropped the weapon and fled in the storm.

Four balls struck Boggs, two entering the brain. The first news of the affair to reach Nauvoo was that he had been killed. But somehow Boggs survived, and his desire for vengeance and retribution became an all-consuming passion.

The deed was attributed to the Mormons. Certainly this was indeed Satan's work, Taylor felt; nothing could have done more damage to the Saints than this rash act.

Gentiles said the gunman was Joseph's bodyguard, Porter Rockwell. Port had been at Independence, the home of his wife's parents, but under the name of "Brown."[3] "Brown" had been in a store several times to examine the pepperbox pistol that fired the balls; he hadn't purchased it, but it had been stolen from the store.

Shortly afterwards John C. Bennett, mayor of Nauvoo, general of the Nauvoo Legion, and assistant president of the church, defected from the faith and attacked Joseph in a series of sensational newspaper articles. "In accordance with your request, I now proceed to give you some account of the attempt on the life of Ex-Governor Boggs," he wrote to Earl Francis, editor of the *Sangamo Journal*.

> Joseph Smith, the Mormon prophet, in a public congregation in Nauvoo, last season (1841), *prophesied* that Lilburn W. Boggs, Ex-Governor of Missouri, should die by *violent hands* within a year. . . .
> In the spring of 1842, Smith offered a reward of five hundred dollars to any man that would kill Boggs. I heard the offer made to some of the Danites, and told Smith that if he persisted in such a course, it would result in his ruin. . . .
> Mr. O. P. Rockwell left Nauvoo from one to two months prior to the attempted assassination of Governor Boggs. . . . I asked Smith where he had gone. *"Gone,"* said he, *"gone to fulfill PROPHECY."* . . .

Though the prophet denied this charge, and though Rockwell himself confronted Bennett to insist that Joseph had nothing to do with his going to Missouri, in the public mind Joseph Smith remained the instigator, Rockwell the instrument of vengeance.[4]

Bennett proved to be a tenacious and most vindictive enemy, as he put his considerable talents to the task of destroying Joseph and the church. He spread the most closely-guarded secrets of Mormonism across the front pages of the nation's press, then amplified the material into a book, *The History of the Saints; or, an Exposé of Joe Smith and Mormonism*. Meanwhile, he toured the country lecturing on the abominations at Nauvoo and the prophet's bad character. He joined forces with Boggs in schemes to capture Joseph and get him across the river to Missouri justice.

---

[3] Joseph said that Rockwell didn't do it: "Port wouldn't have missed." This is a nice quip, but it ignores the fact that the gunman *didn't* miss; the survival of Boggs was something of a medical miracle.

[4] Rockwell subsequently was arrested, tried, and released for lack of evidence. His defense was simple: "If I done it, they've got to prove it on me." He was a man of very few words; he either told the truth or remained silent. Thus it is significant that he never denied having shot Boggs, but was emphatic in insisting that Joseph hadn't commissioned the deed. In later years Rockwell admitted that he did it; his only regret was that he "hadn't killed the son-of-a-bitch." Members of the Rockwell family have said that, at home, he was wont to boast about shooting Boggs.

At a council meeting Taylor supported the prophet's plan to issue an extra of the *Wasp* to refute Bennett's lies and to send the elders into the world to counter them with the truth.

While Bennett's book was self-serving and obviously written with malice, he *had* been assistant president of the church and knew whereof he spoke, even though he put the worst possible face on it. He buttressed his assertions with affidavits, quotations from books and documents, letters, and newspaper reports, which made an impressive documentation of his sensational charges.[5]

The most lurid section of the book concerned the system of polygamy as practiced at Nauvoo. To refute this, Taylor reprinted in *Times and Seasons* the revelation on marriage from the *Doctrine and Covenants* which said that all marriages in the church should be public, and that "one man should have one wife; and one woman, but one husband."[6] This was buttressed by affidavits from twelve men holding church office and by nineteen women of the Female Relief Society declaring that they knew of no system of marriage except that published in the *Doctrine and Covenants*, and that "Dr. J. C. Bennett's 'secret wife system' is a creature of his own make." Taylor signed this with other polygamists and men who had been entrusted with the great secret; Leonora was among the signers of the Relief Society knowing that, among its officers, president Emma Smith, counselor Sarah M. Cleveland, and secretary Eliza R. Snow were all wives of the prophet and that second counselor Elizabeth Ann Whitney was the mother of another. At all costs, the Principle must be kept from the world.

With internal affairs in a precarious balance, the prophet eased his brash brother, William, from editorship of the *Wasp*, putting Taylor in charge of both it and *Times and Seasons*. After a few issues, Taylor changed the name of the weekly to the Nauvoo *Neighbor*, enlarged it to a six-column format, and moderated its belligerent tone.

Under Taylor's editorship, the two papers exhibited a subtle quality: literary style. He valued the manner in which a thing was stated, as well as the substance. Also, for the very first time in the history of the church, he brought humor into its literature.

Elizabeth Kaighin sometimes clucked at the tongue-in-cheek items in the Lord's newspapers—they weren't quite dignified, she felt. Leonora, however, liked to search them out for a good laugh. One thing for sure, though, John Taylor put out papers that were read thoroughly.

---

[5] A curious convention among pro-Mormon scholars is to reject the Bennett book completely. Thus it is never used as documentation. However, these same scholars draw upon it for material that can be found nowhere else.

[6] This subsequently was removed and replaced by the prophet's revelation on plural marriage (Section 132).

Taylor soberly reported a mouse that sang popular ballads in Albany, others at London and elsewhere. He told of a man who lost a leg, but who carved a limb so cunningly that the joints worked as well as had the real one; in fact, the artificial leg became so much part of him that when he got the wooden foot wet he caught cold. A similar story was about a man who learned how to imitate the crowing of a rooster so well that he caused the sun to rise two hours early. Taylor asked if anyone ever knew a settled minister to have a "call" to a poorer congregation? When a farmer's wife died, he noted, his neighbors brought around their daughters. But when his cow died, nobody brought around a calf. Did you ever know a man, he asked, who didn't think he could poke a fire better than you could?

The Nauvoo papers reveled in calamities throughout the world—earthquake, fire, flood, epidemic—signs of the imminence of the great and dreadful day of the Lord. At the same time, Taylor kept a sharp eye on progress. After twenty years of development, he reported, watches were being made by machine in London. And there was the invention of the marvelous self-paying tobacco box—you put a penny in the slot and a drawer popped open containing tobacco and paper. Flying machines were soon expected to fill the skies, and even sail to the moon. The problem, Taylor explained, was developing an engine to get them airborne, after which they would sail like a kite or a hawk, needing very little power to keep in motion.[7]

Taylor deplored the disappearance of childhood in modern life. Boys exchanged the nipple for the cigar; girls either were babies or ladies—clout or bustle. There were no more apprentices. Girls read novels and had parties instead of learning how to cook and knit. The giddy young things frittered away their time playing the piano instead of working at the spinning wheel.

While Taylor held his editorial position by appointment, he was required to make a living through the enterprise. He and his business manager, Wilford Woodruff, announced that they did printing, stereotyping, and book binding; the printing office also sold books, English boots, and garden seeds. The printers joined with the prosperous merchant, Wilson Law, to purchase patent rights for Hancock County of Neal's Lard Lamp, a simple and cheap model which burned cold lard with a brilliant flame.

---

[7] The moon was believed to be inhabited. A newspaper hoax of the day in a New York paper reported activities of moon people as seen through a newly-developed telescope. Joseph himself described the moon people as being six feet tall, dressing like Quakers, and living 1,000 years. A missionary was set apart to go to the moon and bring its people to the true gospel, just as soon as the expected flying machines were perfected.

Times were hard. Taylor accepted wood, corn, flour, potatoes, elderberries, and goose feathers for subscriptions. He chided delinquent subscribers with a bit of doggerel: "Your other bills you promptly pay,/ Wherever you do go, sir,/The butcher for his meat is paid,/For sundries is the grocer,/The tailor and the shoemaker,/The hatter and the vintner,/All get their pay, then why neglect,/To settle with the printer?"

Work on the temple was hampered for want of necessities. Taylor printed appeals for provisions and goods, to be contributed as tithing. A cooking stove was needed by the temple committee, also "MEAL, FLOUR, AND PROVISIONS OF EVERY KIND WANTED ON TITHING."

> The brethren abroad will remember that those who devote the whole of their time to work on the Temple must be fed; they cannot live and work without provisions, and we are growing very scarce; and especially so with regard to MEAL and FLOUR.

Most everyone, including the prophet, was entangled in financial problems. Taylor was on hand opening day when Joseph started his store in the red brick building on Water Street near the river. It was stocked with the best St. Louis merchandise, brought upstream by river boat to Warsaw then hauled around the rapids to Nauvoo in thirteen wagons.

The upper floor of the building was one of the most important places in Nauvoo. Here was the prophet's office and a large room used for meetings of the Masonic Lodge, city council headquarters, schoolroom, church business office, and lecture hall. It was here that Taylor attended secret meetings of the Council of Fifty, an organization of select men charged with implementing the establishment of the Kingdom of God upon earth.[8] And it was here that he helped perform sacred ordinances, including endowments and marriages in the new and everlasting covenant, which would be performed in the temple when it was finished.

As a storekeeper, the prophet proved to be entirely too open-handed. He found it impossible to refuse credit to anyone in need or to press for settlement of accounts. Before long Joseph turned the business over to others and took out bankruptcy.

Taylor made a deal with Joseph to assume liabilities of an estate in return for the printing office. He moved Leonora and the children into the two-story brick mansion adjoining the *Times and Seasons* plant, which came as part of the deal.

John Taylor found that living the Principle correctly was even more difficult than he had imagined. The requirement of bringing his wives

---

[8] This ultra-secret organization was very powerful during the pioneer period. It was commonly referred to as the YTFIF—"Fifty" spelled backwards.

together as sisters in the Principle seemed beyond his abilities, and his appeals to the Lord for guidance brought no answer. While Leonora and Elizabeth were cousins and had been good friends before they both became his wives, Leonora found it difficult to be civil to Elizabeth, while the second wife, rebuffed, withdrew from any association with the first.

Then Taylor learned a final requirement of the Principle, one that tested his soul to the utmost. The members of the Twelve, Joseph told him, must consecrate their wives to the Lord—they must offer their spouses to the Lord's prophet, Joseph.

Taylor was aware that several women with living husbands had also been married to Joseph, evidently on the premise that no marriage was valid except under the new and everlasting covenant, just as no baptism was accepted by the church except that done by authority of its priesthood.[9] But while Taylor could understand this in theory, it was quite another thing to be required to deliver Leonora to Joseph.

When Taylor had made peace with his own soul, he approached Leonora with the prophet's ukase. Worn with worry over the sick baby, smouldering at her husband's license to chase after pretty girls, she exploded in a pan-throwing rage.

A window shattered as she smashed a fist through it. Then suddenly all was quiet as the blood gushed. Taylor wrapped the hand and took her to Dr. Weld's house.

Infection set in; the hand swelled, red lines moved up the arm to the shoulder.

Elizabeth Kaighin came to nurse Leonora and take care of the sick baby.

Dr. Weld did all he could, but the baby died. And as blood poisoning set in, the doctor amputated the middle finger of Leonora's left hand.

On a bleak morning Taylor stood with Leonora and Elizabeth in the graveyard just off the Carthage road, as the clods thumped hollowly on the tiny casket containing the baby and the finger.

As a final irony, when Heber C. Kimball presented Vilate to the prophet: "Joseph wept at this proof of devotion, and, embracing Heber, told him that was all that the Lord required." It had been a test of faith.

Once Heber and Vilate had passed the test, word got out and it wasn't necessary for the wives of other apostles to meet it.[10] Leonora

---

[9] This aspect of plural marriage at Nauvoo was documented by Fawn M. Brodie, *No man knows my history*, and by Jerald and Sandra Tanner, *Joseph Smith and Polygamy*, among others. It has also been confirmed by church sources. For the case of Mary Elizabeth Rollins Lightner, married to Adam Lightner and subsequently married to Joseph by Brigham Young, see *Newsletter*, "Friends of the Brigham Young University Library," March 1971. She remained married to Lightner and bore him ten children.

[10] Orson F. Whitney, *Life of Heber C. Kimball.*

had the feeling that her baby, and her finger, had been sacrificed for the Principle.

If that were so, Taylor believed it was not entirely in vain. The ordeal and the grief had again drawn Leonora and her cousin together. She and Elizabeth had become sisters in the Principle.

When Joseph presented a written copy of the revelation on polygamy for adoption by the church hierarchy, the leadership split wide open on the issue. William Law, Joseph's counselor in the presidency, broke away with a group of dissidents who formed their own church on the premise that Joseph was a fallen prophet, whose early revelations were of God, the recent ones of Satan.

Meanwhile, crime increased in the holy city, until even a force of 500 policemen were unable to root out the well-entrenched banditti. (The underworld had, in fact, infiltrated the police.)

Mobs were rising against the Mormons, as had been the case in Ohio and Missouri. There were robberies, kidnappings, and house-burnings, mostly of Mormon farmers in outlying settlements. The anti-Mormon movement had enlisted powerful support from surrounding counties, who had come together with the resolve that the Mormons must go.

Joseph's solution to this predicament was so unexpected and audacious that John Taylor was sure it had to be inspired by the Lord. No mortal man could have dreamed up so bold a stroke to solve everything with one grand gambit.

Joseph Smith would become a candidate for the presidency of the United States!

The political Kingdom of God was within grasp. Already, in the ultra-secret sessions of the YTFIF, plans had been made for the Mormon takeover. The election would provide the first great stepping stone toward this dazzling concept. Truly, the last days were at hand.

The prophet selected John Taylor as his campaign manager. "You must send every man in the city, who is able to speak in public, throughout the land to electioneer," Joseph told him. Here the Saints were fortunate, for practically all adult males had been trained in public speaking through missionary work. "There is enough oratory in the church to carry me into the presidential chair the first slide," the prophet said with enthusiasm.

Taylor fostered the campaign with a long editorial in the *Times and Seasons*, "WHO SHALL BE OUR NEXT PRESIDENT?"

As for the two candidates, Martin Van Buren and Henry Clay, neither would make an acceptable president. Clay's "politics are diametrically opposed to ours." Van Buren, who had refused to consider the Mormon petition for redress for property losses in Missouri, would be worse.

"Under these circumstances the question arises, who shall we support?" Taylor asked, and immediately supplied the obvious answer: "General Joseph Smith."[11]

That evening Taylor and Leonora walked down Main Street in the brisk cold to the corner of Water, where the newly-built "Mansion" stood. Two stories high, gleaming white with fresh paint in the moonlight, with green shutters and red brick chimneys, enclosed by a white picket fence with lamps on the gateposts, this was a handsome building of twenty-two rooms, the largest in Nauvoo. It now was the official residence of the prophet and, until the Nauvoo House should be completed, served as a hotel. Joseph had become a tavern keeper because, he explained, "I found myself unable to support so much company free of charge." However, as a host he had the same failings he had shown as a storekeeper—his open-handed generosity was his financial undoing. Just this month he had leased the Mansion to Ebenezer Robinson, former editor of the *Times and Seasons*, for $1,000 a year.

The Taylors went inside, took off their wraps, and joined the guests in a glass of wine before dinner. After the meal, there were several speeches and many flowery toasts. Taylor's role, as was customary at such affairs, was master of ceremonies. After the formal speeches, the *Neighbor* noted,

> the next called was Elder John Taylor, who alone was capable of putting on the top stone of the entertainment. His address was highly interesting, combining, like a Laocoon, a volume in every gesture.

Taylor treasured this happy evening, for he was haunted by the knowledge that there could not be many more like it. The stage was set for disaster at Nauvoo.

Taylor scheduled a state-wide nominating convention at Nauvoo, beginning May 17, 1844. As the delegates gathered for a good time, few were aware of the internal crisis. Amid charge and countercharge, the church had recently been purged of some of its most capable and prominent members. Nauvoo was a smouldering volcano; the inevitable explosion had been forecast just four days ago by publication of the prospectus for an opposition newspaper within the city, the *Expositor*, to foster the views of the apostates. Taylor knew that this was the most serious conflict within the Society since the apostasy at Kirtland.

Leaders of the apostate group were now at Carthage, swearing out warrants against Joseph. Citizens of that city were holding mass meetings, threatening to storm Nauvoo by force and take the prophet, if he again

---

[11] Joseph was general of the Nauvoo Legion; in fact, as commander of this local militia he had the self-appointed rank superior to any officer in the U.S. Army.

slipped through the legal net by the too-convenient loophole of the *habeas corpus* in his own court.

Joseph's political power, the incredible growth of Nauvoo as a city-state, and his candidacy for the presidency, had rallied the anti-Mormons. It was just possible that the prophet *might* become president—then all the wild talk about the Kingdom of God would come true as Mormonism took over the nation.

No mention of internal stresses marred the convention, and Joseph's nomination for president went like clockwork. Delegates were chosen for the various states, and a national convention was scheduled for Baltimore on July 13. Because Emma was sick, Joseph was unable to attend the caucus scheduled for 6 P.M. After it was dismissed, Taylor led its members in a demonstration. Joseph wrote:

> At night a large assemblage burned a barrel of tar in the street. I went out to see what was the matter and found they were giving me toasts; and as soon as they became aware of my presence, they carried me on their shoulders twice round the fire, and escorted me to the Mansion by a band of music.[12]

Taylor remembered this as the high point of Joseph's political career, and a memorable event of his own lifetime. The national convention was never held. Prior to that date, the *Expositor* provided the spark to explode the Nauvoo powder keg.

On June 7, it began blowing up another storm. Leonora wondered if the rain would ever stop. It had been a cold, wet spring, creeks and rivers swelling, roads becoming virtually impassable except by horseback. The Saints had been fortunate in having the Law brothers' steam gristmill, for meal and flour elsewhere was becoming scarce as hundreds of water-wheels were washed away by flooding creeks and rivers. And if that weren't enough, on this day the *Expositor* hit the streets of Nauvoo.

John was late for supper; when he finally arrived he merely picked at the food. She knew he'd been in council with the brethren regarding the scandal sheet, which called for separation of church and state; rejection of "political revelations"; repeal of the Nauvoo city charter, with curtailment of the abuses it had encouraged; an end to "the insupportable oppression of the Ministerial powers"; freedom of speech and of worship; and abolition of the "gross moral imperfections" of the "spiritual wife system." In appalling detail, the *Expositor* confirmed John C. Bennett's sensational charges of polygamy within the holy city.

Though John generally was asleep within a minute after his head hit the pillow, on this night he turned and tossed for an hour or more, then

---

[12] CHC, 6:397; May 17, 1844.

got out of bed and paced the floor while the wind howled outside. Leonora got up, coaxed the coals of the fire into flame, and put on the teakettle. As they drank a cup of tea, hot and black as they liked it, John at last began to talk.

This, he said, was the most serious situation the church had ever faced. The exposé by the *Expositor* invited far more trouble than the Bennett vendetta, for the man's own venom and personal background had largely destroyed his credibility. The *Expositor*, on the other hand, was sponsored by responsible men who recently were of good standing and high church office, respected as prominent citizens. Whereas Bennett had weakened his case by claiming that Joseph was a complete fraud whose doctrines Bennett had never believed for an instant, William Law's faction accepted the gospel as originally restored to earth, and called upon Joseph to repent of his recent abominations. The *Expositor*'s list of grievances would touch a responsive chord with many thinking people within the church and would inflame the enemies without.

This, on the eve of the presidential campaign, was the very thing the prophet had feared—that he would be betrayed by a Judas, that "some little dough-head of a fool" would scatter the grand concept of the Kingdom of God on earth.

Leonora asked, what was to be done?

John took a sip of tea, his face like iron. There was only one thing *to* do, destroy the credibility of the apostates.

Having unburdened himself, he went to bed and was asleep within minutes. Leonora lay awake, wondering.

Next morning was blustery, low clouds scudding across the bend of the broad Mississippi. In company with Vilate Kimball, Leonora attended the two meetings where the men behind the *Expositor* were tried *in absentia*, and cut to ribbons. They had made bogus; they had oppressed the poor; there was spicy testimony regarding conduct with girls; and, it was charged, Francis Higbee and John C. Bennett had ruined young men. Bennett had treated Francis for a dose of pox contracted from a French harlot on the hill.

Polygamy, for the record, was denied.

The meetings were climaxed by Mayor Joseph Smith's order to the city marshal to destroy the *Expositor* press.

News that the *Expositor* press had been smashed and the papers burned inflamed the countryside. When the Nauvoo court exonerated Joseph for the act, mobs gathered, threatening to level the city, if necessary, to bring the prophet to justice. Gov. Thomas Ford called out the state militia to maintain law and order. Joseph and Hyrum surrendered to authorities at Carthage and were lodged in the county jail there.

Two days later, Governor Ford left Carthage to investigate conditions at Nauvoo, leaving behind a detail of the local militia, the Carthage Greys, to protect the jail.

John Taylor and Willard Richards were with the prisoners in an upstairs room of the jail that afternoon at 5:20, when from the window "I saw a number of men, with painted faces, coming round the corner of the jail, and aiming towards the stairs," Taylor recorded.

The attack by the mob was prearranged. The guards at the jail, under command of Sgt. Frank Worrell, fired a round of blanks into the air, then stepped aside and allowed the mob entry. The Carthage Greys stood by in the public square, making no defense and, in fact, taking pot shots at the men inside when they came into view at the window.

As the mob stormed upstairs, Richards and Hyrum put shoulders to the door. This was a visiting room, not a cell; the door had no lock. Two shots blasted through the door, one killing Hyrum. A visitor had smuggled a pistol in to Joseph, and, as his brother fell, the prophet sprang to the door and emptied it; three shots found marks, three cartridges misfired. The mob fell back; Taylor grabbed a rascal-beater and stood by the door, knocking down the muskets as the assault came again. The mob shoved the door open. Taylor ran to the window, then collapsed on the sill from a shot. The Carthage Greys took pot shots at the man teetering on the windowsill. One struck Taylor's watch pocket, knocking him back into the room. He began crawling toward a cot in the corner as the mob continued firing from the doorway. Three more bullets hit him.

> I had a very painful idea of becoming lame and decrepit, and being an object of pity; and I felt as though I had rather die than be placed in such circumstances.[18]

Joseph in turn sprang to the window. Riddled by fire from both directions, he fell dead outside. Suddenly all was quiet. The mob had fled. The assault on the jail was over in two minutes. Of the four men in the jail, only the corpulent Richards, the largest target, remained uninjured.

A local doctor, Thomas L. Barnes, removed a bullet from Taylor's hand with a dull penknife and a pair of carpenter's compasses. When people proposed carrying Taylor to the hotel, he retorted, "I don't know you. Who am I among? I am surrounded by assassins and murderers; witness your deeds! Don't talk to me of kindness and comfort, look at your murdered victims. Look at me! I want none of your counsel or comfort."

He lay on a pile of straw from a jail mattress while a coroner's jury assembled. When the name of Francis M. Higbee came up during the

---

18 DHC, 7:105.

inquest, Taylor rose up, despite his wounds, and declared, "I want to swear my life against him!"[14]

Higbee, however, had left town, along with almost everyone else. Fearing Mormon retaliation, the population of Carthage went into hiding. After the inquest, when Willard Richards prevailed upon Taylor to go to the hotel, Richards had a hard time finding people to carry him there,

> for immediately after the murder a great fear fell upon all the people, and men, women, and children fled . . . leaving . . . but two or three women and children and one or two sick persons.
>
> It was with great difficulty that Brother Richards prevailed upon Mr. Hamilton, the hotel-keeper, and his family, to stay; they would not until Brother Richards had given a solemn promise that he would see them protected, and hence I was looked upon as a hostage. . . .
>
> Fearing that when the people heard that their Prophet and Patriarch had been murdered . . . they would lay the country waste before them, and take a terrible vengeance . . . Dr. Richards, after consulting with me, wrote the following note. Fearing that my family might be seriously affected by the news, I told him to insert that I was slightly wounded.

> Carthage Jail, 8 o'clock 5 min. P.M.
> June 27th, 1844
>
> Joseph and Hyrum are dead. Taylor wounded, not very badly. I am well. Our guard was forced, as we believe, by a band of Missourians, from 100 to 200. The job was done in an instant, and the party fled towards Nauvoo instantly. This is as I believe it. The citizens here are afraid of the Mormons attacking them; I promise them, no!
>
> W. Richards
>
> N.B.—The citizens promise us protection; alarm guns have been fired.
>
> John Taylor

"I remember signing my name as quickly as possible," Taylor said, "lest the tremor of my hand should be noticed."

He lay for almost eight hours—until two the next morning—before his wounds were dressed. He got but little sleep afterwards, for the slug in his left thigh gave him a constantly throbbing pain as the leg swelled.[15]

With morning, Taylor was visited by several prominent Gentiles, as the populace drifted back into town. Among the callers was General Deming of the Hancock County militia, "very much a gentleman, and

---

[14] The Higbee brothers were among sixteen Mormon apostates who had joined the mob at Carthage. Others included the Law and Foster brothers, Joseph H. Jackson, and Augustine Spencer.

[15] It seems rather curious that, although Richards was a practicing physician, he made no attempt to dress Taylor's wounds or extract the balls. Evidently the scope of Botanic medicine didn't encompass surgery.

showed me every courtesy," together with Colonel Jones of his command, who "also was very solicitous about my welfare." Taylor was reminded of the danger of his situation when Colonel Jones, in saying good-bye, left two loaded pistols on the table. Taylor slipped them under the pillow.

Leonora arrived from Nauvoo in the afternoon, bringing a physician, Dr. Samuel Bennet. As he prepared to extract the slug from Taylor's thigh, the patient refused whiskey as an anesthetic.

> The doctor asked me if I would be tied during the operation; I told him, no; that I could endure the cutting associated with the operation as well without, and I did so; indeed, so great was the pain I endured, that the cutting was rather a relief than otherwise.

During the ordeal, Leonora went into an adjoining room to pray. While on her knees,

> a Mrs. Bedell, an old lady of the Methodist association, entered, and patting Mrs. Taylor on her back with her hand, said, "There's a good lady, pray for God to forgive your sins; pray that you may be converted, and the Lord may have mercy on your soul."

When Leonora went in to report this to her husband, their laughter echoed through the hallway, causing Gentiles to wonder what the pair could possibly find funny in their situation.

As the townspeople returned to Carthage, it was apparent that public sentiment tacitly approved of the attack on the jail. The death of the prophet would settle the Mormon problem once and for all. Leonora reported that the Hamilton family "rejoiced at the murder"; nor was Taylor himself free from danger. As he lay wounded he learned that the notorious Joseph H. Jackson arrived at the hotel "with a design to murder me," but was prevented from ascending the stairs by a Gentile lawyer named Backman.

> There were others also of whom I heard, that said I ought to be killed, and they would do it, but that it was too damned cowardly to shoot a wounded man; and thus by the chivalry of murderers I was prevented from being a second time mutilated or killed.

Taylor was suspicious when "many of the mob too came around and treated me with apparent respect," because

> the officers and people generally looked upon me as a hostage, and feared that my removal would be the signal for the rising of the Mormons.

Word that he was being held hostage reached Nauvoo, and Alexander Williams arrived at the Hamilton Hotel to tell Taylor there were fifty armed Mormons in the woods, "and that if I would say the word he would raise another fifty, and fetch me out of there."

Wanting to prevent open conflict, "I thanked him," Taylor said, "but told him I thought there was no need."

After several days a contingent of Mormons arrived on horseback, together with two vehicles, William Marks in a carriage and James Allred driving a wagon.

> I was very weak at the time, occasioned by loss of blood and the great discharge of my wounds, so that when Mrs. Taylor asked me if I could talk I could barely whisper no. Quite a discussion arose as to the propriety of my removal, the physicians and people of Carthage protesting it would be my death, whilst my friends were anxious for my removal if possible. . . .
>
> It was finally agreed, however, that I should go, but as it was thought that I could not stand riding in a wagon or carriage, they prepared a litter for me; I was carried downstairs and put upon it.

Taylor was apprehensive because several of the men who had volunteered to carry the litter had been in the mob. From the outskirts of town he saw woods ahead. Fearing ambush, he summoned a Mormon, Dr. Ells, who was mounted on a very good horse.

> I said: "Doctor, I perceive that the people are getting fatigued with carrying me; a number of Mormons live about two or three miles from here, near our route; will you ride to their settlement as quick as possible, and have them come and meet us." He started off at a gallop immediately.

The ruse worked. "Very soon after," he reported, "the men from Carthage made one excuse after another, until they had all left, and I felt glad to get rid of them."

The jolting of the litter became intolerable to the wounded man, so

> a sleigh was produced and attached to the hind end of Brother James Allred's waggon, a bed placed upon it, and I propped up on the bed. Mrs. Taylor rode with me, applying ice and ice water to my wounds. As the sleigh was dragged over the grass of the prairie, which was quite tall, it moved very easily and gave me very little pain.
>
> When I got within five or six miles of Nauvoo, the brethren commenced to meet me from the city, and they increased in number as we grew nearer, until there was a very large company.

The heavy rains of the spring season had left the low places in the prairie in water from one to three feet deep. Here,

> the brethren took hold of the sleigh, lifted it, and carried it over the water; and when we arrived in the neighborhood of the city, where the roads were excessively muddy and bad, the brethren tore down the fences, and we passed through the fields.

"What was very remarkable," Taylor reported,

I found myself very much better after my arrival at Nauvoo than I was when I started on my journey, although I had traveled eighteen miles.... Never shall I forget the difference of feeling that I experienced between the place that I had left and the one that I now had arrived at. I had left a lot of reckless, blood-thirsty murderers, and had come to the City of the Saints, the People of the Living God, Friends of Truth and Righteousness, thousands of whom stood there with warm, true hearts, to offer their friendship and services, and to welcome my return.

John Taylor would always have a special place in the hearts of his people. He had fallen in defense of the martyred prophets and mingled his blood with theirs.

7

Winter Quarters

THE EIGHT COVERED WAGONS and the carriage made a line along Main Street reaching from the *Times and Seasons* office past John Taylor's house and up the block beyond the gunsmith shop of John Browning. Taylor moved from wagon to wagon, checking the yoked ox teams, the loads, the condition of the wagons. George, now twelve, was teamster of the first wagon. Leonora sat between him and ten-year-old Mary Ann. Taylor gave the signal, and George headed the line of wagons toward the lower river landing. Leonora looked straight ahead as the oxen plodded past the red brick mansion that had been her home. She never looked back.

It was Monday morning, February 16, 1846. John Taylor with eight wagons was joining the exodus from Nauvoo. Under the leadership of Brigham Young, the Saints were abandoning the largest city of Illinois, leaving the United States, heading into the wilderness for Mexican territory and an unknown destination in California.

Taylor climbed into his carriage and nodded to Joseph James. The seven-year-old slapped the reins on the rumps of the horses. Taylor told the boy there were several calls he had to make before joining the company at the river landing. He didn't explain that he wanted to say farewell to four of the ten women he had married who wouldn't be leaving with him.

His first call was on Elizabeth Kaighin. She was eight months pregnant. Ever since her condition became obvious she had adopted a fictitious name, posing as the wife of an absent missionary. He told Elizabeth that everything was arranged for her to follow in a later company, after the baby was born.

After kissing Elizabeth good-bye he drove north through town to the wooden store of Hiram Kimball, one of the original buildings of the town of Commerce, to see if Lydia Dibble Granger Smith was provided for and content. Lydia, now fifty-four, had had seven children by her first marriage to Oliver Granger. After Granger's death, she married Hyrum Smith, the ceremony signifying a type of guardianship. After the martyrdom of the patriarch, Taylor had assumed this responsibility. (Two of his other marriages had been of this nature, to Mercy Rachel Fielding Thompson Smith, widow of Robert B. Thompson and Hyrum Smith; and to Sarah Thornton Coleman, widow of Prime Coleman.)[1]

Lydia's oldest daughter, Sarah, was married to the storekeeper, Hiram Kimball, who had built her a fine home and had a prosperous business. Inasmuch as Kimball was a Gentile and an old-time resident, his family wouldn't be molested by the mob. Under the circumstances, Lydia told Taylor, she was happy to remain at Nauvoo, at least for the present.[2]

Taylor drove next to visit Mary Amanda Utley and Mary Ramsbottom. At twenty-four and nineteen, they had entered a true marriage relationship with their husband; however, both now were firm in the decision not to accompany him. He said good-bye to them for this lifetime, comforted by the thought that they would be with him in the next world.[3]

As his carriage rattled south through town toward the lower landing, Taylor wondered what might have been different.

---

[1] The nature of such marriages was indicated by subsequent testimony of Mercy Rachel Fielding Thompson Smith Taylor in the Temple Lot case, wherein she testified that she never had lived in the marriage relationship with John Taylor.

[2] Lydia subsequently came to Utah with her family in the early 1850s.

[3] Nothing more is known of these two wives. It is possible that the two young ladies were dissatisfied with their status as secret plural wives; however, just a month previously they were among all ten of Taylor's wives who were sealed to him in the Nauvoo temple.

Evidently, there was a winnowing process during the period when the Saints were preparing to leave Nauvoo. John D. Lee in his *Confessions* says, "Meetings were held all over the city," where "families entered into covenants with each other—the man to stand by his wife and the woman to cleave unto her husband." Others, Lee said, "agreed to separate from each other." There is evidence that the plural relationship was by many considered as part of the Nauvoo culture, a practice which was either ended or reaffirmed when the Saints decided to move. A notable case in point is the family of Brigham Young. Although he married forty-one living women at Nauvoo, he took only seventeen of them to Utah.

It is doubtful if the tangled marital arrangements at Nauvoo ever will be completely explained. Lee said that during the period of decision, reaffirmation, and rejection, "Some have mutually agreed to exchange wives," the new partners being "sealed to each other as husband and wife."

Quite obviously plural marriage was not only secret but experimental and subject to variations during this period.

In the nineteen months since the martyrdom at Carthage his own wounds had healed; and during this time the holy city had prospered as never before, in population growth, in the abundance of material blessings, and in spiritual zeal. Most of the sturdy edifices of red brick had been built during this period, designed for permanence as the brethren predicted a glowing future for the center stake of Zion. On the bluff, the white temple was visible for thirty miles up and down the river, complete with belfry—the bell donated by the Saints in England—and with

---

The ten wives to whom Taylor was married at the time were:

Leonora Cannon, b Oct. 6, 1796 at Peel, Isle of Man. Married Jan. 28, 1833 at Toronto.

Elizabeth Kaighin, b Sept. 11, 1811 at Peel, Isle of Man. Married Dec. 12, 1843 at Nauvoo.

Jane Ballantyne, b Apr. 11, 1813 at Sheffield, Scotland. Married Feb. 25, 1844 at Nauvoo.

Mary Ann Oakley, b Mar. 20, 1826 at Long Island, New York. Married Apr. 1845 at Nauvoo temple, and sealed there Jan. 14, 1846.

Marriage dates of the next six wives are unknown; however, we have dates when the marriages were sealed in the Nauvoo temple.

Mary Amanda Utley, b Nov. 7, 1821 at Humphrey County, Tenn. Sealed Jan. 17, 1846.

Mercy Rachel Thompson, b June 15, 1807 at Honiden, England. Sealed Jan. 23, 1846.

Mary Ramsbottom, b July 15, 1826 at Nottingham, England. Sealed Jan. 23, 1846.

Sarah Thornton, b June 11, 1807 at Huntington, England. Sealed Jan. 30, 1846.

Lydia Dibble Smith, b Apr. 5, 1790 at Hartford, Conn. Sealed Jan. 30, 1846. (Sealed only "for time," not eternity.)

Ann Hughlings Pitchforth, b June 30, 1801 at Grantham, England. Sealed Jan. 30, 1846.

Subsequent marriages were:

Ann Ballantyne, b Sept. 2, 1819 at Roxburgh, Scotland. Married at Winter Quarters, date unknown. She came west with the Pratt-Taylor company in 1847, and was divorced Nov. 9, 1852. Her name on the roster of the Pratt-Taylor company was listed as "Taylor."

Sophia Whitaker, b Apr. 21, 1825 at Blakedown, England. Married Apr. 23, 1847 at Winter Quarters. (This was the "official" marriage. The actual ceremony was performed by Parley Pratt en route from England; date unknown.)

Harriet Whitaker, b July 30, 1816 at Blakedown, England. Married Dec. 4, 1847 at Salt Lake City.

Caroline Hooper Saunders Gilliam, b Jan. 3, 1813 at West Maryville, Va. Married at Springville, Utah, date unknown. Sealed in the Endowment House, Salt Lake, Dec. 9, 1852.

Margaret Young, b Apr. 24, 1837 at Westport, Conn. Married Sept. 27, 1856 at Westport.

Josephine Elizabeth Roueche, b Mar. 3, 1860 at Kaysville, Utah. Married at Kaysville, Dec. 19, 1886.

The "official" wives of John Taylor, acknowledged as such during his lifetime and listed by his biographers, were Leonora Cannon, Elizabeth Kaighin, Jane Ballantyne, Mary Ann Oakley, Sophia Whitaker, Harriet Whitaker, and Margaret Young.

See "Lesser known wives of John Taylor," BYU Special Collections.

the Angel Moroni with his trumpet flying supine at the spire, heralding the great and dreadful day of the Lord.

Taylor would always have to take care, however, after sitting awhile, not to limp on the leg which still held the embedded bullet; and the wounds of Carthage to the Society of the Saints would always fester. The seeds of disaster which led to the martyrdom came to full flower afterwards, until the only course open was for the Mormons to leave Nauvoo.

Internally, affairs had degenerated to the point of chaos. Joseph had been the great unifying figure, the living prophet; yet there had been revolt even under him, and since his death the Society had been rent with dissention. Various prophets led off groups of adherents.[4] The underworld burgeoned until even with 500 men on the police force (in a city of some 12,000 population) it was impossible to cope with it. Chief of Police Hosea Stout reported that a plot was afoot to assassinate the Twelve; but he could not guarantee their safety because spies had infiltrated his own police force.

The Saints had agreed to leave the following spring, when water ran and grass grew, making travel possible for their livestock. Events, however, boiled to a climax before that time. Mob violence increased. The Twelve were indicted for counterfeiting. And then a letter from Samuel Brannan—in New York preparing to sail around the Horn with a colony of Saints to San Francisco Bay to prepare a place for those coming overland from Nauvoo—precipitated the evacuation of Nauvoo in midwinter.

In the east, there was strong sentiment against allowing the Saints to leave Illinois; it was feared they might join forces with Mexican, British, or Indian enemies of the nation.

Brannan wrote that he'd been to Washington, where he'd

> learned that the secretary of war and other members of the cabinet . . . were determined to prevent our moving west. . . .
> They say it will not do to let the Mormons go to California or Oregon, neither will it do to let them tarry in the states. . . .[5]

The U.S. Army would go upriver from New Orleans to prevent the exodus from Nauvoo, Brannan warned. The troops would disarm the Saints, and leave them helpless in the midst of their enemies.

Taylor attended the tense meeting in Brigham Young's office on the upper floor of the temple. With pistols on the table, the Twelve reviewed the situation, and then issued a directive for the people to put things in order and be ready to move out on four-hour alert. No army could come upriver so long as the Mississippi remained frozen, but when the ice broke

---

[4] Less than half the Saints were to follow Brigham Young to Utah.

[5] DHC, 7:544.

the exodus must begin. There could be no waiting for spring, when water flowed and grass grew.[6]

In January there was an unseasonal thaw. As the snow grew mushy underfoot Taylor walked down to the Mississippi several times a day, looking across the frozen surface for signs of the breakup. Late in January the ice began to buckle, pile up, then move downriver. On February 4 large hunks of ice were still running when Brigham issued the order, and the pioneer party crossed into Iowa.[7]

The departing Saints had been streaming across the Mississippi for almost two weeks, while Taylor and other brethren remained behind, working night and day in the temple in order that the Saints should have their endowments before leaving. Now the apostles were going. Brigham had crossed with his party yesterday.

Taylor reined the team to a walk as the carriage approached the lower landing. Clustered about the dock were a hundred covered wagons. Herd boys tended the loose livestock. A small fleet was at hand—four ferries, several lighters, a number of flatboats, a dozen skiffs—to transport the outfits and livestock across the mile-wide expanse of slate-gray water.

As Taylor swung down his boots squished in slushy snow. He cast a look at the leaden sky. There was a soft feel to the wind, and the ache of the slug in his leg presaged a storm. He crossed onto the dock for a word with Hosea Stout, whose men were superintending the embarkation. The chief of police, tall, gaunt, with the eyes of a zealot, said that this was a good company: sturdy wagons, well provisioned with seeds, tools, clothing, medicine, books, nails, implements, food—all the essentials to sustain life en route and maintain civilization in an unknown wilderness.

Taylor crossed to a covered wagon to exchange a few words with a young couple, Sam and Mary Pitchforth, then he ducked under the canvas to say hello to Ann Pitchforth, Sam's mother and Taylor's tenth wife. A lady of quality and accomplishment, Ann had a special place in Taylor's affections. The middle-aged Jewish convert had given recitals and taught the pianoforte at Nauvoo, though protesting that in the entire city she hadn't yet found an instrument in tune. Taylor, who admired her refusal to lower standards because of circumstance, had secured the best piano in Nauvoo for her use and had instructed departing missionaries to seek out a piano tuner, take the gospel to him, and bring him to Zion.

The piano, covered with a quilt, stood tall in the wagon. With a smile

---

[6] In making the decision to take the population of the city into the wilderness during the worst months of winter, the Twelve didn't accept one man's unsupported word. Three envoys had gone east to investigate. Governor Ford had warned also that the federal army would prevent the exodus; eastern newspapers confirmed this.

[7] That same day, by coincidence, Sam Brannan's colony sailed from New York aboard the *Brooklyn*.

he reminded Ann that it still wasn't too late to exchange it for the cook stove. She returned the smile without changing her mind. Man cannot live by bread alone, she reminded him. If members of Capt. William Pitt's band could bring their instruments along, why couldn't she take her piano?

The ferry operation moved smoothly during the morning. Taylor was near the Montrose shore on his third crossing when a cry came from behind. A flatboat was foundering in midriver. He recognized it as the one containing Joseph James and a group of boys who had been giggling over a box of snuff one of them had obtained. The flatboat carried a wagon outfit, several cattle, poultry cages, and pens of pigs. One of the boys began getting sick and spat out his snuff directly into the eyes of an ox. The animal recoiled, bellowing with pain, flailing with its horns. The other cattle spooked, and looking back, Taylor saw the railing of the flatboat give way. As the cattle stampeded off the side the craft tilted, shipped water, and began sinking.

Taylor was in a skiff, rowing toward the mishap, as the stern of the flatboat rose up. The covered wagon rolled off and vanished into the river; the boat slipped below the surface, while boxes, barrels, pens, cages of chickens, and a feather mattress bobbed down the river among the swimming livestock and the heads of people who grasped at any floating object.

As a number of skiffs converged on the mishap, Taylor gave a silent prayer of thankfulness when he pulled his youngest son from the water. Joseph James was none the worse from the experience, though scared, and sick from the snuff. As Taylor rowed toward the Iowa shore the boy huddled miserably in the skiff, once leaning over the side to vomit into the Mississippi. Leonora was waiting at the shore; she took the boy into the wagon for a change into dry clothing.

Two oxen drowned in the mishap. A young man dived into the icy river to locate the sunken wagon and fasten a rope. Taylor was helping haul the wagon from the river when a small figure tugged at his coat. Joseph James was looking up, the boy's face white and pinched.

"Papa? Where's Rol?"

Rollo White had been among the boys playing with the snuff. But he hadn't been pulled from the river.

Taylor immediately led several men to the skiffs at the bank. They were rowing out when a hail came from shore. Taylor recognized a wet and shivering figure at the campfire as the missing boy.

Returning, Taylor found Rollo White full of praise for his dog, a yellow mutt named Tiger. As Leonora put him in dry clothing and gave him a hot cup of tea, he told about being swept downstream, but by clinging to Tiger's tail he'd made the bank. Rollo and his dog were the admiration of other boys, who envied his adventure.

By midafternoon the company was assembled on the Iowa shore, yoked up and headed toward the camp at Sugar Creek. The thaw made travel heavy, wagon wheels sloshing through slush and muck. It took several hours of hard work to bring the company up the steep road to the summit of the bluffs. From there, the people looked back across the river at Nauvoo, the Beautiful, with its red brick homes enclosed by white picket fences, wide streets lined by locust, catalpa, and elm, and on the bluff the white limestone temple, the house of the Lord, built as the Lord's residence during his millennial reign in the City of Joseph. Golden in the setting sun, cherished in memory, this view of the city that had symbolized their faith would never be forgotten.

But no time for looking back. Taylor called the order; whips cracked; drivers whooped at their teams; herd boys yelled at the livestock; wagons screaked and jolted as the company pushed on through snow and mud toward Sugar Creek.

Nauvoo was no longer Zion. When Taylor had joined the church, Zion was at Kirtland. He had been in the exodus to Missouri, and he had been in the expulsion from Missouri to Illinois. Nauvoo had been Zion only when the gathering of the Society was there. Now the Saints were gathering on the trail, taking Zion along with them. The temple bell had been buried, the figure of Moroni removed from the spire, boxed, and hidden;[8] the records of endowments were in the wagons, as were seeds and cuttings to transplant the living spark of Mother Earth to another patch of soil. Zion wasn't real estate, brick, mortar, shingles, or limestone. Zion was the abode of the gospel in the gathering of the Saints. Zion would be at Sugar Creek and other way stations in the wilderness, until the chosen people found the promised land.

Taylor was up early, tending his teams. As he walked back through camp dozens of fires were going, men chopping wood, women cooking breakfast, children hauling water. Some 2,000 Saints were gathered at Sugar Creek waiting to move on, and Taylor knew, from the council meeting last night, that Brigham Young was getting highly impatient at the delays. Although people had been counseled to carry food for a year, already some families were on short rations. It was impossible for a company this size to live off the country. Wild game—deer and turkey—had become very scarce. The condition of the livestock was critical. With snow on the ground the only forage for the teams and herds consisted of green twigs and the bark stripped from young cottonwoods. The corn brought in the wagons was melting away at an alarming rate. And though the Saints had been able to purchase a little timothy hay

---

[8] The temple bell was exhumed and transported to Utah. It subsequently cracked, was melted down, mixed with other metals, and recast. The figure of Moroni was lost for more than a century, but found again.

from local farmers, the supply was short and so was money to pay for it.

As Taylor ate breakfast at Leonora's campfire, Tiger came up, tail wagging, begging a bite. Joseph James gave him a crust, then took the dog back to Rollo White's wagon with the reminder that Brother Brigham had warned that all loose dogs would be killed.

"Attention!" boomed Brigham's voice at ten minutes after ten that morning. "Attention, the whole Camp of Israel!" The people left their tents, wagons, and campfires to gather near the bridge over Sugar Creek, where the stocky figure of the president of the Twelve stood on a wagon. Edgy and impatient with the strain, Brigham complained at the delay: several companies weren't ready or were waiting to secure and bring along church property. Others had been here waiting for two weeks. "I should have been here sooner," he declared, "if I had to come without a shirt on my back."

At this point a cat streaked through the crowd, a yellow dog yapping in pursuit. As Tiger chased the cat into the woods Brigham followed the hound with a pointing finger, reminding the owner that loose dogs should be killed. Milo White, father of the dog's owner, spoke up immediately, telling Brother Brigham that he'd take care of it. Milo hurried to his wagon, emerging with his gun. As he strode into the woods two apprehensive boys tagged along, Rollo and Joseph James.

As Brigham continued talking, Taylor listened with one ear and with the other awaited the shot from the woods. Brigham exhorted the brethren to "stop running to Nauvoo, hunting, fishing, roasting their shins, idling away their time." Instead, they should "fix nosebags for their horses, and save their corn, and fix comfortable places for their wives and children to ride, and never borrow without asking leave." Distemper was rife among horses in the camp, and he threatened that any man who kept a sick horse should forfeit all his teams.

Captains of hundreds, Brigham counseled, should raise money in their companies for tent canvas and wagon covers. On the march, the job of the pioneer company was to go ahead to prepare roads, select camp grounds, dig wells, find where corn and hay was available for purchase. There must be perfect order in the camp, Brigham advised; anyone not willing to submit to discipline had better leave now and go back. Captains of hundreds should form their companies in circles at night. Every captain of ten should detail a man to night watch. After dark no one could leave camp without the countersign, nor approach a guard abruptly. And, Brigham concluded, every family must call on the Lord night and morning at every tent and wagon.

The sharp report of a rifle came from the woods. Taylor went over the bridge and was near the woods when Milo White appeared, gun in one hand and the other clutching the legs of a big tom turkey. Tagging behind were two proud boys and Tiger.

A ram in the thicket, Milo White said. He had the dog in his sights when Tiger flushed the turkey from the brush. A good hunting dog like that would be invaluable to the camp, wouldn't he, Brother Taylor? And besides, he was fixing a leash with a heavy leather collar for Tiger.

Taylor looked from the man to the wide-eyed faces of the boys. The yellow dog came up, nuzzling to be petted. Then White said he'd be happy to invite Brother Brigham to a turkey dinner this evening, and, he added, he hoped Taylor could also be present.

Mail arrived from Nauvoo in the early afternoon, bringing a packet from Samuel Brannan. Taylor went with the Twelve and members of the Council of Fifty up the creek east of camp about a half mile for a meeting. They built a fire in the snow by the creek and sat on rocks and a fallen log discussing the nefarious deal in which Sam Brannan had involved the Society. It began when Brannan first commenced negotiations for hiring the ship *Brooklyn* to take his colony of Saints to San Francisco Bay. He was looking for freight and mail contracts to defray rental on the vessel of $1,200 a month, and the captain of the *Brooklyn* graciously introduced Sam Brannan to a New York businessman, A. G. Benson, who in turn put Brannan in touch with a Washington expeditor, Amos Kendall. Kendall, a former postmaster-general, was known as the "man to see" at the capital; he could get things done.

The first of Brannan's two letters in the packet, written a month ago on January 12, warned that Amos Kendall had visited him at New York and "positively declared" that

> it is the intention of the government to disarm you after you have taken up your line of march in the spring, on the grounds of the law of nations, or the treaty existing between the United States and Mexico, "That an armed *posse* of men shall not be allowed to invade the territory of a foreign nation."

However, Kendall was using his influence in high places, working for some sort of compromise, Brannan wrote. And, because of his association with Kendall, "I now have it in my power to learn every movement of the government in relation to us." Kendall would again be in New York the following Thursday. "I will make you acquainted with the result before I leave."

Brannan's second letter, written two weeks later, said:

> I had an interview with Amos Kendall, in company with Mr. Benson, which resulted in a compromise, the conditions of which you will learn by reading the contract, between them and us, which I shall forward by this mail.

Kendall had been very cooperative in helping Brannan, for the sharp-witted expeditor saw the opportunity to make a killing from the Mormon migration. With a knowing smile Kendall told Brannan that, while the government was officially firm in its resolve to prevent the Saints from leaving Illinois, there was always a way around the situation if the right strings were pulled. It just happened, Kendall confided, that he belonged to a coterie of prominent businessmen and influential politicians—including, he claimed, President Polk himself—who would cooperate in the best interests of the Mormons, for a consideration. If the Saints would agree to give title to half the land settled in their new location to Kendall's syndicate, then Washington wouldn't oppose the migration.

Of course the matter must be strictly confidential. Although twenty-seven men were involved in the coterie, only one name would appear on the contract, that of the New York shipper, A. G. Benson & Co. And, Taylor said, as the council sitting around the campfire discussed the attempted extortion, it was highly probable that Sam Brannan, who had an eye for a fast dollar, wouldn't have become involved in the mess unless he was himself a partner to it.

The council decided that

> as our trust was in God and that we looked to him for protection, we would not sign any such unjust and oppressive agreement.
>
> This was a plan of political demagogues to rob the Latter-day Saints of millions and compel them to submit to it, by threats of federal bayonets.

However, nothing would be said about rejection of the contract. Open refusal might bring retaliation. As long as the Benson–Kendall coterie held hopes of the contract being signed, the Saints had powerful friends in Washington.

The storm came. The wind shrieked through the camp at Sugar Creek, blowing down tents and tearing off wagon covers. And on the worst night of it Ann Pitchforth got no sleep at all, for Patty Sessions needed help with the nine babies born between darkness and dawn.

When the skies cleared the cold settled in, a penetrating enemy that flowed like water through the smallest crack, turning everything it touched white and solid. The English winters of Ann's homeland were raw and chilly, but this massive coldness turned the world to stone. The Camp of Israel resembled the Arctic expeditions she'd read about, except that explorers went prepared for it and didn't try to move the entire population of a city.

"They began their march in midwinter," commented Col. Thomas L. Kane, "many of their wagons having crossed the Mississippi on the ice."[9]

> Under the most favorable circumstances, an expedition of this sort, undertaken at such a season of the year, could scarcely fail to be disas-

---

[9] *The Mormons*; Kane's account of the exodus from Nauvoo is a powerful statement and a classic of Mormon literature.

trous. But the pioneer company had set out in haste, and were very imperfectly supplied with necessaries. The cold was intense. They moved in the teeth of the keen-edged northwest winds, such as sweep down the Iowa peninsula from the ice-bound regions of the timber-shaded Slave Lake and Lake of the Woods; on the Bald Prairie there, nothing above the dead grass breaks their free course over the hard rolled hills. Even along the scattered water-courses, where they broke the thick ice to give their cattle drink, the annual autumn fires had left little wood of value. The party, therefore, often wanted for good camp-fires, the first luxury of all travellers; but to men insufficiently furnished with tents and other appliances of shelter, almost an essential to life. After days of fatigue, their nights were often freezing. Their stock of food, also, proved inadequate; and as their systems became impoverished, their suffering from the cold increased.

As she waded through the powder snow gathering twigs and bark for the team, as she cooked for her family over an open fire in zero weather, as she huddled in the wagon at night with the frost creeping through the bedclothes, Ann Pitchforth wondered if she'd ever be warm again.

Sickened with catarrhal affections, manacled by the fetters of dreadfully acute rheumatism, some contrived for a while to get over the shortening day's march, and drag along some others. But the sign of an impaired circulation soon began to show itself in the liability of all to be dreadfully frostbitten. The hardiest and strongest became helplessly crippled.

The skin peeled from her frostbitten toes and fingers, the joints swelled gnarled and red. Ann wondered if she should have brought the cook stove. Of what use was the piano if she could never again play well?

About the same time, the strength of their beasts of draught began to fail. The small supply of provender they could carry with them had given out. The winter-bleached prairie straw proved devoid of nourishment; and they could only keep them from starving by seeking for the *browse*, as it is called, a green bark and tender buds, and branches of the cottonwood, and other stunted growth in the hollows.

Limping toward camp with an armload of browse, Ann remembered that on the march with the Camp of Israel—Sugar Creek, Lick Creek, Richardson's Point, Evans' Camp—there were memorable times of joy. After a day's march no banquet could compare to wild game cooked at a great fire, followed by a talk by one of the Lord's prophets. And one night, when the camp sang together, accompanied by Capt. William Pitt's brass band, she went inside the wagon, took the quilt off the piano, and played along with them.

The spring came at last [Kane wrote]. It overtook them in the Sac and Fox country, still on the naked prairie, not yet half way over the trail they were following between the Mississippi and Missouri rivers. But it brought its own share of troubles with it. The months with which it opened proved nearly as trying as the worst of winter.

The snow and sleet and rain which fell, as it appeared to them, without intermission, made the road over the rich prairie soil as impassable as one vast bog of heavy black mud. Sometimes they would fasten the horses and oxen of four or five wagons to one, and attempt to get ahead in this way, taking turns; but at the close of a day of hard toil for themselves and their cattle, they would find themselves a quarter or half a mile from the place they had left in the morning. The heavy rains raised all water-courses; the most trifling streams were impassable. Wood fit for bridging was often not to be had, and in such cases the only recourse was to halt for freshets to subside—a matter in the case of the headwaters of the Chariton, for instance, of over three weeks' delay.

Rain hammered like surf against the canvas of the covered wagon. Three teams and a dozen men struggled knee deep in mud at a bad spot of the route. Sam was on the seat, with the reins. Inside, Ann and Sam's wife, Mary, steadied the top-heavy piano as the wagon pitched and jolted. Ann spoke sharply to her oldest girl, warning Mercy to make sure that Sarah and little Annie were out of the way of the piano, should the wagon upset.

John Taylor's voice called a halt for a breather. His head, drenched and muddy, appeared at the rear opening. Best for the women and children to get out, he advised; the worst spot was just ahead, and he didn't want anyone to risk getting hurt. Ann stubbornly insisted on staying with her piano, so Mary decided to remain inside also. As Taylor took the three girls piggyback through the mud to a high spot under a tree, Ann wondered when it would be possible to tell them that this was their new papa.

As the rain beat against the canvas cover, Ann and Mary braced themselves at opposite ends of the piano, steadying it as Sam whooped at the teams; the bull whip cracked; men grunted as they strained at the wheels. The right front end rose on a hidden boulder, then suddenly the opposite wheel dropped into a hole. "Stand clear!" Taylor shouted. "Ann! Mary! Get out!" There was no time. The piano slid down the tilted bed, then the top-heavy wagon went over. Ann found herself face down in the mud, held helpless by the wagon cover, unable to breathe. Then someone slashed the cover, dragged her out, held her on his knee while wiping mud from her face. She couldn't see him, but the booming laugh could belong only to John Taylor.

When she could see again, she found that Mary was safe. The piano lay deep in the mud beside the overturned wagon. The men got the wagon righted, then with poles began prying the piano out of the muck. As they raised it upright, Ann saw that the front panels had shattered in the fall; the works were filled with mud; the shock of the upset and the work of the pry-poles had left broken pieces of the action scattered about.

Leave it there, Ann said; lay it down again, to be part of the roadbed. Silly to try to take a piano in the first place; she should have brought her cooking stove.

"Stout girl," Taylor said. When they reached California, he promised, he'd have the finest piano in New York shipped around the Horn.

That night, Ann stood in the rain with Leonora and several other women, holding a quilt and horse blanket as shelter while Patty Sessions delivered a baby. Ann decided that her own lot wasn't so bad, after all.

Next morning she had a cold. It got worse on the trail. When they arrived at Garden Grove, Taylor advised her to stay awhile at this "traveling stake of Zion" until she regained her strength. Here the Saints began breaking sod and planting 715 acres to supply the exodus. Sam was one of 359 men reporting for work duty: 100 needed to split rails; 10 to build fences; 48 to make houses; 12 to dig wells; 10 to build bridges; and the remainder to clear land, plow, and plant.

Taylor left his company at Garden Grove and returned by carriage to Nauvoo for the final and official dedication of the temple, to be held the first three days of May. The workmen who had remained behind to finish the job got a barrel of wine as reward, and after the dedication Taylor joined in their big party—with dancing, cakes, and wine—that lasted far into the night. Now the use for which the temple had been built was accomplished, and the Saints were through with it. It would be sold, and the money used to help the poor to emigrate.[10] In a letter to England,[11] Taylor told of walking through the deserted building a final time before leaving: "My feelings were very peculiar while standing in the font, which is of stone, and passing through the rooms, when I thought how the Saints had labored and strove to complete this building, and then be forced to leave it, together with their comfortable homes, in the hands of their enemies." On the return trip from Nauvoo he passed "eight hundred teams" moving across Iowa, "together with cattle and sheep in abundance."

At Garden Grove, he found that Ann Pitchforth had recovered from her cold; but she looked drawn. The rigors of the march were particularly difficult for a lady of middle age who never before in her life had done physical labor. They said farewell here, and Taylor went on with his

---

[10] This plan didn't materialize. Negotiations for disposal of the temple went on for two and a half years, hampered by lawsuits which clouded the title. Finally, in October 1848, the Home Mission Society of New York agreed to rent the building for fifteen years. However, before final arrangements were made, an arsonist put the torch to the temple, destroying it.

[11] *Millennial Star*, 8:30.

company, without knowing that they never would see each other again on this earth.

It was May; the route was improving. A week's travel brought Taylor's company to the middle fork of the Grand, where at Mount Pisgah another traveling stake began enclosing and planting a farm of several thousand acres. After staying two weeks to help with the work, he headed west again with his company, and in mid-June made camp on Mosquito Creek at Council Bluffs. This was near a straggling Indian village on the banks of the Missouri River at Point aux Poules—which the Saints called "Pull Point"—headquarters for the government Indian agent of the Potawatomies and trading post of the American Fur Company, managed by P. A. Sarpy. Here Taylor planned to regroup his camp and rest the teams before crossing the flood-swollen Missouri. He was glad to put teams and livestock to graze on the lush forage of the vicinity. Thomas Speirs, the camp blacksmith, set up his forge to repair damaged wagons. The women had an opportunity to boil clothing and bedding. Taylor put two dozen men to work with scythes, swinging rhythmically in line as they cut the head-high wild hay growing in the bottomland.

A week after arrival Brigham called a meeting to discuss the building of a ferry, after which the council called for six counter hewers, four carpenters, eight choppers, and twelve spadesmen for construction; also six yoke of oxen to haul the side pieces, twelve yoke to snake the logs to the Indian sawmill, and two wagons to transport planks from the mill to the construction site.

Brigham Young had had his forty-fifth birthday on the first of June. On the last day of the month, as Taylor assembled his company to begin crossing on the new ferry, he remembered that this was the forty-fifth birthday of Ann Pitchforth.

As the ferry began loading—capacity, three wagons—herd boys brought cattle down the bank to swim them across. But ·the livestock milled at the water's edge, refusing to plunge into the broad river, swollen and swift from recent rains. Then Taylor saw his son, George, with a companion, charge into the herd on their ponies, whooping and flailing sticks. At the water's edge they slipped from their horses onto the backs of bulls, with a yell and a slash of their sticks. The bulls plunged into the current, and the herd followed. Other boys rushed in, scrambling onto the backs of the swimming cattle. One youth stood up, stepping from animal to animal. He slipped and fell among the tossing horns, then bobbed up, laughing, climbed astride a cow, stood up again and ran along the backs to be the first one across. Taylor breathed a sigh of relief as the boys and the cattle climbed onto the Nebraska shore.

Taylor accompanied the first wagons across on the ferry, and on returning looked at the encampment of the Mormons:

This landing, and the large flat or bottom on the east side of the river, were crowded with covered carts and wagons; and each one of the Council Bluff hills opposite was crowned with its own great camp, gay with bright white canvas, and alive with the busy stir of swarming occupants. In the clear blue morning air, the smoke streamed up from more than a thousand cooking fires. Countless roads and bypaths checkered all manner of geometric figures on the hillsides. Herd boys were dozing upon the slopes; sheep and horses, cows and oxen, were feeding around them, and other herds in the luxuriant meadow of the then swollen river. From a single point I counted four thousand head of cattle in view at one time. As I approached the camps, it seemed to me the children there were to prove still more numerous. Along a little creek I had to cross were women in greater force than blanchisseuses upon the Seine, washing and rinsing all manner of white muslins, red flannels and parti-colored calicoes, and hanging them to bleach upon a greater area of grass and bushes than we can display in all our Washington Square.[12]

Stepping from the empty ferry at Pull Point, Taylor walked to the Mosquito Creek camp and took a wagon with a wobbly wheel to Tom Speirs' forge. The blacksmith took off the iron tire, set it on the ground and laid a circle of kindling over it, igniting the circle with coals from the forge. While the fire heated the rim, he and Taylor shimmed the circumference of the wheel with rawhide strips; then with tongs they set the hot tire onto the wheel, where it shrank tight when quenched with a bucket of water.

That wheel, Speirs declared, would stay tight from here to California. Then the burly blacksmith looked over at the outfits clustered at the ferry landing and shrugged. Among the sturdy wagons were too many makeshift turnouts, carts, two-wheeled trundles. Iron had been in desperately short supply at Nauvoo. Many families had set out to cross prairie, mountain, and desert in rigs with wooden rims held together with rawhide and faith. Outfits were strung out for the entire 275 miles from here to Nauvoo. How many jerry-built rigs had already broken down en route, he hated to reckon. The Saints had been traveling almost five months, now; how did the brethren expect to cross the Rockies this summer?

Taylor told him to trust in the Lord. He climbed into the wagon and drove toward the ferry landing. The council had decided to stay in this vicinity, put up hay, grow crops, and get outfits in shape; they'd start across the plains next spring.[13]

---

12 Thomas L. Kane, *The Mormons.*

13 The actual plan was to go on another 250 miles to Grand Island, and Bishop George Miller had been sent ahead with a pioneer party to that location. However, it became apparent that there simply wasn't time to travel farther this summer if adequate preparations for winter were to be made.

Taylor hadn't driven far from the forge when he heard shouting behind him. He reined as a boy galloped up on a pony. "The army is coming, Brother Taylor! United States troops are upon us!"

Taylor looked back to see a captain of infantry with three dragoons and a baggage wagon coming into view. Was this the vanguard of the army which had been sent to disarm the Saints and escort them back to Nauvoo? Sam Brannan had warned that the attempted land-grab of the Amos Kendall–A. G. Benson coterie was "no gammon." Brigham Young hadn't signed the contract, and now . . .

Handing the lines of the team to the boy, Taylor shinnied bareback onto the youngster's pony and rode to meet the official detail. But Capt. James Allen, from Col. S. F. Kearney's command at Fort Leavenworth, greeted him with a smile and outstretched hand; he was the bearer of good news.

Brigham and the brethren met with Captain Allen in Taylor's tent on Mosquito creek, where the officer presented his orders:

> Sir:
>
> It is understood that there is a large body of Mormons who are desirous of emigrating to California, for the purpose of settling in that country, and I have, therefore, to direct that you will proceed to their camps and endeavor to raise from among them four or five companies of volunteers to join me in my expedition to that country. . . .

Each company would choose its own officers and would be mustered into service with the pay, rations, and allowances of infantry volunteers.

> You will have the Mormons distinctly to understand that I wish to have them as volunteers for twelve months; that they will be marched to California, receiving pay and allowances during the above time, and at its expiration they will be discharged, and allowed to retain, as their private property, the guns and accoutrements furnished them at this post.

Taylor exchanged delighted smiles with the brethren. Before leaving Nauvoo, the council had directed Jesse C. Little, president of the Eastern States Mission, to see what help could be had from Washington for the exodus. The council had been hopeful of a contract to construct forts and stockades on the route to Oregon, or to obtain freighting contracts to California. While failing in this, Little had succeeded—due largely to the efforts of Amos Kendall and A. G. Benson—in getting President Polk to authorize the mustering of five hundred Mormon volunteers for the war that had broken out between the United States and Mexico.[14]

---

[14] The original plan, as presented by Amos Kendall before the president and the cabinet, was for 2,000 Mormon volunteers. The preponderance of such a Mormon force, however, caused misgivings. James K. Polk recorded in his diary: "The mormons . . . will constitute not more than ¼ of Col. Kearney's command, and the main

The pay and cash clothing allowance of the Mormon Battalion would be literally a godsend to the hard-pressed Saints. Taylor felt awed at the mysterious way of the Lord his wonders to perform. Amos Kendall and A. G. Benson, the very men who had schemed to extort great wealth from the misfortune of the Saints, had saved them in their hour of extremity.

Brigham was so enthusiastic that he declared, "After we get through talking, we will call out the companies, and if there are not young men enough, we will take old men, and if they are not enough, we will take women!" The meeting broke up with a laugh.

Two weeks later there was a grand dance under the bowery, after which the Mormon Battalion marched off to the tune of "The Girl I Left Behind Me."[15]

Meanwhile, the council called for old men and boys to replace the teamsters who had joined the army. The wagons of the Saints which stretched out along the route must be brought up. Before winter, hay must be put up, crops planted, a stockade built, cabins and dugouts constructed, and the Saints gathered at the Camp of Israel. Until next spring, Zion would be at Council Bluffs and at Winter Quarters (quickly called "Misery Bottom") across the Missouri.

Relations within the council of the Twelve became increasingly strained because of Brigham's desire to restore the first presidency as it had been in Joseph's time, with himself church president. Taylor insisted that it had been agreed that Joseph's place could never be filled. The church would be governed by the Quorum of the Twelve, with Brigham as president of the Twelve. When Brigham called for a showdown vote to restore the first presidency, Taylor, supported by Orson Hyde and the Pratt brothers "offered manly opposition."[16] Since any decision of the Twelve had to be unanimous, this blocked Brigham's ambition.

Taylor was not too surprised when, a short while later, he, Parley, and Hyde were called to the English mission. There had been increasing friction between Brigham and Parley, who had been severely criticized several times during the exodus.[17] The relationship between Taylor and Brigham, always prickly, had worn paper thin. There was open rupture at a dance

---

object of taking them into service would be to conciliate them, and prevent them from assuming a hostile attitude towards the U.S. after their arrival in California." See *Diary* of James K. Polk for June 2, 3, and 5, 1846.

[15] For many years in Utah, the recruitment of the Mormon Battalion was considered an example of persecution, the government requisitioning the flower of the youth at a time the Saints needed every man. It is now considered a remarkable example of patriotism.

[16] Stenhouse, *Rocky Mountain Saints*. Brigham, he said, had "never forgiven that hostility."

[17] Pratt, *Autobiography*.

in the bowery. While Pitt's band furnished music for French fours, Copenhagen jigs, and Virginia reels, a sudden commotion at the rear found Brigham Young and John Taylor locked in struggle. Taylor being bigger, younger, and stronger, would have made short work of it, except that men leaped in to separate the pair. Standing aside from the fray was the toothsome cause of the conflict, pretty Ann Ballantyne, the very picture of lovely consternation. When, after the scuffle, she accepted Taylor's arm and whirled away with him in the dance, Taylor realized that Brigham would not forget this public humiliation.[18]

As Taylor prepared to leave for England, plague struck the Camp of Israel. He had seen nothing like it since the first dreadful summer at Nauvoo. Among the sick was Col. Thomas L. Kane, a frail and theatrically handsome young man, who had arrived at the camp in quest of adventure; he planned to accompany the Mormon migration to California. Through Jesse Little, Kane had become interested in the Saints, and he had helped expedite Little's negotiations at Washington. At Winter Quarters, Kane was felled by "congestive fever" and forced to return home, expecting to die; but he lived to write the classic description of the exodus. At Winter Quarters, Kane said,

> I found, as early as the 31st of July, that 37 per cent of its inhabitants were down with the Fever and a sort of strange scorbutic disease, frequently fatal, which they named the Black Canker. The camps . . . on the eastern side of the Missouri were yet worse fated.[19]
> In some of these, the fever prevailed to such an extent that hardly any escaped it. They let their cows go unmilked. They wanted for voices to raise the Psalm of Sundays. The few who were able to keep their feet, went about among the tents and wagons with food and water, like nurses through the wards of an Infirmary. Here at one time the digging got behind hand: burials were slow; and you might see women sitting in the open tents keeping the flies off their dead children, sometimes after decomposition had set in. . . .

---

[18] Ann Ballantyne married Taylor at Winter Quarters, but Brigham had the last laugh. Four years after the Saints arrived in Utah, Brigham granted Ann Ballantyne a divorce from Taylor. See divorce certificate, dated November 9, 1852, at Utah Historical Society. The $10 charge for divorces reputedly kept Brigham in pocket money.

Ann was the younger sister of Taylor's wife Jane Ballantyne, whom he'd married at Nauvoo.

[19] Black canker was scurvy, brought on by a diet of salt meat, wheat, and corn. The large farms at Garden Grove and Mount Pisgah were planted almost exclusively to cereal grains. Potatoes and other vegetables were considered too perishable for the trail. The Saints were under the illusion that they could subsist in health indefinitely upon the severely restricted diet of their stored food. Much of the provisions carried in the wagons from Nauvoo already was a year or more old before the march began.

Amid such conditions, Taylor was frustrated in trying to provide security for his families during his mission to England. The economy of this frontier outpost was dislocated by the overwhelming influx of the Mormon migration. He could find nobody to trade him corn and flour for horses. "I now find myself in the wilderness without means of procuring the necessary provisions for a year and a half," he recorded. He'd sent two men into Missouri with the last of his money and a number of horses, to purchase corn and wheat and to trade the horses for cattle; but the men returned having spent the money on traveling expenses, with no wheat, no corn, and no cattle. Then on the eve of departure, a fellow Saint named Stewart offered him a loan; Taylor accepted, "thankful to the Lord that he had opened my way, as he always does in time of need." On August 13, he, Parley Pratt, and Orson Hyde took passage on a flatboat carrying a party of Presbyterian missionaries returning from their labors with the Pawnee Indians. At Fort Leavenworth the three apostles found the Mormon Battalion preparing for the march west. The men had received a bounty of $40 each, and from this they gave the brethren some traveling money, while Parley returned to Winter Quarters with $5,800 for the families of the troops. Taylor and Hyde continued on, by way of the eastern branches of the church.

In the east, Taylor found wolves among the sheep. Strangism, reported W. J. Appleby, presiding elder at Philadelphia, was "making a division of the branch." J. J. Strang had popped up shortly after the prophet's death with a purported revelation from Joseph appointing Strang his successor. The letter exhibited as proof by Strang was proved spurious by reason of its postmark, the type being larger than the stamp used at Nauvoo, the ink black instead of red. This temporarily demolished Strang's claims, but he bounced back, stronger than ever, with tales of heavenly visitors and with impressive manifestations from above. Strang's adherents now included ten of the eleven witnesses to the Book of Mormon (the other one had died). In fact one of them, Martin Harris, was now a missionary for Strang. Harris had been one of the first three witnesses, and he had mortgaged his farm to publish the Book of Mormon; but now he was en route to England to reconvert the Saints there to a new prophet. Joseph's brother, William, former apostle, had joined Strang's clan, as did his mother. One of the strangest fish in Strang's net was John C. Bennett, "whose known corruption and wickedness relieves me from the necessity of commenting on his character," Appleby said. Bennett had "joined Mr. Strang as the successor to Joseph Smith, and had become his right-hand man."

Taylor spent a busy fortnight refuting Strangism in Philadelphia and New York, before sailing on the packet ship *Patrick Henry* on September 8. But he wasn't too busy to inscribe blank verse in the album of Miss Abby Jane Hart.

> *Abby: Knowest thou whence thou camest? Thine*
> *Origin? Who thou art? What? and whither*
> *Thou art bound? . . .*
> *Thou in the*
> *Bosom of thy Father bask'd, and lived, and*
> *Mov'd thousands of years ago. . . .*
> *Thou liv'd*
> *But to continue life eternal—to . . .*
> *Tread in the*
> *Footsteps of thine elder brother, Jesus—*
> *The "Prince of Peace," for whom a body was*
> *Prepared . . .*
> *Thou came! Thou came to live! . . .*
> *Until thou gain once more*
> *Thy Father's breast; raised, quicken'd, immortal;*
> *Body, spirit, all; a God among the*
> *Gods forever bles't. . . .*
> *Abby: the cup's within thy reach; drink thou*
> *The vital balm and live.*[20]

Taylor and Hyde arrived at Liverpool the morning of October 3, and within an hour had taken steps to put an end to the scandal of the "British and American Commercial Joint Stock Company." This grandiose enterprise, sponsored by the mission presidency, had degenerated into a stock-selling operation. "The poor Saints were laying up their pennies, their sixpences, their shillings &c, . . . thinking they were paying their passage to America," reported Taylor and Hyde; but the money arriving at the Joint Stock Company "was received by a set of men who ate and drank it up and squandered it away as fast as it came in." Of a total of £1,644 received for stock sales, £1,418 had been expended on overhead.

Taylor and Hyde went from the docks to the new church headquarters on Bath Street. As they entered the palatial suite in the Stanley building, the two apostles exchanged a glance. Taylor couldn't help contrast the opulent surroundings with the modest quarters on Chapel Street that he had known on his previous mission.

A receptionist informed the visitors that Brother Hedlock was out, but that Brother Ward would be happy to see them. Thomas Ward rose rather unsteadily from his desk in the editorial office of the *Millennial*

---

[20] While Taylor thought enough of the *"LINES, Written in the Album of Miss Abby Jane Hart, of New York City,"* to publish them in the *Millennial Star* (8:178, Dec. 19, 1846), he supplied no background information. Unfortunately, we don't know whether or not Abby drank the "vital balm."

Star to shake hands. From his appearance and slurred speech it was obvious that he had fortified himself for this confrontation.

Taylor and Hyde immediately assumed control. Hyde would edit the *Star*, in Ward's place. And, in case the man hadn't been notified, Taylor presented Ward with a copy of the quorum's action at Council Bluffs, where the Twelve voted on July 16 "that Reuben Hedlock, and Thomas Ward, be disfellowshipped." Ward took his departure. Hedlock already had fled to London "with a loose woman," Taylor learned.[21]

It was still raining in the morning as the wagons waited at Pull Point to cross the swollen Missouri on the ferry. It was a raw and driving storm of late October, and to Ann Pitchforth, huddled by the breakfast fire, it seemed that she never had been warm, never had been dry and comfortable. When, since leaving Nauvoo, had she really felt well? After the nightmare of winter travel and the endless mud of spring, she'd hoped to rest up and gain her strength at Garden Grove; but with hot weather came the sickly season, and like many others she was felled with the ague. She still had the chills and fever when, with the coming of autumn, black canker swelled and discolored her legs; her gums became tender; her teeth began falling out.

Across the fire, Sam began coughing, his thin body racked by the paroxysm. Mary cooked breakfast—porridge, tea, bread, and a bit of boiled meat from the brine barrel. Sam had married a sweet girl. She would mother the children, when. . . . Ann caught herself. She mustn't think that way. She was only forty-five. Perhaps someone at Winter Quarters had some potatoes; they were marvelous in curing the black canker, though scarce as diamonds. And she'd heard that at an abandoned fort above Winter Quarters horseradish was growing. It was also a cure. Somehow, she'd be well again when she and John Taylor were once more together.

Mercy served breakfast. She was almost fourteen, developing into a woman. Men's eyes lingered on her in camp. Sarah, not yet twelve, was the serious one, sitting now under the wagon to keep her notebook dry while making the daily entry. Little Annie, at five, was the camp pet; bright-eyed and happy, she was thoroughly spoiled by everyone.

Steam rising from her plate almost made Ann Pitchforth's stomach turn. She forced herself to eat, knowing she must keep up her strength, though all she really wanted was a hot cup of tea.

It was late at night when the caravan moved along the muddy street

---

[21] Taylor was incredulous that Hedlock, who "might have occupied a high and exalted situation in the church," had "cast from his head the crown." Ward, who had become an alcoholic, died soon afterwards.

of the new Zion. Rain now was coming down in sheets, lashed by gusty winds. The wagon cover had been rent by the disaster with the piano; it leaked streams where Ann and Mary had stitched it together. Winter Quarters was a town of log cabins, most of them with dirt roofs, while along the bluffs dugouts were scooped out of the face of the bank and closed with sticks, brush, quilts, and horse blankets.

A figure with a lantern moved along the line of the newly arrived company, pausing briefly at each wagon. At Sam's outfit he gave the message: There was no accommodation in town. Every cabin and dugout was full, several families in a single room. They'd have to camp in their wagons until they built shelters.

As the wagons moved on toward the camp ground a brawny figure came out of the storm. Was this Ann Pitchforth's outfit? Tom Speirs, the blacksmith, climbed onto the wheel and into the seat beside Sam. Before leaving, Elder Taylor had charged him with making sure there was a place for Sister Pitchforth and her family when they arrived. Wasn't much to boast about, Speirs admitted, but best he'd been able to do, considering.

He drove the yoke of oxen to the bluffs. Inside it was dry, with a pile of clean straw for mattresses. Before leaving, Speirs said he had a few seed potatoes; he'd bring over a couple in the morning. And when the storm stopped he'd take Brother Sam up to the old fort for some horseradish. They'd have Sister Pitchforth's black canker cured before Brother Taylor got back next spring.

Except for a cup of tea, Ann refused supper. As she lay in the dry straw, she began to get warm; the hot tea seemed to spread to her legs and chest. She no longer coughed, while the pain went from her limbs; even her gums were no longer tender. She was warm and cozy in the night, listening to the storm outside.

Lying there, remembering, she was with him again on that last evening they were together before the exodus from Nauvoo. John Taylor had written a sprightly song for the trail. As she played, he sang in his strong baritone:

> *The Upper California, O! that's the land for me,*
> *It lies between the Mountains and great Pacific Sea:*
> *The Saints can be supported there,*
> *   And taste the sweets of liberty.*
> *In Upper California—O! that's the land for me.*

His voice now seemed to fill the dugout, singing of the promised land, where "Our towers and temples there shall rise/Along the great Pacific Sea." She would meet him there, Ann knew; she would meet him at the final gathering of Zion in the golden never-never land.

The storm died in the night. Next morning when Tom Speirs called at the dugout with seed potatoes, the ladies of the Female Relief Society were preparing the body of Ann Pitchforth in her burial robes. Tom Speirs took a shovel and went up on the bluff to help Sam dig her last resting place among the hundreds of unmarked graves.

8

The Promised Land

Upon taking control of the *Millennial Star*, the three apostles[1] immediately moved the office of the magazine to more modest quarters at number 6, Goree Piazza. Here, the new editor found himself plagued by a curious problem. With the English custom of dropping and adding the letter h, it was impossible for many Saints, on hearing the name "Orson Hyde," to comprehend its spelling. The *Star* carried a notice that, when renewing subscriptions,

> Persons procuring post-office orders to send to us are requested to be particular in giving our name correctly. Some orders have come payable to "Horse and Hide," some to "Horson Ide." To avoid giving an incorrect pronounciation of our name, the person wishing to procure an order for us had better write our name on a paper, in a plain legible hand, and present it to the Post Master issuing the order. This will save us trouble. Remember that our name is—ORSON HYDE.[2]

Martin Harris, one of the original three witnesses to the Book of Mormon, had arrived in England as a missionary for James Strang's faction. However, the *Star* reported, Harris soon got his comeuppance. When he showed up at Birmingham, where the Saints were assembled,

> He introduced himself to their conference meeting and wished to speak, but on being politely informed by Elder Banks that the season of the year had come when *Martins* sought a more genial climate than England, he had better follow. On being rejected by the united voice of the confer-

---

[1] Parley had joined Taylor and Hyde in England.

[2] While this is written from Hyde's viewpoint, it is characteristic of Taylor's pixie humor.

ence, he went out into the street, and began to proclaim the corruption of the Twelve; but here the officers of government honored him with their presence—two policemen came and very gently took hold of each arm and led Martin away to the Lock-Up.

Meanwhile, Taylor was busy with what might well have been the prime purpose of his mission to England, which was to present a petition to Queen Victoria asking her government to sponsor emigration of British Saints to "the island of Vancouver, or to the great territory of Oregon." He published a copy of the petition in the *Star*, urging presiding elders at the various conferences to get "all the signatures they can" to it. Response was overwhelming. It required little urging for victims of the industrial revolution to put their names to a petition asking the queen to send them, at crown expense, to a new country and free land. When Taylor had assembled the signatures with scissors and paste-pot, he had a petition 168 feet long.

The English Saints were mostly of the working class, those with jobs working dawn to dusk at starvation wages, while for the swarms of unemployed it was root, hog, or die. During the potato famine in Ireland the previous year, two million people of a total population of eight million had either emigrated or starved.

In return for free passage, the emigrants would reserve half of the newly-settled land for the crown. The country would be surveyed, the Saints settling on even-numbered sections, the government retaining odd. Improvements to occupied lands would enhance the value of crown property more than enough to repay "your majesty's gracious interference and Royal aid."[3]

However, when he obtained an interview with the Earl of Dartmouth, Taylor learned that the British government had problems of its own. Trade depression had brought the kingdom to the brink of revolution. The crown was in no position to sponsor the settlement by Mormons of land already in dispute with the United States.

Taylor's official mission was completed by presentation of the petition. In his personal life, however, he was just beginning a new chapter. When he and Parley embarked at Liverpool on the *America* in January 1847, with a party of fourteen Saints, it quickly was apparent that Parley was courting two nubile beauties of the group, Martha Monks and Ann Agatha Walker, while Taylor was paying attention to Sophia Whitaker, a small girl with a beautifully curving figure, who was emigrating with

---

[3] Genesis of this proposition quite obviously was the infamous A. G. Benson deal. The difference, of course, was that the Kendall–Benson plot attempted to use the misfortune of the Mormons to extort lands to which the coterie had no rights. In petitioning the queen, the Saints offered half the settled territory—which already was crown land—in return for transportation, survey of the area, and permission to occupy.

her two sisters, Harriet and Elizabeth. Lively and quick, full of fun, and with a keen sense of humor, Sophia Whitaker completely captivated John Taylor.

As far back as she could remember, there had been unrest over hard times. Sophia Whitaker lived at the tiny hamlet of Blakedown, near the industrial city of Birmingham. This was the "Black Country" noted for its iron-works, the production of hardware and machinery of every description—from pen nibs to locomotives—and characterized by the smoke and grime that filled the sky, coated the brick houses, blackened the cobblestones, and impregnated the clothing and the faces of men employed in the iron works.

Sophia grew up with demonstrations, torch-light parades of protest, strikes, and riots stemming from misery and want.

She was the seventh of nine children born to Thomas and Sophia Turner Whitaker. Her father, a tool-edger, was one of the many "small masters" of the area, proprietor of his own workshop. His five boys learned the trade early and helped in the business. By prudent management, Thomas Whitaker made an adequate income for his large family.

At fifteen, Sophia was at Liverpool, helping in the household of her oldest sister, Mary Ann, who was married to Richard Harrison, when John Taylor arrived on his first mission to England. Sophia was among his early converts, being baptized in April 1840, along with Mary Ann and Richard Harrison.

Her mother died the following summer, and Sophia returned to Blakedown to keep house for her father. She brought the gospel with her, and began proselyting with the family at home. When Parley Pratt arrived at Birmingham to preach, she coaxed her brother George to go with her to hear him. George was so impressed he was baptized the next day. When missionaries arrived at Blakedown, she and George invited them to hold meetings at the Whitaker home. Soon all the family had converted.

Sophia never forgot the spirit of these cottage meetings, when the Lord seemed close, and the Adversary fought for possession of souls. Her brother George wrote about an evening when some forty to fifty people gathered at the house. After tea and biscuits they began the prayer meeting, and while a woman was speaking in tongues she suddenly was possessed by evil spirits. By dawn, the possessed woman lay exhausted on a bed upstairs, while George and the brethren wrestled with Satan's demons.

Use of the home for meetings ended abruptly when Sophia's father married again. The new wife forbade such carryings-on in her home. She enjoyed ridiculing Mormonism and would allow no back talk under her roof. The home became a hell for Sophia. The family scattered. Several of her siblings, including George and Mary Ann, embarked for the gathering of the Saints at Nauvoo. Sophia and two sisters, Harriet and Elizabeth, left home to live at Birmingham. The three girls were thrilled when Apostles Parley Pratt and John Taylor, accompanied by Elder Joseph Cain, visited the city. Sitting in meeting, the girls were rapt as the visiting brethren spoke.

The girls pushed forward among the people clustered about the stand. Sophia found that John Taylor not only remembered her, but brought news from Mary Ann and George. George, in fact, had driven one of Parley's wagons from Nauvoo to Winter Quarters. Just a few days before the apostles left for England, Parley had married George to Eveline Robinson. And, Taylor said, he and his companions would be most happy to accept the invitation for dinner tomorrow.

Sophia never forgot that meal, as she became acquainted with John Taylor as a man rather than an apostle. Elizabeth in turn was simply fascinated by Joseph Cain. Before the evening was over, the three sisters agreed to join the small party of Saints who would accompany the visiting brethren on their return to Winter Quarters on the *America*.

The sea was calm and the weather perfect during the thirty-six-day voyage to New Orleans. A most memorable trip, for during the voyage John Taylor told the sisters the tremendous secret of the celestial order of marriage according to the law of Abraham, Isaac, and Jacob.

The voyage became the honeymoon trip for two of the girls, Sophia marrying John Taylor and Elizabeth becoming the bride of Joseph Cain; Parley Pratt performed the ceremonies aboard ship.

The party took passage upriver from New Orleans. Taylor left the riverboat at St. Joseph to hurry overland by carriage with the surveying instruments needed by Brigham Young's pioneer company. Taylor also carried in a money belt a most welcome contribution to the cause: 469 gold sovereigns, tithing from the British Saints.

When Sophia arrived a week later the pioneer party of young men was already on their way to found a new Zion in the Rockies. Taylor and Parley were busy organizing a company of emigrant families to follow. Brigham's pioneers would break the trail, locate the new Zion, and plant crops for the emigrants to harvest. Then the pioneers would return to Winter Quarters; the Pratt–Taylor emigrants were the families who would actually settle and live in the new Zion.

Sophia's brother George was at Winter Quarters, preparing to emigrate with the Pratt–Taylor company. His wife, Eveline, was big with child. Early one morning George came to the dugout where Sophia was staying with her two sisters and Elizabeth's husband, Joseph Cain, and led them to a patch of wild strawberries at a secluded spot by the bluff. Nothing had ever tasted so delicious. As they sat eating, they saw John Taylor, some distance away, walking slowly among the mounds of the graveyard together with the blacksmith, Tom Speirs. Speirs paused and indicated a grave. Taylor took off his hat, then placed flowers on the mound. Sophia found her husband quiet and preoccupied for several days, but he never explained why.

Families joining the Pratt–Taylor emigrant company had to have two yoke of oxen for each wagon, flour and corn enough for a year's bread, seed grain, cattle, farming implements, and cooking utensils. While the company got ready, Taylor and Pratt pitched in to help plow and plant a large acreage to supply those remaining at Winter Quarters.

Taylor found his sleep disturbed by a problem that grew day by day, as he received reports of the progress of Brigham's pioneer party. There had been a change of plans that invited disaster.

When Taylor left for England, everything had been arranged: An advance party under Bishop George Miller would winter at Grand Island, 250 miles along the way, plant crops next spring for emigrants to harvest, then the Miller company would push on to the Great Basin. Another company would try to cross the Rockies that fall, but, if unable to, would winter at Fort Laramie, plant crops there in the spring, and move on. With the way "now prepared," Taylor reported in the *Millennial Star*, emigrant companies who followed would find

> the roads, bridges, and ferry boats made; there are stopping places also on the way, where they can rest, obtain vegetables and corn, and when they arrive at the far end, instead of finding a wild waste, they will meet with friends, provisions, and a home.

Such was the plan when Taylor left in the fall. When he returned the following spring, he was stunned to discover that the advance parties had been recalled to Winter Quarters.[4]

Regardless of the reasons for recalling these outposts, their return to Winter Quarters meant that no pioneers were at Grand Island (250 miles), nor at Fort Laramie (500 miles), putting in crops and then making a dash across the mountains to grow a crop for the emigrant families who would arrive in the fall.

Everything now depended upon the pioneer company led by Brigham Young. This group of hand-picked young men (only three women),

---

[4] According to Miller, this resulted from a power struggle between him and Brigham. Miller had been "greatly disgusted" at Brigham's ambition to take Joseph's former position as president of the church. The recall of the advance companies, Miller said, grew "out of the jealousy of Brigham Young, lest I should lead away a body of the Saints." Miller was so furious at the change of plans that he left the church, leading a group of disaffected Saints to join Lyman Wight's colony in Texas. For Miller's viewpoint, see his "Correspondence with the Northern Islander," and "De Tal Palo Tal Astrilla."

traveling light with the best teams and outfits, started their forced march at the earliest possible chance "in their anxiety to get to their destination in the mountains in time to plant crops that season."[5]

Considering the urgency, Taylor was dismayed to learn that the pioneers decided to travel along the north bank of the Platte River, instead of the south. This made rapid travel impossible.

Running along the south bank of the Platte was the well-traveled Oregon Trail, where the Indians were friendly, the road good, bridges made, and forage ample. Across the river, on the north, the situation was entirely different. Here, no road existed; and the Pawnees resented intrusion on their territory. The Indians lurked about, stealing livestock.

The Mormons increased the guard and the Indians began burning the prairie ahead of them. Day after day Brigham's party made camp on blackened ground. Except for two quarts of corn each day, the horses subsisted on the bark and browse of cottonwoods the men chopped down. As teams weakened, the forced march slowed to a crawl.

Charles Beaumont, traveling east from Fort Laramie with a company of French fur traders and three freight wagons, told of his amazement at spotting a wagon train breaking new road along the north side of the river. When he crossed over, he learned that Brigham's party had been traveling an entire month, yet was only now to Grand Island, and with the teams in sorry shape. Beaumont explained to Brigham that there was good road on the south side, plenty of feed, and that his party had encountered no Indians since leaving Fort Laramie sixteen days previously. Brigham thanked him for the report—and ordered the pioneers to continue along the north bank. Beaumont joined his company across the river and headed east along the Oregon Trail, completely bewildered.

Taylor knew the reason underlying the decision to break new road north of the river despite hell or high water. After being driven from Ohio, Missouri, and Illinois, Brigham's aversion to mingling with Gentiles was so strong as to overwhelm all other considerations. Even the hostility of the Pawnees was attributed to the evil influence of outsiders.

Taylor and Pratt, however, assembling a big company of emigrant families dependent upon the pioneers to prepare the way, could not help questioning whether the avoidance of hypothetical future friction with Gentiles on the trail was worth the present delays. Instead of reaching the Great Basin in the estimated thirty-five days, it would take almost twice that long for the pioneers to get to Fort Laramie, the halfway mark.[6] And this was the easy half of the journey—across the plains. From Laramie they would face the Rockies.

---

[5] For the well-known story of the pioneer company, see CHC, vol 3, where Roberts devotes more than 125 pages to the subject.

[6] It was to take sixty days.

With her brother George and Joseph Cain away trading for supplies, Harriet Whitaker had to do a man's work about the household at Winter Quarters, while also preparing for the journey across the plains. While Sophia and Elizabeth were willing, both were pregnant. It was close to Elizabeth's time of delivery, while Sophia was having morning sickness and was easily upset.

Slender and fastidious, Harriet was accomplished in needlework, cooking, housekeeping, and other feminine tasks. Never before in her life had she used a saw and hammer, chopped firewood, spaded a garden, split a log, milked a cow, cleaned a cowpen, or killed a rattlesnake. She learned fast, of necessity, but her strength was inadequate for the calls upon it. As blisters swelled and broke on her hands she grew more and more exhausted. Every muscle ached.

She was chopping wood when the axe glanced off a knot and the handle rammed into her body. It was as if she had been shot. She sank to the ground, gasping with pain. Sophia found her lying by the woodpile and with Elizabeth's help got her inside. A boy went running for Patty Sessions. After the midwife examined Harriet, she shook her head dubiously. A blood vessel had ruptured. There was nothing to be done.

Harriet woke up in the dugout, very weak. At the bedside were Sophia and Elizabeth, together with John Taylor and Parley Pratt. Her voice was thin and barely audible as she requested the elders to consign her soul to eternity.

The two men put hands on her head. Taylor blessed her, then promised that she would recover to bear progeny that would people the celestial realm where she would be queen.

Weak as she was, Harriet smiled at this. Who would marry an old maid of thirty?

"When you are fully recovered, my dear," Taylor said, "I will."

From that moment Harriet knew that she wouldn't die.

George Whitaker and Joseph Cain returned only partly successful from their Missouri trading expedition. The influx of emigrants into the sparsely settled region had cleaned out the countryside. However, they'd found some wheat and had traded a saddle for sixty bushels of corn. Now they had provisions enough for the trip, but needed another wagon and two yoke of oxen.

Harriet donated her life savings for the wagon. Cain traded for one oxen, then George's father-in-law donated the other three. George and Cain loaded up the wagons, had the outfit inspected, and were ready for the trip across the plains.

Taylor and Parley walked slowly among the covered wagons, checking with captains of hundreds, fifties, and tens. Five hundred seventy outfits were assembled at the Elkhorn River, twenty-seven miles west of Winter Quarters; this was the staging area to which the emigrants came after their outfits had passed inspection. Taylor and Pratt had organized the Camp of Israel into four "hundreds," and nine "fifties," the extra fifty being a company of artillery from the Nauvoo Legion under command of Charles C. Rich. Now everything was bustle as the men yoked up oxen and the women put out campfires and stowed away bedding and breakfast dishes in the wagons. Herd boys scoured the hills, rounding up livestock.

It was June 21, and today the emigrant train would start west. It was late to begin a journey of a thousand miles across prairie and mountain, but the size of the company had made it impossible to get away sooner. All that mattered, really, was to get through the Rockies before the passes were blocked with snow. The pioneers had taken the best teams and crack outfits for their forced march. The Pratt–Taylor company had what was left. Parley, though co-leader of the expedition, had traded his last horse for corn to provide for his families; he would walk to the Great Basin. Taylor was in somewhat better shape—he had arranged to borrow a saddle horse.

Moving through the bustle of preparation, Taylor wished the wagons were more sturdy, the oxen in better shape. There could be no turning back, no replenishing of stores. The oxen had wintered in the rushes, without corn, and were bony and weak.

Bishop Edward Hunter, captain of the second hundred, stepped up and handed Taylor a tally sheet. There were 1,553 men, women, and children in the company; 2,213 oxen, 124 horses, 887 cows; 358 sheep; 716 chickens; and an indefinite number of pigs (several sows were pregnant).

Taylor checked with Parley, then asked Hunter if he was ready. Hunter reported that each person had 300 pounds of breadstuff; every man had a gun with a hundred rounds of ammunition; all outfits had seeds and agricultural implements.

"Move out."

The temple bell began to toll. This signaled that the wagons would roll in fifteen minutes.[7]

Contention and bickering broke out regarding the order of march and delegated authority. Before leaving, Brigham had designated his brother, John Young, as president of the emigrant company, with John Van Cott marshal. While these men had deferred authority to the two apostles, some men of the company were confused about rank and refused to obey

---

[7] The bell from the Nauvoo temple had been buried when the Saints left the city. Subsequently it was unearthed and now was in the custody of the Pratt–Taylor company. It would signal morning prayer, breakfast, stopping time, and at night would serve as a warning "if Indians are hovering about."

orders. Murmuring grew until, after two weeks of travel, Pratt and Taylor called a halt to straighten things out. By three that afternoon everyone was in such harmony that Taylor baptized eleven, some being children, and rebaptized others as affirmation of faith.

Parley then performed the marriage ceremony for Sanford Bingham and Martha Lewis, after which Taylor officiated in marrying his younger sister, Elizabeth, to George Boyes. Each newlywed couple left in a carriage ride over the prairie, and returned an hour or so later, the honeymoon over, to celebrate at a feast and dance on the banks of the Platte.

The forests began giving way to endless prairie. Buffalo country. At Loup Fork the Pawnees had abandoned their two villages for the summer. The burning of the dry prairie grass of the previous year, which had so hampered the pioneer party, encouraged the new growth, and the emigrants moved through good forage.

As they forded Loup Fork two boys fell out of the wagons and under the wheels. Fortunately, the bottom was sandy; after being administered to, both youngsters seemed little worse for the experience.

A few days later the Camp of Israel stopped at another deserted Indian village opposite Grand Island. The Lamanites used Grand Island for wintering their livestock. While the Saints had seen no Indians en route, that didn't mean they weren't lurking about. This had been proved the first day of travel, when Jacob Weatherby decided to return to Winter Quarters for something he'd forgotten, while the wagons were crossing the Elkhorn. He was waylaid en route, killed, and scalped.

As they traveled alongside Grand Island they saw immense herds of buffalo. Spotted among them were horses, mules, and cattle, strays from various wagon trains. Taylor warned the herd boys to keep close watch on the livestock to prevent mingling with the buffalo herds.

As the emigrant company approached the South Fork of the Platte the afternoon of July 8, Taylor spotted a board planted in the sand where the pioneers had camped. Swinging off his borrowed horse, he read the penciled message: At this point the pioneers had encountered a war party of several hundred Pawnee braves, hostile that the whites were traveling through their lands.

A wild whoop came from the sandy bluffs bordering the river channel. Two beautiful mares came into view, a herd boy chasing them on his pony. "Strays!" he yelled.

Taylor sprang into the saddle and joined the chase. He succeeded in heading the two strays back toward the bluffs. One was a bay, the other a sorrel, both fat and spirited. As he chased them into the heavy sand, another herd boy rode into view atop the bluff. The mares whirled and tried to charge past. Taylor dropped the loop of his rope over the bay's neck and snubbed it close to the saddle horn.

Parley came running up, admiring the bay. If only they could get the sorrel also, he said. Taylor handed Parley the reins of his own horse, and, as Pratt galloped away in chase, Taylor slipped a half hitch on the muzzle of the bay and sprang astride it. The mare hadn't been ridden for awhile and began crow-hopping, but he kicked it in the ribs, whacked it with the end of the rope, and let out a wild whoop. The mare broke into a gallop.

The company was circling the wagons for the night when Taylor rode in astride the bay, with Parley leading the sorrel. While the women cooked supper, the two apostles were busy putting shoes on the mares and currying them. Men came by to admire the horses and joke about the cowboy apostles. Taylor noted a new respect in the attitude of several who had been most rebellious about authority.

At the campfire, Leonora complained that it was difficult to cook a meal with nothing to burn but buffalo chips. On the other hand, her husband pointed out, the smudge kept mosquitos away.

Sarah Pitchforth ran up to the campfire, breathless. The eleven-year-old asked if Annie was having supper with the Taylors. Where was Annie? While Aunt Mercy was fixing supper, Sarah said that she went with her sisters, Mary and Annie, to gather buffalo chips. Annie hadn't returned to camp.

Taylor put down his plate and joined the search for the missing child. In a dozen ways Annie might have encountered an accident or misfortune; she could have slipped into the river, fallen into a wash, become confused and wandered away, been kidnapped by lurking Pawnees, or . . .

The sun had set as he prowled the brush at the base of the sandy bluffs. As he crossed a wash he suddenly froze at a warning sound, the whirr of a rattlesnake. Only his eyes moved as he tried to locate the source. Then he saw, up the wash a bit, the missing child. Annie Pitchforth was crouched by a bush, prodding a big rattler with a stick. The massive body writhed in a coil as the triangular head moved slowly back and forth, beady eyes fixed on the tormentor. Then the snake struck. The thick body uncoiled while the mouth gasped wide as the fangs lashed out. The strike was inches short. Annie giggled, poking with the stick as the rattler coiled again.

Taylor kicked sand at the snake and snatched up the girl. He held Annie tightly as the rattler slid away into the brush. As he carried the child toward camp he asked if she didn't understand; didn't she know a rattlesnake bite could kill her?

Annie's face—so much like her mother's—was wide-eyed with innocence as she asked if it would be so bad to die. Then she'd be with Mommie, wouldn't she? On the night Mommie died, she'd said she was going to a wonderful place to wait for the children.

Then with a finger the child touched his cheek. Was this a tear? Was

Brother Taylor crying? Men didn't cry, did they? Only children cried, and women.

Just a grain of sand in the eye, Taylor said huskily. He put the child down and they walked hand in hand to the camp.

At dusk the herders brought the livestock inside the circled wagons, an armed guard and a herd boy standing watch at the opening.

Taylor walked the circle of wagons with the captain of his company, Edward Hunter, checking with captains of fifties and tens. Everything was in order. He said good night to Hunter, then spread his bedroll under his wagon and crawled into the blankets. It had been a full day.

The clanging of the temple bell awakened him. For a confused moment he thought it was a thunderstorm; then he realized it was the hammering of hooves that shook the earth. The cattle within the wagon circle of his company moved restlessly, bawling, spooked by the sound of the stampede. Taylor rolled from his bed under the wagon, wondering if a buffalo herd would overwhelm them. The thunder of hooves came close in the night, shaking the earth; then as the stampede poured past he realized that the animals weren't buffalo, but cattle from one of the other companies, running wild, while several men on horseback tried to control them.

Taylor and a dozen riders from his own company joined the chase after the spooked cattle, through brush, across washes, among thickets of the river bottom, up the sandy bluffs. By daybreak they'd rounded up the herd and were headed back for Capt. Jedediah Grant's company, where the stampede had originated.

Washington Cook, who'd been on guard at the wagon opening of the Grant company, rode alongside Taylor, saying he'd take the blame. It wasn't really the boy's fault. He and the lad, Amenzo Baker, were sitting on guard when something spooked the cattle and some of them tried to break out of the circle. Amenzo had a sheepskin over his shoulder, and he sprang up, shaking it to haze the critters back. Well, that dry sheepskin crackled like a nest of rattlesnakes. The cattle bolted. Nothing could hold them. But the boy didn't mean any harm, Cook said; if there was any blame, he'd take it himself.

Accidents happen, Taylor told him; fortunately, no one was hurt.

At the Grant company he found one wagon overturned by the stampede—Robert Pierce's outfit, loaded with three thousand pounds, was knocked fifty feet into the brush—while Willard Snow's wagon, in the path of the stampede, was smashed to pieces, with seven broken ox horns lying among the spokes of the wheels.

But that wasn't the worst. When the herd was tallied, the count showed forty-six cattle missing.

The entire Camp of Israel spent a week at the forks of the Platte, scouring the country in search of the strays. But forty-six cattle had vanished, to melt into the roving buffalo herds. Members of other companies donated oxen to help make up the loss. When the bell tolled to move on, some of the wagons were yoked to milch cows.

That night they camped in the last of the timber they would see for two hundred miles, except for one lone tree.

The Camp of Israel lived well on the march. Fish could be had from the Platte or any tributary by throwing in a baited hook. In buffalo country fresh meat was plentiful, though tough compared to beef. However, Taylor missed the fresh vegetables that might have been ready at Grand Island, and he thought of the other harvest that could have been waiting ahead at Fort Laramie.

Young men on their ponies chased after wild horses in the buffalo herds, but without success. When one youth narrowly escaped death when his horse stumbled, Taylor counseled against the sport. Buffalo was so easily had, with rifles, that men brought six tongues into camp, leaving the huge bodies on the plains for the wolves. Pratt and Taylor issued orders that there would be no hunting without specific appointment; to waste game was "a disgrace to the people and displeasing to the Lord."

In late July they came onto an Indian village near Chimney Rock, the first Lamanites they'd seen since leaving Winter Quarters. These were friendly, and a hundred came into camp that afternoon, one bearing an American flag. The Indians sang and danced, then the Mormons did likewise, to the music of violin, fife, and drums, climaxed by the firing of two cannon by Captain Rich's artillery. The natives traded buffalo robes, moccasins, and gloves for corn, tobacco, coffee, salt, and fish hooks. Then as a gesture of friendship, the Indians invited the whites to enjoy the wild currants near the bluffs across the river. Taylor with several wives joined a picnic party, fording the Platte to enjoy the fresh berries and bring back a harvest for pie.

As the company passed Indians on the trail the next few days, dragging their luggage on travois harnessed to horses, mules, and dogs, Taylor was reminded that autumn was at hand and winter coming on.

In early August a squad of fourteen members of the Mormon Battalion came into camp from the east, escort of Gen. S. F. Kearney, en route from San Francisco Bay to Fort Leavenworth with Col. John C. Fremont in custody to stand charges of insubordination.

It was not until the Camp of Israel reached Fort Laramie that the emigrant train followed Brigham's pioneers across the Platte to the well-worn Oregon Trail. Taylor learned that the pioneers had followed the Oregon Trail four hundred miles to Fort Bridger, then taken the Hastings cut-off to the Salt Lake valley. He and Pratt were decidedly of mixed feelings regarding the wisdom of the pioneer party in breaking new road for five hundred miles to avoid contact with Gentiles, when it was inevitable that the next four hundred would be along the Oregon Trail.

Taylor was chilled by news that the resulting delay threw the pioneers so far behind schedule that they didn't enter Salt Lake valley until July 24. Was there time to mature a crop?

Meanwhile, Brigham had become impatient with the slow progress of the Pratt–Taylor company. Taylor ignored the first letter, feeling that Brigham had little room for criticism, considering that the select party of pioneers had taken three and a half months instead of the estimated thirty-five days. Brigham then dispatched three men with another letter, with orders to bring a reply. Taylor wrote,

> Our numbers far exceed what we anticipated, for instead of numbering 100 wagons, we have near 600; the cattle were generally weak in coming off the rushes; we had to recruit more cattle and send to Missouri for bread stuffs. You know, Brethren, that it takes a little labor and time to start a large wheel.

He pointed out, further, that "You may expect also on your return to find an abundance of corn and vegetables; . . . we plowed and enclosed a large tract of land before we left." And if Brigham wanted to take this as a gentle reminder of the failure of the plan for pioneer parties to do the same thing along the trail, let him.

In council with the visitors, Taylor and Pratt learned that the pioneers were encountering unexpected difficulties in trying to grow crops in the Salt Lake valley. They had to learn practical irrigation from scratch. Then, after they had had the land watered and the seeds planted, voracious crickets swarmed over the sprouting crop. Yes, they'd get a harvest, but not what they'd hoped for. And despite the lateness of the season, they'd planted eighty-four acres.

It snowed the morning of September 4, in the high elevation near South Pass, still 300 miles from the destination. That afternoon Brigham rode into camp, en route back to Winter Quarters with the pioneer company and a contingent of Mormon Battalion men returning to their families.

Brigham was steaming mad. While behind a shelter of bushes the women fixed a surprise banquet for the visiting brethren, the council of the Twelve met in private session, and Brigham blistered the ears of Parley and Taylor. Parley ranked ahead of Taylor in the Quorum, so therefore was technically responsible for what displeased the president of the Twelve, which was quite a list.

Before leaving Winter Quarters, the council had appointed Brigham's brother, John, as leader of the emigrant company, with John Van Cott marshal. However, the arrival of Pratt and Taylor from England caused these men to defer to the two apostles. "Parley was severely censured by Brigham, who was highly incensed because Parley had assumed any superintendency over the company," wrote Reva Stanley.

> Brigham made it plain that he had issued orders before his departure regarding the leadership of the company and he resented Parley's interference. He blamed him for all the trouble which had developed at the beginning of the trip. In short, everything that went wrong was Parley's fault. And that was not all Brigham had to say to him. Parley had married two women without first asking Brigham's consent, and this was the act which infuriated Brigham most. He told Parley in no uncertain terms that no man, whatever his position in the church, would be allowed to make plural marriages without first obtaining the consent of Brigham. Parley realized then that he must continue to knuckle to Brigham whether he was right or wrong. If he did not bow to Brigham's iron will Brigham would try to break him. Parley loved peace and would keep it at any price. He asked Brigham's forgiveness, and they parted as friends.[8]

With difficulty Taylor held his temper during this tongue-lashing. He knew that Brigham's fury was provoked by a deeper motive than the acceptance of leadership, slowness of travel, or marrying plural wives. What really stuck in Brigham's craw was not that his authority had been flouted, but that he actually didn't *have* the authority, thanks primarily to Taylor and Pratt. Taylor reminded Brigham that he wasn't president of the church, and that the Twelve, as a body, governed the Society of Saints.[9] As for authority, according to Brigham's own revelation the companies were to be organized under direction of the apostles; Brigham himself had made no bones about who was in charge of the pioneers, regardless of the formal organization.

During this hectic council meeting, Roberts records,

---

[8] Reva Stanley, *The Archer of Paradise*. The author was Parley Pratt's grand-daughter.

It is curious that although Parley admits in his *Autobiography* that "I humbled myself, acknowledged my faults and errors, and asked forgiveness," there is no record of Taylor doing likewise. He evidently slugged it out with Brigham, toe to toe.

It might be well to point out, also, that despite Brigham's severe criticism of the slowness of the Pratt–Taylor company of emigrants, when Brigham subsequently was in charge of a similar party the following spring, it took exactly the same time en route as the Pratt–Taylor company.

[9] Reva Stanley says that because of the opposition by Parley and Taylor, "Brigham never completely forgave either of those men for their attitude that day." Throughout the remainder of his life Brigham also took pot shots at Hyde and Orson Pratt. He declared that Hyde had as much right to his church standing as "my old mule"; while "He despised Orson Pratt," says Hirshson in his *Lion of the Lord*; "the prophet twice publicly reprimanded him for his appearance and twice gave him clothes suitable for the Tabernacle. Distrusting Pratt's intellectualism, Young sent him on an endless string of missions."

the clouds cleared away, and before the warm sunshine the snow soon disappeared. There was nervous activity in the camp, mysterious movements among the sisters. Trunks that had been undisturbed on the journey were opened, their contents investigated and certain articles hurriedly conveyed to a beautiful, natural lawn enclosed by a dense growth of bushes.

When the meeting adjourned, the members "were led by Elder Taylor through a natural opening in the bushes," where they found improvised banquet tables laid with snow-white linen and gleaming tableware, groaning under "roast beef, pies, cakes, biscuits, butter, peach-sauce, coffee, tea, sugar, and a great variety of good things."

Supper over and cleared away, preparations were made for dancing; and soon was added to the sweet confusion of laughter and cheerful conversation the merry strains of the violin, and the strong, clear voice of the prompter. . . . Dancing was interspersed with songs and recitations. "We felt mutually edified and blessed," writes Elder Taylor; "we praised the Lord and blessed one another."[10]

During the festivities, the wily Lamanites ran off twenty-one horses and mules, mostly belonging to Brigham's party. This meant that a number of the pioneers would have to walk the 760 miles back to Winter Quarters.

The Camp of Israel pushed on toward the promised land. When a large number of oxen died from drinking alkali water near Devil's Gate, more cows went under the yoke. The various companies of the great wagon train reached the Salt Lake valley in late September and early October.

In the valley the pioneers had located the site of Great Salt Lake City. Orson Pratt, using the instruments Taylor had brought from England, had surveyed Zion into blocks of ten acres each, with enormously wide streets. The pioneers had partially completed a stockade, with houses of adobe and log forming a continuous wall on its perimeter. All this was good; but when Taylor and Pratt inspected the acreage put into crops, they experienced a sickening shock.

They walked through cornfields that hadn't come into tassel, the scrubby stocks denuded by crickets. No vegetables had matured; the plantings of beans, peas, squash, melon, cabbage, carrots, and other row crops were complete failures. Clouds of crickets flew up before them as they walked through a field of buckwheat that had never come to head. At a potato patch, the plants blackened by early frost, Taylor dug in the dry soil and found "a few small potatoes, from the size of a pea upward to that of a half inch in diameter," Parley reported. These tiny pellets,

---

[10] Roberts' *The Life of John Taylor* . . . ; also Wilford Woodruff's *Journal*.

resembling a boy's marbles, constituted the entire harvest of the eighty-four acres planted by the pioneers. The prime purpose of the pioneer expedition, which was to put in crops for the emigrants, was a complete failure.[11]

There was no turning back. With winter coming on, the emigrants were trapped between the Rockies and the Sierras, dependent for a second winter upon the grain stored in their wagons, facing the possibility of another epidemic of blackleg and other ailments of deficient diet which had made Winter Quarters a nightmare.

On Sunday, October 31, the pioneer party returned to Winter Quarters. Brigham stopped the company on the outskirs of town to congratulate them on the expedition:

> Brethren, I will say to the Pioneers, I wish you to receive my thanks for your kindness and willingness to obey orders; I am satisfied with you; you have done well. We have accomplished more than we expected. . . . I feel to bless you all in the name of the Lord God of Israel. You are dismissed to go to your own homes.[12]

Early in December, Brigham once again attempted to achieve his most cherished ambition: to be named president of the church, prophet, seer, and revelator. Taylor and Parley Pratt, ringleaders of the opposition within the quorum, were in far-off Utah. Orson Hyde, who had sided with them, was appeased by the prestige of becoming president of the quorum when Brigham became head of the church and took the two men ahead of Hyde in the quorum—Heber C. Kimball and Willard Richards —into the presidency with him. This left only Orson Pratt among the original dissenters at Winter Quarters when Brigham brought the matter to a vote on December 5. He was unanimously approved as president of the Church of Jesus Christ of Latter-day Saints.[13]

---

11 CHC, 3:237. Roberts buries the crop failure in a brief footnote, terming the putting in of crops "an experiment," and admitting that "From this planting nothing matured."

12 DHC, 7:616.

13 It is uncertain whether Orson Pratt attended this council meeting. The DHC and Andrew Jenson's *Church Chronology* omit his name as among those present. Later accounts, notably CHC, list him as present. There is some indication that whether at the meeting or not, he voiced objection, for the very next day he was called on a mission to England, as had Hyde, Parley Pratt, and Taylor previously.

9

Years of the Locust

AFTER SIX HOURS, Taylor was glad when the last log was whipsawed. He climbed out of the saw pit, took the netting from over his head, and with a handkerchief wiped at the fine sawdust that had sifted through to smart his eyes and rim his lips. Young George Whitaker, top man on the saw, was still fresh; but at forty Taylor was glad to be finished. He hoped this would be the last house he'd have to build with his own hands.

Whitaker went for his wagon, to haul away his share of the lumber. Taylor slapped the sawdust from his clothing. As he crossed to Leonora's tent, he observed the ant-like activity of the Saints preparing for winter and protecting themselves against possible Indian trouble. Men notched logs and laid adobe brick for houses whose walls joined together to form a rectangular fort, all windows facing inward, the outside solid except for loop holes. Brigham's pioneers had partly enclosed a ten-acre fort before returning to Winter Quarters. Now the permanent residents worked at finishing this and building a thirty-acre addition adjoining the south side.

Taylor had staked off ninety feet of the new fort for his own residence, which would consist of three apartments for his families, who were now living in tents and wagons. Both Sophia Whitaker and Jane Ballantyne, Ann's sister, were big with child, and he was courting Sophia's sister, Harriet. As their condition became apparent, both Sophia and Jane had adopted the usual fiction of being married to an absent missionary.

For his own house, he had whipsawed a four-inch plank from the center of each log. The outer slabs would form the exterior walls, the planks used for partitions and—a rare luxury—wooden floors. With the interior plastered with fine white clay, his would be one of the finest dwellings of the fort.

Sophia and Jane kept after him to have the house completed before their babies came; but a man could do only so much, and it was probable that Sophia's first child would at some future time, when Great Salt Lake City was a metropolis, boast of having been born in a wagon.

Leonora had the noon meal ready when he entered the tent. Taylor washed up at the basin beside the doorway, then sat down to boiled beef and corn dodger. The meat was stringy, devoid of fat. It was so tough and dry that when he butchered the bony animal he'd said wryly that the saw should be greased.

What, Leonora asked as he ate, was he going to do about Sophia and Jane? Did he expect them, in their delicate condition, to subsist on tough beef, old corn meal, and flour? The brethren preached that people store provisions for a year ahead, two, even seven years; but without fresh food people got sick and died. Sophia and Jane needed vegetables, greens, fresh living food. Sophia in particular had cravings which showed that her unborn child needed nourishment it wasn't getting.

Taylor sighed and held out his teacup for a refill. The situation haunted him, but what could he do about it?

All a man cared about was starting the baby, Leonora said scathingly; then he left the rest of it to the woman. What if Sophia and Jane gave birth to babies mentally deficient or physically deformed—a living rebuke to the father who neglected them?

He was glad of the interruption when visitors arrived. Young George Bean came in with an ancient Indian, whom Bean introduced as a Gosiute medicine man. Bean had a knack for Lamanite dialects and sign language, and could communicate with any tribe. After Leonora served them tea and corn dodgers, Bean explained that the Gosiutes were camped at the hot springs at the north end of the valley, where they were being ravaged by measles. This white man's disease, for which they had no immunity, was killing them by the dozens. The skills of the medicine man were ineffective, the waters of the hot springs didn't help, and he had come seeking stronger medicine. Yellow Bird, twelve-year-old son of Chief Little Face and his father's favorite child, was deathly sick. The Lamanites had heard of miraculous cures effected by the Mormonites with the laying on of hands. Would Brother Taylor cure the sick boy?

Taylor agreed to try. He went out for a horse and found that George Whitaker had returned with his wagon for the lumber. When Taylor asked if he'd like to help administer to Yellow Bird, Whitaker was dubious. Did Brother John realize the responsibility? If the child died, he'd be blamed, and there could be Indian trouble. However, Whitaker said, he'd come along and assist if Brother John wished.

Taylor advised him to keep on with the lumber hauling. Faith healing depended upon faith, and he didn't want anyone to assist with reservations. Young Bean could help with the ordinance.

At the Lamanite encampment, sick Indians were soaking in the hot springs, while about thirty corpses with their dogs lay about the pools; except for killing their dogs, the Indians had been too overwhelmed by the epidemic to take care of their dead. Taylor told Bean to get a detail of men to attend to the burial, as soon as they got back to the fort.

The medicine man took them to the wickiup of Chief Little Face. As he opened the flap the shaft of light caused a cry of pain from the sick boy within. The chief and two squaws sat by Yellow Bird, whose eyes were red-rimmed and body splotched with patches of ugly rash. His quick breathing came in wheezing gasps, broken by a dry cough.

Bean anointed the boy's head with consecrated oil, then both men laid hands on the fever-flushed head while Taylor administered a healing blessing. The following morning Bean took a detail of men to bury the dead Lamanites, and on returning reported that Yellow Bird was considerably better. Several days later Chief Little Face and Yellow Bird arrived with several braves to offer gifts of appreciation—deerskin moccasins and gloves, together with sego lily and camus bulbs, thistle roots, sunflower seeds, pine nuts, wild honey, and a bag of meal which had the rich flavor of cracklings. Taylor accompanied them to the places where the bulbs and thistle roots could be dug up; and he returned with the comfortable knowledge that it needn't be a winter of famine after all. The Saints could live off the land, just as the Indians did. Their vegetables grew wild; their meat was to be had for the hunting.

The fresh vegetables filled a hollow spot within Taylor and his family. While the Indian meal lasted, Sophia and Jane found their food craving satisfied, but when it was gone they once again were gnawed by persistent yearning. Taylor went with George Bean to find the secret of the meal from Chief Little Face. The chief said they were just in time, for a harvest was planned that very afternoon.

The two Saints went with the Lamanites to a wheat field the pioneers had planted but which hadn't matured. The Indians lighted torches, then encircled the field, igniting it with a ring of fire. As the dry straw burned, millions of crickets leaped up and fell back into the flames. The Indians moved across the blackened ground, collecting the roasted crickets in baskets. Then at their village the squaws ground the insects into meal with stones and mixed it with honey for the delicious cakes.

Taylor took some fresh meal home for his pregnant wives. While he knew that John the Baptist had lived on locusts and honey, he found his own appetite for the fare gone. However, if Sophia and Jane craved it, what they didn't know wouldn't hurt them.

Fortunately, it was an open winter. The house still was unfinished when, on December 7, Sophia presented her husband with a daughter, which he blessed and christened Harriet Ann.

Three days previously, in a ceremony known only to the family and recorded on secret books, he had married Sophia's older sister, Harriet.

The family moved into the house in time for Christmas.

On the morning after Christmas, Taylor crossed the rectangle of the fort for a meeting at the home of John Smith, the stake president. There was no code of laws in the valley, and in consequence numerous problems had arisen.

As he crossed the fort the brisk air was like wine. Though surrounding mountains glittered white with snow, there was none in the valley. Certainly Brigham had been inspired to select this spot, with its mild climate, beauty, canyon streams, fertile soil, its timber and coal, and its isolation from the world, where the Saints could live the gospel unmolested.

At council meeting, Parley Pratt spoke "at some length on the disaffected spirits in the valley." The burly apostle said that too many—particularly people of means with good outfits and ample provisions—were joining emigrant trains headed for California. Taylor voted with the council to order the marshal to stop them from leaving, and "appointed a committee to inform Mr. Miles Goodyear why Samuel Brown, Elijah Shockley and son, and Samuel Shepherd and son were stopped."

Taylor was a member of a committee appointed "to draft such laws as were needed immediately." By the following day they had prepared the first legal code of the valley, consisting of five ordinances enacted "for the peace, welfare, and good order of the community." The first made "idling away his time" a serious charge against a man, for which his property could be taken over by trustees and the loafer put in custody and caused "to be industriously employed."

The second, third, and fourth ordinances provided sentences of "a certain number of lashes on the bare back, not exceeding thirty-nine," for violence, threats, or riot; for adultery and fornication; and for arson or theft. In addition, violence could receive a fine of $500, adultery $1,000, while thieves and arsonists must "restore four fold" and give security for good behavior.

The final ordinance provided a fine of not less than $25 for "drunkeness, cursing, swearing . . . unnecessary firing of guns . . . or in any other way disturbing the quiet or peace of the community."[1]

The whipping post provided rough justice in a country without a jail and with no spare manpower to construct and maintain one. Taylor knew that in practice it would be rarely used. The overwhelming weight

---

[1] JH, December 27, 1847.

of group disapproval in the fastness kept almost everyone in line. In a few cases the lash was necessary, such as to punish a young man for a shocking breach of decency—riding a horse with a young lady seated ahead of him.

The Nauvoo temple bell, which had called the Saints together on the march, served the same purpose at the fort. Ironically, the 100-foot standard on which it was mounted, called the Liberty Pole, became the whipping post.

The ordinance providing for four-fold repayment for stealing caused knotty legal problems in the case of a thieving dog.

> This dog stole some biscuits from a man and the fellow borrowed a shot gun and shot the dog. The case was brought before me for arbitration, and I gave the man who had lost the biscuits the full benefit of the law, namely allowed him four-fold—or 16 biscuits, which kept the fellow for a whole week.[2]

On March 6, the high council wrote to Brigham and the council at Winter Quarters that the population in the valley was 1,671, with 423 houses; that animals which had run loose during the winter were in fine condition; the brethren were busy with their gardens, and had thrifty tomato, cabbage, and other plants ready to set out; 872 acres were sown to winter wheat, with 4,260 acres designed for spring and summer crops.

> We will state as to machinery, that Bro Charles Crismon has a small gristmill, with one run of small stones, in operation on City Creek. . . . Bro John Neff intends to build a good flouring mill, to be ready to grind by harvest, if possible. Bro Chase has a sawmill in operation on a spring a short distance from the Pioneer garden. Archibald and Robert Gardner have a sawmill nearly ready for sawing on Mill Creek. Bro Crismon has the frame and gearing of a sawmill nearly ready to put up. Bro Nebeker, Riter, and Wallace are progressing rapidly with a sawmill, in a canyon some ten miles north of the city. Bro Amasa Russell has leave to put up a frame for the carding machine near Bro Gardener's sawmill. Several of our mechanics have been busy through the winter making kitchen chairs, tables, bedsteads, washtubs, churns, a few bureaus, &c.[3]

The future looked prosperous. Aside from tight rations until crops matured, the major problem came from rodents and vermin. The houses crawled with bedbugs and wood ticks. With an acute shortage of cats, mice thrived, burrowing under foundations and honeycombing the dirt roofs.

Then on the first of April the air turned soft and clouds hung low. It quietly began to snow, and before the storm was over a foot of snow lay

---

[2] Nebeker, "Early Utah Justice," UHQ, July 1930.

[3] JH, March 6, 1848.

in the valley. As the sky cleared, bitter cold closed in, freezing the new crops. Taylor realized that the Saints had misjudged the capricious mountain climate; they had just happened to arrive at an unusually mild winter. The spring made up for it. There was more heavy snow the following week. Then came soaking rains. The dirt roofs didn't have sufficient slope; rain ran through the honeycomb of mouse runways and dripped from the ceiling; foundations shifted and settled as water softened rodent tunnels. Taylor ruefully watched his plaster of fine white clay melt and fall in sticky gobs from ceiling and walls. Leonora had to carry an umbrella while cooking and doing housework. "Some people began to pray for rain before they ascertained that their houses were not waterproof," he wrote to Brigham and the Twelve on May 22, "and almost wished that they had deferred their supplications a little longer."

Because of the weather, wheat would harvest only from ten to fifteen bushels to the acre, he estimated, but "barley, oats, rye, buckwheat, and other grains look well. Flax, and especially peas look very promising. Crickets and other insects in some isolated districts have been very destructive to the rising vegetation, but their ravages are limited and their operations not such as to create any general alarm."[4]

While the harvest would have been adequate for the residents then in the valley, emigration would more than double the population before winter. Taylor put his wives to spinning a seine a hundred feet long, while he built a boat. He hauled the equipment thirty miles south to Utah Lake and launched a fishing operation.

Brigham arrived in September with a company of 1,229. Other emigrant trains swelled the valley population by 2,500, and another hard winter was ahead.

Meanwhile, members of the Mormon Battalion changed the course of history. Employed to dig the race for a sawmill in California near Sutter's Fort, they struck gold. The rush was on. Brigham's dream of isolation in the Great Basin was shattered, as Salt Lake became the way station of the western migration.

During the summer of 1849 the Saints formed the provisional State of Deseret. At this time there were fewer than 4,500 people in the valley, but they had vision. The State of Deseret was in essence the Great Basin,

---

4 JH, May 22, 1848. It should be noted that neither Taylor nor Pratt made mention of the well-known miracle of the seagulls, who saved the Saints from starvation by devouring the cricket hordes. No doubt the gulls ate crickets; but the insects remained a destructive pest in subsequent years. The legend of the miracle evidently improved with hindsight. The *Journal History* contains two letters on the subject, one dated 1869 and the other 1920—written twenty-one and seventy-two years after the event.

an immense territory comprising the entire drainage area of the Colorado River.[5]

John Taylor became associate justice of the supreme court of Deseret, whose other members were Heber C. Kimball of the first presidency and Presiding Bishop Newel K. Whitney. None of these men had studied law.[6] The Mormons very simply transformed their ecclesiastical hierarchy into a political government. The three men of the first presidency of the church became the most powerful civil officers, Brigham Young governor, Heber C. Kimball lieutenant-governor, and Willard Richards secretary of state.

The Saints expected that when Deseret was admitted as a state, the Kingdom of God would reign, the only perfect government since the city of Enoch.

The problem was to gain admission to the Union. This attempt involved Taylor in one of the great ironies of Mormon history. Because of a snowstorm, the state of Deseret never was admitted to the Union. In consequence, the course of western history was most drastically altered. The "Mormon question" became a political football, and the Saints had to struggle for another forty-five years to gain admission of Utah as a state.

When Gen. John Wilson, Indian Agent for the California region, arrived at Salt Lake August 30, it seemed a dream come true. Wilson presented a proposal from President Zachary Taylor. To overcome the opposition of slavery advocates, the president planned that the combined territory of Deseret and California (known as Eastern and Western California) be admitted as a single state, the option remaining with the people as to whether it should be slave or free—thus avoiding a fight over the issue in Congress. After admission to the Union, California and Deseret would, in 1851, be dissolved into two states, each "becoming a

---

[5] "Deseret," a term from the Book of Mormon meaning "honey bee," comprised "virtually all of modern Utah, most of modern Nevada and Arizona, much of Wyoming, Colorado, and New Mexico, small portions of modern Oregon and Idaho, and all that portion of southern California between the Mexican border and 118° 30′ west longitude, including the sea coast in the vicinity of San Diego, which was to serve as a seaport." Morgan, "The State of Deseret," *UHQ*, vol. VII, numbers 2, 3, 4.

Despite what might seem a grandiloquent concept, the State of Deseret made good geographical sense. Had it been adopted, the Colorado River basin could have been developed as a complete entity, instead of being dismembered by the long and bitter fight between the western states over the apportionment of the water.

[6] Ibid. No qualifications as to legal training were set up. "This omission is significant when it is remembered that the Mormons regarded lawyers as an abomination. . . . The judiciary had no legal background whatever, but all three men were possessed of great practical experience and trusted by the people, and therefore were eminently qualified, in the homely sense, for judicial office."

free, sovereign, independent State, without any further action of Congress."[7]

Taylor was one of a committee who negotiated with General Wilson. "We acceded to his request and agreed to form this union, on condition that we were each, within two years, to form separate State constitutions and governments."[8]

The first presidency immediately dispatched a letter to Amasa M. Lyman, church leader in California, to support the plan, pointing out that "while the government is using us to save the nation, we are using them to save ourselves." The letter concluded with sound political advice regarding formation of the new state: "Don't get too much in a constitution, lest it tie your hands. This has been the grand difficulty with almost all constitution-makers."[9]

Meanwhile Bvt. Brig. Gen. Bennett Riley had gone by water to California to prepare the conglomerate citizenry—native Mexicans and the gold-rushers drawn from every strata of society—for the plan. General Wilson left Salt Lake late in the fall to coordinate affairs in California with General Riley. However, a severe snowstorm in the Sierras "prevented his arrival in California at the time specified."

Meanwhile, General Riley,

> not being able to wait for him, made other arrangements with the people of California, and his [Wilson's] mission was thus frustrated. Had it not been for a snowstorm, we should have been a free people; as it is, we have been living under the worst species of despotism—a satrapy—from that time to the present.[10]

On September 5, 1849, John Taylor made affidavit of his intention of becoming a United States citizen, swearing

---

[7] JH, September 6, 1849.

[8] *Millennial Star*, 33:769.

[9] JH, September 6, 1849.

[10] *Millennial Star*, 33:769. Taylor was herein telling of the event three decades later.

The monograph, "The State of Deseret," op. cit., states: "In an unorganized California the proposal by Wilson and the Mormons might have found interested ears. In a California already organized as a state, the proposal was at once dismissed as presumptuous and impossible." California was admitted to statehood the following year, while "Deseret stood as the moving symbol of forty-five years of struggle for admission. It can only be conjectured how the problems of Utah in relation with the nation might have been resolved had Congress approved Deseret in 1850. Had Deseret been spared the bitter attacks which between 1850 and 1890 so powerfully shaped the Mormons as a distinct and separate group, the problems of Utah 'treason,' like that of polygamy, might have found a more quiet solution. . . . One may well wonder what the course of history of the West would have taken had Deseret, like California, been admitted to the Union in 1850."

to renounce for ever all allegiance and fidelity to all and any foreign Prince, Potentate, State, and Sovereignty whatever; and particularly to Victoria, Queen of the United Kingdom of Great Britain and Ireland.

One month later he was called on a mission that would take him to foreign soil for three years. He was to open France and Germany to the gospel, though he knew neither language.

The mission would also involve him in a project to establish the first beet-sugar industry in the United States, a nightmare experience of heroic endeavor and grand achievement, of loyalty and treachery, sacrifice and bribery, of betrayal and happenstance so involved and complex that the full story hasn't to this day been told.

10

Mission I:
Fried Froth

TAYLOR WROTE HIS FAMILY from St. Louis, while en route "to Washington, New York, and thence to France," that he was sending a wagonload of supplies in care of Brother Hoagland. The sale of this shipment of items, badly needed in the valley, would provide "everything to make you comfortable" during his absence on the mission. He helped load Brother Hoagland's wagon with 500 pounds of sugar, 3 dozen bags of coffee beans, and 100 pounds of tea. Then, with the welfare of his family attended to, he sailed with clear conscience on the *Westervelt*, arriving at Liverpool May 27, 1850.

After a few weeks tilling the vineyard in the Channel Islands, which were scheduled to be attached to the French mission when it was organized, Taylor arrived in France at Boulogne-sur-Mer. At this fortified seaport on the Pas de Calais, he quickly became involved in the most famous event of the entire mission—his public debate with three Protestant ministers.[1]

---

[1] This event remains highly controversial to this day. Taylor's report of it was widely distributed as a faith-promoting tract in England, and was reprinted in Orson Pratt's *Works*. In Roberts' *Life of John Taylor* and also his *Comprehensive History of the Church*, he gives it due homage—the classic confrontation, so loved in Mormon lore, where by simple truth and inspiration from above the humble missionary confounds the men of vast learning.

On the other hand, anti-Mormon writers never tire of using the Boulogne debate

Accompanying Taylor to France were two missionaries, William Howell and Curtis E. Bolton; a third, John Pack, was due from Jersey within a few days. Bolton and Pack had traveled from Utah with Taylor. Howell, a zealous Welshman, had organized at Boulogne the first branch of the church on continental Europe just two months previously.[2]

The very first thing that had to be attended to in France was obtaining permission to preach. The nation was on the verge of revolution. The authorities imposed stringent restrictions on public assembly, while the powerful Jesuits were vigilant in hamstringing non-Catholic activities. It was illegal to hold any religious meeting outside a consecrated church without written permission from the mayor of the city.

Taylor made an appointment to see Mayor M. S. Fontaine. While waiting, he and Bolton took a walk along the sea coast, visiting the remains of Napoleon's fortifications against the English across the Channel and the ruins of an ancient brick tower built by the Romans. Returning to the Basse Ville, or lower town, they visited the church of St.-Nicolas at the Place Dalton, then ascended the steep Grande Rue to the Haute Ville to see the Cathédrale Notre Dame, still unfinished after twenty-three years of labor by the dedicated monks; and they saw the old Chateau where Louis Napoleon, now president of France, had been confined just ten years previously.

Bolton was limping by the time they returned to their quarters at No. 15, Rue de la Lanipe. Taylor wondered if he'd made the wrong decision in not sending Bolton back to the valley at the time the missionary badly sprained his ankle in New York. Bolton had made such an impassioned plea that, despite misgivings, Taylor had permitted him to stay on the mission. Bolton's familiarity with French, from having lived in the country several years, would be invaluable as interpreter and also for translating the Book of Mormon.[3]

After an initial setback, the visit with Mayor Fontaine turned out well. At first Bolton acted as interpreter; but it quickly was apparent that this

---

as a classic example of the evasion, deceit, and outright falsehood practiced by missionaries of that time.

New light on the event has been shed by availability in recent years of Curtis E. Bolton's journal, a candid and unvarnished record by a fellow missionary.

[2] Joseph Smith had first organized the church April 6, 1830, with six members. Howell organized the branch at Boulogne April 6, 1850, with six members. It might seem that this presaged great things in France; however, that country has remained stony soil in the vineyard from that day to this.

[3] Bolton's ankle continued to bother him during the entire period of his mission, swelling if he walked much. Very possibly he had broken it. He never saw a doctor about it, the only treatment being that Taylor had laid hands upon it at the time of the injury.

supposed fluency with French either was greatly overestimated or else he was terribly rusty in its use. However, Boulogne was a bilingual city— its newspaper *Interpreter Anglais et Francais* published stories in both languages—so the mayor took the opportunity of displaying his erudition by continuing the interview in fearfully broken English. Not to be outdone, Taylor replied in extremely fractured French. Despite the handicap of communication—or perhaps because of it—the two men charmed each other, and Taylor received official permission to preach.

Presently Taylor was out tacking up handbills announcing meetings three times a week at the Concert Hall, No. 21, Rue Montsigny. Meanwhile to stir up interest, he wrote several letters to the *Interpreter*, sending copies in both English and French. While he planned a bilingual meeting, "Bro. Bolton did not feel himself competent without a little more experience to preach in French," he wrote Brigham. So Taylor, beginning to wonder about Bolton's competence, decided to conduct the meetings in English.

Before the first meeting, John Pack arrived from Jersey, and Taylor immediately took the missionary to task. In a stormy session, Taylor accused Pack of casting pearls before swine—of discussing the doctrine of plural marriage in public meeting. Pack replied that the Principle was essential to celestial glory, and he certainly wasn't ashamed of the gospel. Taylor told him to remember Joseph's admonition that, above all, a man mustn't betray his brethren. The Principle was not for the world; it was the privilege of a select few. At all costs it must be kept secret. When Pack quickly repented, Taylor accepted this, and assumed the matter was finished. It wasn't.

When only thirty people turned out for the first meeting, despite the publicity, it was obvious that religious interest in France was at low ebb. Even whispers of polygamy among the Mormons couldn't attract a good audience. The French just didn't care one way or another. However, three English ministers were on hand, heckling—C. W. Cleave, James Robertson, and Philip Cater (the latter described by Bolton as "a deformed bowlegged diminutive foul spirit"). They heckled the meeting, and afterwards followed the missionaries home, insolently trying to provoke a confrontation.

Taylor ignored them that night, but two days later on receiving a letter from the ministers ("a most abusive unpleasant missive," Bolton recorded), Taylor was most happy to accept the challenge to a public discussion. He hadn't forgotten the remarkable results at Douglas, on the Isle of Man, from ministerial opposition.

The debate was to run for three nights, seven to ten, each party having thirty minutes alternately, with three officials of the Church of England as chairmen. The subjects would be, first, Joseph Smith: "Was he a truthful and honest man, or a blasphemous and daring imposter?"; second, the

Book of Mormon: "Is it . . . a revelation from God . . . [or] stupid and ignorant farago of nonsense?" and third, "Yourselves! The pretended facts of your Direct Appointment by God, to preach what you call the Gospel."

Admission, one-half franc; after expenses the surplus to be divided between the mayor and the English consul for the benefit of the poor.

While Taylor and fellow elders were preparing for the debate, a Jesuit priest called around to offer help. "When they ask about the character of your founders," he said, "just examine into theirs, and I will furnish you all the testimony you want."

Taylor said he was much obliged, but could handle the situation. "I thought if I could not get along without the help of a Jesuit priest," he explained, "it was a poor case."[4]

The *Interpreter*, reporting the debate, said that the Rev. C. W. Cleave

cited Mr. Taylor and his friends, not as teachers of any form of Christianity, but as emissaries and advocates of the vilest imposture since the days of Mahomet; . . . it was numbering its victims by tens of thousands, and it became the duty of every one to expose its audacious and fatal errors.

The first question is, was Joseph Smith an imposter? For if he was, there was an end of Mormonism. . . . The Rev. gentleman then proceeded to read general extracts from a work by the Rev. Henry Caswall, General Bennett, and others, . . . charging Joseph Smith and the Mormonites with a number of crimes and immoralities.[5]

"Whatever may be the views of men in relation to our principles," Taylor said in rebuttal, "all must accord that our being here on such a mission, so far from our families and homes, is evidence, at least, of our sincerity. Neither do I consider that the foundation of eternal truth rests upon the character of any man, much less upon false reports, newspaper stories, and the unauthorized statements of wicked and corrupt men."

"Truth," Taylor pointed out, "has always been opposed by the children of men," because it conflicts with wicked practices and corrupt hearts. "The prophets have always been persecuted—and why? Because they dared to tell the word of the Lord to the people. Stephen, in speaking on the same subject, says, 'Which of the prophets have not your forefathers killed who testified before of the coming of the Just One, of whom ye have been the betrayers and murderers?'" In this age, Taylor declared, people say, "'We would not have done that.' So said the Jews to Jesus, and yet they crucified him."

---

[4] JD, 1:16.

[5] The books cited were Caswall's *The City of the Mormons*; J. B. Turner's *Mormonism in All Ages*; and John C. Bennett's *History of the Saints*. Of the three authors, only Bennett possessed the background for an authentic exposé.

His opponents, in attacking Joseph Smith, "instead of meeting what they call error with the scriptures, and testing it with the touchstone of truth, seek to undermine the character of a good, honorable, and virtuous man. Hence we hear the hue-and-cry of false prophet, impostor, deceiver, blasphemer, adulterer, &c. Gentlemen, men of your calling ought to use other weapons," he advised the three ministers. "For men to descend to such means as my opponents have done, I consider too degrading for gentlemen, much more for men calling themselves by the name of Reverend."

Taylor then made the important point that the character of Joseph Smith had nothing to do with his standing as a prophet of God. Even if all they had said against him were true, the eternal truths of God which he preached could not be assailed. Though defying them to prove anything against the character of Joseph Smith, he emphasized that this was not the test. "What would become of the Psalms with such a test? David not only committed adultery, but murder. For certain designs of the Lord, Hosea was told to take unto him a wife of whoredoms, and children of whoredoms. Shall we reject his testimony because of this? We read of Elijah taking four hundred and fifty of the prophets of Baal, and slaying them at the brook Kishon. This certainly was a bloody deed; are we to reject his testimony because of this? Joseph Smith never slew so many false teachers. What would you say of Joshua and Samuel hewing prisoners down in cold blood? What of the disciples wishing to call down fire from heaven to slay their enemies? What of Peter smiting off the man's ear, and of his cursing and swearing, and saying that he did not know Jesus?"[6]

---

[6] Eduard Meyer subsequently stated this proposition admirably in his *Origin and History of the Mormons*:

"The opponents of the church have often raised a question as to how the absurd tales of the Book of Mormon, and the foolish revelations of the Prophet, which contradict all reason, could be literally accepted as God's communication to man; the question further expresses incredulity that Smith's followers could have deluded themselves by believing in their prophet's divine calling in view of his human weaknesses and the crimes which he committed. The answer which they offer is decisive and irrefutable. The Bible also contains numerous stories which are as absurd as those of the Book of Mormon if they are to be literally accepted—and such circles, whether Mormon or Gentile, admit of no other interpretation. But God's ways are not those of man, and a human scale of values may not be imposed upon his actions; man shall rather humble himself and accept the divine will and its manifestations as such, without exalting his own intelligence. . . . Looking at the moral scruples of Smith, there is again no problem for the believer. Assuming that all of the accusations brought against him *are* true, does not the Bible tell of grave sins and misdeeds committed by Abraham, Moses, David, and Solomon, men who were nevertheless chosen prophets of God? . . . God chooses whom He will, without having to give an account of Himself; apparently, as these stories teach, He has a predilection for sinners and

As to hearsay, Taylor said, "If we come to reports, they said that Jesus was born of fornication; that he was the associate and friend of publicans and sinners; a gluttonous man and a wine bibber, that he was associated with Beelzebub, the prince of devils. When he rose, they said that his disciples stole him away. They whipped St. Peter and St. John, banished St. John to the Isle of Patmos, whipped and imprisoned St. Paul, and killed all of the Apostles except St. John, because they were everywhere spoken evil of. Are we to reject their testimony because of this? Are we to reject Joseph Smith's testimony on account of false reports? I say no."[7]

Had the debate ended there, it might have lived on its merits of Taylor's defense of the faith. However, his opponents didn't neglect the opportunity to attack the church at its most vulnerable point—the charge of polygamy, so graphically detailed in Bennett's book. Taylor's reply to this was destined to survive to haunt the church. Although he had at least ten wives at this time, and while he believed the Principle to be essential to the gospel and necessary to celestial exaltation, the practice was so secret and sacred that he must deny it to the world.

In outraged tones he said, "We are accused here of polygamy, and actions the most indelicate, obscene, and disgusting, such that none but a corrupt and depraved heart could have contrived." Such things "are too outrageous to admit of belief." In refutation, he read the church's official attitude toward marriage, from *Doctrine and Covenants*, Section 101:

> ... All marriages in this church should be solemnized in a public meeting. ...
>
> Inasmuch as this Church of Jesus Christ has been reproached with the crime of fornication and polygamy, we declare that we believe that one

---

criminals. Thus, all reproaches made against Smith's character can cast no suspicion upon his inspiration. He remains the chosen instrument of God, who chose him as His mouthpiece. Herein lay the main strength of the Church, and the secret of the powerful propaganda which it exerted; in its midst was a genuine Prophet, from whom the living word of God resounded, a steady source of advice for every contingency which might arise, and a fulfillment of the ancient Biblical prophecies which others vainly sought to discredit."

[7] This summation of the three nights' discussion has been condensed in the same spirit with which Taylor elaborated it. While he is scrupulous in quoting the *Interpreter* regarding the arguments of his opponents, he quite obviously embellished his own. This is apparent from the pamphlet he published of the debate: The arguments of his opponents are summarized by the newspaper in third person, while Taylor quotes his own statements verbatim, first person. Thus it is obvious from internal evidence that the pamphlet is not, as might appear, a reprint of the *Interpreter* article. Also, Bolton in his diary notes that "Bro. Taylor and I are writing a pamphlet of his Boulogne Discussion to be published in England"; and a week later states that Taylor "left for England to finish his pamphlet."

man should have one wife, and one woman but one husband, except in case of death, when either is at liberty to marry again. . . .[8]

According to a young missionary who had labored with Taylor in the Channel Islands, John Hyde, the apostle also quoted from Section 42 of the D&C:

> Thou shalt love thy wife with all thy heart, and shalt cleave unto her and none else. And he that looketh upon a woman to lust after her shall deny the faith, and shall not have the Spirit; and if he repents not he shall be cast out.[9]

Although Taylor's pamphlet clearly establishes that he confounded the learned ministers in debate, his fellow missionary had an entirely different evaluation of the affair. "I feel in my own bosom," Bolton wrote, "that we were most signally defeated."[10] The debate sparked no public interest. On the following night only two persons in all of Boulogne came to the Concert Hall to hear him talk on the Book of Mormon. Taylor gave up the hall. "Bro. Taylor preached in his own room to three persons." Bolton wrote the next night. "Mormonism is dead here."

Taylor left Boulogne, and established headquarters in Paris.

If Bolton was critical of his superior, Taylor in turn was having problems with the missionary, who simply couldn't sustain himself in the mission field.[11] Taylor left him in Paris to translate the Book of Mormon, while he himself went to England to raise funds for publication. He hoped Bolton would rise to the responsibility, but, on returning to Paris, found that the fellow had been living two weeks on dry bread.

---

[8] Taylor was fully aware that this section of the D&C was completely obsolete. Subsequent to its reception, temple marriage had been instituted, which was a private rather than a public ceremony, and so secret that marriage records more than a century old are still inaccessible, despite Mormon emphasis on genealogy.

A subsequent revelation, not yet published, had been received by Joseph Smith "relating to the new and everlasting covenant, including the eternity of the marriage covenant, as also plurality of wives." When plural marriage was officially acknowledged as church doctrine, the revelation concerning it became Section 132 of the D&C, while Section 101, denying it, was deleted.

[9] Hyde, *Mormonism, Its Leaders and Designs*. Hyde was cut off because of his contrary spirit.

[10] In Roberts' *The Life of John Taylor* he declares, "The Champion of Truth was triumphant." However, considering Bolton's reaction, we must wonder how much the event was improved in the telling. Regardless of this, the pamphlet was a powerful missionary tract; so perhaps it hardly matters whether the exact words were or were not said before a handful of disinterested people at Boulogne.

[11] Bolton had left the Salt Lake valley without an overcoat. His clothing was so threadbare that by the time he reached St. Louis Taylor gave him a pair of pants and vest.

When Bolton finished the translation, Taylor showed it to a French scholar he'd converted named Wilhelm. The man put on his glasses and began reading. Presently he pursed his lips and began shaking his head. Then he began dipping here and there in the manuscript. Before long he took off his glasses and said quietly that it just wouldn't do. Bolton wasn't competent enough to make the translation.[12]

Taylor put Wilhelm to work on the translation, trying to save Bolton's face by having the two collaborate. Bolton was furious at having his script revised and fought Wilhelm every page and line. Wilhelm had so harrowing a time that he quit after three and a half futile months. The experience soured him on the church, and he was cut off after a disagreement over payment for his work, the sum in question being $26.

Taylor put Louis Bertrand, his first convert in Paris, on the job, and began personally checking every line. He wrote that

> there are some points that could not be translated correctly without me or someone else as well acquainted with the doctrinal points being present. . . . You are aware that it requires more than a knowledge of words to translate the Book of Mormon, Bible, or any inspired record; we must know the ideas intended to be conveyed before we can represent them correctly in another language.[13]

Meanwhile, Bolton was beset by personal problems. There was discord among his wives at home "that filled me with the most bitter anguish." His romance with the beautiful daughter of Louis Vanlembrouck, to whom he was teaching English, was aborted when the neighbors began gossiping. Bolton also was trying to promote the manufacture of a repeating rifle of his own invention.

Then, from England, Taylor dealt the crowning blow with a letter "for which he will be sorry some day or other." Taylor wanted his own name as translator on the French edition of the Book of Mormon. "God knows, and so do the Brethren here and Mr. Auge"—Auge was latest of several scholars who had engaged in the formidable task of collaboration—"that the translation of the Book of Mormon into French is literally, emphatically, truly, and essentially my own work." Bolton obviously envied and resented Taylor's commanding presence, handsome appearance, and enormous personal charm. The missionary wrote that the apostle

> has the greatest knack I ever saw to make everybody think him some great one! *but only for a time*, for they find him out after a while. I

---

[12] Taylor reported to Brigham that Bolton's translation "needs a revision. He was not sufficiently acquainted with the French to prepare it for the press" (March 13, 1851).

[13] To George Viett, July 15, 1851.

verily believe it is that spirit which he manifests is one chief cause why this mission does not prosper. . . . I write this, being determined that these facts shall be on my journal for the benefit of posterity.

The practical problems of the French mission went considerably deeper than Bolton's self-oriented analysis. The press was muzzled. Bolton recorded endless trouble dealing with pettifogging bureaucracy in publishing and distributing the innocent little periodical *Etoile du Deseret.* Severe press laws required the deposit of "caution money" by editors, which could be confiscated as fines for violating censorship restrictions. For ten years France was to be characterized as "a sickroom in which people spoke in lowered voices."

When Taylor applied for official permission to preach throughout France, the authorities "treated me with the greatest courtesy," he wrote to the family. Then instead of expected permission,

> they have utterly prohibited us from preaching anywhere throughout the country. I presume they are afraid of excitement for just about the time that the ministry had it [the application] in consideration there was a mob broke out in Denmark that tore down the Saints' meeting house and very much abused many of the Saints. If the French authorities have seen this, which I suppose they have, it would be quite sufficient to deter them from allowing us the privilege of preaching in France.

Taylor simply ignored the official ukase—born of Satan, in his opinion. He held secret meetings in Paris twice a week and sent Elders throughout France to bore from within. Before long he organized branches in Paris, Le Havre, and Calais, in addition to the one at Boulogne. The Channel Islands, containing several branches, came under the jurisdiction of the French mission, as scheduled, considerably increasing its strength.

The cloak-and-dagger aspect terrified Bolton, but added spice for Taylor. "I have published a pamphlet on the first principles of the gospel," he wrote the family in Utah. "It is not lawful to circulate them, but I contrive to do it."

The French people, however, were not opposed to Mormonism so much as faintly amused by it. To believe that celestial beings had appeared to an unlettered youth in the howling wilderness of frontier America, of all places, to restore the true gospel—it was to smile. Taylor found the sophistication of the French a much more formidable obstacle to missionary work than legal restrictions. Opposition always helped the cause; but he found it difficult to combat amused apathy. There was only one successful approach, he found, to the French:

> When they come to see it [the gospel], they rejoice in it, but we do not preach religion much to them, for a great many of them are philosophers, and, of course, we must be philosophers too, and make it appear

that our philosophy is better than theirs, and then show them that religion is at the bottom of it. . . . When they once get interested in the work of God, and get the spirit of God, they rejoice exceedingly in the blessings of the Gospel.[14]

Among French intellectuals, "philosophy is about every tenth word they speak," Taylor said.

I was almost buried up in it while I was in Paris. I was walking about one day in the *Jardin des Plantes*—a splendid garden. There they had a sort of exceedingly light cake; it was so thin and light that you could blow it away, and you could eat all day of it, and never be satisfied. Somebody asked me what the name of that was. I said, I don't know the proper name, but in the absence of one, I can give you a name—I will call it philosophy, or fried froth.

At last the Book of Mormon began going to press. "I gave the first 50 pages of the manuscript to the printer, Marc Decloux," Bolton wrote as of September 8, 1851. "What a glorious day in my eventful life." In a letter to his family Taylor said, "You will have some little idea of the trouble when I tell you it has been written three times over."

Taylor went to England to arrange financing for both the French and German publishing projects. Left on his own, Bolton again almost starved. He couldn't pay bills or buy food. When he learned the prohibitive cost of a French patent on his repeating rifle, his dream of wealth collapsed.

In England, Taylor made arrangements for publication, obtaining funds from several wealthy members. One investor, a young convert from Jersey named Phillip de LaMare, donated $1,000, and soon was involved with Taylor in the beet sugar project. Taylor's independence is indicated by his letter to Franklin D. Richards, who offered financial aid from the British mission. Taylor thanked him, but said that in view of

the many calls that have been made upon the brethren, I have been seeking to make other arrangements without troubling them, which I am very happy to inform you I have accomplished. . . . The scriptures say that "It is more blessed to give than to receive," and if in making the above move, I may have deprived some of an anticipated blessing, I hope they will excuse me; for perhaps there may be an opportunity afforded them of assisting some of my brethren in another way. If not, the world is large, and there is ample opportunity to do good.

After being away six weeks, Taylor returned to Paris. He "gave me money to pay off Mr. Decloux," Bolton wrote, and the happy printer invited them to dinner. Richards had arrived in Paris with Taylor, and next day Bolton "took a very long walk with Elder Richards," pouring

---

14 JD, 1:16.

out his woes, the prime one being lack of credit for the French translation. Taylor's refusal

> cut me so to the heart that I have been broken hearted and sick ever since. . . . God knows, and the Saints here know too, that I have labored with the most faithful unceasing diligence to do what I thought was required of me and have invariantly done right as far as the light and intelligence God has given me, and that too, much of the time half fed and half clothed, which has kept me weak in mind and body.

Taylor remained firm in refusing credit to a man whose contribution had been to hamper and hamstring the project, first through incompetence and then by his tenacious fight to save face.[15]

On the eve of going to Germany, Taylor wrote his family,

> I don't know but what I shall have to go alone into that land, for there is no one in England that I can find that will be of any use to me. . . . However, it makes but very little difference to me. The Lord can control affairs in one place the same as another, and all will be well.

With such faith, it was not surprising that he left for Hamburg with two competent German scholars, George Viett and George P. Dykes, and soon after arrival converted another, Charles Miller. The translation proceeded rapidly. Taylor showed the manuscript to professors at the university of Hamburg, who found very few corrections necessary. The printed text was designed to coincide page by page with the French edition, so that in bilingual regions the two translations could be bound together, the French and German texts facing each other.

In contrast to the French attitude, "Among the German people," Taylor said, "we find very much sterling integrity, and there will be thousands and tens of thousands of people in that country who will embrace the faith, and rejoice in the blessings of the gospel."

The one man Taylor had wanted above all others to help with the translation, Daniel Carn, arrived at Hamburg. He fulfilled all expectations. When Taylor showed a copy of the monthly periodical, *Zion's Panier*, to a university professor, he said "he would not have known it was written in English and translated; he should, if not told to the contrary, have supposed it written originally in German." After two months the Book of Mormon was half translated (in contrast to the French edition, which Bolton and various collaborators had been working on for a year and a half). Taylor left the work under Carn's supervision and returned to Paris in mid-December.

Just two weeks previously, Louis Napoleon's *coup d'etat* had over-

---

[15] After returning, Taylor gave public praise for Bolton's work on the translation. This saved Bolton's face and preserved the official facade of utmost harmony among the tillers of the Lord's vineyard. See JD, 1:25.

thrown the republic. Paris was filled with troops. Taylor didn't miss the irony of the situation. " 'Liberty, Equality, Fraternity' were written upon almost every door," he said. "You had liberty to speak, but might be put in prison for doing so. You had liberty to print, but they might burn what you had printed and put you in confinement for it."[16]

Taylor found Bolton hungry and dressed in castoffs. The man would have been barefoot and in rags except that T. B. H. Stenhouse, president of the Swiss mission, had visited Paris and exhorted the Saints to "feed and clothe Bro. Bolton." Taylor suspected there would be more trouble with Bolton's good friend, Elder Pack, who wrote from Jersey that he wouldn't be able to attend the Paris conference. Bolton admitted that Pack had "openly taught the plurality of wives" in the Channel Islands "and declared that those who would not believe in this doctrine would go to hell."

On learning of Taylor's wrath, Pack "was seized with fear and trembling," Bolton recorded. At Jersey he

> called a grand council, . . . denied he had ever taught such doctrine and said anybody who did believe in it would go to hell. So you'll be damned if you don't and damned if you do.[17]

Taylor cannily scheduled the conference for a date on which the authorities would be occupied with other matters—election day. "At the very time they were voting for their president," Taylor said with a grin, "we were voting for our president, and building up the Kingdom of God; and I prophesied that our cause would stand when theirs was crushed to pieces."

Because of the political situation, Taylor held the conference in secret, with only officers of the church in attendance. Before the meeting a member drew Taylor aside and whispered the information that the police had a complete dossier on his illegal religious activities and were going to arrest him the following day. Taylor quickly made up his mind to leave the next morning for England to finish up business details of the sugar and woolen factories he was transporting to the valley, and then go home. At the conference he appointed Bolton president of the French mission, with Louis Bertrand first counselor; he packed up that night.

Taylor and Bolton had hardly left their quarters for the station when the police arrived. From the landlord the authorities learned that Taylor was involved with business dealings with a printer, Marc Decloux.

Taylor and Bolton stopped at the Decloux establishment to arrange

---

[16] Ibid.

[17] Bolton says that Pack "cut off very many from the church in consequence and had left Jersey for England on his way to the Valley before Elder Taylor got to Jersey."

final financial details. Taylor said goodbye, and the rattle of the hack on the cobblestones could still be faintly heard when the gendarmes rushed in. Decloux was most cooperative with the authorities. He explained in detail all of his dealings with Taylor. In fact, he gave them so much information that it took almost half an hour. Then, when he was sure the train had gone, he told them that Taylor was leaving France that morning.

Taylor realized that if the police tried to apprehend him before he left the country, they would watch major routes of travel. So he stopped at Le Havre a week (holding another secret conference while there), then went to the island of Jersey (to hold another), and from there to England.

Left on his own resources, Bolton realized how much he had depended upon Taylor's support. After saying good-bye at the railroad station, he said, he

> never felt more utterly alone. . . . Elder Taylor had rolled off of him on to my shoulders the whole burden of the French Mission and had left me. He was going to the Valley. I should be deprived of his godlike counsels and assistance. I stood alone. Oh, God protect me . . .

The longer Taylor was gone, the more Bolton missed him. After a visit by T. B. H. Stenhouse, Bolton said, "He and God have alone stood my firm friends since Elder Taylor left. God knows what I have suffered for want of means to carry on my work here." As his clothing wore out, the president of the French mission went about in rags, the soles of his broken shoes entirely gone. He appealed to the English mission for help, but after giving him £25 to settle the printing bill, the brethren there told him to stand on his own two feet in his own mission.

Bolton somehow managed to survive another year in the field before returning to Zion.

II

Mission II: "Damn Miserable Company"

DURING THE FINAL WEEKS of his mission in Europe, Taylor maintained an outward calm as he struggled to attend to a thousand details before sailing. He had promised to finish a book, *The Government of God*, proceeds to go to the British mission. He had commissioned a London sculptor to make busts of the martyrs, Joseph and Hyrum Smith. And he had undertaken to establish two new industries in Utah, a woolen mill and a beet-sugar factory.[1] This involved having the machinery made, shipping it by water from Liverpool to New Orleans and upriver to Fort Leavenworth. Since freight for the 1,200 miles from there to the valley was $500 a ton, he planned to build his own wagons—fifty-two of them —and to purchase and break to the yoke 600 head of wild cattle to pull them. He had shipped sugar beet seed ahead for the Saints to plant and grow during the summer, and he planned on shipping two thousand merino sheep to the valley to provide fine wool for the best worsted textiles. In addition to raising the money, organizing, and supervising these projects, Taylor had to find, hire, and transport the skilled help to man the enterprises—from shepherds to sugar-makers, weavers to wagon-

---

[1] From the time they had first settled in the valley, the Saints had known the importance of making their own sugar. Shortly before leaving on his mission, Taylor had sat in the legislature of Deseret while Gov. Brigham Young urged the founding of this industry. Brigham estimated that the freight alone on sufficient sugar to supply only one ounce per day for each individual would amount to $45,000 a year, a sum "adequate to construct the most extensive sugar manufactory."

builders, dyers to drovers. Finally, every last person involved had to be a Saint. John Taylor would have no truck with Gentiles in these enterprises vital to the welfare of his people.

"I found this affair as difficult to arrange as anything I have had to do," he admitted with laconic understatement.[2]

In the spring of 1851, Taylor's second year in the mission field, he had received a letter from Brigham Young urging him to find industry suitable for the valley. Taylor already had been investigating several projects and had formed a company "for the purpose of establishing a large woolen manufactory," he wrote Brigham on March 13, 1851.

> The best machinery will be bought that can be purchased in England & men brought to work it. If fine merino wool can be obtained, as good cloth can be manufactured as in the west of England. . . . The company will probably bring one or two thousand sheep, merinos . . . as fine wool is absolutely necessary for broadcloth and fine women's wear.

It was a cold day in February when the beet-sugar industry literally walked into the Paris mission headquarters at No. 7, Rue de Tournon. "We were visited today by a manufacturer of sugar from the sugar beet, who is desirous to go to the Valley," Bolton recorded in his journal. Taylor believed that the Lord had directed the man to his doorstep, and immediately went into action.[3]

For the next eight months Bolton continually complained of being kept running about on the sugar business. A typical entry of his journal says,

> I have had to give all my time and attention to the sugar manufacturing of Elder Taylor. He runs me to death. My ankle pains me at night so I can scarcely sleep. I am really ill, not able to go, but go I must. I am too hoarse to speak more than a few words at a time and that only in a whisper.

Under the strain of Taylor's investigations, Bolton took to bed, "too sick to sit up." Taylor bustled in at eleven next morning, and "told me to rise in the name of the Lord," to "go to Arras (seven hours ride per railroad) with him to visit a number of sugar manufacturers from the sugar beet and serve as interpreter."

Accompanying them were Phillip De LaMare, the well-to-do convert from Jersey who had come to Paris to help with the translation work,

---

[2] JD, 1:16.

[3] The line in Bolton's journal is the only record of this anonymous caller whose visit was to have such important consequences. Very possibly, he refused to convert, for Taylor went elsewhere for information about the industry. It is interesting to speculate what might have happened to the DMC (Deseret Manufacturing Company) if this knowledgable man had remained in the project.

and Taylor's brother-in-law, M. Mollenhauer, an Englishman who worked in a British sugar factory.

At Arras they visited the Crespel-Delisse refinery, the oldest beet-sugar plant in France, then subsequently called at the home of the manager, Crespel, in Paris, "who received us with a great deal of kindness and offered to give all the knowledge that he could." Crespel gave Taylor plans of the machinery at the Arras plant.

De LaMare and Mollenhauer actively joined Taylor in the eight months of investigation, from soil analysis to beet cultivation. The French manufacturers were the soul of affability. Taylor did not have the slightest suspicion that they were holding back vital details of the refining process.

In all innocence he had wandered into a ruthless commercial jungle that for centuries had been characterized by power politics, conniving, subterfuge, monopoly, bribery, and war.

The native beet grew wild in the coastal regions of Europe. Called the mangel-wurzel or mangold, it had long been known to yield a juice which, when boiled down, was "similar to syrup of sugar," as Olivier de Serres, a Frenchman, noted in the 1600s. Then, in 1747, a German chemist, Andreas Marggraf, succeeded in obtaining pure sucrose crystals from beet juice. Though a scientific breakthrough, producing a few crystals in a flask of juice had no commercial possibilities. It remained for one of Marggraf's pupils, Franz Karl Achard, to develop beet sugar as a competitor to cane, some forty years later. After extensive cultivation to improve the sugar content of the beet and perfection of a method for its extraction, Achard made the startling announcement that beet sugar could be produced for about 6¢ a pound. Skeptical members of the French Institute investigated his claims, and while estimating the price at 18¢, confirmed the fact that beet sugar was commercially possible.

Frederick the Great subsidized Achard's early experiments. Within a reasonable range, the price of beet sugar actually was immaterial. With England controlling the seas, sugar was a weapon of war. Frederick's son, Frederick William III, continued supporting Achard's work, and financed building of the world's first beet-sugar factory—at Achard's estate in Curnern, Silesia—which began operations in 1802.

Meanwhile, British sugarcane interests tried to buy Achard off. When Achard refused a bribe of £6,000 to abandon his work and announce failure, the ante was raised to £25,000—a stupendous fortune.[4]

The beet sugar industry was first developed on a commercial basis, competitive with cane, when, as a result of the Napoleonic wars, the entire European coastline was closed to British trade.

---

[4] *The Beet Sugar Story*. U.S. Beet Sugar Association.

Napoleon, with the stroke of a pen, had decreed that 79,000 acres be planted to beets. As a result of this encouragement, during the next three years 334 beet-sugar factories sprang up in France.

The boom in beet sugar lasted a total of only four years, from Napoleon's sponsorship on March 18, 1811 to June 18, 1815. His defeat, by British troops under Wellington, at Waterloo

> crushed an industry as well as an Emperor. With the downfall of Napoleon, the blockade was lifted and ships from the West Indies hastened to dump their cargoes of accumulated sugar into the ports of the Continent. Prices collapsed. The newly established beet-sugar factories were hit hard by the war's aftermath. Struggling with primitive processing methods and raw materials of low quality, the homeland industry was unable to withstand the effects of this wholesale dumping of cane sugar produced by slave labor.[5]

As a footnote on international sugar politics, it should be noted that Wellington's troops systematically destroyed French sugar factories. A year after Waterloo, only one single refinery remained in operation in the country, the one at Arras.

For the next three decades, the industry thrived or withered according to the political climate. By the time John Taylor became interested, political leaders had realized that the value of the sugar beet as a farm crop in providing labor, cash income, and livestock feed, was too important to the economy to be considered only as a "war baby." Under Louis Philippe and his successor, Napoleon III, the industry had been flourishing for twenty years with government support. It was at this time that Taylor began investigating it as an enterprise for the Saints.

Taking the French offer of cooperation at face value, Taylor decided that the beet-sugar industry was ideal for the valley. It would give farmers a much-needed cash crop while providing employment with the vast amount of hand labor required in seeding, blocking, thinning, irrigating, weeding, digging, and topping the beets. And, of course, the factory would produce a commodity in desperately short supply.

Before going to Germany to arrange translation and publication of the Book of Mormon, Taylor spent a week at Arras with De LaMare and Mollenhauer. He left the two men there for further study while he was away. On returning, he took them to England, where he formed the Deseret Manufacturing Company and set out to raise capital for the enterprise. De LaMare and three other investors subscribed to $60,000 in stock, while Taylor took $10,000 worth. Capt. Joseph H. Russell, a shipbuilder (who, incidentally, had constructed the *Brooklyn* in which Sam Brannan and his company sailed from New York to the Golden Gate), subscribed to stock worth $45,000. John W. Coward, a salt

---

[5] Ibid.

dealer; De LaMare; and a boot manufacturer named Collison each took $5,000. Coward was the only member who paid outright for his shares. De LaMare put up $1,750 cash against his shares, and Collison nothing. Russell, who was given the contract to construct the wagons for freighting the machinery, put up $25,000 against his stock. It is possible that part of this sum was credited for his construction of the wagons. At any event, less than half the value of the capital stock was put up in cash. Taylor was severely handicapped for want of ready money.

Orders for the machinery, totaling $12,500, were placed with Fawcett-Preston & Co. of Liverpool, specifying that some of the massive castings used in the hydraulic presses be forged from wrought iron, to save weight.[6] Plans were complete in every detail, and even included a still for making alcohol from by-products of the sugar process. Taylor wrote Brigham that the hydraulic presses could be adapted to "manufacture oil from the sunflower seed, linseed, or anything that will make oil."

He sent De LaMare and Russell ahead to prepare for freighting the factory the 1,200 miles from Fort Leavenworth to the valley. Russell began making the wagons, while De LaMare ranged the countryside for hundreds of miles, with a money belt containing $6,000 in gold, to find and purchase 600 oxen to pull the wagons.

Loren Babbitt, a returning missionary, had meanwhile left for the valley, taking along 1,200 pounds of the best French beet seed in tin-lined boxes. While the machinery was en route, the seed was distributed at the Tithing Office, planted and tilled, the beets grown, dug, topped, and stored for processing.

Taylor needed competent help to erect and run the factory. He selected Elias Morris, a young man who had learned the building trade from his father, to construct the building. John Vernon, who had worked with Fawcett-Preston during the manufacture of the machinery, would install it. Mollenhauer, "an expert sugar maker and refiner," would operate the plant, assisted by "John Bollwinkel and Mr. Conner, who had worked in a sugar factory in Liverpool."[7]

In all, Taylor assembled a crew of about thirty men for the project, including his future secretary and son-in-law, L. John Nuttall. When the cargo was loaded aboard the sailing ship *Rockaway* at Liverpool, it included not only the sugar factory, woolen mill, and still, but three zinc-lined caskets marked "machinery" containing the bodies of missionaries who had died in the field. (One of them sprang a leak en route, and was in bad shape before reaching Zion.) Leaving Elias Morris and Nuttall in

---

[6] This innovation proved so successful that the use of wrought iron became general practice thereafter. Fawcett-Preston also adapted this method to the manufacture of cannons, which formerly had been cast.

[7] *Utah Genealogical Magazine*, 21:88. Other sources give Bollwinkel's name as Fred.

charge of the *Rockaway* cargo, Taylor somehow managed to complete *The Government of God*; deliver the manuscript to Samuel W. Richards at mission headquarters at Walton Street, near Hyde Park; get the busts of Joseph and Hyrum from the artist, Gahagan; and embark on the steamship, *Niagara.*

Up to this point, everything had gone like clockwork.

Taylor was blissfully unaware of a curious circumstance connected with attempts to manufacture beet sugar in America. Although commercial production had been successful in Europe from the time of Achard's first factory in 1802—exactly half a century—repeated attempts to transplant the industry to the United States had invariably failed. Americans tried time and again to produce commercial beet sugar in the United States. They imported the best beet seed. They received gracious cooperation from European producers. They had machinery built to European specifications. They even imported European experts to install the machinery and run the plant. But, by some mysterious circumstance, they just couldn't make sugar.[8]

The first indication that the project was ill-starred came when the *Rockaway* docked at New Orleans. The Internal Revenue office clapped an import duty of $4,056.10 on the machinery. Taylor was flabbergasted. America was short of sugar. The government was proverbially eager to foster new industry. It simply was incredible that a tax of 40 percent of the assessed value of the machinery should be imposed.

In discussing things with Morris and Nuttall, Taylor realized that Satan never sleeps. Talk along the waterfront hinted that somebody in Washington had been "reached." They had no proof, but this would explain the astounding duty.

It took several paddle-wheel riverboats to carry the cargo upriver, together with the shipload of emigrants from the *Rockaway* who would accompany the sugar train to the valley.

At St. Louis, he found that Phillip De LaMare's task of securing teams for the freight wagons had been interrupted by the sickness of his wife, Mary Ann, and his children, who had come down with cholera. The oldest child had died of the disease, but thanks to the devoted nursing care of a pretty French convert, Marie Chevalier, the others had recovered. De

---

[8] During this fifty year period, six American companies had been formed to produce beet sugar; all had failed because of an inability to make the product. DMC was number seven.

Before the first successful plant—at Alvarado, California—began production in 1879, no less than sixteen attempts to establish the industry in America had been flat failures. Why did it take seventy-seven years to transplant the industry across the Atlantic? There can be no other explanation except that Europe had a monopoly and made every effort to maintain it.

LaMare now was ready to embark again on his cattle-buying mission, and he promised to have the oxen by the time Captain Russell completed building the wagons upriver at Kanesville.

Taylor appointed De LaMare captain of the sugar train, and at the same time exhorted him to magnify his calling in the priesthood. Phillip accepted counsel, asked Mary Ann, then Marie, and with his first wife's blessing took a second; Taylor officiated in joining Phillip and Marie in holy wedlock under the new and everlasting covenant.

There wouldn't be enough wagons to haul both factories to the valley this summer; the woolen mill would have to wait another year. Taylor put a crew to work storing the textile machinery in a warehouse, and another crew to loading the huge DMC crates with the sugar factory onto riverboats heading up the Missouri to Fort Leavenworth. Taylor then went ahead with Elias Morris to Kanesville to hurry Captain Russell's slow progress with the freight wagons. Time was of the essence if the sugar train was to cross the plains this summer.

As the convoy of paddle-wheel riverboats carrying machinery and converts headed up the Missouri from St. Louis, disaster struck. Suddenly there was a great explosion, a blast of flame, steam, and smoke; one of the craft, the *Saluta*, was blown apart by a bursting boiler. Twenty-six Mormon emigrants were killed, including several members of Taylor's sugar crew. The *Saluta*'s cargo of sugar machinery went to the bottom. Some was recovered from the river. But was all of it? Were vital cogs of the sugar factory buried in the mud?

The Mormon outpost of Kanesville at Council Bluffs was reduced in size since Taylor had last seen it; Fort Leavenworth had replaced it as the departure point for wagon trains. Capt. Joseph Russell took him to a long shed where workmen were making the freight wagons. As Taylor walked through the shop an icy hand seemed to close inside him. He knew wagons. He'd made them with his own hands. He also knew first-hand the brutal stress and strain which twelve hundred miles of rough trail across plains, through rivers, over mountains, could put on every part of a vehicle. Only the best and most sturdy wagons could handle the heavy loads of massive machinery. And, examining the ones being made by Russell, Taylor saw they were neither sturdy in design nor well-made. The rigs were flimsy, put together of green lumber. While Russell was a competent shipbuilder, he quite obviously was an incompetent novice at wagon construction.

When Taylor expressed doubts about the vehicles, Russell flew into a rage. He'd fulfilled his contract, he roared, and what's more, he had a controlling interest in DMC stock. He could take the company away from Taylor any time he wanted to.

There was nothing to be gained from a shouting match. It was too late to rebuild the wagons; they would have to be used.

Morris' fiancee, Mary Parry of New Market, had sailed ahead from England on the *Ellen Maria* and was waiting for him at Kanesville. Taylor went with the couple to the home of Mary's uncle, Joseph Parry, and stood witness while Orson Hyde performed the marriage ceremony. Hyde had been in charge of this outpost, publishing the *Frontier Guardian* and overseeing the outfitting of emigrants using the northern route to the valley. Now he was preparing to return to Zion.

Taylor's relations with Hyde were outwardly cordial, but he had little use for the man; Hyde had turned twice against the prophet and the Saints, once after the banking disaster at Kirtland, again in Missouri. Twice repented and forgiven, Taylor could accept Hyde as one of the brethren but found it impossible to be his friend. During the wedding reception Hyde and Captain Russell stood apart, engaged in serious discussion. Taylor thought little of it at the time, but would remember it later.

Despite his best efforts, it took Taylor another month to get the finished wagons and ox-teams to Fort Leavenworth. He saw the DMC equipment loaded onto the creaking wagons, and, on July 4, the sugar train headed west.

Taylor turned the other way and traveled east to Washington where, with the aid of Col. Thomas L. Kane and the Utah delegate to Congress, John M. Bernhisel, he engaged in a futile attempt to get the 40 percent duty on the machinery rescinded. After a few days of being shunted from office to office, he realized he was getting nowhere. The impossibility of getting a hearing made him wonder if the whispers about a bribe were true. He left Washington and headed for Utah to arrange things for the arrival of the machinery.

As his carriage overtook the sugar train on the prairie, he was dismayed at its slow progress. In camp that night, he and Phillip De LaMare sat late by the campfire, while the young man told of the obstacles, accidents, and misfortunes that had plagued the journey.

With cattle wild, teamsters green, and the normal delays involved in getting a large company underway, the first day's travel was less than five miles. Even so, in this short distance Captain Russell's wagons began breaking down. Loaded with huge crates weighing from 5,000 to 9,000 pounds, green axles broke and wheels collapsed. De LaMare unloaded the machinery and turned the wagons over to emigrant families. He then went back and made a deal with a trader, Charles H. Perry, for forty sturdy Santa Fe prairie schooners. Though a Gentile, Perry let him have the wagons on credit.

Everything, De LaMare said with a perplexed shake of his head, seemed to go wrong. Even the flour he bought for the expedition—

again on credit—was infested with worms. While the weevils could be sifted out, the bread turned to stone in the oven; the flour was adulterated with plaster of paris. It was as if, Phillip said, the Devil was at work. Too much had happened for it to be merely bad luck.

The fire had burned low. Taylor tossed a couple of buffalo chips on the coals to keep it going. He admitted that he'd had somewhat the same feeling. While going from office to office in Washington he was strongly impressed with the feeling that he was up against impossible opposition. He'd wondered if powerful forces were at work to hamstring the DMC.

When Phillip asked just what he meant, Taylor countered with a question: Just why hadn't Captain Russell been able to make better wagons?

He was a shipbuilder, not a wagon-maker, De LaMare said; he was a novice at the trade.

Admitted; but Russell was a competent craftsman, Taylor pointed out; he knew woods; he knew stress and strain. And he hadn't undertaken to design and build the wagons by himself. He'd hired a crew of experienced wagon-makers, who could have duplicated the Santa Fe design to the last nut and bolt had he required it. Russell knew the loads the wagons must carry. How could he approve flimsy design and the use of green timber?

Perplexed, the younger man met Taylor's eye. Was Brother John doubting Russell's loyalty? After all, the captain had the largest financial interest in the DMC.

Taylor slowly shook his head, baffled. Nothing added up, he admitted; but by now he was convinced that there was hidden opposition to the project.

Next morning Taylor was up early, with breakfast over and carriage hitched up before sunrise. He promised De LaMare to send supplies from the valley, for with the heavy loads and poor cattle, plus the late start, winter was sure to catch the sugar train in the mountains.

Taylor climbed into the carriage and headed west at a trot. He arrived at Great Salt Lake late in August, and immediately sent Joseph Horne back with a wagonload of supplies.

Taylor had looked forward to the valley as a haven. Now, with his people solidly behind him, he expected to defeat whatever evil forces were in opposition. He had performed a miracle of financing—putting together two much-needed industries from scratch on a shoestring in foreign lands.

However, he encountered severe criticism instead of praise. Brigham was greatly dissatisfied with the way the DMC had been handled. Orson Hyde, Captain Russell, and John Coward had arrived in the valley ahead of Taylor, claiming he had mishandled affairs and squandered company money. They'd told their story first and, perhaps because of the personal antagonism between Brigham and Taylor, the church president was inclined to believe critics of the project.

In deciding where to locate the sugar factory, Brigham and Taylor visited the spacious carpenter shop at Temple Square. "I want a building like this to put up my machinery in," Taylor said.

All right, Brigham agreed; a corner of the shop could be spared for the factory. When Taylor explained that he would need the entire building, Brigham was scornful. "You might as well take the whole territory to put it in," he retorted.[9]

Taylor held his gorge. It was typical that Brigham should assume more knowledge of a sugar factory by intuition than Taylor had learned during eight months of investigation.

Taylor decided to locate the plant at Provo, forty-five miles south— and away from Brigham's immediate supervision.

The internal struggle over the affairs of the DMC remained entirely below the serene surface when Taylor reported on his mission at the tabernacle, August 22.

> . . . I organized a society to make sugar, and a woolen manufactory. The sugar factory will be here soon. If you will only provide us with beets and wood, we will make you sugar enough to preserve yourself with. We can have as good sugar in this country as anywhere else; we have as good machinery as is in the world, . . . nor [are there] better men to make sugar than those who are coming.

The woolen machinery, he explained, would arrive next year.

> I can say of this that it is as good machinery as there is in the world. It is the same kind of machinery that is made use of in the west of England to make the best kind of broadcloth; also a worsted manufactory to manufacture cloth for ladies' wear, such as merinoes, and alpacas, and other sorts of pacas—I don't know the name of them all—and various kinds of shawls, blankets, carpets, &c, &c, if we can only command the wool.[10]

The audience chuckled at Taylor's humor, and looked forward happily to an abundance of sugar and factory woolens.

The first hint that all was not well with the sugar train came with arrival of the emigrants who had been with the company. The forty Santa Fe wagons containing the machinery had been left in the mountains.

---

[9] *Minutes*, Sugar Company meeting, March 17, 1853.

[10] JD, 1:16.

By the time the sugar train had reached the Platte River, provisions were so short as to threaten disaster. Fortunately, trail scouts killed three buffalo.

With the late start and heavy loads, the company was still in the Rockies, three hundred miles from the valley, when a blizzard engulfed the wagons as they crawled along near the last crossing of the Sweetwater. "We came to camp about nine o'clock at night," Elias Morris recorded.

It was very dark and stormy and there were but very little provisions in camp. As soon as the cattle were fed and unyoked, all hands turned to bed, tired, cold, and hungry. The morning was no better. A deep snow was on the ground, and still falling, so that we could not kindle fire until noon. The storm ceased. We turned out in search of the cattle. Before going a quarter mile from camp, we found ten of them dead—about eighty had gone astray.

The emigrant wagons continued on with the remaining teams, leaving behind the schooners containing the heavy machinery, together with teamsters to search for the lost cattle as well as hunt for their own food.

After two days of searching through deep snow, the hunters found most of the strays; but they missed the trail on returning and had to make a forty-mile detour through the mountains, which involved fording the icy Green River several times.

As they started on again, freight wagons short-teamed and out of food, they began slaughtering oxen for meat—the sugar train was eating its own teams.

Joseph Horne met the train in Wyoming with the wagonload of supplies sent by Taylor, a welcome relief to lean men reduced to a diet of stringy ox.

At Green River, De LaMare replenished the cattle supply from the stock of two trappers, Descampe and Garnier, who were engaged in a curious but profitable enterprise. They bought for a song exhausted cattle from wagon companies, rested and fattened the stock, then re-sold it at high prices to other companies. Theirs was a type of used-ox business, where travelers could turn in decrepit oxen on the price of fat teams.

At Fort Bridger, De LaMare was happy to find A. O. Smoot with another wagonload of supplies dispatched by Taylor. The flour of this consignment was also short in the valley, selling for $50 a hundred.

Shortly after reaching the Bear River, De LaMare found the roads so rugged and the snow so deep that he ordered the men to heave off some of the heaviest machinery while the wagons struggled on. It was not until November that the Santa Fe schooners came out of the canyon and into the valley of the Great Salt Lake. Nothing better illustrates the weakened condition of the teams, the weight of the loads, and severity of the weather than the fact that it took three more weeks to travel the forty-five miles to Provo.

Once there, the sugar crew, under John Vernon, built a number of houses to be used by the permanent workers and staked out the plan for the factory and its water power near by on the Provo River.

At this point, John Taylor's world collapsed. The two largest stockholders of the Deseret Manufacturing Company turned their shares over to the Public Works Department of the church. Brigham was now in control of the DMC. Taylor was completely and suddenly out.

Brigham dispatched a crew of "tithing hands" to take over. These men, working at the rate of $1.50 a day in tithing credit—$3 with teams—replaced Taylor's crew at Provo. Following Brigham's orders, they piled the machinery again into the Santa Fe wagons, hauled it back to Salt Lake, and installed it in the blacksmith shop at Temple Square and on the banks of City Creek. Brigham now would do things his own way.

Taylor's crew was largely left high and dry. While tithing hands hauled beets to the makeshift factory and prepared to make sugar from them, Phillip De LaMare returned to Salt Lake and went to work for the city's leading merchants, Kinkaid and Livingston. L. John Nuttall and a number of others remained at Provo; Elias Morris, engaged to erect the factory, was called away to the Iron mission in southern Utah. Other workmen imported by Taylor found themselves suddenly out of work and twelve hundred miles from nowhere. It was a humbling experience for everyone involved in the Deseret Manufacturing Company, which now was being called the "Damn Miserable Company."

Brigham placed Orson Hyde in charge of the sugar works, because, he explained, "He is a snug business man," while "Brother Taylor will be left out entirely. He will have no more to do with it."[11] Only the chief sugar-maker, Mollenhauer, and John Vernon, the engineer, remained of the skilled personnel comprising the original crew.

The tithing hands hauled beets to the blacksmith shop and put the jumble of machinery into operation. But, somehow, things went wrong. Evidently it took more than snug business judgment and inspiration to make beet sugar. The juice turned black, went sour, then fermented. Nothing came from the vile stuff except foul-smelling molasses that even the hogs wouldn't eat. It was all too obvious that there was more to the process than putting beets in at one end and scooping out white sugar crystals from the other.

After this complete failure, Brigham called a meeting, March 17, 1853,

---

11 *Minutes*, op cit.

attended by himself, Heber C. Kimball, Orson Hyde, John Taylor, and Daniel H. Wells of the church hierarchy, together with "Joseph Russell, John W. Coward, and the sugar operatives."

Russell and Coward, Brigham explained, had signed over their interests in the DMC to the church. To the crew, he said they wouldn't work for wages, but for the "upbuilding of the common cause." Others were ready to take their place. "Mormonism will take a tailor from his shop and straightway set him to making wagons."

Taylor held his tongue, though doubting that the gospel would endow a man with the skills for manufacturing sugar.

He felt it was entirely uncalled-for when Brigham began belittling his business methods: "A Frenchman came to my office and presented a bill of $3 or $300 that he had against Brother Taylor, perhaps for looking at the machinery as it passed along," Brigham said mockingly, while the roomful of men grinned. "I know not but it was some person or other who had been bowing and scraping to Brother Taylor once or twice."

As the men guffawed, Taylor's face burned. Why was he being ridiculed before this group? He knew nothing about the Frenchman and his bill. Brigham might have referred the fellow to Taylor, the man responsible.

Then as the meeting continued, Taylor found his own motives questioned—as if his only purpose for undertaking the entire enterprise was personal profit; as if any profit at all was somehow sinister. Of course Taylor had hoped the DMC would be highly profitable, to farmers in the valley, to field hands cultivating the beets, to workers in the sugar factory, and to backers of the enterprise. There was absolutely nothing wrong with this; it was in the Mormon tradition. A financially successful project would benefit the people of the valley, which was the prime purpose of the DMC.

But as he tried to present his views, Joseph Russell heckled him with venom, as if Taylor had no right to speak because he, Russell, had full control of the machinery by reason of his investment. Taylor ignored the man and addressed Brigham: "As far as profits arising from this affair are concerned, there is just as much as I calculated on," he declared. Then his rage boiled over as he declared that "if President Young wants the whole—profits and all—he can take it, for all I care about it."

It was Brigham's turn to flush. Furious, Taylor said, "Brother Brigham, you have mentioned that you do not want me to have anything to do with the matter, in the future arrangements." Brigham agreed emphatically that he didn't. "Then," Taylor said, "if you rid me from any responsibility, I shall be glad of it."

"I shall free you from all responsibility," Brigham retorted sharply. "You have shown too much already; and, therefore, I do not wish you to have any more dictation about this machinery." If they couldn't make sugar without Taylor meddling in the business affairs, "It will be better to let it alone altogether."

Brigham added that if Taylor wanted to debate the issue, "I am ready to prove it before the people at the approaching conference." And he would prove "that you do not know any more about business than a child."

With his church membership in the balance, Taylor held his gorge. A public keel-hauling at conference would require public repentance, which Taylor would never do. Better to say nothing than lose what he valued most, his church standing.

As was customary, the meeting was closed with prayer. A good soldier, Taylor walked out bleeding and naked, but with head high.[12] He was completely disassociated from the sugar and woolen projects. Brigham made sure of it three weeks later by calling him as a missionary "in the valleys of the mountains," requiring him to visit nearly every settlement of Mormon country. Then, the following year, Brigham sent him to New York to publish a newspaper, *The Mormon.*

With Orson Hyde in charge, tithing hands hauled forty wagonloads of machinery to the church farm southeast of the city and dumped it at a point which became known as Sugar House. Truman O. Angell, the church architect, looked over the mass of machinery heaped upon two acres of ground and began designing a factory to put it in. Elias Morris, who had been engaged by Taylor to put up the factory, remained at the Iron mission. Neither Taylor nor De LaMare were asked advice. None of the imported crew was consulted, except the sugar-maker, Mollenhauer, and the engineer, John Vernon. Curiously, they both had a lapse of memory. They couldn't understand the plans, nor identify what went where.

No beets were planted that year, as Angell wrestled with the puzzle of the factory. Two years had elapsed and Taylor was in New York when the Sugar House factory finally began operations. Everything was ready. There had been plenty of time to correct previous mistakes. But the factory couldn't make sugar.

Brigham had had enough. At his orders, the factory was dismantled. The hydraulic presses were put to use in the book binding department of the church newspaper, the vacuum pans utilized in the paper mill. Some

---

[12] In his *Life of John Taylor*, Roberts has a somewhat different account of Taylor's homecoming, "where he was welcomed by his family, and by his brethren in the priesthood, who heartily approved of all his labors, blessed him for his faithfulness, his untiring zeal, and the energy he had manifested. How sweet to the ear! How joyous to the soul! How gratifying to the heart is that grandest of all salutations—'Well done thou good and faithful servant!'"

of the equipment was installed in Brigham's woolen mill. The *Deseret News* reported that the apparatus for distilling alcohol was "the first still and worm ever brought to the West. They were used for the manufacture of liquor, Jeter Clinton and others operating them for years."[13]

Aside from the tremendous effort involved, the enterprise had cost in cash about $100,000. Failure was a heart-wrenching disappointment to the pioneers in the valley.

ADDENDUM

As previously noted, the DMC was one of sixteen companies which tried and failed, over a period of seventy-seven years, to produce beet sugar in America. On the face of things, there seems no good reason why sugar couldn't be made in the new world. Fred G. Taylor, an official in the beet-sugar industry, whose *A Saga of Sugar* remains the definitive work on the DMC, concluded that,

> It is safe to say that, notwithstanding the poor quality of their sugar beets, knowledge of a few minor mechanical and chemical adjustments would have made the Sugar House project a great frontier success.

If there is no *good* reason why it was impossible to transfer knowledge of a few minor mechanical and chemical adjustments from Europe to America over a period of three-quarters of a century, the obvious question is: could there have been a *bad* reason?

The author of *A Saga of Sugar* says as much:

> In those days, and even in the long years that followed, masters of the art of sugar making jealously guarded their secrets from others, particularly from prospective competitors. Taylor and De LaMare stated that they "received the courtesy and assistance of the French sugar manufacturers" while working out their mechanical plans, but nowhere does the record show that they obtained any information regarding the chemistry or chemical controls employed in sugar making.

To put it bluntly, they were gulled.

The man who finally made beet sugar in America was E. H. Dyer. Dyer had failed with a previous attempt, when his $250,000-factory, erected on his farm at Alvarado, failed to solve the peculiar chemical puzzle of beets grown in American soil. A decade later, he raised more capital and collected machinery from various bankrupt sugar enterprises (one being a plant at nearby Isleton, which had attempted to make sugar from watermelons); it was on this second effort that Dyer established the first successful beet-sugar factory in the United States.

---

[13] March 27, 1897.

The know-how had finally crossed the Atlantic.

The secret of Dyer's success seems almost too simple. He imported the customary "expert sugar-maker" from Europe. However, Dyer's man, an Austrian named W. Kollburg, was different from all the other imported experts in one vital respect: He not only knew how to make beet sugar, but actually did so. Because of Kollburg's skill, the Alvarado plant was a commercial success.

This poses the obvious question which must nag the sugar historian: Was every single one of the "expert sugar-makers" imported from Europe prior to Kollburg's arrival incompetent? This seems highly unlikely. A more reasonable explanation is that while some might have professed to knowledge which they didn't have, others undoubtedly were expert enough to make sure of the failure of American factories.

It would be interesting to know Kollburg's background and motivations in breaking the long-established European monopoly.

Dyer fully realized the importance of Kollburg's skill. He put his son, Edward, under the Austrian's wing to learn the secrets of the craft. Edward clung to Kollburg like a shadow, all day every day, making notes of everything the Austrian did, however trivial.

Then, when the factory's first season was over, Dyer and Edward visited France and Germany to examine sugar factories. Now that they had the background for evaluation, the trip was highly beneficial. It didn't matter that an occasional fact or process was omitted by their hosts; the Dyers had the great secret, and from this point it was only a matter of minor improvement in detail. Subsequently, Edward and his cousin, Harold, went to Germany for several additional months of study. At the beginning of the third season at Alvarado, Edward took over the superintendency, with Kollburg retained in an advisory capacity.

E. H. Dyer himself built the second beet-sugar factory in Utah, a quarter century after the failure of the DMC. By this time, John Taylor was dead; but his oldest boy, George, was on hand for the successful opening of this plant at Lehi. Like the DMC, the Lehi operation was sponsored by the church. It became the first unit of the Utah–Idaho Sugar Co.

12

To Make a Spoon or Spoil a Horn

JOHN TAYLOR'S MISSION to New York was for the purpose of countering repercussions of the greatest bombshell ever to rock Mormonism.

On the hot Sunday morning of August 29, 1852, just nine days after returning from France, Taylor had been seated with the authorities on the rostrum of the new adobe tabernacle as Orson Pratt, church historian and leading theologian of the faith, arose to speak. The audience that filled the hall and overflowed to the outside bowery had no intimation of what was to come. Pratt admitted it was "quite unexpected" to be called upon to speak, "and still more so to address you upon the principle which has been named: namely, a plurality of wives."

Taylor felt as if a great burden was taken from his shoulders. At long last, after some twenty years of evasion, denial, and doubletalk, the Principle was acknowledged as church doctrine. John Taylor wasn't ashamed of the gospel, nor was he afraid to fight for it; but he'd always hated the requirement that he lie for it.[1]

Brigham dispatched eighty elders throughout the world to explain the Principle and defend the faith; but an outraged world gave them short shrift. Traveling as they were without purse or scrip, the missionaries found it difficult to find food and lodging, let alone make conversions.

---

[1] Denials of the secret practice were so emphatic that the Reorganized LDS Church used them to "prove" that there was no polygamy practiced during Joseph Smith's lifetime.

Many of the elders suffered great privations, and returned to the valley emaciated and in rags.

The impact on foreign missions was devastating. In the United Kingdom, John Taylor's repudiation of polygamy during the famous debate at Boulogne had sustained British Saints, who refuted whispers of plural marriage in Utah as lies of Satan. Stenhouse reported that when the revelation concerning plurality of wives was first published, on January 1, 1853 in the *Millennial Star*,

> It fell like a thunderbolt upon the Saints . . . and the mission that once was the glory of the Mormon Church has withered and shriveled into comparative insignificance.[2]

The official endorsement of polygamy was no less a shock to the majority of the Saints of Deseret. While the practice was common knowledge, it was largely confined to the church hierarchy and considered a privilege of rank. "The outside world misjudges the Mormon people when it imagines that polygamy was ever a favourite doctrine," Stenhouse said. "The great majority of both men and women have fought against it, and its acceptance at all has been a terrible trial of faith."

Within a few months after the public endorsement of plural marriage, John Taylor's own marital situation underwent adjustment as he lost one wife and gained another. With Taylor's blessing, one of his "lesser known" wives, Sarah Thornton Coleman, divorced him and married David Evans.[3]

During his labors to organize the sugar train at Fort Leavenworth, Taylor had not been too busy to notice a most attractive emigrant. Caroline Hooper Saunders Gilliam at thirty-nine had the mature beauty that had attracted him to his first wife, Leonora. Caroline had left her husband when he refused to join the church or gather with the Saints in Deseret, and Taylor admired her spunk.

Soon after Caroline arrived with the sugar train emigrants, Taylor married her at the home of his friend, Luman Shurtliff, at Springville.[4]

---

[2] *The Rocky Mountain Saints*. Stenhouse himself was a polygamist, while his daughter became a plural wife of Brigham's son. See Fanny Stenhouse, *Tell It All*.

[3] A widow with eight children, Sarah Coleman had been one of three women for whom Taylor had assumed responsibility, through marriage, just prior to the exodus from Nauvoo, the other two being widows of the martyred Hyrum Smith. Fellow brethren assumed responsibility, in the same manner, for other relicts of Joseph and Hyrum. During Taylor's three-year absence in Europe, Sarah Coleman had become acquainted with a man interested in her as a person, not merely a responsibility. On divorcing Taylor, she was sealed as wife to her first husband, Prime Coleman, for eternity in the hereafter, while marrying David Evans for the time remaining on this earth.

[4] "Notes" on "the lesser-known wives of President John Taylor," BYU Library, Special Collections.

Taylor was elected to the Territorial legislature, but before that body assembled Brigham called him to supervise the eastern states mission and publish a newspaper there to explain polygamy to an outraged public.

Taylor left in the fall of 1854 accompanied by his son, George, and four other men, Jeter Clinton, Nathaniel H. Felt, Alexander Robbins, and Angus M. Cannon. He found the church in New York shattered by the polygamy disclosure. When he called upon eastern Saints to help finance the newspaper, the response reminded him of a man who claimed, "I can call spirits from the vasty deep." "So can I," replied another, "but they won't come."

However, Taylor reported to Brigham, he sold the teams and wagons; then with the help of the missionaries scraped up enough to set up a printing shop at the corner of Nassau and Ann streets—the very heart of New York's publishing district, with the *Herald* on one side and the *Tribune* on the other.

"I find it one thing to preach the gospel without purse or scrip," he wrote Brigham; but it was "another thing to publish a paper on the same terms." However, he was determined "to fulfill our mission, and either make a spoon or spoil a horn."

According to custom, the first issue of the paper was supplied free to newsboys to stimulate circulation. On February 17, 1855, hundreds of eager urchins jammed the premises and filled the street. Soon they were running through the city hawking a publishing explosion.

Taylor made no pretense of backing into the subject. He called the paper *The Mormon*, with a striking masthead occupying a quarter of the seven-column front page.[5]

"We are Mormon," Taylor announced, "inside and outside; at home or abroad; in public and private—everywhere. . . . We are such, not because we believe it to be the most popular, lucrative, or honorable (as the world has it); but because we believe it to be true, and . . . more calculated to promote the happiness and well-being of humanity, in time and throughout eternity, than any other system which we have met with."

However, he made no converts on newspaper row. The *Mirror* proclaimed:

---

[5] The design, created by his son, showed an eagle with outstretched wings atop the Deseret beehive, clutching an American flag in each talon. Above this was an all-seeing eye amid shafts of sunshine, with the words, "And he said let there be light and there was light." Two scrolls flanked the beehive, one saying, "Constitution of the U.S., given by inspiration of God.—Joseph Smith"; and the other, "Mormon creed: Mind your own business.—Brigham Young." The white stripes of one flag bore the inscription, "Truth will prevail.—H. C. Kimball"; the other said, "Truth, Intelligence, Virtue, and Faith.—John Taylor." A streamer in bold letters beneath this design stated, "IT IS BETTER TO REPRESENT OURSELVES, THAN TO BE REPRESENTED BY OTHERS."

While our public moralists and reformers are making war upon the hotels and taverns and private property of our citizens, a hideous system —an immoral excrescence—is allowed to spring up and overtop the Constitution itself. Why are there no public meetings convened in the tabernacle to denounce Mormonism?

The *Herald* proposed a meeting of ministers at Tammany Hall to expose the fallacies and abominations of the Saints. When Taylor welcomed the opportunity of a debate, the ministers backed down, apparently reluctant to be drawn into a brouhaha with the small and upstart sect.

The *Sun* joined the anti-Mormon crusade with vitriolic zeal. The attack by the entire eastern press was so bitter, in fact, that when Utah was threatened by famine because of crop failure caused by drought and another cricket plague (the seagulls apparently refusing salvation), this desperate plight was hailed as an automatic solution to the Mormon question—the Saints simply would starve.

Such attacks brought Mormon support from a most unexpected source, the *Woman's Advocate*. This paper, devoted to female rights, might be expected to be the last to rally to a sect espousing polygamy. However, the *Woman's Advocate* was the only voice on newspaper row to show compassion:

We need not be surprised if we learn next spring that thousands have perished miserably of starvation. . . . But not one word is spoken any where [by the press] of regret or sympathy; on the contrary there are frequent manifestations of satisfaction that the problem of Mormonism and its destiny is likely to be settled by the grasshoppers. What little comment we have noticed here and there has a tone of delighted chuckle that chills the blood. *There is the spirit of murder in it . . .*

Taylor reprinted the *Advocate* item, to which the *Sun* responded that there had been "no appeal for help from Utah." If the Mormons asked, the American public would respond, despite "the degrading and disgusting doctrines of Brigham Young and others of the priesthood."

"An appeal for help indeed!" Taylor retorted. Should the Saints seek charity from

those that robbed and despoiled them of their goods and murdered their best men? We have been robbed of millions and driven from our own firesides into the cold, wintry blasts of the desert to starve by your charitable institutions, and shall we now crave your paltry sixpences? . . . The Mormons neither need your sympathy nor your cankered gold.

Reciprocating the support of the *Woman's Advocate*, Taylor published an article advocating female rights, deploring the double standard and showing compassion for "the case of the fallen woman." Why was it that

when two people commit the same sin, one shall be received into favor again and the other remorselessly driven to destruction? . . . As the two have sinned alike, punish them both or forgive them both; have for both equal mercy, equal good nature, equal condemnation; above all, equal justice.[6]

To Taylor's dismay, polygamy became tied to slavery as a political football. The Democratic party supported the policy of "Popular Sovereignty," which meant that the question of slavery in the territories would be settled by allowing the inhabitants to adopt or reject it upon becoming states. The Abolition party pounced upon this proposition, pointing out that it would allow the people of Utah to legalize polygamy. To avoid being tarred with this stick, the pro-slavery party became more vindictive than the Abolitionists regarding polygamy. The newly organized Republican party coined a vote-getting catch phrase with its platform denouncing the "twin relics of barbarism; slavery and polygamy." It was "the imperative duty of Congress" to prohibit both in the territories.

Among the various schemes to overthrow Mormonism was the plan of the American Bible Society to drown the abominations of Deseret by flooding Utah with Bibles. Taylor was delighted. He called at the Society's office to offer assistance, and he advised that the books should be well bound, for they would get hard use. In *The Mormon*, he added:

> Our mountaineers never do things by halves or for appearance; if they carry Bibles they mean to use them; they'll read them frequently and thoroughly, too. We have a Bible that has kept us company many years on our pilgrimage through life; it has dangled in our pockets many a thousand miles, when, for the gospel's sake, we have visited towns, cities, and hamlets. We have had to patch it together frequently, and in fact our friend has got so covered over with our notes and references, that a white spot is scarcely discernible. We would, therefore, respectfully suggest to the managers of the American Bible Society—if they propose doing real good to the inhabitants of Utah in the Bible line—do it, gentlemen, respectably, for the inhabitants of that Territory will probably use them as we have ours.

In the face of this endorsement, the Bible project was quietly dropped. When the *Sun* called upon the city's churches to send missionaries to darkest Utah to bring the deluded Mormons to the true faith, Taylor again endorsed the project, but expressed doubts that it would be implemented.

> The Bible Society got up a report about two months ago, that they were going to send a Bible agent to Utah. We then hastened to offer them our cooperation, but as we advanced to receive the precious gifts, they vanished into their original element—gas!

The scheme of the *Herald* was perhaps the most practical. A detachment of U.S. troops under Lt. Col. E. J. Steptoe, en route to California,

---

[6] *The Mormon*, October 20, 1855.

had wintered at Salt Lake. Like soldiers everywhere, they had seduced a number of women, both white and Indian. On receipt of this news, the *Herald* proclaimed:

> It shows that the Mormon women are ripe for rebellion, and that a detachment of the regular army is a greater terror to the patriarch of the Mormon Jerusalem than Indians or drouth or grasshoppers. It indicates the way, too, for the abolishment of the peculiar institution of Utah. The astonishing results of the expedition of Colonel Steptoe, in this view, do most distinctly suggest the future policy of the government. . . . It is to send out to the Great Salt Lake, a fresh detachment of young, good-looking soldiers, and at the end of two or three months, order them off to California and replace them by a new detachment at Salt Lake City and so on until those Turks of the desert are reduced, by female desertions, to the standard Christian regulation of one wife apiece.

Enthusiasm increased as the idea grew, and the *Herald* even suggested the dispatch of a Women's Auxiliary Force to Utah.

> Unquestionably, if . . . the President were to send out to Utah at this crisis of impending famine, a corps of regular disciplined women's rights women, to lay down the law to their sisters among the Mormons, they would soon compel the patriarchal authorities of Salt Lake to an exodus to some other region beyond the reach of our gallant army, and our heroic warriors in petticoats, who know their rights, and knowing, dare maintain them. . . . Thus even should the grasshoppers fail to conquer the Territory in the expulsion of the Saints, the work may be done by a revolution among the wives of the apostles.

It was entirely possible that James Gordon Bennett, editor of the *Herald*, had tongue-in-cheek with this proposal. Taylor's sense of humor, however, entirely deserted him. With biting sarcasm he replied to this plan to introduce into Utah

> Christianity in all its beauty as practiced in the United States: that she may be crowded with voluptuaries, and prostitutes, like all other good Christian states and cities; that debauchery and corruption may run riot; that we may have our procuresses, pimps, cyprians, hotel accommodations, and houses of assignation; that virtue, chastity and purity may be banished from Utah; that our daughters may be prostituted and our wives debauched; that we may have our *nymphis du pave*, our "Five points," our Randall's Island, our infanticides, our *maisons d'accouchement*, our diseases, doctors and hospitals, and all the other appliances of a good Christian community.[7]

---

[7] Roberts reminds us that Randall's Island was "Famous in those years for its hospital for the unfortunate victims of man's licentiousness." Both he and Taylor ignore the fact that newspapers of the Mormon environment, both at Nauvoo and at Salt Lake, carried ads for the cure of "secret diseases."

"There seems to be a deadly hostility against us," Taylor reported to Brigham, February 24, 1857. All editors were in bondage, compelled to pander to public desire; in particular "we have not a more virulent, bitter, and unscrupulous enemy than Greeley of the *Tribune*."

Despite loud talk about liberty, he declared,

> There is a species of bondage that is associated with every grade of society. It is with the mercantile community, the editorial fraternity, the political world, up to members of Congress and the President of the United States. There are yokes made for men of every grade to put their necks into; and every one bows down to them willingly, and they are driven in their turn according to circumstances.[8]

When Taylor preached in the New York area, he had no difficulty filling the hall. He was a forceful speaker; the audience never went to sleep. Mormonism was in the public eye; everyone wanted to know something about it. And not just the poorer classes. The carriage trade flocked to his meetings; in New Jersey some 200 vehicles lined the streets in the vicinity of the hall where he preached. The crowd was so great, in fact, that an enterprising hawker set up a portable bar and sold drinks—a nuisance which Taylor quickly abated.

Despite the interest, Taylor and his missionary companions made precious few converts. It was fashionable to know something about this curious sect. It was the smart thing to have heard Mormons preach. But to accept their faith—hardly.

"They do not love the truth," Taylor concluded.

He made a few converts among the rural citizenry of Connecticut. Yet some fell away within a week or two. A farmer's wife joined, and was helpful in providing a place for meetings; but before long she defected, and offered $500 for anyone to prove Mormonism untrue. On hearing of this, "I said I would do it for half that sum," Taylor said; "if she wanted a lie, she should have it."[9]

Taylor made a number of trips to Washington, where, with George A. Smith and Utah's delegate to Congress, Dr. John M. Bernhisel, he lobbied for a bill that would admit Utah Territory as a state. As a political reality, such a bill had absolutely no chance of passage. He wrote Brigham of interviewing President Franklin Pierce on the matter: "He was very sociable and seemed desirous to conciliate; but like all other public men he will be governed by the tide and will sacrifice all else to popularity."

He reported scornfully on the manner in which political hangers-on were appointed as officials to Utah:

---

[8] JD, 5:119.

[9] See his report of the New York mission, JD, 5:112.

When a president is elected, a crowd of men press around him, like so many hungry dogs, for a division of the spoils, . . . mean, contemptible pups, doggery men, broken-down lawyers, or common, dirty, political hacks . . . come to the table for fragments, and, with a hungry maw and not very delicate stomach, whine out, "Won't you give me a place, if it is only in Utah?" In order to stop the howling, the president says, "Throw a bone to that dog, and let him go out"; and he comes out a great big "United States officer," dressed in lion's garb, it is true, but with the bray of an ass. He comes out here, carrying out his groggery and whoring operations, and seeking to introduce among us eastern civilization.[10]

During Taylor's first year in New York, emigration of European converts became a flood, as the church initiated the "ten pound" plan and established the Perpetual Emigration Fund. For the price of £10 ($50), the emigrant would get transportation from Europe to the Salt Lake valley. If he couldn't raise the money, the PE Fund would advance it, as a loan.

There were no frills to the £10 plan. Passengers were so jam-packed on the Atlantic voyage that a convert ship, like a slaver, could be smelled downwind for miles before appearing on the horizon. On the final 1,200 miles by ox team, every able-bodied person had to walk; the wagons were reserved for supplies and the 100 pounds of personal gear allowed each emigrant.

Under the stimulus of cheap fare and easy credit, some 5,000 European Saints arrived for the gathering during Taylor's first year in New York. While some stayed in the east, 4,225 of them crossed the plains to Zion during the summer of 1855.

Taking care of the new arrivals, keeping them out of breadlines, finding employment, and outfitting them for the overland trip was a demanding job for which, as ranking church authority in the east, Taylor was ultimately responsible.

Among the arrivals from Europe was a missionary and his family, T. B. H. Stenhouse, his wife, Fanny, and their children. Taylor gave Stenhouse a job on *The Mormon*, which started him on his career as newspaperman and writer. Both he and Fanny were becoming disgruntled and were taking notes for books they would write.[11]

---

10 JD, 5:120.

11 T. B. H. Stenhouse's *Rocky Mountain Saints* is an unvarnished history of the church that is perceptive and penetrating. While it was denounced for many years as an "apostate" book, modern scholars have come to accept a good deal of it. His wife's *"Tell it All": The Story of a Life's Experience in Mormonism*, while not of the stature of her husband's monumental work, is filled with first-hand sidelights and anecdotes of the Mormon culture.

It is curious that while T. B. H. Stenhouse admires John Taylor, Fanny hates him.

Hard times were upon the land. Taylor reported to Brigham that there were 30,000 unemployed in New York City. Part of the job problem for emigrants was solved by Ebenezer Young (no relation to Brigham), a convert who owned a cotton mill at Westport, Connecticut, "around which," Taylor suggested to Brigham, "a nucleus might be formed for manufacturing purposes."

Ebenezer also had an attractive daughter. Margaret Young, first of eight children, was a happy girl of twenty, beautiful, with wide brown eyes and auburn hair. As an author, Taylor evidently admired his own love letters, for he published one to Margaret in *The Mormon* under the title, "The Origin and Destiny of Woman," just as his "Lines Written in the Album of Miss Abby Jane Hart of New York City" had previously been printed in the *Millennial Star*. And a comparison of the two shows that he used the same route to the girl's emotions in each case. His "Lines" to Abby Jane said,

> *Abby: Knowest thou whence thou camest? Thine*
> *Origin? Why thou art? What? and whither thou*
> *Art bound? . . .*
> *Thou in the*
> *Bosom of thy Father bask'd and lived, and*
> *Mov'd thousands of years ago. Yes, e'er this*
> *Mundane sphere from chaos sprung . . . thou liv'dst.*
> *Thou liv'dst to live again . . .*

For Margaret, the blank verse became prose:

> Lady, whence comest thou? Thine origin? What art thou doing here? Whither art thou going, and what is thy destiny? . . .
> Knowest thou not that eternities ago thy spirit, pure and holy, dwelt in thy Heavenly Father's bosom, and in His presence . . . surrounded by thy brother and sister spirits of the spirit world, among the Gods?

In either case, it was good Mormon doctrine and an effective love letter. On September 27, 1856, Margaret Young became John Taylor's seventh and final "official" wife, George A. Smith performing the ceremony at Westport.

"Miss Young," Fanny Stenhouse reported, made Taylor "an excellent housekeeper in the handsomely furnished house in Brooklyn."

The success of the ten-pound plan had a severe impact upon the Utah economy. The Perpetual Emigration Fund was a direct drain on the church's treasury, for poverty-stricken emigrants arriving in the valley had no immediate way to repay. The trip by ship and railroad could be

---

Fanny's antipathy stemmed from an incident when the emigrants of her party arrived destitute in New York, and John Taylor censured them for begging in the streets. Fanny was unaware that Taylor was legally responsible for keeping church emigrants off public welfare.

made on commercial carriers; but the last leg of the journey, more than a thousand miles from Iowa City to Salt Lake, required the purchase of hundreds of wagons with several yoke of oxen for each.

Thousands of emigrants arriving in the valley during the autumn found Zion facing a severe crop failure; the Saints went on rations during the winter of 1855–56.

With hard times, the church simply couldn't afford the heavy expense of wagon trains the following summer. Taylor wrote to Brigham suggesting one way to beat the high cost of ox teams—capture buffalo from the roving bands and break them to the yoke.[12]

For some time, though, Brigham had nurtured another plan. After the flood of emigrants during the 1855 season, "The question now is how we shall operate another year," Brigham wrote to Taylor.

> We cannot afford to purchase wagons and teams, as in times past. I am consequently thrown back upon my old plan—to make handcarts, and let the emigration foot it. . . . They can come just as quick, if not quicker, and much cheaper—can start earlier and escape the prevailing sickness which annually lays so many of our brethren in the dust.

With characteristic attention to detail, Brigham sent Taylor specifications for construction of the carts, "to be made strong but as light as possible." To avoid risk of mishap, Brigham said, men from the valley could meet the handcart companies with provisions midway on the journey.[13]

Taylor was less than enthusiastic about the handcart plan. Almost its only virtue was low cost. Wagons would accompany the handcart train and carry a surplus of provisions and livestock to aid survival of accidents and misfortune and to transport tents and a limited amount of foodstuffs. But the handcart train would have only one wagon to twenty-five carts. Men, women, and children would be required to drag handcarts more than a thousand miles; and they would arrive in Zion with almost nothing except the clothing on their backs. Personal belongings of handcart emigrants were limited to seventeen pounds, including bedding and cooking utensils. Trunks, organs, books, china, linen, furniture, rugs, treasured souvenirs, must be left behind. Then en route, the weight limit was reduced from seventeen pounds to ten, which made a hard choice between a Bible and a pair of boots, a violin or a frying pan.

The arrival of a wagon train in the valley had been a definite asset, bringing goods in short supply—farm implements, hand tools, sugar,

---

12 Whether or not this was possible will never be known. However, there were instances of buffalo being broken to harness.

13 Ninety-three men volunteered to meet the handcarts midway. However, for some reason this part of the plan was never put into effect.

coffee, tea, manufactured goods. Iron was so scarce that the Saints took the rims off the wagon wheels to use in forging tools, hardware, and implements. A handcart company would arrive as a dead weight on the overburdened resources of the valley. The decision had been made, however; it was the will of the Lord.

Franklin D. Richards, in England, had charge of the emigration and was custodian of the Perpetual Emigration Fund disbursements. He sent Daniel Spencer to oversee affairs at Iowa City—the building of the handcarts, outfitting the companies, and dispatching them across the plains. Taylor pitched in to expedite operations at New York. "I have had it drummed into my ears all the day long that I had nothing to do with the emigration," he wrote Brigham; "but if the poor were to be fed, the destitute provided for, the sick taken care of, or money wanted, it was generally found that I had something to do."

Taylor was deluged by shiploads of emigrants pouring into eastern ports, week after week. He saw them housed and fed, then dispatched by railroad to Iowa City. But there, their numbers overwhelmed the handcart-building operation. The first three companies started on schedule and arrived at the valley without difficulty. Brigham wrote Taylor that all the single girls had found husbands. The last two companies, however, waited at the railhead for long weeks that stretched into months, as handcarts were being constructed. These two companies pulled out with their handcarts terribly late—the last one not leaving until early September.

Disaster overtook these two companies. They lost their wagon teams when the livestock bolted in the night with buffalo stampedes. Tents and foodstuffs carried by the wagons had to be loaded onto the carts—400 to 500 pounds on vehicles designed for lightness rather than strength. Fall storms made travel slow and laborious. A sickness called cholera ran through the camps—nine out of ten of the victims died within two days. This further slowed the daily travel. Now it was a race against starvation. Once the food on the carts was gone, there was no more; entire daily food ration for adults became one cup of flour. The two companies were caught in the Rockies by winter storms. Before supplies reached them from Salt Lake, more than 200 people perished, while many more were crippled for life with frozen feet and hands.

Taylor was appalled by news of the tragedy and infuriated by a letter from Brigham implying that Taylor had delayed the operation and added to the expense. "In regard to detaining the emigration, or any portion of it—either directly or indirectly—I positively deny it," Taylor replied hotly.

> To avoid all delay, collision and difficulty, I appointed Br. Daniel Spencer, simply because he was Br. Richards' agent, to take charge of all the emigration, as well as that of the PE Fund; he had his own men exclusively.

... I rendered him all the assistance that lay in my power. If he could not carry out his own arrangements, it certainly was not my fault.

The handcart system was to me, and to all of us, a new operation. I considered that the utmost care and precaution were necessary. I wanted, if a train started, to know that it would get through. I knew of the weakness and infirmity of many women, children & aged persons that were calculated to go. I did not consider that a few dollars were to be put into competition with the lives of human beings. I felt it better for a small company to go through safe than for a larger one to perish on the way. I felt that if there was a short outfit that we should have famine, sickness & death, and I shrank from the responsibility. . . .

Taylor reminded Brigham that he was on record in believing plans for the handcart expeditions were inadequate:

I positively believed that the calculations for the emigration were too small; my object was to increase them. I wrote and made an offer to this effect, before the companies started. It was rejected. . . .

I would just remark in conclusion that I have occupied a position which I never wish to do again. . . . I feel willing all the time & have a strong desire to submit to legally constituted authority; but . . . on the death of Br. [Orson] Spencer and in the absence of Br. [Erastus] Snow, without being able to obtain communication from you I knew that the responsibility rested somewhere.[14] There was no one here of the Twelve but myself & I could not see how, upon any principle of reason, that those responsibilities could revert to Europe. If I was responsible I wished to have some say in the direction, if not, I wanted to know it. . . .

I felt, and said, that I would give $500 for five minutes conversation with you. You must excuse me here, Br. Young; I may be obtuse & so may those who were with me; but however plain your words might be to yourself on this matter, neither I nor my associates could understand them.

Brigham absolved Taylor, and at the tabernacle on November 2 he cleared his own skirts of the matter:

If any man, or woman, complains of me or of my counselors, in regard to the lateness of some of this season's immigration, let the curse of God be on them and blast their substance with mildew and destruction, until their names are forgotten from the earth. I never thought of my being accused of advising or having anything to do with so late a start. . . . There is not a person, who knows anything about the counsel of the First Presidency concerning the immigration, but what knows that we have recommended it to start in season.

---

[14] Orson Spencer, connected with the *Luminary* at St. Louis, had died the previous October. Erastus Snow was in charge of church affairs at St. Louis. It was Orson's brother, Daniel Spencer, who oversaw the handcart emigration at Iowa City.

Furthermore, he declared, those responsible for delayed starts in the future "shall be severed from the church."

The real culprit for the handcart disaster was difficulty of communication at a time when the flood of emigrants overwhelmed machinery set up for equipping them. But Richards had had overall responsibility for the emigration, and Daniel Spencer had been in charge at Iowa City. Brigham castigated them from the rostrum:

> . . . I do not know that I will attach blame to either of them. But if, while at the Missouri River, they had received a hint from any person on this earth, or even a bird had chirped it in the ears of Brs. Richards and Spencer, they would have known better than to rush men, women, and children on to the prairie in the autumn months, on the third of September, to travel over a thousand miles. I repeat that if a bird had chirped the inconsistency of such a course in their ears, they would have thought and considered for one moment, and would have stopped those men, women, and children there until another year.[15]

On the day before Christmas, Taylor was at the *Mormon* office when a burly man of middle age walked in with a carpetbag clutched in a massive fist—his old and dear friend, fellow apostle Parley P. Pratt, dispatched by Brigham on a mission "to travel and preach the gospel in different places, as you shall be led by the spirit of the Lord." His letter of appointment also stated:

> Owing to the extra duties of delegate [to Washington] being placed upon brother John Taylor, it is suggested that you also aid him in writing for *The Mormon*, and such other duties as may devolve upon you by the united counsel of brethren now in charge of that mission.[16]

Taylor took Parley home to Brooklyn, where the new bride, Margaret, made him welcome and served a fine supper. That evening the two men

---

[15] *Deseret News*, November 12, 1856. To the newspaper account of the speech was appended Brigham's comment: "The above is all of the remarks made at this time, that I deem proper to print at present. B.Y."

According to Stenhouse, the remarks not deemed proper to print pertained to Richards and Spencer:

"On the arrival of the apostle Richards, Brigham attacked him in the tabernacle, held him up to ridicule and contempt, and cursed him in the name of Israel's God. Elder Daniel Spencer, who had been the counselor of Richards, came in for his share of the contempt and anathemas. For years after, the apostle could scarcely lift up his head; he absented himself from the public meetings and was rarely seen in times of rejoicing. . . . For ten years Richards and Spencer were under a heavy cloud, and silently bore heavy grief. At length it told upon the riper years of elder Spencer, and he went to his grave a broken-hearted man, the object of much sympathy in the community."

[16] Letter of appointment dated September 10, 1856.

had a glass of wine and talked for hours of old times and new problems. It was a memorable evening, at once pleasurable and apprehensive. Taylor tried to savor every moment, remember every word, for he was ridden with the presentiment that Parley's days were numbered.

He would have said nothing about this feeling; but then Parley himself brought up the subject. Though only forty-nine, Parley had written out detailed instructions for his burial. He also had been working on his *Auto-biography* and was ridden by the fear that he'd be unable to finish it.[17]

Taylor had been out of touch with Parley for some time. As they sipped the wine, he listened with growing concern as the burly apostle told of events leading to his feelings of doom.

At the time Taylor was called to go to New York and establish *The Mormon*, Parley was sent to San Francisco to found the *Western Standard*. While waiting for the press to arrive from the Hawaiian mission, Parley became involved in the personal problems of one of the most devout and attractive members of his little congregation. Elenore McLean apparently had everything that makes for happiness. Her husband, Hector, was a customs house official and respected citizen. She had three beautiful children, aged ten, eight, and seven. And, to complete her good fortune, she had found the true gospel. Parley learned that her home life was a veritable hell. Hector McLean drank to excess every night and became a brute when intoxicated.

Suspecting that his wife was in love with Parley, McLean retaliated by shipping the children to New Orleans, where her father lived. In wild despair, she told Parley that if she tried to follow, her husband threatened that "he would have me in an Insane Asylum in twenty-four hours."[18] Parley helped spirit her aboard the next ship for New Orleans.

Parley was called back to Utah; three months later Elenore arrived. Her family hadn't allowed her to be with her children a minute, for fear she might teach them Mormon doctrine or plot escape. She had come to Zion alone. Before long, she became the twelfth wife of Parley Pratt.

As Parley told this, Taylor studied his wine glass and said nothing. There had been no divorce. Hector McLean now held all the legal cards. Whatever the husband might do, to regain his wife or enact vengeance on the polygamist who had stolen her, would have full support of the police and public sympathy.

Elenore had returned to New Orleans. The plan was that at her father's home she would give the impression that she was disillusioned with

---

[17] Entries in Parley's journal at this time show that he lived day by day expecting death.

[18] Letter to the Van Buren, Arkansas, *Intelligence*, May 18, 1857. Regarding Parley, Elenore said that "I am free to declare, before angels and men," there was nothing improper in their relationship.

Mormonism and had come home to stay. In this manner she would disarm suspicion, while awaiting an opportunity to spirit the children away to the home of friends at Houston for the winter. In the spring she would find transportation with someone going overland to Fort Smith, Arkansas. Parley would meet her there, and they would go to Utah with a Mormon wagon company forming in the vicinity.

Parley remained with Taylor only a few days. As the two old friends shook hands in farewell, Taylor advised: Be careful, Brother Parley; and may the Lord protect you.

Parley kept in touch. He sent contributions to *The Mormon*, one being a poem written on his birthday, April 12:

My Fiftieth Year

> *I am fifty years old! I have lived to see*
> *Seven times seven and a Jubilee. . . .*
> *I have wandered far, over land and sea,*
> *To proclaim to the world its destiny—*
> *To cry to the nations, repent and live,*
> *And be ready the bridegroom to receive. . . .*
> *I have lain in a dungeon, bound in chains,*
> *And been honored in Courts where Justice reigns.*
> *In a thousand joys, and a thousand fears*
> *I have struggled on through fifty years.*
> *And now, by the law of God, I am free;*
> *I will seek to enjoy my Jubilee.*
> *I will hie me home, to my mountain dell,*
> *And I will say to the "Christian" world—farewell!*
> *I have served ye long—; 'twas a thankless task;*
> *To retire in peace is all I ask.*

But word from Arkansas made Taylor fear that Parley's jubilee might be in the next world, not this. Hector McLean had arrived in the vicinity, searching for his family. At the Fort Smith post office, he obtained letters that Parley had written to Elenore. Parley, meanwhile, had written her at Houston, advising her to come in a Gentile's wagon. He would patrol the Texas road in Indian territory, to meet her before she arrived at Fort Smith.

Taylor published his farewell in *The Mormon*:

A Response to P. P. Pratt's "Fiftieth Year"

> *. . . If a wish from a sincere friendly heart*
> *Can to thee any comfort or joy impart;*
> *If a fervent prayer to God of grace*
> *Could smooth thy path in thy onward race,*
> *That prayer would be, may grace be given*
> *To wend thy onward course to Heaven.*

May'st thou abound in corn and wine,
And the blessings of plenty now be thine;
May thy family all be free from care,
And a husband's and father's plenty share;
May thy sun go down with glory rife,
And dying, may'st thou burst into life;
And, when sleeping among the silent dead,
Have the blessings of millions on thy head;
And, living with God, may'st thou be free,
And partake of an endless Jubilee.

A few weeks later Taylor learned that Parley had been murdered by McLean.

Soon afterwards, Taylor left for Utah. President James Buchanan had dispatched an army to suppress the "Mormon rebellion." The Saints were at war with the United States government. Taylor said little to Margaret on the train ride to Iowa City, where they joined a Mormon emigrant train. Parley's death had hit him hard. It was a time for casting up accounts. He himself would be fifty in another year and a half. Though he had married sixteen women, there had been only a few months during the past eight years when he was at home and with the opportunity of making a living. The remainder of the time he had been traveling as a missionary, without purse or scrip. More than that, he was charged personally for funds expended on missionary activities, until now the church books showed that John Taylor owed Brigham Young, Trustee-in-Trust, the sum of $4,943.88.

When the company reached the Missouri River at Florence—which he remembered as Winter Quarters—he visited Ann Pitchforth's grave. What a price she had paid for her faith. Why did the Lord require such sacrifice?

He returned to the encampment in the late afternoon. Fires were going, and the breeze brought the smell of cooking food. Then he noticed an old man with a cane standing apart, raptly watching the busy scene as the emigrants prepared for the evening camp. Then the old man called to him in a quavering voice: "Brother John! John Taylor!" and hobbled toward him, one foot dragging, an arm dangling. "Do you remember me, Brother John? I'm Thomas B. Marsh."

Thomas B. Marsh, former president of the Twelve, the office to which Brigham Young succeeded when Marsh apostatized during the times of violence and persecution eighteen years ago in Missouri. Marsh was only nine years older than Taylor; yet at fifty-seven was a shattered wreck of his former self. With a pathetic eagerness he asked Taylor if it was too late; could he hope for re-baptism, be forgiven his mistakes, accepted into fellowship once more?

It was never too late for repentance, Taylor said, and invited Marsh to supper. As they ate, Marsh told of the rocky road back from apostasy. For several years he was stiff-necked. "But the Lord loved me too much to let me go without whipping," he said. "I have seen the hand of the Lord in the chastisement which I have received. I have seen and known that it has proved he loved me; for if he had not cared anything about me, he would not have taken me by the arm and given me such a shaking."

Later that evening around the central campfire, Thomas B. Marsh addressed the emigrants bound for the gathering. Hold to the faith, he advised, "If you want to see the fruits of apostasy, look at me."[19]

Next morning as the wagon company started the journey across the plains, John Taylor was his old self, buoyant, eager, with a ready quip and a hearty laugh. The frustrations and setbacks of his eight years in the mission field was evidence that the Lord loved him too much to let him go without whipping.[20]

[19] Upon reaching Utah, Marsh spoke the same way to the Saints assembled at the bowery, and in fact from then on adopted the role of one who had reaped the fruits of apostasy.

[20] Shortly after Taylor returned, his debt of $4,943.88 was cancelled on the church books, "In consideration of John Taylor's faithful labors in the ministry."

13

Latter-Day Joshua

SUNDAY MORNING was too hot for the Saints to assemble in the adobe tabernacle; they gathered out back at the bowery, shaded by the canopy of fresh tree branches. As John Taylor arose to speak, every bench was crowded, while the overflow stood about the pole framework. On this September 13, 1857, the U.S. Army was bivouacked in Wyoming at Ham's Fork on the Green River, only 143 miles away, awaiting the order to march on Utah. The Saints were gathered for counsel at this time of crisis.

Seated among the brethren on the rostrum was a U.S. Army officer. The audience anticipated that, while Taylor would address the congregation, his every word would be directed to Capt. Stewart Van Vliet, whose report to his superiors would reflect the Mormon attitude toward the threat of armed invasion.

Van Vliet, assistant quartermaster, had been in Great Salt Lake City several days, vainly trying to secure supplies for the men and livestock of the Utah Expedition—2,500 troops, with as many more teamsters and camp followers, the gamblers and prostitutes. Taylor had previously known Captain Van Vliet a decade ago at Winter Quarters, where the officer had helped the impoverished Saints by furnishing employment. But while Van Vliet was regarded with personal cordiality, Brigham and the Twelve refused to sell him provisions and lumber for the army of occupation.

Taylor began his remarks with a discussion seemingly unrelated to the problem at hand. However, his purpose was to reassure the Saints of Divine protection and at the same time put a flea in Van Vliet's ear. He mentioned "rather a strange anomaly" in comparing various social experiments in Utopian colonies, which invariably had failed, with Mormonism, which despite everything had thrived. The answer, he said, was that the others didn't have "the gospel as it existed in its purity."

With the people in a confident and happy mood—they couldn't hear too often of their superiority over the Gentiles or of being persecuted for righteousness sake—Taylor asked, "What was your object in coming here? Was it to rebel against the general government?"

From behind him, Brigham supplied the answer: "To get away from Christians."

The bowery exploded in laughter. "Brother Young says it was to get away from Christians," Taylor said, "—from that unbounded charity which you had experienced amongst them. . . ."

> We came here because we could not help it, and now we have got an idea to stay here because we *can* help it: this is about the feeling.

"Why do this people feel so comfortable when an army is approaching?" he asked.

> Are you not afraid of being killed? No, not a great deal. . . . Because you have got a principle within you that cannot be conquered in time nor in eternity: you possess the principles of eternal life in your bosoms, that cannot be subdued.

The Saints had been driven out before, and might be again; but they never had been conquered. "Talk to us of bowing to the Gentile yoke! Nonsense!"

> What would be your feeling if the United States wanted to have the honor of driving us from our homes and bringing us subject to their depraved standard of moral and religious truth? Would you, if necessary, brethren, put the torch to your buildings, and lay them in ashes, and wander homeless into the mountains?

Brigham spoke up behind him: "Try the vote."

Taylor asked: "All you that are willing to set fire to your property and lay it in ashes, rather than submit to their military rule and oppression, manifest it by raising your hands."

A forest of hands shot up. Taylor turned to look at Captain Van Vliet. The officer sat with military erectness, his face impassive. To the congregation, Taylor said, "I know what your feelings are. We have been persecuted and robbed long enough; and, in the name of Israel's God, we will be free!"

"Amen!" came the echoed response. Brigham spoke up: "I say amen all the time to that."

While the Saints had been charged with rebellion, Taylor asked what were the real reasons for the U.S. Army being dispatched to Utah. In the east, it was common knowledge that Secretary of War John B. Floyd was a red-hot secessionist, favoring the impending rebellion of the southern states. This great civil conflict had been predicted by revelation to Joseph the prophet. The Utah Expedition would go down in history as part of Secretary Floyd's efforts to disarm the North and fortify the South, in anticipation of the impending civil war.[1]

The audience was with him now. This was the John Taylor they characterized as a latter-day Joshua, who like the Old Testament prophet wanted the sun, moon, and stars to stand still while he demolished the enemy.

Ostensibly, the purpose of the army was merely to protect the authority of appointed federal officials—but was a force of 2,500 troops, with artillery, necessary for this? Of the real designs of the invading force, Taylor declared, church leaders for some time had been "well informed."

> We had men in all the camps, and knew what was intended. There was a continued boast among the men and officers, even before they left the Missouri River, of what they intended to do with the Mormons. The houses were picked out that certain persons were to inhabit; farms, property, and women were to be distributed. "Beauty and Booty" were their watchwords. We were to have another grand Mormon conquest, and our houses, gardens, orchards, vineyards, and daughters were to be the spoils.[2]

The Utah Expedition was called the "contractor's war" in the east, Taylor said, because of the enormous graft and waste in supplying the army. No force ever dispatched by the United States was so well equipped and provisioned. For 2,500 troops, two thousand head of beef cattle had been sent ahead, together with a huge wagon convoy freighting enough supplies for 10,000 men. Contractors were being paid 22¢ a pound for transporting stores, provisions, and armaments, a rate that would make fortunes for those with the government contracts.

Even worse than the army of occupation, Taylor said, would be the rabble that would accompany it. A thousand teamsters would be discharged upon arrival—dangerous men, the scum of frontier cities, becoming desperate upon being thrown out of work in the middle of

---

[1] Taylor subsequently repeated this assertion in the *Taylor–Colfax Discussion*, stating that President Buchanan "had another object in view, and Mr. J. B. Floyd, Secretary of War, had also his ax to grind"; that "part of this grand tableau originated in the desire of Secretary Floyd to scatter United States forces and arms preparatory to the Confederate Rebellion. Such is history and such are facts."

Whitney supports Taylor's view in the *History of Utah*: "It was doubtless due to Floyd's advice that Buchanan sent the troops to Utah, ostensibly to suppress a rebellion in this distant Territory, but in reality to favor a rebellion in the Southern States."

[2] From *Taylor–Colfax Discussion*. Taylor's talk as reported in the *Journal of Discourses* bears evidence of war-time censorship. JD, 5:237.

nowhere. And traveling with the army was the usual horde of camp followers, the gamblers, bootleggers, whores, pimps, ruffians, and sharp traders who would form the nucleus of a Utah underworld.

The men who supplied the army would receive freight costs regardless of where they purchased supplies. The contract for flour was an example. The political huckster who was awarded this choice plum agreed to supply the army at $28.40 per hundredweight—$6.40 for the cost of the flour, plus $22 freight. But flour could be purchased in Salt Lake and delivered to Ham's Fork for a total cost of $7, providing a profit of $21.10 on every barrel.[3]

As for Captain Van Vliet, Taylor said, he was only obeying orders. However, his mission in the valley to obtain provisions and supplies for the army would only fatten the purses of the contractors. Was it any wonder that the brethren had refused to deal with him?

At this, Captain Van Vliet's face flushed brick red. Brigham leaned forward and jerked Taylor's jacket. But the latter-day Joshua was not to be shushed.

"Brother Brigham, let go my coattail!" Taylor cried. "I tell you, the bullets in me yet hurt!"[4]

Upon arriving home from New York the previous month, Taylor had learned of an incredible irony of circumstance: the U.S. Army had been ordered to march against the Saints as a result of a card game at Fillmore, Utah, between a local shopkeeper and the visiting judge of the district court.

The merchant was Levi Abrams, a Jewish convert called Abraham the Jew. Holding the other hand of cards was W. W. Drummond, appointed to the federal office of Associate Justice of the Territorial Supreme Court. Both were in southern Utah because the Territorial capital had been moved from Salt Lake to Fillmore. Abrams set up a small store and gaming house. The judge dropped in for a drink and stayed for a game of stud poker with the proprietor.

Judge Drummond went home that night in an ugly mood. By morning the incident had festered and he sent his strapping servant, Cato, the only Negro in the territory south of Salt Lake, with a rawhide to horsewhip the Jew. Arriving at the store, the big black man spat in Abrams' face, pulled his nose, and was dragging him over the counter when Abrams brought out a knife. Cato prudently unhanded him and departed.

---

[3] The possessor of this contract, as it turned out, made a profit of $170,000 on it in a single year. But this was only the beginning. He exercised his option of taking his pay in mules, "at figures ranging from $100 to $150 each," Stenhouse reports. Herds of these animals were driven to California, and sold for nearly six times the purchase price. This case became a public scandal in Washington.

[4] For coattail incident, see *Millennial Star*, 56:389.

Steaming at the assault, Abrams swore out a warrant against Drummond, charging assault with intent to kill. Wild talk swept through the hotheads at Fillmore. Here was a serious offense: this was not simply assault; the assailant was one of the accursed race, "the descendants of Cain and Canan," who had attacked one of the chosen people, not only a Jew but a Mormon.[5]

Extremists had been waiting for just such an incident. Here was the opportunity to get rid of Judge Drummond, as other unpopular federal appointees had been hounded out of Utah by one means or another. Drummond had aroused the antipathy of the Saints before the opening of his first court session, by challenging the jurisdiction of the local probate courts. This struck directly at the heart of the church's authority.

The territorial legislature had increased the jurisdiction of the probate courts—which had Mormon judges—to include civil and criminal matters, thus taking such cases from the district courts presided over by federal judges. The Saints intended to handle their own legal affairs, only territorial law being enforced in Utah, and that through the probate courts.

Judge Drummond, however, announced that he would ignore all proceedings of the probate courts except those pertaining to legitimate probate matters. He ruled that the special powers given by the legislature to probate courts were "founded in ignorance" and without legal status.

As the first federal official to challenge the peculiar judiciary system of Deseret, Drummond was a peril to the front-line defenses of the Saints against Gentile interference. As such, he was a marked man. Soon afterwards, he found himself involved in a nasty scandal.[6]

Before leaving New York, Taylor had received information which caused him to send his assistant editor, William I. Appleby, to Washington to investigate Drummond's past. Upon arrival in Utah, the judge was accompanied by a striking beauty, introduced as his wife, the former Ada Caroll of Washington. He was so attached to the lovely Ada that she sometimes sat beside him on the bench during court. However, when a woman who had known the family in the east called to pay her respects, she was surprised to find that Ada wasn't the Mrs. Drummond of her acquaintance.

The judge explained that he had divorced and remarried. However, the Saints had a most efficient investigative force with their far-flung mis-

---

[5] For this attitude, see William Chandless, *A Visit to Salt Lake.* Jewish converts were highly prized, but very scarce. During the twenty-seven years of the church's existence, only three Jewish families had converted. See Juanita Brooks, *The History of Jews in Utah and Idaho.*

[6] Furniss, in *The Mormon Conflict,* says, "As was their practice with their enemies," the Mormons "investigated his past for evidences of turpitude."

sionary system. Taylor learned that, on going to Utah, Drummond had deserted his wife and children. Who, then, was Ada Caroll?

In Washington, Appleby interviewed the madam of a bordello where Ada had been working when Drummond made her acquaintance. "Ada Caroll" was actually Mrs. Charles Fletcher (born Mary Ridgley) of Baltimore, where the husband she had deserted for a life of shame was a respectable school teacher. Drummond had deserted his family to bring a harlot to Utah.[7]

The Mormon press had a field day. Long under attack for their own peculiar marriage customs, the Saints were eager to pounce upon any irregularity on the part of a Gentile. The cry of outrage regarding the affair of the judge with the luscious tart taxed the vocabulary of vituperation, Drummond being called an "infamous scoundrel and dastardly wretch," a "beastly criminal," "horrible monster," a "black-hearted judge" · who was a "loathsome specimen of humanity," and a "lying, adulterous, murderous fiend."[8]

Such was the shattered character of the man involved in a gambling quarrel at Fillmore with Levi Abrams. When Abraham the Jew filed a complaint of the mistreatment by Drummond's servant, a posse of armed horsemen led by the zealous Hosea Stout, former chief of police at Nauvoo and now attorney general, apprehended Drummond and Cato, then took them to a private home for trial rather than to the courthouse. Surrounded by what he believed to be the Danite band of Avenging Angels, Drummond found himself on trial, where "During the prosecution of the case, the judge gave some sort of stipulation that he would not interfere any further with the probate courts."[9]

Inasmuch as the trial presumably was about the scuffle between his servant, Cato, and Abrams, the verdict might have boggled the legal mind of the Associate Justice of the Supreme Court. However, thoroughly intimidated, Drummond got the message, made the deal, and was vastly relieved to leave the house alive.[10]

Taylor, known as Champion of Rights, was distinctly not in favor of such bully-boy tactics. The attempt to render Drummond impotent backfired when the judge slipped out of Utah, evidently in fear of his life. In

---

[7] Appleby to Taylor, April 25, 1857. By coincidence, while Taylor was in New York his oldest daughter, Mary Ann, married a Gentile named Drummond. This has caused family genealogists to assume her husband was the infamous judge. However, it was another man; she married before Judge Drummond arrived in Utah. See Brigham to Taylor, April 20, 1855: "Her husband . . . has been very highly recommended by Judge Kinney, who states that he is of a good family, and respectable character."

[8] *Millennial Star*, May 23, 1857.

[9] See Mrs. C. V. Waite's *The Mormon Prophet and His Harem.*

[10] Roberts reflects the official version in the CHC: "The case was never brought to trial, the matter being in some way, not very clearly set forth, 'smothered' in court."

resigning his position Drummond sent a blistering report to Washington regarding conditions in Utah. This letter proved to be the spark that ignited the powder keg of the Utah War.

Drummond made six major charges: (1) The Mormons looked to Brigham Young, "and to him alone, for the *law* by which they are governed; therefore no law of Congress is by them considered binding in any manner." (2) "There is a secret oath-bound organization among all male members of the church to resist the laws of the country, and to acknowledge no law save the law of the 'Holy Priesthood,' which comes to the people through Brigham Young direct from God." (3) "There is a set of men, set apart by special order of the church, to take both the lives and property of persons who may question the authority of the church." (4) "The records, papers, etc., of the Supreme Court have been destroyed by order of the church, with the direct knowledge and approbation of Governor B. Young, and the federal officers grossly insulted for presuming to raise a single question about the treasonable act." (5) "The federal officers of the Territory are constantly insulted, harassed, and annoyed by the Mormons, and for these insults there is no redress." (6) "The federal officers are daily compelled to hear the forms of the American government traduced, the chief executives of the nation, both living and dead, slandered and abused from the masses, as well as from all the leading members of the church, in the most vulgar, loathsome, and wicked manner that the evil passions of men can possibly conceive."

Drummond added that Brigham Young pardoned Mormon criminals while throwing innocent Gentiles into jail; that he dominated federal courts, "directing the grand jury whom to indict and whom to not"; and that several murders had been committed "under the particular and special order" of the first presidency, and performed by "members of the Danite Band," who were "bound to do the will of Brigham Young . . . or forfeit their lives."

He concluded his bombshell by recommending that a Gentile governor be appointed to replace Brigham, "and be supported with a *sufficient* military aid"; otherwise, "it is noonday madness and folly to attempt to administer the law in that Territory," where "the judiciary is only treated as a farce," by "those despots who rule with an iron hand," and where federal officers "are insulted, harassed, and murdered for doing their duty, and [for] not recognizing Brigham Young as the only lawgiver and lawmaker on earth."[11]

---

11 Drummond to U.S. Attorney General Jeremiah S. Black, March 30, 1857 in *House Executive Document No. 71*, 35th Congress, 1st Session, 1858, pp. 212–14. The Mormon refutation of the charges, written by Taylor's former mission associate, Curtis E. Bolton, was futile. Before it was dispatched, President Buchanan had already appointed a new governor, Alfred Cumming, and dispatched the U.S. Army to uphold his authority.

Taylor was aware that, although Drummond's letter precipitated the war, the way had been paved with other incidents. When Colonel E. J. Steptoe had wintered in Utah with his detachment of troops whose romantic conquests had seemed, in the east, a possible solution to the Mormon problem, the colonel had been offered the position of governor. Steptoe had declined the nomination, signing a petition favoring Young's continuation in office. But the inside gossip of why he did so, while circumstantial, certainly ruffled official feathers in Washington. In her *Mormon Prophet*, Mrs. C. B. Waite said that two Utah beauties were favorites of Steptoe and his fellow officers; upon learning of the colonel's appointment as governor, the Saints used the two girls to frame him, they being surprised with him in his office at night under compromising circumstances. To avoid disgrace and possible Danite retribution for bespoiling two of the fairest flowers of Zion, Steptoe declined his own nomination and supported Brigham in office.[12]

The Reformation had swept Utah during Taylor's stay in New York, an upsurge of religious zeal that increased tensions between the Saints and the federal government. Like Drummond's famous card game with Abraham the Jew, the Reformation began with an insignificant incident, the loan of a mule. Jedediah M. Grant, counselor to Brigham in the first presidency, loaned his mule to a Salt Lake man to attend a local conference at Kaysville, twenty-five miles north. Upon arrival, the mule was lathered, as were the mounts of others in the party. Grant chastened the men from the rostrum for abusing the animals. Then, warming up, he

> assailed the bishop and his counselors for inactivity and carelessness, and charged the congregation generally with all manner of wickedness, calling upon them to repent and "do their first works over again," or God's judgment would overtake them speedily. Thus began the noted "Reformation" in Utah, and "accusation of the brethren became forthwith a mania with this reformer."[18]

---

[12] Beadle's *Life in Utah* repeats the story, adding that "Utah now began to be regarded as the 'Botany Bay of worn-out politicians'; if a man was fit for nothing else, and yet had to be rewarded for political service, he was sent to Utah."

In the CHC, Roberts rejects gossip of the badger game as "an incredible story" without foundation. Whether true or not, Washington believed it. CHC, 4:184.

[18] Stenhouse, *Rocky Mountain Saints* (p. 293). In John D. Lee's *Confessions* he says members were required to arise in open meeting and confess all sins, and any attempt at concealment "was an unpardonable sin." It was the duty of others to tell of anything omitted. "The right thing to do with a sinner who did not repent . . . was to take the life of the offending party, and thus save his everlasting soul." This was called "blood atonement." The members who fully confessed their sins were again admitted into the church and rebaptized, taking new covenants to obey any and all orders of the priesthood, and to refuse all manner of assistance, friendship, or communication with those who refused a strict obedience to the authorities of the church.

Ironically, Grant gave his life to the Reformation. Rebaptizing penitents in bitter weather, he died of exposure. But the Reformation continued. Taylor had received letters in New York from Brigham, exhorting him to cleanse the Saints in the east; Brigham had also required Taylor to restate his own belief in and adherence to the principles of the gospel.[14]

Following close on Drummond's heels in getting out of Utah was the surveyor general of the Territory, David H. Burr, whose stay among the Saints had been as brief and as stormy as that of the judge. Burr's arrival with a survey crew caused apprehension among the Saints, who held title to the land merely as squatters. Burr claimed that the Saints stirred up Indian trouble against his crew, removed corner posts, stole his animals, stoned his quarters, and did other obstructive acts. Brigham was openly opposed to the survey; there was no redress in the Mormon-controlled courts. When one of Burr's deputies was severely beaten, Burr attributed it to three Danites directed by the notorious Bill Hickman, acting on orders from higher up. As soon as the snow melted in the mountain passes, Burr headed east, fearing for his life. The only remaining Gentile official in the entire Territory was the Indian agent, Garland Hurt.[15]

Amid charge and countercharge, with the piling up of incidents of violence, the excessive zeal of the Reformation, the hatred of Gentiles, and with the typical hysteria of war gripping the Saints as the U.S. Army marched on Utah—with all this combined, Taylor felt a tension among the people and was apprehensive that something might trigger off a catastrophic incident of violence.

He soon learned that his worst fears had been more than realized. John D. Lee arrived in Salt Lake from southern Utah with news to chill the blood. At a grassy hollow called Mountain Meadows, an emigrant train of some 140 people en route to California had been attacked by a combined force of Mormons and Indians, and all except seventeen children

---

"The most deadly sin among the people was adultery," Lee says, "and many men were killed in Utah for that crime" (pp. 281–82).

In the CHC, Roberts denies that "blood atonement" was ever practiced, giving the rather curious reason that the only evidence of such deeds comes from "confessed murderers." Yet if the evidence of men implicated in such deeds must be rejected, then where can we go for the truth? To deny the hysteria of the Reformation and the practice of blood atonement is to make the massacre at Mountain Meadows utterly incomprehensible.

14 Taylor's letter to Brigham from New York (no date), would be completely bewildering unless the circumstances surrounding it were understood. Why should a member of the Twelve who had dedicated his life to the church for more than twenty years affirm his faith to Brigham at great length and detail? It is also noteworthy that Taylor did not confess to or repent of any sins in the missive.

15 In his *History of Utah* (p. 492), Bancroft added, "and none were found willing to accept office in a territory where it was believed they could only perform their duty at peril of their lives."

under the age of eight had been slaughtered. The massacre occurred September 11, at the very time Captain Van Vliet was in Salt Lake negotiating with the brethren.

One thing was certain. The enormity of Mountain Meadows spelled the end of the policy of blood atonement; the Reformation was over.

Sophia Whitaker felt like a fifth wheel, useless amid all the activity of the move south. As John and his other wives prepared to evacuate "Taylor Row," she wasn't allowed to carry anything out to the wagons, nor to stoop, to pack, or strain herself in any way.

Patty Sessions, the midwife, had predicted that it would be a large baby. Now nearly eight months along, Sophia didn't have much energy to spare anyhow. Patty had prescribed a long walk each afternoon, and as Sophia put on wrap and bonnet, hammering filled the air; she winced at the scream of nails as a window frame was wrenched free. All over Salt Lake men were taking out windows and doors, to cache away with mirrors, organs, and other belongings that couldn't be carried in the wagons during the move south.

"Sophia!" It was Mary Ann Oakley at the door. She came in, dressed for the walk; the noise, she said, was hard on her nerves. With all the hammering, Sophia hadn't even heard her knock.

As the two pregnant wives went outside, the air struck Sophia's face like ice water. It had been a hard winter and a stormy spring. There was still snow lying on the north side of buildings, slush underfoot; the mountains rising abruptly to the east of the city glittered with unbroken white in the afternoon sun.

John Taylor, in shirtsleeves, was helping a crew of men board up Taylor Row. In the yards were two piles, one of essentials to be taken along in the wagons, the other of things to be cached. Sophia's piano stood tall in its box among the latter category. She hated to think of its condition on her return; it was to be buried. She'd suggested leaving it in the house, but John had vetoed that.

Two men were pitching straw across the fence from a hayrack. This was to put inside the houses upon leaving. The city was being evacuated ahead of the advancing army. Only a standing guard of select men would remain, with axe and torch, ready to burn every building and cut down every tree, if the army attempted to occupy the city. The troops under Gen. Albert Sidney Johnston would find the Salt Lake valley in the same condition it had been when the Saints arrived.

Other wives—Leonora Cannon, Jane Ballantyne, Harriet Whitaker, "Aunt Caroline" Gilliam, and the new bride, Margaret Young—were hurrying in and out of their quarters, towels around their hair, getting ready for the move, children helping. Sophia felt helpless, pampered, and useless. Leonora, as first wife, was directing things. Passing Elizabeth

Kaighin's door, Sophia saw her inside on hands and knees, scrubbing the floor before leaving. Sophia and Mary Ann exchanged a smile. How like the fastidious Elizabeth; her place had to be spotless before being burned down.

John paused in his work to ask if the two wives were warmly dressed for the walk. Be back before sundown, he advised; don't take a chill. Sophia told him not to fret. As they walked north along First West toward Brigham Street Sophia said that men always worried more about having a baby than the wives. Presently she was puffing as she kept alongside. Tall and slender, Mary Ann stepped along lightly at a brisk pace. Though she was six months along it scarcely showed with her coat on. In contrast, Sophia felt dowdy. Short and stocky, she was conscious of waddling.

They turned east along Brigham Street and walked the long block to Temple Square. As they came along the high wall to the south gate, Sophia was glad to catch her breath while they peered through. During the past four years the distinctive feature of the square had been the work on the temple foundation, the deep excavations, the great blocks of granite sitting about, with the cranes and gear for setting them in place. Now everything had been cleared away. The stone and the construction gear was gone, the excavation filled in and leveled. When the troops marched in, they would find nothing to defile or destroy, as had happened to the temples abandoned at Kirtland and Nauvoo.

Poor Leonora, Mary Ann said; she'd been through this four times— Kirtland, Missouri, Nauvoo, Winter Quarters—and now forced to move again.

Where to, this time, Sophia wondered; where would the Saints find refuge?

South, to the promised land, Mary Ann said confidently. Brother Brigham had told of a fertile oasis in the desert, unknown to whites and even to Indians, yet larger than any eastern state, where a half million people could live in peace and plenty. The surrounding desert, Brigham declared, would provide better protection than an army of forty thousand men.

Sophia knew that John held definite reservations about Brigham's mysterious land of promise; but one had to be careful about showing skepticism toward the inspired words of the prophet, even among the family, so she asked why couldn't the great oasis be found? Brigham had sent out David Evans with an exploring party, and when he couldn't locate it had dispatched two other parties, under George W. Bean and W. H. Dame, who also had been unsuccessful. Were the Saints to strike off into the wilderness without knowing their destination? What if thirty thousand people perished in the desert?

Mary Ann admitted that she didn't like the uncertainty; but, she said, we must trust our leaders. Many things she didn't understand, such as the secret lands where the lost tribes of Israel lived. But in proper time, such things would be known. In the move south the Saints would be guided and sheltered as were the Israelites under Moses. And we're better off than they were; Brother Brigham had said there were 40,000 bushels of wheat stored. The Saints wouldn't have to depend upon manna from heaven.

The two wives continued their walk. The shadows lengthened and slush underfoot froze hard. When they returned to Taylor Row at sunset the furniture and supplies had been cleared from the yards. A line of wagons in the street held everything that would be taken along, the things to be cached—including Sophia's piano—taken away to be buried in a gravel bank. Only the piles of straw remained in the yards, to be put inside after the family left in the morning. The houses of the row had windows boarded over, just one door remaining on hinges for use one last time.

Conscious that her eyes were smarting, Sophia ducked her head and hurried inside.

A storm blew up during the night. Next morning the wagons started south in a blizzard. With roads heavy with snow and mud, the teams became exhausted within a few miles. John scouted around for a place to stay, but every home in the vicinity was already crowded with refugees. For two days Sophia stayed in the wagon with Harriet and their children until the storm cleared.

As travel continued, every jolt of the wagon became a torment. The four cooped-up children, her two and Harriet's, were always in an uproar. With nerves on edge, the clatter and bang of the gear made her want to scream. When weather permitted, Sophia escaped the turmoil and jolting by walking; but, heavy as she was, this was only possible for perhaps a half hour in the morning and again in the afternoon. Harriet did all she could to make things easy for her sister, and their two daughters were big enough to take turns with the reins and be of real help around the camp in the evening. But—*where was this promised land in the desert? How far?*

She got out for an afternoon walk when the wagon was at the Point of the Mountain. Here from the elevation above the Jordan Narrows Sophia could look for miles along the road both north and south. As far as she could see the road was crowded with refugees. All of northern Utah was on the move, some 30,000 people in one continuous line of travel. They came by wagon, buggy, and various rigs drawn by horses, cows, oxen, and even yearling steers. A number of families pushed handcarts. Alongside the roadway were the livestock, cows, sheep, geese, pigs, tended by children.

Not only the people were on the road, but they brought their culture along with them. Freight wagons rumbled along with the presses and equipment of the *Deseret News*; looms, carding machines, and spinning jennies of the woolen mill; lathes and equipment from the machine shop. Tithing grain came in wooden bins holding seventy-three bushels each. The papers, books, documents, and records of the church archives were boxed and accompanying the Peculiar People to the promised land, wherever that might be.

One aspect of the exodus made Sophia ashamed of herself. She was so heavy, so miserable, so prone to self pity. Yet almost everyone was cheerful, making a lark of the move as if going to a corn husking. Fortitude, she reminded herself, was one of the cardinal virtues.

It seemed an eternity before they reached Provo, only forty-five miles south. Most of the refugees were camped on the Bottoms west of town, awaiting directions to the land of milk and honey. Sophia's heart sank at first sight of "Shanghai," the squalid jumble of tents, dugouts, shelters of log and of mud and willow. Many people lived in wagon boxes. Brigham and some other officials had temporary housing in the city square.

John was approaching, pushing through the crowd of arrivals. He'd gone ahead to find a place, and by some miracle had located a house in the jam-packed town. It wasn't much, he cautioned as she and Harriet rode with him in the carriage—with *springs* on it—but anything at all at such a time was a godsend.

The dwelling, belonging to Roger Farrar, was in the back of the lot. It had been used as an outbuilding after a new house was built in front. As she went in, Sophia caught the scent of a chicken coop. The window panes which weren't broken were black with grime. It wasn't much, John said, but they were lucky to find anything.

They lived in the wagon box behind the house; after three days of scrubbing, cleaning, and whitewashing the walls, they moved in. Sophia awoke in the night scratching. The light of a match showed the sheets crawling with bedbugs. They moved back into the wagon. John brought a can of coal oil and everyone worked, going over every crack in floor and walls with rags wet with it. Then John set rocks around the floor and on them put pans smouldering with sulphur, pepper, tar, and horse manure. Two days later they again moved into the house.

John attended a meeting with men from New York, who wanted the Saints to colonize a tract of land in Central America. Sophia was relieved when he returned with news that the brethren had turned it down. The Saints stemmed from northern European stock; they weren't tropical people. And anyhow, John said, with a quirk to his lips, why go to the jungles when Brigham knew of the promised land awaiting?

Then where, she asked, *are* we going?

Back to Salt Lake, he said, before long. The move south had received wide publicity, and there was an upsurge of sympathy for the Saints. Buchanan was realizing his blunder.

The following month, on May 15, Sophia gave birth in the chicken coop to a baby boy, whom the father blessed and christened John Whitaker.[16]

A few weeks later Johnston's army marched through Salt Lake, without pausing to molest or plunder, and continued on forty miles to Cedar valley to establish a garrison, Camp Floyd. A delegation from Washington arrived at Provo with presidential amnesty for Taylor, Brigham, and other church officials under indictment for treason.

The Utah War was over. The move back began. After months of squalor at Shanghai, many of the refugees were ragged and barefoot. But on every face Sophia saw blooming joy. It hadn't been necessary, people said, for Brigham to lead the people to the hidden sanctuary in the desert. For the first time in their history, the Saints were *returning* to homes they had been forced to leave. Around the campfire they talked of prophecy. This was the turning point, the beginning of the back track which eventually would bring them again to Jackson County, Missouri, site of the Garden of Eden and gathering place of the chosen people in the last days, as foretold by Joseph the prophet.

---

[16] John Whitaker Taylor was the father of the author.

14

The Kingdom
or Nothing

As THE WIVES and children sat on the bleachers before the Beehive House, awaiting the parade, Leonora smiled indulgently at the way the young children were being fussed over—spoiled rotten. During a period of eight years prior to the Utah War, John had been away on missions almost constantly. In consequence, the wives had been denied the blessing of children who would be treasured on earth and jewels in their crowns during the hereafter. If it took a war to have him home, then the war was a blessing in disguise.

Mary Ann Oakley and Sophia Whitaker each had presented John with two babies since his return, while Margaret Young was five months pregnant with her second. As for Leonora herself, at age sixty-five babies were a thing of the past; her youngest, Joseph James, was twenty-three. But as she watched Elizabeth Kaighin, Jane Ballantyne, and Harriet Whitaker spoiling the babies, she felt a pang of compassion. These three had discovered that during the years of John's continual missions they also had passed childbearing age. Though the purpose of marriage was to provide opportunity for as many souls as possible to experience their earthly trials, Elizabeth, Jane, Harriet, and Leonora had had opportunity to bear only a combined total of thirteen children, two of whom had died in infancy.[1]

---

[1] John Taylor was to have a total of thirty-four children by his seven acknowledged wives, plus an adopted daughter. There is no available record of his progeny by his "little-known" wives.

It was the Fourth of July, 1861. The fretting children on the bleachers came alert as the Martial Band began playing a spirited march. Stepping briskly around the corner of State Street came a company of 1847 pioneers under the command of Capt. Seth Taft, resplendent in his Nauvoo Legion uniform. The crowd lining both sides of South Temple Street (formerly Brigham) broke into a cheer.

Abraham Lincoln was president of the nation, and the country was engaged in the Civil War. In Utah, all signs pointed to the establishment of the Kingdom of God on earth, as foretold by revelation. When asked what his policy would be toward the Saints, Lincoln had said, "I propose to let them alone." The Mormon question was like a green hemlock stump on a newly-cleared farm—too heavy to remove, too knotty to split, and too wet to burn; so he'd plow around it. And when the struggle between the North and the South prostrated both sides, the Saints were prepared to step in and save the constitution as prophesied.

As the '47 pioneers marched by the Beehive House, Captain Taft delivered a smart salute to Brigham Young and members of his family on the balcony. The Martial Band came next, led by Maj. Dimick B. Huntington. Then came a company of light infantry, under command of Capt. George Romney. Captain Romney had designed his own uniform, glittering with gold braid and brass buttons, and his men also were attired by individual taste, most of them in portions of the U.S. Army uniform from Camp Floyd.

Floats and marchers followed: the Deseret Agricultural and Manufacturing Society, the stock raisers, horticulturists, chemists, millwrights, bridge-builders, and the Deseret Foundry. Then came crafts and trades; forty-six skills were represented, from bakers and brick makers to tanners, turners, and upholsterers.

Ballo's Band came along, fortunately, for the children were getting restless. Then the larger kids swarmed around the wagon of the Typographical Association, fitted with press and fixtures, the pressmen striking off copies of a patriotic song composed for the occasion by Eliza R. Snow and handing them out.

"Here's Papa!"

John Taylor, orator of the day, sat in the leading carriage of a procession of dignitaries.

This was followed by teachers and pupils of select and district schools. Near the end of the parade marched a company of neatly dressed Indian children, under direction of John Alger, carrying a banner with the book of Mormon prediction:

Considering the example of their father, and the importance of marriage in the Mormon culture, it is curious that three sons and three daughters never married. Only five sons entered the Principle.

WE SHALL BECOME A WHITE AND DELIGHTSOME PEOPLE.[2]

Leonora, matriarch of the clan, admonished the children to keep close to their mamas as the family moved with the crowd to the bowery at Temple Square. Sitting in the shade of freshly-cut branches, she enjoyed "The Star-Spangled Banner" by the Nauvoo Brass Band, prayer by Chaplain David Pettigrew, "Hail Columbia" by Ballo's Band, the reading of the Declaration of Independence by John R. Clawson, and "Yankee Doodle" by Major Huntington's Martial Band.

Then came the major event of the day, the oration by Apostle John Taylor. As he arose, tall, commanding, dressed in cutaway with velvet collar, ruffled shirt, heavy gold watch chain gleaming against a figured waistcoat, Leonora knew that feminine hearts fluttered. It was not remarkable that he had married so many times, but that, with his opportunities it had been so few, compared to such *confrères* as Brigham with over fifty, Heber C. Kimball with forty-five—and nobody knew the number of Joseph's wives. But Mary Ann Angell, the first wife, was the only Mrs. Brigham Young; Vilate Murray the only Mrs. Heber C. Kimball; Emma Hale the only Mrs. Joseph Smith; and Leonora Cannon the only Mrs. John Taylor.

She was happy that John had entered a new phase of church work. His missionary period was over. During the eight years he'd been absent, she'd suspected that Brigham sent John on one mission after another to get him out of sight. However, his labors in New York with *The Mormon* had received Brigham's hard-won approval.

"With regard to brother John Taylor," she'd heard Brigham tell the assembled Saints while John was in the east,

> I will say that he has one of the strongest intellects of any man that can be found; he is a powerful man; he is a mighty man. And we may say that he is a powerful editor—but I will use a term to suit myself, and say that he is one of the strongest editors that ever wrote.

Brigham praised John Taylor as one of the old-time buttermilk-and-potatoes missionaries, who started from Nauvoo walking without purse or scrip, en route to England, took sick and "was left to die by the roadside"—not like the prissy modern elders, stylishly attired in broadcloth, who "must start from here with a full purse," Brigham said scornfully, and who must "hire first-cabin passages in the best ocean steamers—and after all this many think it is hard times."[3]

It was John's pugnacious loyalty during the Utah War, she believed, that at long last outweighed the personality clash that had made propin-

---

[2] As a practical approach to the fulfillment of prophecy, Mormon men were encouraged to take a Lamanite wife or two. Joseph Smith's first revelation on plural marriage (1831) advocated this.

[3] JD, 4:33.

quity irritating. With the war over, Johnston's Army at Camp Floyd had marched off for duty in the Civil War. But with government troops gone, Brigham hadn't sent back the colonists from California, Nevada, and other outlying areas, who had been called to Zion when the U.S. Army marched on Utah. Nor had he sent John to far-off missions. As first wife of a member of the Twelve, Leonora knew why.

It had been predicted that the United States should fall, and with the constitution hanging by a thread, the Kingdom of God—under control of the Council of Fifty—would rescue the constitution and take control of the country. Even in Joseph's time, the organization had been assembled; and now, with the nation destroying itself, the YTFIF was busy with preparations for the takeover.

First the nation, then the world; like the little stone of Daniel, the Kingdom of God would fill the earth.

"It is folly to make stereotyped speeches about Washington or American liberty," John told the assembled Saints, at a time such as this, when states were seceding from the Union and "our Nation has fallen from the highest pinnacle of union, power, fame, and wealth to the lowest depth of angry, malignant, bloodthirsty, fratricidal war."

He attributed this to "a loss of national integrity, the increase of crime and corruption, and a want of proper administration of the law."

Politicians "pandered to the basest passions," offering their patriotism "as unblushing as a harlot does her charms." Pugilists intimidated the polls, until ballot-stuffing "became almost the rule instead of the exception." Congress degenerated into "the theater for the display of all the baser passions of humanity." Political appointments were bought and sold. As a result,

> The United States of America—that boasted justly of its greatness; its power; its commerce, trade, and agriculture; its cities and states; its mineral and agricultural wealth; its civil and religious institutions—the last born, as it were, among nations; the glory and pride of the world—is fallen and dismembered, severed, shattered, and broken.

What part should Utah take in the conflict?

> Shall we join the North to fight against the South? No! Shall we join the South against the North? As emphatically: No! Why? They have both . . . brought it upon themselves, and we have had no hand in the matter.

However, though the nation had fallen, the constitution would survive. Joseph Smith said it was given by inspiration of God. When hanging by a thread it would be saved by the Saints.

It was a powerful speech, and Leonora noted that Brigham and the other brethren behind John on the rostrum kept nodding affirmatively.

For thirty years the elders had warned the world "that their kingdoms would be overthrown, and their nations would be destroyed, and that God would speedily arise and shake terribly the earth."

The time was now at hand. Despite opposition and persecution, "no power, no reverses, no influence that can be brought against the Kingdom of God will withstand its onward progress."

And then, typically, John brought the grand plan down to practical detail. With the characteristic quirk to his lips, he said,

> Men who are talking of possessing thrones, principalities, and powers, of becoming kings and priests unto God, ought to know how to take care of enough wheat to supply the wants of themselves and their families.

We would "be kings and priests unto God and rule with him," John Taylor said, "—and yet we are obliged to have guardians placed over us to teach us how to take care of a bushel of wheat."

This sugar-coated the message, and the audience chuckled. After the meeting the people surged to the stand, everyone wanting to congratulate the Champion of Rights and shake his hand.

While waiting for him, Leonora wondered what position John would have when the Kingdom of God held sway. During the prophet's time, Joseph Smith had been anointed king of the world, Brigham president of the nation, with John vice president. Would Brigham now be emperor of the entire earth, and John president of the nation? It was a heady prospect. But she couldn't ask John about this. He never talked with the family about the secret meetings of the YTFIF.[4]

As Leonora waited for John at the bowery, a man in his mid-twenties introduced himself; he was Thomas Quayle from the Isle of Man. She remembered his father's family there and reminded him that her brother had married a Quayle.

Whenever he saw John Taylor on the rostrum, Quayle said, he remembered him as a missionary visiting the home, when Quayle was a boy of five. Sweets were a luxury on the Isle of Man, and his father put the sugar bowl on the table only for company. The boy would watch his chance to filch a pinch of it.

---

4 Klaus J. Hansen in his *Quest for Empire* points out that at the time of the exodus from Nauvoo the Council of Fifty intended to set up a kingdom independent from the United States. He says,

"The error in the work of apologist historians is that they have written Mormon history from hindsight. The image of Mormons leaving the United States in order to set up an independent Kingdom of God conflicts with the subsequent self-conscious Mormon view of themselves as loyal citizens. . . . What these writers fail to acknowledge, simply, is that a transformation has taken place in the attitude of the Mormons toward the United States. This shift, while patently apparent, has in fact served to obscure Mormon understanding of their own past."

See the *Journal of Discourses* for many statements from the rostrum by church authorities assailing the government and predicting its downfall.

"Every day that the missionaries were with us, that prize rested upon our dining room table," Quayle said. "I can see John Taylor now, as he paced the room preaching the gospel to the family. With his thumbs in the armholes of his vest, head erect, stride prolonged and sturdy, he paced the room. And every time he passed the table, he reached out and took a pinch of sugar. How I envied him!" Quayle chuckled. "I wanted to grow up to be a missionary, and live on sugar."[5]

As a member of the YTFIF, an apostle, and speaker of the house in the territorial legislature, John Taylor took an active part in secret preparations for the Council of Fifty to rescue the constitution and take charge of the nation when the government should collapse.

Gentiles blinked in amazement when the Saints revived the defunct "State of Deseret." When the legislature voted to hold a constitutional convention, the suspicious governor promptly vetoed it. However, expectation of the imminent collapse of the nation made it imperative to prepare for the Kingdom, so the YTFIF held the convention despite the veto. The delegates nominated Brigham Young for governor of the State of Deseret, and the same men composing the territorial legislature became candidates for identical positions in the State of Deseret.

With numbered ballots, results were predictable: of 9,880 votes cast, 9,880 were for Brigham, the legislature, and the State of Deseret.

As Gentiles glowered suspiciously, the "ghost government" began operation. At the close of each legislative session, members remained seated and convened as the legislature of the State of Deseret. By resolution the ghost legislature reenacted the identical laws for Deseret that the same body of men had enacted for Utah Territory.

"Many may not be able to tell why we are in this capacity," Brigham admitted with remarkable understatement in a private message to the ghost legislature. But the organization would be maintained, and "hold fast to it," he exhorted in his capacity as ghost governor, "for this is the Kingdom of God."

> Our government is going to pieces and . . . I do not want you to lose any part of this government which you have organized. For the time will come when we will give laws to the nations of the earth. . . . We should get all things ready, and when the time comes, we should let the water on the wheel and start the machine in motion.[6]

Gentile reaction ranged from alarmist charges of treason to ridicule. In an item headed "BRIGHAM AS COMEDIAN," the *Daily Union Vedette* at Camp Douglas called it farce.

---

[5] Daughters of Utah Pioneers pamphlet, "Isles of Man—Wight—Jersey," 1973.
[6] JH, January 19, 1863.

... It has been our notion all along that the role of the big villain was his particular forte, but we were mistaken. His talents are of the versatile order which descends from the higher flights of tragedy and takes to comedy naturally as a duck does to water. ... His last appearance was as "Governor" in that immensely funny affair, the farce entitled "The State of Deseret." He took his role with that ridiculous gravity he knows so well how to assume when playing the fool, and delivered his message in a style superbly comic. The audience, who were also actors, ... went through the farce with a serious decorum ... appearing to lose themselves completely in their parts and evidently forgetful that it was not reality. ... For a full description of the affair ... we refer our readers to the "Dead Sea Telegraph," the comic paper published in town."[7]

With the government of God so close to reality, Taylor anticipated that Satan would throw every resource into desperate attempts to block it. He looked upon federal carpetbaggers not merely as political hacks, but as emissaries of the Prince of Darkness.

Certainly Associate Justice John Cradlebaugh qualified as one of the Devil's minions, in Taylor's estimate. The judge had arrived from Washington at the time Camp Floyd was still garrisoned by Johnston's army, and he had requisitioned a detachment of a hundred soldiers to guard witnesses and secure prisoners when he convened a grand jury at the Second Judicial District Court in Provo. Reason for this extraordinary precaution was that the judge intended to investigate the massacre at Mountain Meadows and a number of unsolved murders at the town of Springville, near Provo; Cradlebaugh frankly was attempting to implicate Brigham Young and other church leaders.

As Brigham's trouble-shooter, Taylor arrived at Provo to find troops bivouacked on the grounds of the Seminary building—the church school —officers quartered on the lower floor and Judge Cradlebaugh presiding at court above. Local citizens were quick to let Taylor know they were thoroughly aroused at this show of force, just another outrage of carpetbag government. As the investigation proceeded, Taylor received confidential reports of doings in grand jury sessions, and on the basis of these sent word to Brigham that there was little to worry about. Cradlebaugh rather naively expected a grand jury composed of Mormon stalwarts to indict the church leadership.

Meanwhile Governor Cumming, whose relations with General Johnston already were strained because of conflict of authority, made formal protest; the governor claimed that he, and only he, had authority to call out troops. General Johnston ignored this, and acceeded to Judge Cradlebaugh's call for military reinforcements. Eight companies of infantry, an artillery company and a cavalry unit arrived at Provo and stationed

---

[7] January 26, 1865. The "comic paper" is the Salt Lake *Telegraph*, published by T. B. H. Stenhouse.

themselves near the courthouse. Whereupon, Judge Cradlebaugh discharged the grand jury with a severe tongue-lashing:

> Until I commenced the examination of the testimony in this case, I always supposed that I lived in a land of civil and religious liberty. . . . But I regret to say that the evidence in this case proves that, so far as Utah is concerned, I have been mistaken. . . . Men are murdered here. Coolly, deliberately, premeditatedly murdered—their murder is deliberated and determined upon by church council-meetings, and that, too, for no other reason than that they had apostatized from your church, and were striving to leave the Territory.
>
> You are the tools, the dupes, the instruments of a tyrannical church despotism. The heads of your church order and direct you. You are taught to obey their orders and commit these horrid murders. Deprived of your liberty, you have lost your manhood, and become the willing instruments of bad men.
>
> I say to you it will be my earnest effort, while with you, to knock off your ecclesiastical shackles and set you free.[8]

As Judge Cradlebaugh continued examining witnesses without a grand jury, Taylor was apprehensive. The rising resentment against military occupation of Provo, together with the judge's high-handed methods, presented a real danger that some spark might ignite the Utah War again.

Then in the night a messenger awakened Taylor. It was his faithful friend, Sam Bateman, with information that Cradlebaugh had issued secret bench warrants and that the U.S. Marshal, accompanied by the U.S. Army and the judge, would be in Springville before daylight to apprehend the wanted men.

Taylor made a fire and got dressed while Bateman hitched up the carriage. After a hot cup of tea, they set out through the cold night of early spring, driving south. The carriage was on the outskirts of Springville

---

[8] Stenhouse says that "the members of the grand jury . . . were themselves accused of participating in the very crimes they were instructed to investigate," and that "immediately after they were dismissed, several of them betook themselves to concealment, and Judge Cradlebaugh expressed his sorrow that he did not keep them when he had them." The Mormon viewpoint (given by Whitney, Roberts, Bancroft) refutes this; and Stenhouse admits their guilt remained unproved. Modern apologists avoid the subject entirely.

The grand jury, replying to Judge Cradlebaugh's assertions, said that they were surrounded during deliberations by a detachment of the army, whose officers were quartered within earshot of witnesses being examined in the jury room; that indictments voted by the jury had been treated with contempt by the judge, who liberated prisoners without trial; that witnesses subpoenaed by the grand jury had been arrested and prevented from giving evidence; and that they were dismissed with a slanderous and insulting harangue.

The names of the men on the grand jury constitute a list of solid and substantial citizens of impeccable reputation.

The Springville murders have never been solved.

when they heard a trumpet call. Bateman turned to Taylor with a wink. The trumpet was warning of danger. The men wanted by the bench warrants (which weren't as secret as the judge supposed) would take to the canyons.

Before dawn troops surrounded Springville, and accompanied the U.S. Marshal in searching the town. None of the wanted men were to be found. The cavalry headed for the canyons in pursuit, but deep snow caused the horse troops to turn back. To avoid complete frustration, the marshal arrested a couple of Gentile loafers and three surprised Indians. Cradlebaugh dismissed them and closed his court. Taylor returned to Salt Lake.

But the judge wasn't through yet. A counterfeiting case gave the eager feds a "chance to get the deadwood on Brigham."

A soldier at Camp Floyd named Brewer had enlisted a young Mormon artist to counterfeit the U.S. Treasury notes issued by the quartermaster. The counterfeit was clever, but the scheme discovered. When arrested Brewer turned state's evidence, and, pandering to his custodians, named a clerk in the church offices as having furnished the paper. On this extremely tenuous evidence, federal officials planned to arrest Brigham, calling upon General Johnston to supply two regiments and a battery of artillery to apprehend and secure the prisoner.

All Utah was in an uproar. Three hundred armed guards surrounded the high stone wall of Brigham's fortress day and night. As an officer in the Nauvoo Legion, Taylor found himself mustered into service by Governor Cumming, who called up the Mormon militia to repel the threatened assault by the U.S. Army. Gen. Daniel H. Wells, commander of the Legion, mustered five thousand furious Mormon troops to defend their prophet, seer, and revelator.

It looked as if the Utah War was beginning again.

However, at this juncture a dispatch arrived from U.S. Attorney General Jeremiah S. Black, reprimanding Cradlebaugh for exceeding his authority as judge. The governor had sole authority, Black stated, to call out troops. Members of the Nauvoo Legion went back to their spring plowing. Judge Cradlebaugh, smarting with humiliation, was transferred to the Western Judicial District, with headquarters in Carson City.

Cradlebaugh fought back with the dangerous fury of a wounded man; he agitated for the Nevada area to "throw off the Mormon yoke" and become an independent Territory. With his eager help, this happened, and as a reward Nevada sent Cradlebaugh to Congress, where he carried on a vendetta to prevent the Mormon takeover.

Taylor, reading a dispatch from the New York *Tribune* at the breakfast table, suddenly let out a howl and slapped the table so hard the teapot jumped. Margaret Young gasped; her two children reacted with fright, three-year-old Ebenezer's lower lip trembling, while the baby, Frank Y., burst into a wail. Margaret took Frank Y. from the high chair and offered her breast, soothing the infant. She told her husband that he really *shouldn't* read Gentile lies at the table.

But, Taylor cried, just listen to what that fiendish son of Satan, Cradlebaugh, told Congress! Muttering impassioned interpolations, he read aloud:

> "Brigham Young is the *Pontifex Maximus*—the God Almighty, it might truthfully be said—of this modern Israel. His will permeates the whole mass of his followers, and before his unrelenting tyranny the souls and bodies of all are bowed. . . . He is commander-in-chief of the armies of the Lord; holds the power of the purse; he controls the decisions of the courts, rebukes and counsels juries; is omnipotent in the Legislative Assembly—whose members are simply registers of his imperial edicts. The power of life and death is in his hands, and the crooking of his little finger sends his enemies to swift destruction. The sick he heals by the laying on of hands, and the widow and (virgin) orphan he comforts by procuring them future exaltation. Is it any wonder that a man so pampered, worshipped, and flattered should grow proud, arrogant, and should offer a menial position in spirit life to a President of the United States (Franklin Pierce was to black the prophet's boots in the next world), and that he should claim the honor of deification? . . ."⁹

Taylor looked up from the paper as Margaret burst into laughter. When he demanded to know what was funny, she reminded him that while he hadn't used quite that language, she'd heard the Champion of Rights utter similar sentiments regarding Brigham's oppressive rule.

Taylor began sputtering, then his big frame began shaking and he joined Margaret in a real belly laugh. The baby gurgled happily. Ebenezer chortled, beating upon the table with his porridge spoon.

New Year's eve was a pleasant event for the family. With youngsters in bed, the older siblings attending various social affairs, Taylor and his wives—both official and secret—gathered for a rare evening together. He disliked subterfuge; but somehow the time never seemed right to bring the lesser-known wives into the official family. Right now there was again agitation in Congress for anti-polygamy legislation; this time it appeared sure of passage.

All in all, however, 1861 had been a good year, Taylor reflected as he raised his glass together with his wives at midnight. Outside, guns fired into the night, whistles blew, sleigh bells jingled as young people dashed along the streets whooping the old year out and the new one in. The Cradlebaugh affair had been settled, the judge banished to Nevada; the attempt to arrest Brigham had aborted; and a new governor, John W.

---

⁹ *Congressional Globe*, February 7, 1863.

Dawson, a troublemaker, was leaving Salt Lake this very night on the Overland stage, headed east.

Just three weeks previously, Dawson had arrived to govern the Territory—followed by ill-repute. He had been editor and publisher of the Fort Wayne *Times*, a Republican newspaper, but was known as a political meddler of shady morality. It was said he was rewarded with the governorship of Utah on the recommendation of high-ranking Indiana politicians who wanted to be rid of him.

Dawson wasted no time making himself unpopular. Three days after his arrival on December 7, he infuriated the legislature by implying disloyalty and urging passage of a special federal war tax to vindicate the territorial patriotism. As speaker of the House, Taylor listened to the long tirade with ill-concealed displeasure.

Dawson added to the ill-will by vetoing a bill for a state convention and by rejecting a memorial to congress, which Taylor had helped frame, for Deseret's admission as a state. It was obvious that the new governor wouldn't stay long.

He hardly had got himself settled in his quarters when a scandal broke —he'd made "improper advances" to a pretty widow employed as housekeeper. This was enough to ensure that his days would be short in the land of Zion.

Violence of the Mormon reaction to the alleged gallantry devastated the governor. Instead of denying the charge, or trying to brazen it out, Dawson locked himself in his quarters, terrified by wild tales of Avenging Angels. The press reported him both sick and insane—which he certainly must be, Taylor agreed, to have insulted a respectable woman in Salt Lake City.

On hearing Gentile insinuations that it was a case of entrapment, Taylor had his good friend on the Salt Lake police force, Sam Bateman, investigate. Bateman, chuckling in his beard, reported that it was indeed a put-up job—however, not by the Mormons, but by Dawson's fellow appointees from Washington, to whom he was an embarrassment.[10]

Before retiring after the New Year's Eve party, Taylor offered a prayer of thanks for deliverance from the unwelcome presence of the new governor. On this very night, Dawson was slipping out of Utah, after a term of office lasting only three weeks, so terrified that he'd hired several local ruffians at $100 apiece as bodyguards to see him safely out of Utah.

It seemed that Taylor's head had hardly touched the pillow when there was sharp rapping at the window. It was Sam Bateman. The city policeman reported that while Dawson was waiting for the Overland stage in Hank's Mail Station at Mountain Dell, his hired rowdies turned

---

[10] Stenhouse and others corroborate this.

on him and administered a severe beating. Bateman lowered his voice to a whisper, and added that he'd heard they also emasculated the governor. A doctor accompanying Dawson revived him, and the two lost no time climbing aboard the eastbound stage when it arrived.

Taylor was appalled. Nothing worse could have happened at the very time Utah Territory was bending every effort to become the State of Deseret. He had been on the committee which prepared the address to the constitutional convention at the tabernacle, reviewing past grievances and prevailing conditions in support of the right to self-government. He had framed the proposed constitution for the State of Deseret, forwarded to Congress for approval. William H. Hooper and George Q. Cannon already had been chosen U.S. Senators to represent the new state.

And now this outrage on the governor.

The hoodlums responsible must be apprehended quickly, and punished, he told Bateman.

On the complaint of Judge W. W. Drummond, Washington had sent Johnston's Army against Utah. Recently Judge Cradlebaugh had fired off grave charges about conditions in Utah. Now this. The governor beaten and emasculated. What would be the nation's reaction?

Sam Bateman returned in the morning to report that the city police had joined forces with the sheriff in search of the hoodlums. Also on the trail was a longtime deputy sheriff of the State of Deseret, Porter Rockwell, legendary gunman. Bateman said that six men were involved in the assault. One of them, Wood Reynolds, was related to the widow who had repulsed Dawson's advances. Identities of all the hoodlums were known; but they were in hiding.

When the *Deseret News* came out, later in the day, Taylor's heart sank. An editorial on Dawson's departure added fuel to Gentile claims of frame-up. The paper said that the governor took with him his physician and four guards, to "prevent his being killed or becoming qualified for the office of chamberlain in the King's palace"—a direct allusion to emasculation. Then, asserting that Dawson had committed an offense which under common law "would have caused him to have bitten the dust," the *News* added: "Why he selected the individuals named for his bodyguard no one with whom we have conversed has been able to determine. That they will do him justice, and see him safely out of the Territory, there can be no doubt." This constituted a broad hint that the hired rowdies would do exactly the opposite.

That the Mormon paper had come out with such a statement—written and set in type *before* the assault—was proof to Gentiles of fore-knowledge.

Despite the best efforts of the law officers, joined by the U.S. Marshal's office, and with the cooperation of the entire Mormon population, two weeks went by without apprehension of the wanted men. Meanwhile,

Dawson had fired a furious letter to the *Deseret News*, and to Washington, during the stage stop at Bear River.

A break in the case came when Lot Huntington, ringleader of the gang, took off for California with two confederates. Huntington's mistake was to steal a horse as a parting gesture, particularly since this animal was a beautiful mare, famous in the valley, called Brown Sal. It was impossible to remain inconspicuous on such a mount; soon Porter Rockwell was on the trail with a small posse. Rockwell trapped the three desperadoes at Faust's Mail Station, on the desert west of Camp Floyd. Huntington made the fatal mistake of trying to shoot it out with Rockwell, and was riddled by Port's sawed-off revolver, loaded with buckshot for close work. The other two men surrendered. Rockwell delivered them to the city police, and was putting up Brown Sal in the livery stable when shots blasted in the street. Hurrying out, he found that the police had killed the two while they were trying to escape.[11] The other wanted men were taken into custody and given prison terms.

Punishment of the hoodlums did little to improve the Mormon image in Washington. Congress denied seats to Senators Hooper and Cannon, and rejected the petition of the State of Deseret for admission to the Union.

A few months later Congress enacted legislation against polygamy in the territories. Until then the territories, like the states, had jurisdiction over marriage laws. On July 2, 1862, President Lincoln signed the law making polygamy in the territories a felony subject to $500 fine and five years imprisonment.[12] The act also dissolved the LDS Church as a legal corporation and limited the value of its property to $50,000—all real estate of greater value to "be forfeited and escheat to the United States."[13]

Three months after the passage of this bill, the U.S. Army again occupied Utah. Mormon preparations for the takeover upon the nation's expected collapse caused the Secretary of War to put Utah Territory once more under military supervision.[14]

---

[11] In his *Brigham's Destroying Angel*, Bill Hickman said, "They were both powder-burnt, and one of them was shot in the face. How could that be, and they running?" Stenhouse said that this type of "legal" shooting was commonplace; it "saved the county the expenses of a trial and . . . subsequent boarding in the penitentiary."

[12] An old-time Mormon told the author some years ago that when he was born the government charged his father a $500 "amusement tax."

[13] The dissolution of the church's legal entity, and the escheatment provision, weren't enforced at this time; but they remained a threat, and subsequently became key factors in forcing capitulation.

[14] In an address to the Saints, December 31, 1861, John Taylor expressed the prevailing attitude regarding preparations for statehood: "The dismemberment of our common country we regard as the greatest of crimes which can be committed against

Taylor stood among the sullen crowd lining the sidewalks as Col. Patrick Edward Connor led his California Volunteers into Salt Lake City. The onlookers were grimly silent, and not a flag flew in the city except over the official residence of the latest governor, Stephen S. Harding. At the governor's residence the battalion formed into two lines; Governor Harding, standing in the buggy in which he had ridden out to greet the troops, exhorted them to maintain peace, security, and the strictest discipline. The colonel then led his men in three cheers for country, flag, and the governor, after which the column marched east to the base of the Wasatch mountains and set up Camp Douglas, the city below in range of its artillery.

The kingdom of the Saints was definitely in the public eye; anything at all about the Mormons was news. Travelers, authors, newspapermen, political figures, notoriety seekers—practically everyone who could wangle stagecoach fare, it seemed to Taylor, came to visit Zion. And just about all of them, apparently, turned out books about polygamy and the Mormon menace, even if their stay was only a day or so. Salt Lake was red hot copy. Sir Richard Burton, the famous explorer, adventurer, and author, was surprised to find Taylor affable and good company, despite his truculent reputation. In turn, Taylor was attracted by Burton's detached and tolerant view of Mormon polygamy. Burton had studied plural marriage first-hand in Africa and the Near East. He had stayed with a jungle tribe whose chief had 300 wives. He had visited Turkish harems, disguised as a doctor from India. In Utah, he gathered data on the Mormon practice with the urbanity of a scholar having vast background on the subject.

Taylor appreciated the opportunity, so rare in frontier Utah, of having an afternoon in company with a fellow Englishman with whom he had so much in common as author, scholar, and intellectual. There also was an unspoken bond: both were, in a sense, outcasts. Taylor had embraced an unpopular cult that had been banished to the desert. Burton had come to Utah under a cloud. His reputation was based on books that came from personal adventure requiring enormous courage in the face of appalling risks. Impersonating a pilgrim, he had penetrated the sacred cities of Mecca and Medina. He was the first European to explore the forbidden city of Harar in Somaliland, and he was the first to discover and identify Lake Tanganyika. His books, combining high adventure, intrepid daring, deep scholarship, and research into exotic subjects, were highly popular.

But then Burton's reputation became tarnished as a result of the

human laws; *but the judgment of the Almighty must be satisfied*, and then peace will follow."

Tanganyika expedition. He incorrectly designated the lake as the true source of the Nile, and subsequently was discredited by his companion, who had pushed on to find the source at Lake Victoria. Disgraced, Burton abruptly fled London for America and the city of the Saints, pouring his immense scholarship and talent for research into a book that would, he hoped, rehabilitate his name.

Burton's hurt was, Taylor felt, Zion's gain; he welcomed so qualified an observer of the local culture. He took Burton on a tour of the city, while answering perceptive and sometimes sharp questions. Burton recorded:

> I told him openly that there must have been some cause for the furious proceedings of the people in Illinois, Missouri, and other places against the Latter-day Saints; that even those who had extended hospitality to them ended by hating and expelling them, and accusing them of all possible iniquities, especially of horse-thieving, forgery, larceny, and offenses against property which on the borders are never pardoned—was this smoke quite without fire?
>
> He heard me courteously and in perfect temper replied that no one claimed immaculateness for the Mormons; that the net cast into the sea brought forth evil as well as good fish. . . . At the same time that when the New Faith was stoutly struggling into existence, it was the object of detraction, odium, persecution—so, said Mr. Taylor, were the Christians in the days of Nero—that the border ruffians, forgers, horse-thieves, and other vile fellows followed the Mormons wherever they went; and finally that every fraud and crime was charged upon those whom the populace were disposed by desire for confiscation's sake to believe guilty. . . . Mr. Taylor remarked that the Saints had been treated by the United States as the colonies had been treated by the Crown: that the persecuted naturally became persecutors, as the Pilgrim Fathers, after flying for their faith, hung the Quakers on Bloody Hill at Boston.

This was the first time Burton had heard this broad viewpoint. He appreciated Taylor's frankness and obtained from him a manuscript account of the martyrdom at Carthage whose "tone of candor, simplicity, and honesty, renders it highly attractive."[15]

When Burton's *The City of the Saints* appeared, Taylor was disappointed by the very sophistication and objectivity he had admired in the author's personality. The book held up a remarkably accurate mirror to Mormonism; and few like so unsparing a reflection. Tongue-in-cheek, Burton dryly reported the incessant Mormon claim to "obeying, honouring, and sustaining the law"—this from a people who had come west

---

[15] Burton published "The Martyrdom of Joseph Smith" in the appendix of his book, where it consisted of forty-eight large pages of fine print. This account subsequently was incorporated into the DHC, and has become the primary source material for all accounts of the event.

to get free of United States jurisdiction, and who treated the Fourth of July, Burton observed, with "silent contempt"; this at a time federal troops which had marched on Utah to quell the "Mormon rebellion" were still garrisoned there; this when federal judges were impotent to secure indictments for Utah murders; and this at the time Utah was being denied admittance to the Union because of being considered an absolute monarchy, with Congress concocting punitive legislation to control it.

Burton was virtually alone among Gentile authors in his understanding and sympathetic treatment of polygamy. He published the text of Joseph's revelation on the subject, and also the excellent Mormon defense of the Principle which followed the revelation in the *Doctrine and Covenants*.[16]

Regarding the busy bees of Deseret, he said, "The object of the young colony is to rear a swarm of healthy working bees," and added a penetrating observation of the culture: "The social hive has as yet no room for drones, bookworms, and gentlemen."

He tempered criticism, however, by admitting that there was in Mormonism, "as in all other exclusive faiths, whether Jewish, Hindu, or other, an inner life into which I cannot flatter myself or deceive the reader with the idea of my having penetrated."

Analyzing the scene, Burton said,

> I must here warn the reader that in Gt. S.L. City there are three distinct opinions concerning, three several reasons for, and three diametrically different accounts of everything that happens, viz: that of the Mormons, which is invariably one-sided; that of the Gentiles, which is sometimes fair and just; and that of the anti-Mormons, which is always prejudiced and violent.

Here, Taylor decided, the author put a prophetic finger on the reception of his book. Mormons rejected the mirror image as unflattering. The outside world was outraged by Burton's sympathetic view of an unpopular people, particularly his dispassionate justification of plural marriage. The book failed to find a large audience or redeem Burton's reputation.[17]

As the nation was torn by civil war, as pestilence, insurrection, fire, famine, slaughter, and earthquake ravaged the world, John Taylor viewed it all as fulfillment of prophecy "that God would speedily arise and shake

---

[16] While the revelation still survives in the D&C, the justification for the practice has been deleted from modern editions. As a result, today's missionaries go out completely ignorant of the pioneer concept.

[17] *The City of the Saints* at last has gained the recognition it deserved. When it was reissued in 1963, edited by Fawn Brodie, she called it "the best book on the Mormons published during the nineteenth century."

terribly the earth," as a prelude to the Kingdom of God which would precede the millennium.

When the Civil War ended with the nation intact, it was evident that the takeover would not come as quickly as anticipated. Taylor's faith remained so firm, however, that some in the audience became bored that he couldn't make a talk "without running on to the one string that they all harp on all the time till I get sick of it," as Frances P. Dyer complained to her father in a letter; "that is the *down fall* of the United States government and the building up of *Mormonism.*"[18]

But then a new threat to Zion loomed, growing greater day by day. As the transcontinental railroad crawled from the east and the west toward a meeting place in Utah, Taylor shared the growing tension among the Saints.

Satan wasn't through; not yet. This was the gravest menace to the LDS people since the beginning of the church. Isolation from the world was the great strength. The stronghold in the Great Basin was guarded on the east by the Rockies and a thousand miles of prairie, on the west by the Sierras and the desert. Only a handful of Gentiles could afford the expense and endure the rigors of a trip to Salt Lake by stage or wagon train. Brigham had forbidden mining, in order that there would be nothing to lure an influx of Gentiles.[19]

But at Camp Douglas the commander, now General Connor, had encouraged his troops to prospect the Utah mountains and canyons, with breath-taking results. Gold was discovered and silver and an entire mountain of copper.

There also was internal unrest. Within the Society of the Saints a "New Movement" was fermenting, intellectuals chafing under repressive controls, seeking human rights of thought, speech, and the press, calling for separation of church and state.

How like Nauvoo, Taylor thought, at the time the *Expositor* touched off the spark.

It was freely predicted by Gentiles, and openly feared by church officials, that when the railroad arrived a stampede of Gentiles would trample Mormonism into the dust.

---

[18] Quoted in Hansen, *Quest for Empire*, p. 168.

[19] According to legend, Porter Rockwell discovered a fabulous gold strike. On Brigham's counsel, he kept the secret to the grave

15

The Beam
and the Mote

STRAWBERRIES WERE RIPE. Early Saturday morning a carriage and a wagon filled with the family left Taylor Row and traveled south to the farm at Taylorsville to pick them.[1] Thus John Taylor was away when a telegram arrived from Schuyler Colfax that was to initiate a series of events of great importance to him and to Deseret.

At the farm, the older boys took charge of crate-making and hauling; the remainder of the family moved along the rows picking berries. Wives and older girls wore sunbonnets and had stockings over their arms to shield their complexions. Taylor himself worked hatless and without a shirt. Though a suntan was the badge of the laborer, generally avoided by gentlemen, he had no patience with the attitude that there was anything wrong with earning the daily bread by the sweat of the brow. He also believed in the healthful qualities of the sun's rays, and, truth to tell, was a bit vain about the striking contrast between his tanned face and his hair which, at fifty-seven, was snow white.

A white-top rig drawn by a span of bay geldings rattled down the lane at midmorning, and a man climbed out at the hitching rack who had the powerful build, ruggedly handsome face, curly gray hair, and neatly trimmed beard reminiscent of a younger John Taylor. This was T. B. H. Stenhouse, associate on *The Mormon* in New York nine years previously. Subsequently, Stenhouse had worked on eastern newspapers before com-

---

[1] Taylorsville is now in Murray, at 4800 South.

223

ing west to join the staff of the *Deseret News*. Just a year ago he had started his own paper, the *Daily Telegraph*.

Taylor considered Stenhouse the foremost literary talent of Zion and was happy to have given him a start in the field. He was a capable and brilliant man who would go far in the church, if he didn't talk too much. Since arriving in the valley Stenhouse had magnified his calling by taking a second wife, Belinda Pratt, Parley's daughter, and had become engaged to one of Brigham's daughters, Zina. He also had passed the most severe test of plurality by giving his own daughter, Clara, in the Principle, as a wife of Brigham's son, Joseph A. Young. With such connections, his future would seem secure, except that Stenhouse was known to be outspoken and to associate with intellectuals, free thinkers, and Gentiles.

Stenhouse frequently went east on business for his paper, and upon returning to the *Telegraph* would display a liberal attitude that sometimes brought a rebuke from Brigham. His first wife, Fanny, had been warned that "Brother Stenhouse is doing himself no good by his constant association with the Gentiles." As a result, his engagement to Zina was endangered, and his attitude toward Brigham was stiffening. Taylor had heard dark whispers that Stenhouse was on the road to apostasy.[2]

But the very independence that made Stenhouse something of a maverick endeared him to Taylor, who shared many of his concepts. In return, Stenhouse held him in great respect.[3]

Stenhouse had driven to Taylorsville with news that Schuyler Colfax, speaker of the House, with a party of distinguished men of the press, were at Fort Bridger and would arrive tomorrow morning on the Overland stage. Stenhouse, a member of the welcoming committee, went over plans for rolling out the red carpet during the week's visit.

Taylor looked forward to meeting Colfax, both as an individual and because of his congressional labors on behalf of the Saints. Though sometimes derisively called "Smiler" Colfax, because of his attitude of righteousness, Taylor respected him as deeply religious and a life-long temperance worker. As speaker of the House, he had done more than anyone in Washington to bridge the isolation of the Saints from the outside world. Despite charges that it was wild extravagance and the road to ruin, he had as chairman of the post office committee sponsored legislation to appropriate $1-million-a-year for a daily mail service across the continent. He then secured an appropriation for a telegraph line, the wires having reached Salt Lake three years ago.

Of most benefit of all was his work for a transcontinental railroad, which the Mormons had ardently desired—before realizing its possible

---

[2] Fanny Stenhouse, *Tell it All*.

[3] Fanny, however, harbored petty resentments, which mar her *Tell it All*, in contrast to her husband's well-documented *Rocky Mountain Saints*.

consequences. The Saints had held a giant mass meeting at the bowery to petition Congress for the railroad; nothing was done about it for eight years until Colfax got behind the project. Now, in the spring of 1865, rails were pushing across the eastern prairies and through the western mountains, with the junction in Zion expected only three years hence.

The following morning a military band and a detachment of cavalry met the Overland stage as it entered the valley and escorted it to Camp Douglas. Schuyler Colfax was accompanied by William Bross, Lieutenant Governor of Illinois and editor of the Chicago *Tribune*; Samuel Bowles, editor of the Springfield (Mass.) *Republican*; and Albert D. Richardson, correspondent for the New York *Tribune*. After paying respects to General Connor, the party went into the city to be welcomed again by the Mormon delegation, and escorted to quarters at the Salt Lake House.

During the week of their stay the visitors attended a performance of the newly-completed Salt Lake Theater, bathed in the brine of the Great Salt Lake, ate strawberries and cream, made and listened to speeches of platitudes and praise. However, it wasn't until Taylor entertained the party at Leonora's residence on Taylor Row that he learned the true feelings of these observers of the Mormon culture.

Taylor had known Albert D. Richardson of the *Tribune* while in New York; and, on visiting New England to court Margaret Young he had become acquainted with Samuel Bowles of the Springfield *Republican*. He also had met Colfax on visiting Washington. Perhaps this was a factor when, after dinner, surface politeness gave way to true feelings on Taylor's urging to be frank.

Bowles said the result of the visit was to increase his appreciation of the Mormons' material progress; to evoke congratulations for their order, frugality, morality, and industry; to excite wonder at the perfection of the church system and enlarge respect for the personal sincerity of its leaders. However, he said frankly, it served on the other hand "to deepen my disgust at their polygamy and strengthen my convictions of its barbaric and degrading influences."

Bowles paused, drawing at his cigar. With a nod Taylor urged him to continue.

The Mormons had fled from New York, Ohio, Missouri, and Illinois, Bowles said. "Nothing can save Mormonism but a new flight and a more complete isolation. The click of the telegraph and the roll of the Overland stage are its death rattle now. The first whistle of the locomotive will sound its requiem; and the pickaxe of the miner will dig its grave."[4]

---

[4] Samuel Bowles, *Across the Continent*. That this reflected the Washington attitude is indicated by the dedication to Colfax, where the author says, "The book is more yours than mine."

The ice broken, Richardson was equally candid. The correspondent for the New York *Tribune* declared that it was "an anomaly of our civilization, that a church more rigid than that of Rome, with a domestic system utterly defying the laws of all enlightened nations in modern times, should exist in the center of our continent, openly nullifying the statutes and authority of the national government." But the problem, he declared, would soon be solved by natural laws. "Polygamy cannot exist without isolation."

Thus far, "Brigham has kept his followers from working the rich mines of silver and gold which the mountains contain. This sagacious policy has preserved his power. But within three years Utah will contain a large mining population, composed exclusively of men." The miners, he declared, would solve polygamy by taking plural wives away from the Saints.

As the iron horse ushered in a new era, "Perchance the splendid Mormon temple now rising may yet be the depot of the great Pacific railroad," Richardson suggested. "Brought in contact with our national civilization, the power of Brigham and his associates will cease forever; and the one repulsive and monstrous feature of their domestic life no longer stain a community whose history contains much to challenge respect and admiration."[5]

The prospect of Mormonism being trampled into the dust by miners' boots caused a growing apprehension that approached panic as the railroad neared Zion. Hysteria gripped the Saints, reminiscent of the Reformation of a decade previously.

From the beginning, there had been conflict between storekeepers and the church. Brigham frowned upon trade; it took a brave Mormon to open a store.[6] When rags were needed to make paper for the *Deseret News*, Brigham summoned a prominent merchant, George Goddard, and informed this startled businessman that the Lord had called him to the "Rag Mission." It would be a calling of three years, during which Goddard would go forth, not with tracts and the word of God but with a bell in one hand and a sack in the other, collecting rags from door to door.[7]

With "states goods" 1,200 miles away by ox team, and freight rates $500 a ton, Gentile merchants could, and sometimes did, charge what

---

[5] Albert D. Richardson, *Beyond the Mississippi.*

[6] "To become a merchant was to antagonize the church and her policies," says Tullidge in his *History of Salt Lake City*; "so that it was almost illegitimate for Mormon men of enterprising character to enter into mercantile pursuits."

[7] Wendell J. Ashton, *Voice in the West.*

the traffic would bear. When sugar sold for $1 a pound, calico for 75¢ a yard, and flour $75 a hundred, Mormons became hostile.

Taylor and other prominent residents sent agents east each spring to purchase a year's supply of states goods and ship them with convert companies; but this was only for those who could afford to buy in quantity.

Mining was another source of conflict with the Gentiles. The discovery by Connor's troops of a fabulous lode of copper at Bingham canyon, 25 miles southwest of Salt Lake, was hailed as a means of solving the "Mormon problem" by inviting a flood of Gentile miners into Zion.[8] Connor himself realized that with commerce largely in Gentile hands, the addition of mining would give outsiders a virtual corner on territorial wealth.

In the first issue of the Camp Douglas newspaper, the *Union Vedette*, obviously founded for the purpose of hastening the Mormon downfall, Connor issued an order declaring "it imperative that the prospecting for minerals should not only be untrammeled and unrestricted, but fostered by every proper means." He promised military protection for prospectors and encouraged his enlisted personnel to join in.

Thus encouraged, troops made strikes in the Tooele valley to the west and laid out Stockton—the first Gentile community in Utah Territory. Connor himself found the first silver ore in Little Cottonwood canyon, adjacent to Salt Lake. Two years later, in 1866, when the Regular Army replaced the California Volunteers at Camp Douglas, Connor's mining interests were so important he resigned his commission and remained in Utah as a private citizen.

The Mormon–Gentile tension came to a head with the murder of Dr. King Robinson, former assistant surgeon at Camp Douglas who had married an apostate Mormon girl. Both were active in the Congregational flock of the Rev. Norman McLeod, who was delivering a series of anti-Mormon lectures at Independence Hall. Robinson had tried to claim-jump the city-owned hot springs on a technicality which, he asserted, put the property in the public domain. In trying to reason with him, Taylor found Robinson obdurate. When ousted by city police, he went to court, and when he lost the case loudly proclaimed his intention of securing justice.

Three nights after the court suit, Dr. Robinson responded to a professional call in the middle of the night. It was a trap. He was waylaid, bludgeoned, and shot. A half-dozen men were seen running from the scene, but nobody was identified and there were no arrests.

---

[8] Robert Joseph Dwyer, *The Gentile Comes to Utah*. The strike at Bingham was an event "of the greatest importance in the subsequent course of affairs in Utah, bearing directly upon the relations between the Mormons and the Gentiles."

Gentiles loudly proclaimed that the murder was by direct command of ecclesiastical power. Mormon reaction was a renewal of sermons preaching nonintercourse with Gentiles. Taylor exhorted the Saints to keep separate and unspotted from the "world."

> We do not look upon things as they exist in the world as being correct, . . . whether relating to morals, politics, religion, philosophy, or anything else. . . . When men come among us we should be very sorry indeed if they found us like the world; we are not like them, neither do we wish to be. . . .[9]

Brigham's reaction to the crisis was drastic: He called for a boycott of all Gentile businesses, urging the Saints not to trade with "the enemies of our church who would seek to destroy us."

The boycott could spell ruin to the Gentile merchants of Main Street (commonly called "Whiskey Row"), who drew up a letter to church authorities offering to sell out and leave the Territory, upon two conditions:

> First—The payment of our outstanding accounts owing by members of your church.
> Secondly—All of our goods, merchandise, chattels, houses, improvements, &c, to be taken at a cash valuation, and we to make a deduction of 25% from total amount.

In reply, Brigham wrote next day:

> I have to say that we will not obligate ourselves to collect your outstanding debts, nor buy your goods. . . . If you could make such sales as you propose, you would make more money than any merchants have ever done in this country, and we, as merchants, would like to find purchasers upon the same basis. Your withdrawal from the Territory is not a matter about which we feel any anxiety; so far as we are concerned you are at liberty to stay or go as you please.

The approach of the railroad furnished the final impetus to the conflict. With railroad transportation, mining would dominate the economy; and Gentiles owned the mines. Brigham, with isolation gone, would find his people in the same relationship with their neighbors that had caused previous expulsion from Ohio, Missouri, and Illinois. But this time there was nowhere left to flee. Mormonism was finished.

"There is growing up in our midst a power that menaces us with utter destruction," declared George Q. Cannon of the first presidency at October conference, 1868. "We are told openly and without disguise that when the railroad is completed there will be such a flood of so-called 'civilization' brought in here that every vestige of us, our church and institutions, shall be completely obliterated."

---

[9] JD, 11:339.

The apprehensive assembly voted to boycott all Gentile businesses, following Brigham's counsel not to trade "another cent" with anyone "who does not pay his tithing."

Following conference, Brigham initiated an active campaign to prepare the people for a cooperative system of Mormon merchandizing. The *Deseret News* published a series of articles, while Taylor and others went out to hold meetings in the wards and stakes. The way had been previously shown by cooperatives in smaller towns, notably the Brigham City Mercantile and Manufacturing Association, which had thrived the past four years under direction of Lorenzo Snow.

As Taylor explained the plan, all merchandizing would be combined under one church-controlled organization. A wholesale house at Salt Lake would supply branches in various parts of Utah, and each settlement would have its own cooperative retail store. The people themselves would own the stores, thereby benefiting from dividends as well as lower prices.

A similar plan was working well among Mormon farmers in southern Utah who supplied outlying mining towns. Men of Cedar City who hauled grain, eggs, and dairy products to Nevada mining towns had been offered appallingly low prices by local merchants—take it or leave it. If the farmer tried to peddle his load door to door, he might be set upon by hoodlums or collared by the local constabulary. If he got rid of his load he might never get home with the money, for holdup men could be waiting at the first bend of the road out of town.

Of necessity, Mormon farmers came together in cooperative marketing. They appointed an agent who handled transactions for the entire produce of the area. Nevada merchants had to send a man to Cedar City to parley with the agent, place orders, and pay in advance, after which Mormon freighters made delivery.

Ten days after the sustaining vote in conference, all Mormon merchants in Salt Lake City were merged into one company, Zion's Cooperative Mercantile Institution (ZCMI), Brigham Young president, other officers selected either because of church office or standing as merchants. Stock in ZCMI was available only to Saints of good character who "have paid their tithing."[10]

Some of the Mormon merchants "invited" to join ZCMI emphatically didn't like it. When one protested that he was in debt, and to join would bankrupt him, Brigham retorted that it served him right; Mormons were supposed to avoid debt. Several merchants didn't relish the prospect of giving up businesses which they'd built through years of hard work, in return for being merely department managers of ZCMI. But they had small choice. When plans for ZCMI were being formulated, Brigham

---

[10] Not until a century later did Mormons realize that ZCMI was actually the first department store in America.

was asked, "What do you think the merchants will do in this matter? Will they fall in with this cooperative idea?"

"I don't know," Brigham said, "but if they don't we shall leave them out in the cold, the same as the Gentiles, and the goods will rot upon their shelves."

To make certain of this, he appointed spies to watch for and report unauthorized trading with anyone except ZCMI.

ZCMI was incorporated just two months before the railroad joined the east and west in Utah in May 1869. The iron horse did not destroy Mormonism, nor did Gentile merchants have their goods rot upon the shelves. Hardheaded shoppers traded where the price was best, and ZCMI was saddled with the built-in inefficiency of church management.

However, the attempted Gentile boycott rallied the opposition into a united front. Now it was Mormon against Gentile, a war to the finish for control of Utah.

Christmas, 1868, was a subdued occasion for the Taylor family. Leonora had died of pneumonia just two weeks previously. She was his first love, in those days of ecstasy when they found both each other and the true faith; and somehow to him the gospel was inseparable from her. As first wife she had undergone the travail of accepting a second. "The Lord often led me by a way that I knew not, and in a path that I naturally did not wish to go," she wrote in her journal. "Every sweet has had its bitter. The way seemed to me narrower every day. Without His almighty power to help me I cannot walk in it. To whom shall I go or look for succor, but unto Thee, my Father and only friend."

Faith had sustained her. She had become matriarch of the family clan, her word final in matters between the wives. And though Taylor had loved and married others, none could ever occupy Leonora's special place, either in the patriarchal order of the family or in his heart.

She had endured much, but the rewards would be great: she would be queen of her own world in the celestial kingdom, when he joined her in eternity; and their family would be as numberless as the sands of the seashore.

Leonora's death meant that Elizabeth Kaighin now became the "official" wife. However, when a Gentile friend suggested to Taylor that it would be wise to avoid possible trouble by going through a civil marriage ceremony with Elizabeth to make things "legal," Taylor regarded him with incredulity. To marry Elizabeth again, after living with her twenty-five years, would infer that something was wrong with the original ceremony.

Taylor was away from Utah at the time Schuyler Colfax paid a second visit. Conditions in Zion were such that the Champion of Rights had acutely mixed feelings, and he was glad to get away from things, if only temporarily on a business trip. A revolt within the Society against Brigham's oppressive one-man rule had put Taylor on the horns of a dilemma. He couldn't, of course, support any attack on church leadership, for the very worst sin in his book was disloyalty. However, the bill of particulars of what was called the "New Movement" coincided with his deepest convictions.

William S. Godbe and Elias L. T. Harrison, both prominent Saints, had started the *Utah Magazine* as a literary journal of protest. Around them rallied some of the most progressive and brilliant men of Utah, including Eli B. Kelsey, Edward W. Tullidge, Henry W. Lawrence, and T. B. H. Stenhouse. All were solid citizens: Godbe, a wealthy druggist; Harrison, a prominent architect; Kelsey, active in civic affairs; Lawrence, a founding director of ZCMI; Stenhouse and Tullidge, newspapermen and authors.

This group realized that the Mormon boycott would stimulate Gentile solidarity in retaliation. It felt that the formation of ZCMI, the railroad contracts, building projects and multitudinous other business activities under Brigham's leadership constituted a dangerous example of one-man power, and was evidence that the church was selling out to mammon. The New Movement advocated a free press, free trade, free speech, and the free vote with secret ballot. It called for the church to return to government by the first presidency and council of the Twelve, in place of the current one-man rule; that it should divorce itself from politics and all temporal matters, devoting all its attention to spiritual affairs.[11]

Though most respectfully submitted, the Godbeite reform movement was a challenge to the existing order. Soon, five thousand Saints had rallied behind it. When the magazine published an article on "The True Development of the Territory," urging the Saints to engage in mining despite the official ban, Brigham called the editor, Harrison, on a mission to get him out of the way. When Harrison refused to go, he, with Godbe and the leadership of the New Movement were cut off from the church.

This attempt to crush criticism was no more successful than had been the destruction of the *Expositor* at Nauvoo a quarter century previously. The Godbeites started a newspaper, the *Mormon Tribune*. Its policy

---

[11] "These men saw the future of Utah in terms of a more tolerant relationship between Mormons and Gentiles," Nels Anderson says in his *Desert Saints*; "but they were ahead of their time."

Subsequently, many of the policies of the New Movement were adopted by the church.

It is curious to compare the platform of the *Utah Magazine* with that of the previous publication of protest, the Nauvoo *Expositor*. Except for the subject of plural marriage, the objectives are remarkably parallel.

hardened, and it came under Gentile control as the Salt Lake *Tribune*, strongly anti-Mormon, and became without doubt the greatest single enemy of the church. The *Trib* was a most potent force in blocking statehood for Utah and in bringing the church to the brink of destruction over the issue of polygamy.

At the height of the Godbeite brouhaha Schuyler Colfax, now the nation's vice president, visited Salt Lake again. Members of the New Movement had his ear. Gen. U. S. Grant was president, and Colfax believed that the man who had crushed the Confederacy should now settle the Mormon question "once and for all with the sword." However, Stenhouse met with the vice president at the Townsend House and strongly urged him to let the Mormons handle their own problems. "For God's sake, Mr. Colfax, keep the United States off," he implored. "If the government interferes and sends troops, you will drive the thousands back into the arms of Brigham Young who are ready to rebel against the one-man power."[12]

Taylor was in Boston, in company with Bishop John Sharp and Brigham's son, Joseph A. Young, to settle claims of Utah sub-contractors with the Union Pacific railroad. After a long and exhausting day of negotiation, he returned to the American House looking forward to a good supper, a hot bath, and a sound night's sleep. At the hotel desk the clerk handed him a copy of the Springfield *Republican*, left for him by a local missionary. It contained the speech of Schuyler Colfax on the Mormon question, delivered on the portico of the Townsend House in Salt Lake, October 5, 1869. Taylor scanned it in the dining room. By the time the waiter brought the meal the three men at the table were in furious discussion, while Taylor jotted notes on the margins of the menu. Taylor hardly touched his supper. After ordering a strong pot of tea sent to his room he left the table and hurried upstairs.

Samuel Bowles, editor of the *Republican*, again was with Colfax on this visit to Utah, and his paper carried the vice president's speech in full. After praising the beauty of the city, the progressive industry of the people, the New Tabernacle ("The largest building in which religious services are held on the continent"), and its organ, Colfax swung into an attack on the very heart of the Mormon Society.

> You have as much right to worship the Creator through . . . your church organization as I have through the ministers and elders and creed of mine. But our country is governed by law, and no assumed revelation justifies any one in trampling on the law.

It was *not* a question of religion, but of law, Colfax told the glowering audience assembled in the street before the Townsend House. "The law

---

12 Whitney, *History of Utah*, 2:334.

which you denounce only reenacts the original prohibition of your Book of Mormon . . . and your book of *Doctrine and Covenants*; and these are the inspired words, as you claim them, on which your church was organized."[13]

After accusing Brigham of denouncing Colfax and President Grant as gamblers and drunkards, the vice president delivered some hard criticism of his own:

> When our party visited you four years ago, we all believed that, under wise counsels, your city might become the great city of the interior. But you must allow me to say you do not seem to have improved these opportunities as you might have done. . . . You should encourage and not discourage competition in trade. You should welcome, and not repel, investments from abroad. You should discourage every effort to drive capital from your midst. You should rejoice at the opening of every new store, or factory, or machine shop, by whomsoever conducted. You should seek to widen the area of country dependent on your city for supplies. You should realize that wealth will come to you only by development, by unfettered competition, by increased capital.
>
> Here I must close. I have spoken to you, face to face, frankly, truthfully, fearlessly. I have said nothing but for your own good.

In his room, working by gaslight far into the night, Taylor covered page upon page of American House stationery with furious rebuttal.

> That our country is governed by law all admit; but when it is said that "no assumed revelation justifies any one in trampling on the law," I should respectfully ask: "What? Not if it interferes with my religious faith, which you state, 'is a matter between God and myself alone?'" Allow me, sir, here to state that the assumed revelation referred to is one of the most vital parts of our religious faith; it emanated from God and cannot be legislated away. It is part of the "Everlasting Covenant" which God has given to man. . . . With us it is "Celestial Marriage." Take this from us and you rob us of our hopes and associations in the resurrection of the just.
>
> This is not religion? You do not see things as we do. . . .

"Are we to understand that Mr. Colfax is created an umpire to decide upon what is religion and what is not?" Taylor wrote, his pen sputtering in fury. "If so, by whom and what authority is he created judge?"

Taylor pointed out that all religious oppression was rationalized.

> Loyola did not invent and put into use the faggot, the flame, the sword, the thumbscrews, the rack and gibbet to persecute anybody; it was to purify the church of heretics, as others would purify Utah. His

---

[13] The Book of Mormon denounces Old Testament prophets for having "many wives and concubines, which thing was abominable before me, saith the Lord." Section 101, D&C, denounced polygamy; but as previously noted it was deleted from the D&C.

zeal was for the Holy Mother Church. The Nonconformists of England and Holland, the Huguenots of France and the Scottish non-Covenanters, were not persecuted or put to death for their religion; it was for being schismatics, turbulents, and unbelievers. . . . All of the persecutors, as Mr. Colfax said about us, did "not concede that the institution they had established, which was condemned by the law, was religion."

The revelation on polygamy was recorded in 1843, Taylor stated,[14] and the Principle was practiced for nineteen years after that before the law of 1862 made it illegal. The law of 1862, "in its inception, progress, and passage, was intended to bring us into collision with the United States, that a pretext might be found for our ruin."

But we are graciously told that we have our appeal [to the Supreme Court]. True, we have an appeal. So had the Hebrew mothers to Pharaoh; so had Daniel to Nebuchadnezzar; so had Jesus to Herod; so had Caesar to Brutus; so had those sufferers on the rack to Loyola; so had the Waldenses and the Albigenses to the Pope; so had the Quakers and Baptists of New England to the Puritans. . . .

But these things were done in barbarous ages. . . . We are told that we are living in a more enlightened age. Our morals are more pure, our ideas more refined and enlarged, our institutions more liberal.

"Ours," says Mr. Colfax, "is a land of civil and religious liberty, and the faith of every man is a matter between himself and God alone,"— providing God doesn't shock our moral ideas by introducing something we don't believe in. If he does, let him look out.

Taylor now turned from defense to attack. "Let me respectfully ask in all sincerity," he said,

is there not plenty of scope for the action of government at home? . . . What of your gambling hells? What of your gold rings, your whiskey rings, your railroad rings, manipulated through the lobby into your con-gressional rings? What of that great moral curse of the land, that great institution of monogamy—*Prostitution*? What of its twin sister—*Infanti-cide*? . . . What of the thirty thousand prostitutes of New York City and the proportionate numbers of other cities, towns, and villages, and their multitudinous pimps and paramours. . . . Would it not be well to cleanse your own Augean stables? . . .

We can teach you a lesson on this matter, polygamists as we are. You acknowledge one wife and her children; what of your other associations unacknowledged? We acknowledge and maintain all of our wives and all of our children; we don't keep a few only, and turn the others out as outcasts. . . . We have no gambling hells, no drunkenness, no infanticide, no houses of assignation, no prostitutes. . . . We believe in the chastity

---

14 An earlier revelation, known only to a select few, came twelve years previously, in 1831. It has never been published by the church.

and virtue of women, and maintain them. There is not, today, in the wide world, a place where female honor, virtue, and chastity are so well protected as in Utah. Would you have us . . . exchange the sobriety, the chastity, the virtue, and honor of our institutions for yours? . . . We have fled from these things, and with great trouble and care have purged ourselves from your evils. Do not try to legislate them upon us nor seek to engulf us in your damning vices.

You may say, "It is not against your purity that we contend, but against polygamy, which we consider a crying evil." Be it so. Why, then, if your system is so much better, does it not bring forth better fruits? . . . Is it too much to say, "Take the beam out of thine own eye and then shalt thou see clearly to remove the mote that is in thy brother's?"

When Taylor left his room next morning he'd had no sleep; but he carried two fat envelopes, one addressed to the New York *Tribune*, the other a copy for the *Deseret News*. He mailed the letters in the lobby, then went in to join Bishop Sharp and Joseph Young for a hearty breakfast. Though his eyes were bloodshot and his hands quivered from the fury of his retort, he never felt better.

On returning to Utah he found himself the lion of the valley. Congratulations showered from all sides. Never, he was told, had the Mormon case been so masterfully presented.

National publicity of Taylor's reply stung Colfax to make rejoinder in the New York *Independent*, December 2. In this, the vice president's grasp of Mormon history and culture was so comprehensive that Taylor was sure he'd had help, no doubt from the Godbeites. Taylor believed that Tullidge had furnished the material, or perhaps had written the Colfax article. From that time, any feeling of sympathy for the recusants vanished. It was one thing to advocate reform within the Society, but unforgivable to join the enemy against their own people.

"I propose in this article to examine, in the light of history, some phases of the Mormon question," wrote Colfax (or his ghost writer), "treating of those especially which are the favorite themes of the Mormon leaders."[15]

I. Their Fertilizing the Desert.

For this they claim great credit. . . . But the solution of it all is in one word—WATER. What seemed to the eye a desert became fruitful when irrigated; and the mountains whose crests are clothed in perpetual snow,

---

[15] Taylor was unfriendly with Tullidge from that time on, though the two were fellow authors with strikingly similar views on many things. Tullidge left Utah the following year when his play, *Oliver Cromwell*, was produced in New York. While in the east he joined the Josephites. He returned to Utah five years later to pursue an active career as author and magazine publisher. Though known as the "rebel historian," his work is today held in high esteem by scholars.

furnished, in the unfailing supplies of their ravines, the necessary fertilizer. . . .

II. Their Persecutions

This is also one of their favorite themes. . . . They have been driven from place to place, they claim, solely on account of their religious belief.

However, Colfax said, at Kirtland financial manipulation was the root cause, not persecution.

A bank was established there by them; large quantities of bills of doubtful value issued; . . . the bank failed; and, to avoid arrest for fraud, the leaders fled in the night for Missouri. Their followers joined them there, and were soon accused by the people of "plundering and burning habitations, and of secret assassinations."

Regarding Danite activities in Missouri, Colfax quoted the damaging affidavit of Thomas B. Marsh, president of the Twelve, corroborated by fellow apostle Orson Hyde, and also the report of Governor Boggs, who said:

These people had violated the laws of the land, by open and armed resistance to them; they had instituted among themselves a government of their own, independent of, and in opposition to, the government of this state; they had, at an inclement season of the year, driven the inhabitants of an entire county from their homes, ravaged their crops, and destroyed their dwellings.

Colfax commented: "There is nothing as to their religion here."

At Nauvoo, Colfax said, destruction of the *Expositor* caused the death of Joseph and Hyrum Smith.

It *was* murder, and nothing else. . . . But the origin of this tragedy can be traced *directly* to the illegal mobbing of a free press for daring to publicly denounce Mormonism and its practices.

The Utah War was caused because the "civil officers of the territory . . . were harassed and threatened," he claimed.

In February 1856, a mob of Mormons, instigated by sermons from the heads of the church, broke into the United States Courtroom, and at the point of the bowie knife compelled Judge Drummond to adjourn his court *sine die*; and very soon all of the United States officers, except the Indian agent, were compelled to flee from the Territory.

As a result, President Buchanan sent the army to protect the new officials "and compel obedience to the law."

Under the third heading, "Their Polygamy," Colfax recited the familiar charges of abuse, excess and scandalous unions that had titilated Gentile readers of sensational literature ever since John C. Bennett's *History of the Saints* pioneered this field. Colfax also emphasized the fact that although the Mormons based their defiance of law on the "assumed revelation of 1843 ... in 1845, *two years after this pretended revelation,*" the church formally denounced polygamy in the *Doctrine and Covenants.*

IV. Is Utah Within the United States?

The Mormons claim the benefit of every law they see fit to approve—homestead, naturalization, protection of property by courts and government, &c—and trample under foot such other laws of the government under whose flag is their home, as they see fit to reject. It is time to understand whether the authority of the nation or the authority of Brigham Young is the supreme power in Utah. ....

In reply to this broadside, Taylor refuted the issues point by point. First of all, he declared flatly that no one ever was cast from the church "for disbelieving in the infallibility of President Young. I do not believe he is infallible, for one; and have taught so publicly. I am in the church yet."

Regarding the charge that water, not the Saints, transformed the desert, Taylor waxed sarcastic about "this wonderful little water nymph," who did it all "with a wave of her magic wand and the mysterious words, 'hickory, dickory, dock.'"

> But to be serious, did water tunnel through our mountains, construct dams, canals, and ditches, lay out our cities and towns, import and plant choice fruit-trees, shrubs, and flowers, cultivate the land and cover it with the cattle on a thousand hills, erect churches, schoolhouses, and factories, and transform a howling wilderness into a fruitful field and garden?

As to repeated claims of persecution, he declared they were "all true; does it falsify a truth to repeat it?"

Concerning Danite activities in Missouri, he simply followed church policy of blanket denial, as had previously been required with polygamy. "It is not true that these things existed, for I was there and knew to the contrary."

> I cannot defend the acts of Thomas B. Marsh or Orson Hyde ... no more than I could defend the acts of Peter when he cursed and swore and denied Jesus; ... but if Peter, after going out and "weeping bitterly," was restored, and was afterwards chief apostle; so did Orson Hyde repent sincerely and weep bitterly, and was restored. .... Thomas B. Marsh returned a poor broken-down man, and begged to live with us; he got up before assembled thousands and stated: "If you wish to see the effects of apostasy, look at me."

The polygamy charge "is simply a rehash of his former arguments," Taylor said. Refuting the final point, regarding lawlessness in Utah, he painted a vivid picture of the crime and immorality tolerated in the nation, then concluded:

> We have now a territory out of debt; . . . we have no gambling, no drunkenness, no prostitution, foeticide nor infanticide. We maintain our wives and children, and we have made the "desert to bloom as the rose."
>
> We are here at peace with ourselves, and with all the world. Whom have we injured? Why can we not be let alone?[16]

---

[16] Taylor's defense of Deseret was thought of so highly in Zion that 2,000 copies of the debate were issued for distribution in Washington and, by missionaries, throughout the world. Roberts says, "Taking it all in all, this is doubtless the most important discussion in the history of the church."

16

"A System is on Trial"

TAYLOR BELIEVED it wasn't merely coincidental that the harshly punitive Cullom bill was introduced in Congress following his keel-hauling of Vice President Colfax. This act would imprison all polygamists, confiscate their property, and take away their wives and children, leaving them destitute. The people of Utah would have no voice in their internal affairs: territorial courts and law enforcement would be under federal control; and inasmuch as all who *believed in* plural marriage, whether they practiced it or not, would be disenfranchised, Mormons would be compelled to deny an essential of the faith in order to vote. And 40,000 U.S. troops would arrive in Utah to enforce the law.

The primary duty of the vice president is to act as presiding officer of the Senate, and Taylor wasn't surprised when the chaplain of that august body took up the cudgels against plural marriage. On Sunday morning, April 24, 1870, the Rev. Dr. J. P. Newman attacked this surviving relic of barbarism from his pulpit at the Metropolitan Methodist Church in Washington, declaring it an abomination in the sight of the Lord and prohibited by the Bible. Nor was it mere happenstance, Taylor knew, that the president of the United States was in the congregation. Gen. U. S. Grant, already bristling about the Mormon question, left the church steaming.[1]

The sermon gained wide newspaper coverage, and Orson Pratt kept the pot boiling by refuting Dr. Newman in a long letter to the New

[1] In the CHC, Roberts says pressure was applied by the Colfax coterie in Washington and the Salt Lake "ring," the latter being "local anti-Mormon agitators who hoped to profit by the conflict they sought to create," primarily composed of lawyers, political adventurers, merchants, and government contractors.

York *Herald*. Taylor enjoyed the exchange as, for months, the two buffeted each other in the press, for when it came to Old Testament sanction of plural wives and concubines, Orson made something of a fool out of the outraged chaplain. But Dr. Newman kept flailing, and in early August accepted the invitation of T. B. H. Stenhouse's Salt Lake *Telegraph* to come to Utah and settle the issue in public debate.

When the train bearing Dr. Newman arrived at Salt Lake, Taylor was at hand, together with his friend on the police force, Sam Bateman, not to welcome the gentleman of the cloth—Gentiles were there in force for this purpose—but to observe and by their presence make sure no untoward incident occurred. Tempers were short and feelings high about a most emotional subject.

In particular, Taylor noted two men among the Mormon-eaters greeting Dr. Newman. R. N. Baskin, a lanky, red-headed young lawyer with an explosive temper, had sworn vengeance against the Saints when his friend and client, Dr. King Robinson, had been murdered. Baskin had personally helped draft the Cullom bill at his Salt Lake office.[2] Hardly less zealous was a tall and massive man, U.S. Deputy Marshal Samuel Gilson, whose implacable ambition was to get the deadwood on Brigham Young, and hang him.

Taylor exchanged a glance with Bateman as the party went to a waiting carriage. Nice company.

The Rev. Dr. J. P. Newman notified Brigham by letter that he was ready for a confrontation. However, the self-taught prophet had no intention of crossing swords with a Biblical scholar. After reminding Newman that the *Telegraph* was not an official church publication, Brigham said that either John Taylor or Orson Pratt stood ready to defend the faith. Newman picked Pratt as the easier adversary. Taylor would have liked the chance to demolish the preacher; however, he knew Orson could do the job.[3] Newman and Pratt agreed to a three-night debate in the tabernacle.

The great hall with its domed roof was packed as Taylor opened the first meeting with prayer. Then he sat back and enjoyed the program as Orson, his bushy beard bristling, cut Dr. Newman's arguments to ribbons. The cleric's repugnance for polygamy evidently had warped his literary

---

2 See his *Reminiscences of Early Utah*. Baskin subsequently became chief justice of the Utah Supreme Court, and mayor of Salt Lake City.

3 Newman was advised: "If he meets Orson Pratt, he will debate a learned man who knows the Bible well, who is familiar with Greek and Latin, and a man who will stick closely to the Bible text. On the other hand, John Taylor wouldn't leave a grease spot left." ("Reminiscences of Prest John Taylor," a talk by Matthias F. Cowley, October 4, 1925.)

judgment. While he sincerely believed polygamy an abomination, there was no way of proving this thesis in the Bible, whose ancient prophets had wives and concubines. The very basis for the Mormon practice was restoration of the primitive church.

After three days of humiliation before a highly appreciative audience, the learned Rev. Dr. J. P. Newman slipped out of Salt Lake with much less fanfare than when he had entered.[4]

Meanwhile the Cullom bill had passed the House. Taylor helped draft an official protest, and at a great mass meeting advocated resistance to the last ditch. If Grant sent troops, he declared, the Saints would leave the United States, scorching the earth behind them.[5] Godbeites and even prominent Gentiles joined in advocating amendments to the harshly punitive bill.

With Brigham away, easing his encroaching rheumatism under the hot sun at St. George, a committee including Godbe and Stenhouse held audience with John Taylor and George Q. Cannon, asking if they would pledge the church to abide by the law if objectional aspects of the Cullom bill were deleted. Taylor and Cannon would make no compromise with the law of God; however, they urged Godbe to go to Washington to present the Mormon viewpoint to Congressman Cullom and President Grant, and, if possible, secure amendments.

While Elizabeth Kaighin was the senior wife, Taylor spent a good deal of his time at the home of his youngest, Margaret Young. He had his library and study at Maggie's home and liked to talk out his thoughts with her.[6]

Reading the reaction of the eastern press, reprinted in the *Deseret News*, Taylor was delighted that the threat to crush a small sect by military might brought an upsurge of public sympathy, as had been the case during the Utah War more than a decade previously. "The Omaha *Herald* says, 'If the Cullom bill shall become a law it will produce war and bloodshed,' " Taylor commented to Maggie at the dinner table. The New York *Herald* denounced the "cruel and tyrannous" objective to overthrow the social, marital, and domestic relations of 150,000 people by the suppression of their religious convictions; and it pointed out the upheaval in the nation's economy if the Saints moved out, leaving Utah "a scene of desolation."

---

[4] For complete text, see *The Bible & Polygamy*.

[5] "This age has never witnessed such example of religious defiance of all earthly governments," Tullidge said in his *Quarterly Magazine*; "not even was that of the Utah War its equal, for this was made, not in isolation now, but in the very face of the American nation, with the railroad completed over which, in a few days, troops could have been hurried by the conquerer of the South."

[6] At this time Margaret had a baby six months old, and she subsequently would give birth to four more, the last when she was forty-four and Taylor seventy-three.

If Grant sent the U.S. Army to Utah, it "means war," warned the New York *World*.

> If we force them into a hostile attitude, the Mormons can give us a very disagreeable, a very wearisome, and tremendously expensive war. Cullom's bill provides for the employment of about 40,000 troops. . . . The Mormons could give such a force two or three years' fighting, at an annual expense to us of no less than two hundred millions of dollars.

The outside papers unanimously believed that polygamy was an anachronism dependent upon isolation, and that the railroad had struck it a death blow. Leave the Mormons alone, the Gentile press urged, and the matter would solve itself.

Taylor was jubilant when the Cullom bill failed to pass the Senate; it vindicated the stand, taken by himself and Cannon, of no compromise.

Like a ghost from the past, a wizened little man of eighty-seven arrived at Salt Lake. This was Martin Harris, one of the three witnesses to the Book of Mormon, who after many detours had come to Zion to die. Edward Stephenson, a missionary who had raised $200 to finance the trip, rebaptized Harris; John Taylor helped confirm him for the third time a member of the church by the laying on of hands.

Harris had had a curiously checkered career since mortgaging his farm to finance the printing of the Book of Mormon, as well as prior to it. Born a Quaker, he became a Universalist, a Restorationer, a Baptist, and a Presbyterian before embracing Mormonism; but after that he followed one avowed prophet and another, changing his religion eight times during the Kirtland period. He joined the Saints again at Nauvoo, but soon defected to the Shakers. After Joseph Smith's death, Taylor remembered meeting Harris in England as a missionary for James Strang's offshoot group.

Harris hopped from there to the faction led by the former apostle, William E. McLellin, who'd been a member of the original Quorum of the Twelve. How many more times Harris had changed brands, Taylor didn't know, except that as a Josephite he was a guide at the Kirtland temple when discovered by Mormon missionaries. He professed to be bitter about the Brighamites, but the offer of free transportation and the chance to visit his children in Utah caused him to change his mind, and once more he returned to the church.

As the shriveled old man bore his testimony in a quavering voice at conference, Taylor was comforted by the thought that Harris was now so near the end he had no time to die outside the true gospel.

Defeat of the Cullom bill was the second setback to President Grant's determination to bring the Mormons to heel. Taylor's great laugh had boomed through Maggie's home when the first measure was introduced —a bill to give Utah women the vote, in expectation that they would throw off the yoke of polygamy. To Grant's consternation, the Saints welcomed the legislation; Utah became the first territory to have female suffrage—and the women voted exactly like the men.

Smarting and under pressure from all sides, Grant began selecting territorial appointees known for their determination to subdue the Saints. The Josephites put in their bid, offering to supply a member of the Reorganized LDS Church to govern Utah.

Even Sidney Rigdon, rejected a quarter century previously at Nauvoo as church leader, generously offered to be Utah's governor. Grant selected J. Wilson Shaffer, a Civil War officer who'd shown zeal in lobbying for the Cullom bill. The appointment was hailed with glee by the Utah ring.

Taylor, paying a courtesy call on the new governor at his quarters in the boarding house of William H. McKay, was shocked by Shaffer's appearance. Ravaged by tuberculosis, he obviously was a dying man. But over a cup of tea the governor showed his iron determination to accomplish one objective in the time remaining. With his predecessors, it had been said that each had been governor of the Territory, but that Brigham was governor of the people. "Never, after me, by God," Shaffer told Taylor, "shall it be said that Brigham Young is governor of Utah."

Taylor could be equally blunt. "Sir, you will be buried in the shades of everlasting infamy. If remembered, your name will be execrated from generation to generation."[7]

Taylor arose, bowed, and left.

Shaffer showed he meant business by taking the Nauvoo Legion from Mormon leadership. He ousted its commander, Daniel H. Wells (who was in the first presidency and also mayor of Salt Lake), giving the post to the well-known Mormon-eater, ex-Gen. Patrick E. Connor, former commander at Camp Douglas. The governor called in all arms of the Legion, leaving the proud organization of 13,000 troops as nothing but a *posse comitatus* to back up the U.S. Marshal.

Ably furthering Grant's get-tough policy was the new chief justice of the Territory, a wiry New Yorker, James B. McKean. Taylor approved the judge's immaculate dress; but when McKean appointed as district attorney the hot-headed Robert N. Baskin, the stage was all too obviously set for trouble. Soon, two prominent Mormons, George Q. Cannon and Henry Lawrence, were indicted for "lewd and lascivious cohabitation," while other warrants were issued by the Gentile grand jury, either on that charge or for being implicated in unsolved murders during the Utah War thirteen years previously.

---

[7] Both men reiterated these views several times in public.

But these, Taylor told Maggie as he paced her kitchen, were considered small-fry by the Utah ring. Brigham Young was the prize trophy of the hunt.

Governor Shaffer died six months after arriving. In the scramble for the office, none other than Shelby M. Cullom put in a bid. He had recently lost his seat as Congressman for Illinois, but considered his sponsorship of the Cullom bill sufficient qualification for keeping the Saints in line. Among the Utah ring, General Connor and O. J. Hollister hoped to succeed Shaffer; Connor because of Grant's appreciation for military men, and Hollister—Utah collector of internal revenue—because he was brother-in-law to Colfax. Grant, however, appointed George L. Woods, a born Missourian and deeply anti-Mormon, recently governor of Oregon.

While the Cullom bill had failed in Congress, the carpetbaggers acted as if it were in effect. Taylor, as judge of the Utah County Territorial Court, found himself stripped of authority to preside in anything except probate and divorce cases, deprived of participation in the selection of grand or petit juries. McKean's federal courts took jurisdiction in territorial cases, rejecting the Utah Marshal and Attorney General in favor of United States appointees; the U.S. Marshal assumed authority for selecting juries top-heavy with Gentiles, and took charge of the penitentiary; the U.S. District Attorney assumed full right to prosecute both territorial and federal cases; and the U.S. Army stood ready to back up the arrogated powers of the carpetbaggers.[8]

A satrapy, Taylor declared, reading outside press reaction by lamplight in Maggie's living room. Even Gentile papers agreed. The Omaha *Herald* called it a conspiracy

> to destroy men and institutions in a territory whose civilizing and industrial achievements are the admiration of mankind.

The San Francisco *Examiner* declared

> These small fry, popinjay politicians, and would-be statesmen, know full well that they will have no show for promotion until the Mormon power is broken. Hence it is that they seek to create a civil war. . . . The whole affair is a disgrace to the American name.[9]

Taylor flung the paper away and began pacing the floor. He'd accompanied an English friend to McKean's court, he said, to witness the naturalization ceremony. "His honor, Chief Justice McKean, informed him that he was now admitted to all the rights of an American citizen." Taylor took a pinch from the sugar bowl, then continued pacing. "What

---

[8] "In all this one cannot fail to see that the evident intention of the group . . . was to accomplish, without the sanctions of the law, what the congress of the United States had refused to sanction," says Roberts, CHC, 5:391.

[9] Quoted in *Deseret News*, October 1871.

are those inestimable rights?—the right to be tried by an imported court before a packed jury of his sworn enemies; the right to the sympathy of the judge while passing sentence of three years hard labor for living with his own wife; the right to have his religion assailed; the right to vote for a legislature to make laws which any political despot can annul at pleasure; the right to pay taxes without representation; the right to be maligned, slandered, and abused; the right to have pimps, whorehouses, gambling saloons, debauchery forced upon us by judicial exertion; the right to live in a satrapy; the right to die and be buried."

He paused to observe her reaction. Maggie was radiant. This was the Champion of Rights in good voice. He wasn't speaking to her, she knew, so much as gathering his ammunition for a broadside attack.[10]

Sam Bateman tapped at the window at dawn of October first. The telegraph had brought news from the New York *Herald*:

BRIGHAM YOUNG HAS BEEN INDICTED.
THE MORMONS ARE ARMING.

The feeling of the Mormon people . . . is unmistakably rebellious and warlike. The *Deseret News*, the official organ for Brigham Young, is extremely bitter and offensive. It advocates—

OPEN RESISTANCE TO THE LAWS,

libels United States officials, and endeavors in every way to insult the people to open rebellion. Under these influences many persons are sending off their wives and children to points where there will be no danger.

What did it mean, Bateman asked? No part of the story was true.

Wishful thinking, Taylor advised. Last night the *Trib* editor had telegraphed the tip to the *Herald*. Alert the police to keep the peace, Taylor counseled, for the ring thought they had the deadwood on Brigham, and his arrest might come at any time.

It wasn't until the following afternoon that U.S. Marshal M. T. Patrick served a warrant of arrest on Brigham for lewd and lascivious cohabitation. There followed a long and stormy session of the presidency and the Twelve, during which Taylor strongly advised against appearing in court. He was supported by Orson Pratt, George A. Smith, and Brigham's brother Joseph. Go underground, Taylor urged, rather than risk confinement in a Gentile prison. The Saints would revolt rather than see the prophet jailed. Resist to the bitter end. If necessary, lead the Saints to Mexico, cutting the irrigation ditches and scorching the earth behind them.

Brigham, however, feeble from diarrhea and with hair frosted by seventy winters, was not the lion of Kirtland, Missouri, Nauvoo, and Winter Quarters. He told Taylor's group that he'd been promised protection and a fair hearing.

---

[10] He spelled out the thought subsequently in the *Deseret News*.

"So was Joseph!" Taylor roared. "I saw the safe treatment they gave him in jail! I still carry the bullets!"

After listening to counsel from both sides, Brigham made the decision: "There will be no resistance. I shall obey the summons."[11] He appeared in court, posted $5,000 bail, and returned home.

Chuckling, Taylor described the scene to Maggie over supper. He accompanied Brigham, the church hierarchy, and nine lawyers to Faust's old stone stable. With the help of a cane and a man on each arm, Brigham climbed the rickety outside stairs to the hayloft, where, permeated by the miasma of the Overland Stage mules in the stalls below, the majesty of the United States judiciary held court. Wrapped in shawls, an overcoat, and wool comforter, Brigham sat on a lumpy divan while the federal officials kept him waiting fifteen minutes before putting in an appearance.

Taylor's lips turned up in glee as he pointed out that two could play the game of lese majesty. The Saints had countered the arrogance of the carpetbaggers by terminating the lease on their previous courtroom; and this hayloft was the only available space in the entire city. With relish he read aloud the dispatch of the reporter for the Cincinnati *Commercial*:

> The judge on the bench, J. B. McKean . . . wore a blue coat and was as trim as a bank president. He sat upon a wooden chair behind a deal table, raised a half foot above the floor. The Marshal stood behind a remnant of dry goods box in one corner, and the jury sat upon two broken settees under a hot stovepipe and behind the stove. . . . They resembled a parcel of baggage smashers warming themselves in a railroad depot between trains. The bar consisted of what appeared to be a large keno party keeping tally on a long pine table. . . . The audience sat upon six rows of damaged settees, and a standing party formed the background, over whose heads was seen a great barren barn-like area of room in the rear, filled with debris of some former fair. One chair to the right of the judge was deputed to witnesses. . . . A polygamous jackass and several unregenerate Lamanite mules in the stall beneath occasionally interrupted the judge with a bray of delight. . . .

But seriously, Maggie pointed out, it was no laughing matter. Taylor agreed; more arrests were due; but, he said, laughs were few and far between these days, so enjoy them.

As the crusade continued a number of prominent Mormons were indicted for u.c. (unlawful cohabitation). Then Sam Bateman brought Taylor news of a far more serious development: they'd got the deadwood for sure on Brigham. The arrest for u.c. was only the first step in a plan to hang him for murder. Bill Hickman, a blow-hard Mormon ruffian, had copped a plea. Hickman had met with Deputy U.S. Marshal Sam Gilson at a roundup shack on the horse ranch owned by Gilson's brother in

---

[11] George Alfred Townsend, *The Mormon Trials in Salt Lake City*.

Ferner valley, west of Nephi. There, after dinner and a few slugs of valley tan, Hickman agreed to save his own hide by implicating Brigham in several murders, which Hickman freely admitted as having committed, but, he claimed, the executions were on Brigham's orders. Deputy Gilson took Hickman to Baskin's office, where the lanky and unkempt prosecuting attorney decided, after several long interviews, that the murder of a man named Yates, fourteen years previously, made the best case against Brigham. Hickman had appeared before the packed grand jury, which indicted Brigham and several other church officials for murder.

And right now, Bateman said, Hickman was in protective custody at Camp Douglas, spilling his guts to a Gentile writer, J. H. Beadle.[12]

That night Maggie sat by as Taylor paced the floor. The Saints could expect no justice from the carpetbag tyranny; so he would plead the case before the bar of public opinion.[13]

With Maggie as the sounding board, he asked, "Why is it that the liberties of our most esteemed citizens are attacked and their characters assailed under the guise of law? Why this palpable attempt to stir up sedition, provoke strife, and, is it too much to say, to inaugurate a scene of desolation and bloodshed?

"I have asked myself: Are governments organized to oppress and enslave their subjects? Are courts instituted to insult, outrage, abuse, and tyrannize the people? If not, why are we subject to this living insult, this crying disgrace, this burning shame, this foetid excrescence on the body politic?"

He paused for a pinch of sugar, glancing at Margaret. She nodded approval. He paced again. The questions, he said, "Have been solved by the very extraordinary and lucid opinion of his honor Chief Justice J. B. McKean, delivered October 13, 1871, at the United States courtroom over Faust's stable."

He drew notes from his pocket, that he had scribbled during the day:

I quote: "It is therefore proper to say, that while the case at the bar is called· The People *vs* Brigham Young, its other and real title is, Federal authority *vs* Polygamic theocracy."

This certainly elucidates the subject. We now have a reason for this crusade against the liberties of the citizens of this territory, this prosecution, persecution, and infamy that has disgraced our courts for some time past.

Some have asserted that it was a religious persecution, and that after the Cullom bill failed the judges were set on by their pious coadjutors to carry out their program. Others have stated that it was a political plot,

---

[12] See Baskin's *Reminiscences of Early Utah*; also Hickman's *Brigham's Destroying Angel*, written by Beadle.

[13] Taylor wrote a series of five letters to the *Deseret News*, for distribution worldwide.

that by the sacrifice of a few thousand Mormons President Grant might be re-elected. Others have thought that it was of a more private and financial nature, gotten up for gain. Judge McKean, however, has dispelled the mists in which it has been shrouded.

Stripped of all tinsel and wrappings, it simply resolves itself into this: that the government of the United States is at war with the Church of Jesus Christ of Latter-day Saints.

Again he glanced at Maggie, who said she was glad that the Champion of Rights was in good voice. Taylor consulted another note.

This point being settled, it may be necessary to inquire into another. We are informed by his honor that "A system is on trial in the person of Brigham Young." His honor gives us to understand that Brigham has been accused of one thing and is being tried for another. Furthermore, he is already prejudged of guilt.

I would not treat his honor discourteously, but quote the language of the Washington *Capitol*: "Thoughtful minds will concur that we procure polygamy's annihilation at heavy cost when we destroy our courts and fetch justice into such contempt."

Maggie applauded. Taylor rounded out his conclusion: "It must be remembered that while the court has persons at its bar, the court itself is at the bar of public opinion. It is becoming a serious question how far the federal authority shall be permitted to lend itself to breaking down all the safeguards and bulwarks of society, while rushing recklessly into the worst kind of anarchy and despotism."

Maggie kissed him good night and went to bed. Taylor went into his study, where his pen sputtered far into the night.

Reaction in the national press caused Taylor to continue the attack. The Saints had had a decided disadvantage with the news media, because Oscar G. Sawyer, special correspondent of the New York *Herald*, was not only a particular friend and partisan of Judge McKean, but also was editor of the Salt Lake *Tribune*. This gave Sawyer inside information on grand jury affairs, and it gave McKean "the editorial stool of the *Tribune*, at his pleasure, to write editorials sustaining his own court decisions."[14]

Taylor's second letter was devoted to discussion of the inherent rights of man. He began with the basic premise that "governments were, at least ostensibly," organized for the benefit of the people. However,

there has been from time immemorial a continual struggle between the governors and the governed, the first trying to usurp power, authority, and dominion, the other to resist these encroachments. . . . The history of France during the last twenty years is an exemplification of this. Napoleon commenced his political career as president of a republic, had himself proclaimed emperor, and left it a vanquished, resigned empire. The

---

[14] Tullidge, *History of Salt Lake City*.

histories of the Babylonians, the Medes and Persians, the Grecians, the Romans and the Russians are all evidence of this fact, nor can we exempt the British, the Prussians, the Austrians, or other European nations.

The "forms or names" of governments made little difference to the liberties of the people.

> While the Russian serfs have been liberated by the edict of an autocrat, republican America imported slaves and kept them in bondage for nearly a century. The greatest outrages and crimes were perpetrated in republican France. . . . Caligula and Nero, as emperors, were no more bloodthirsty than were Robespierre, Marat, and Danton, as republicans. . . . Liberty is not a name but a reality.

"Tyranny is the same, whether in the dictator or the people, the general, the judge, or the preacher." There were certain inalienable rights possessed by man; their infringement had produced "all the oppressions, bloodshed, injustice, war, carnage and dislocation, the tears, groans and misery with which the world has been cursed."

> It is alleged "that all nations have the elements of destruction within themselves," . . . for, so far as they interfere with inherent God-given right, they open the floodgates of error and injustice; tyranny, oppression, and corruption follow in its train; anarchy, confusion, and revolt ensue, and weakness and desolation are the result.

Of the 100,000 people in Utah, "How many of them had a voice in the selection of the present federal officers? Not one." How many Mormons sat on the grand jury? "Not one."

> Liberty does not consist in the clanging of bells, the sound of trumpets, the beat of drums, . . . nor in the declamations of demagogues; . . . but in the preserving of these rights to the people, the preserving intact as the living inheritance of man. Every man that sustains these principles is the friend of freedom and humanity; and every one who opposes them— whether among autocrats, monarchies, or republics—is a disturber of the peace, a sower of discord, an enemy of mankind and of God.

Meanwhile two apparently minor events were as a cloud in the sky no larger than a man's hand. The Salt Lake City police raided the liquor establishment of a Gentile merchant, one Paul Engelbrecht, who was dispensing the foul deceiver both wholesale and by the drink without a license. Because the cops destroyed his stock, Engelbrecht sued the city. Judge McKean and a Gentile jury awarded him triple damages of $59,063.25. The appeal by the city was just one of many going up through higher courts.

The second omen was so apparently insignificant that Taylor could not imagine it as having an effect on the course of history: Ann Eliza

Webb Young, one of the fifty-three living women Brigham had married, was getting unhappy about her lot.

In his third letter, Taylor examined constitutional rights, and the Mormon concept of the Kingdom of God.

> When God's "will shall be done on the earth as it is done in heaven," the shackles will be knocked from every son and daughter of Adam; there will be proclaimed a universal jubilee, and all mankind will be free, every wrong will be suppressed, and every right maintained. The living, glorious, eternal principles of "doing unto all men as we would they should do unto us," will prevail. . . . "Peace on earth and good will to man," shall be proclaimed to every nation. . . . Then all hearts shall be made glad, and the voice of mourning and sorrow be banished from the earth;
>
> > *And every man in every place,*
> > *Shall meet a brother and a friend;*
>
> and as Parley P. Pratt has it—
>
> > *Come, ye sons of doubt and wonder,*
> > *Indian, Moslem, Greek, or Jew;*
> > *All your shackles burst asunder,*
> > *Freedom's banner waves for you.*
>
> This is what the Latter-day Saints are trying to inaugurate. Judge McKean says it is a system that is on trial. He does not know it, but the above *is* the system—what he is pleased to called "Polygamic Theocracy."

In his fourth letter, Taylor challenged the power of Congress to govern territories; for "there is no constitutional authority for such an organization; it is simply an unauthorized jurisdiction." He pointed out that territorial status developed from the slavery question, when both North and South were unwilling to admit a state "without a corresponding equivalent, so as to preserve the balance of power." Prior to that time, Kentucky, Tennessee, Ohio, Louisiana, Indiana, and Mississippi were among states admitted to the Union "without territorial tutelage."

He was galled by the irony of an incident twenty-two years previously, when a storm in the Sierras frustrated Utah's opportunity for statehood.

> Had it not been for a snowstorm, we would have been a free people. As it is, we have been living under the worst species of despotism—a satrapy—from that time to the present. Does freedom depend upon such adventitious circumstances? Are the liberties of men depending upon such contingencies? Is this the popular republican government guaranteed by the Constitution of the United States?

Taylor compared territorial and state governments, concluding that territorial rights under the Organic act "are simply bubbles, playthings for children, to be given and taken at pleasure, just as mamma says, like little boys who don't play marbles 'for keeps.'" Justice in a territory "is simply a courtesy, concession, favor received, . . . [not] from national justice or inherent inalienable rights."

In his fifth and final letter, Taylor asked, "Having commenced with us, the question very naturally arises: where will it end?"

> For if these principles of injustice and inhumanity can be practiced with impunity upon us, . . . it will not be long before the same rule, or misrule, will be applied to others; the sword once unsheathed will clamor for more victims; encroachment will tread on the heels of encroachment . . . [until] the nation will be bound in chains of its own forging. . . .

"Having said so much on this subject, let me now address a few words to the Saints," Taylor counseled.

> You made the roads, killed the snakes, built the bridges, redeemed the sterile desert country and made it "blossom as the rose." . . . But these very beauties and excellencies are your danger. Corrupt men look upon your possessions with greedy eyes, and, like vultures, are ready to pounce upon their prey.

What to do? "Keep quiet!" Taylor counseled. "Don't allow them to insult you. . . . If they send you to prison unjustly, rejoice. Let them have their full swing—and they will hang themselves."

> The lamb is drinking below; the wolf is fouling the water above. The big boy is strutting about with a chip on his shoulder daring you to knock it off. Some pretext is needed. Don't give it to them. They want a pretext to plunder you; their program is to pillage, rob, ravage, lay waste, and destroy. They want your farms, and, although very virtuous, would like to ravish your wives and daughters. Don't give them the opportunity. . . . Don't work into their hands.

Public reaction to Taylor's five letters to the press showed they were important in three areas: They put on record to the nation the Mormon side of the conflict, as it never had previously been presented. They listed by chapter and verse the rape of constitutional rights by Utah carpetbaggers. And, perhaps most important, they acted as a safety valve to let off steam and help quiet the infuriated Saints, at a time when the national press freely predicted civil war.[15]

---

[15] Tullidge says, "It was well known that he [Brigham] had often declared that he never would give himself up to be murdered as his predecessor, the Prophet Joseph, and his brother Hyrum had been, while in the hands of the law; . . . and, ere this could have been repeated, ten thousand Mormon Elders would have gone into the jaws of death with Brigham Young. In a few hours the suspended Nauvoo Legion would have been in arms." (*History of Salt Lake City*; 527.)

The correspondent for the Indianapolis *Journal* wrote: "After a full and free conference with the leading Mormons, federal officers, and businessmen of Salt Lake City, we predict that a dreadful civil war will soon be raging in this fertile region,

In their arrogance, however, the carpetbaggers mistook Taylor's ringing denunciation as the squealing of a pig caught in a gate; they laughed at his malediction. And they went about getting the deadwood on Brigham Young, indicting him on two counts of murder.

Brigham vanished. Gentiles claimed he had fled, Mormons that he simply had made a scheduled trip to St. George. Brigham's chief legal counsel, the swarthy and heavy-set Thomas Fitch, told the new prosecuting attorney, George C. Bates (sympathetic in contrast to the fire-eating Baskin), that Brigham left "not to avoid trial, but to escape confinement in the garrison here and for fear of his life."

When a reporter asked Fitch, "Will he probably return and submit to arrest and incarceration at Camp Douglas, on the unbailable charge of murder?" the attorney replied, "He may. But I shouldn't blame him if he refused to walk into this dead-fall."

"Why do you say dead-fall?"

"Because under the jury-packing system now practiced in Utah, and the rulings and chargings of the court, he has no chance whatever."

Brigham, however, returned for a dramatic appearance in court when his case was called. Inasmuch as there was no jail in the city for United States prisoners—and possibly because of the horde of Saints packing the hayloft and crowding the street below—McKean refrained from putting him in custody at Camp Douglas, allowing him to go home ("The defendant now at the bar is reputed to be the owner of several houses in this city") under custody of the U.S. Marshal.

As the cases of Brigham Young and other prominent Saints indicted for murder were pending trial, Taylor spoke to the assembled Saints in the new tabernacle:

> And who are these men they are now prosecuting and persecuting? Why, here is Brigham Young, for instance. I have traveled with him thousands of miles, preaching the Gospel without purse or scrip. What has he done to anybody? Whom has he injured? Can anybody put a finger on it? Not and tell the truth. I know before God they lie. I have been with him in private and public under all circumstances and I know his feelings. I know they are liars when they make these statements, and this people believe it, too.

"Well, what shall we do, then?" he asked. "Why—do right," he advised. "Don't fight!"

---

resulting in the loss of thousands of lives, the expenditure of millions in public treasure, and the complete devastation of one of the most beautiful and thriving regions on the continent, unless the administration interferes with the schemes of the petty lords of misrule, who are doing their utmost to bring it about. . . .

"We are convinced that the pending prosecutions are conceived in folly, conducted in violation of the law, and with an utter recklessness as to the grave results that must necessarily ensue."

We want no vigilant societies here, nor bloodtubs; no "Plug-uglies," nor Ku-Klux, nor John Brown raids, nor Jayhawkers. . . . We don't want any secret organizations of any kind, nor any infractions of the law.

Let others be breakers of the law, and us the keepers of it. Let others trample underfoot human rights, and us maintain them. . . . If others want to play the part of tyrants, let them do so, and they will find the tyrant's end. . . .

Now, I would rather be the friend and associate of these men whom they call murderers here than of their most honorable men, and so would this people.

The audience responded with a unanimous "aye." "No power in this city nor in these United States, I say—and I will prophesy in the name of Israel's God—shall harm you," Taylor promised the accused. "God will control, direct, and manage all the affairs pertaining to his people, and Israel will rejoice and be triumphant, and the Kingdom of God will be established."

The Saints left the tabernacle full of faith. As Taylor met his wives in the waiting carriage outside the wall of Temple Square, they regarded him with an unspoken question. He gave them a reassuring smile as he climbed in. He'd done his part, he said; now it was up to the Lord.

The following month, with the cases still pending, Taylor was thrilled —as well as vastly relieved—by a message that clicked over the telegraph:

> Washington, D.C., April 15, 1872.
> The judgment of the Supreme Court of Utah in the case of Engelbrecht *vs* Clinton, Mormon test case, was reversed by the Supreme Court of the United States today. Jury unlawfully drawn; summonses invalid; proceedings ordered dismissed. Decision unanimous. All indictments quashed.

The decision voided all criminal proceedings in Utah for the previous eighteen months, and required discharge of 138 prisoners.[16]

Shortly afterwards, another bombshell clicked over the wires from Washington: The vice president was involved in scandal; his reputation suddenly was shattered and his influence terminated. Sanctimonious "Smiler" Colfax, famous for self-righteousness, had while speaker of the House accepted twenty shares of stock under the counter from the infamous Credit Mobilier, the company organized to build the transcontinental railroad—with millions in government subsidies. A congressional investigation revealed that Colfax had accepted a cash stock dividend from Credit Mobilier, which he lied about under oath; and also was involved in kickbacks from government contracts. As chairman of the Committee on Post Offices and Post Roads he had taken a campaign con-

---

[16] Whitney says the Engelbrecht decision was "by far the most important ruling ever given by that august tribunal in relation to the general affairs of the territories."

tribution of $4,000 from a contractor supplying government envelopes.

A resolution to impeach Colfax was narrowly defeated on the technicality that he couldn't be impeached as vice president for bribes taken while speaker of the House. But his name was smeared and his influence gone. The Washington *Post* wrote his political obituary: "A resolution for the impeachment of the bribed and perjured Colfax failed by a majority of three votes."

Taylor saw the hand of the Lord in the downfall of Colfax. Once more his faith was vindicated that if the Saints made no compromise with God's laws, the Almighty would smite their enemies hip and thigh.

The Utah ring wasn't through, however. McKean still controlled the courts, and he prodded Washington into new legislation by "masterly inactivity"—claiming to be unable to empanel grand or petit juries. In response, Congress passed the Poland bill, greatly enlarging the powers of the federal courts, U.S. marshal and attorney general, and giving equal representation on juries to the insignificant (numerically) Gentile minority.

Again Taylor's pen scratched far into the night at Maggie's home, as he wrote another series of letters for the press. To Congress, he said,

> Would you, to gratify a morbid sentimentality, desecrate and tear down one of the most magnificent temples of human liberty ever erected? Would you wantonly deliver up the sacred principles of liberty, equity, and justice, bequeathed by your fathers, to the grim Moloch of party, who is crushing, grinding, and trampling underfoot our God-given rights? . . . Have we not had more than enough trouble already? . . . Can we ever be satisfied? Let us have peace.

Opening his "black book," he listed chapter and verse of cases where officials administering territorial law had aided and abetted criminal activity, summing up:

> Some of the United States officials have shielded and protected criminals, and for this purpose every subterfuge of the law has been brought into requisition. Thus, by writs of error, injunctions, *habeas corpus*, pardons, and officious and indecent interference, they have exhibited themselves as the abettors and protectors of crime. They have liberated felons and murderers, encouraged drunkenness and riot, protected and shielded brothel-houses, winked at and sustained gambling, and so clogged the wheels of justice, in both civil and criminal cases, that they have brought the judiciary into such contempt that it has become a stink in the nostrils of honest men.

By contrast, McKean still viewed himself as a white knight crusading against sin. Having failed to hang Brigham and other officials for murder, the ring zeroed in on polygamy to bring the church to its knees. McKean confidently predicted that "the day is not far in the future when the disloyal high priesthood of the so-called Church of Jesus Christ of Latter-day Saints shall bow to and obey the laws that are elsewhere respected, or else those laws will grind them into powder."[17]

At the very time the anti-polygamy crusade was reaching its peak, a fat plum dropped into McKean's lap. Ann Eliza Webb Young, the toothsome cupcake who styled herself, inaccurately, as Brigham's "wife number 19," became disenchanted and wanted out. Eagerly, the ring sponsored her case, while the national press had a field day. Estimating Brigham's worth at $8-million, and his income $40,000 a month, Ann Eliza asked $1,000 a month while the suit was pending, and an award of $200,000 plus attorney fees of $20,000.

Brigham's defense shocked Taylor. After all the Mormon effort to establish polygamy as a respectable practice, a marriage system necessary for attainment of the celestial glory, entered into for time and all eternity, as defendant Brigham claimed that there could be no divorce nor alimony, because a plural marriage was illegal.[18] He also claimed that, unknown to him at the time of the marriage, Ann Eliza was actually the wife of another Mormon, James L. Dee, by whom she had had two children, and from whom no divorce.[19]

Judge McKean, sitting on the case, ordered Brigham to pay attorney fees of $3,000; $9,500 alimony; and support of $500 a month.

By granting a divorce and alimony, McKean—the dedicated foe of polygamy—had established its legality. Even the outside press realized this. Chuckling, Taylor read to Maggie the reaction of the New York Post:

> By common law of Congress made especially for Utah, and by the common law of the land, any other woman taken by [Brigham] to his bed and board after his first legal marriage is not his wife. This is the very point Judge McKean has heretofore considered it his special mission to establish. . . .
>
> By his decision, the judge recedes from his own principles, and may fairly be hailed by the Mormon Church as a convert to the doctrine of polygamy.

By paying the judgment, the case would close, and the legality of the Principle established. What a tremendous bargain! What a windfall!

---

[17] Kimball Young, *Isn't One Wife Enough?*

[18] In his *Life*, Roberts (himself a polygamist) says blandly, "The marriage between Ann Eliza Webb and Brigham Young was not recognized by the law of the land. It was illegal, and therefore void from the beginning; consequently there could be neither divorce nor alimony."

[19] In *The Twenty-Seventh Wife*, Irving Wallace establishes that Ann Eliza not only was divorced from Dee prior to her marriage to Brigham, but that Brigham himself, and George Q. Cannon, helped expedite the case. On December 25, 1865, Judge Elias Smith of the Salt Lake County Probate Court granted her a divorce from Dee and custody of her children. Brigham married her subsequently, in April 1868.

Taylor's joy didn't last long. Brigham was a fighter. The shrewd empire builder couldn't endure personal defeat—particularly by a woman. To Taylor's complete dismay, Brigham appealed the ruling. McKean ordered him to pay attorney fees of $3,000 meanwhile. Brigham refused to pay anything while the case was under appeal. McKean fined him $25 and sentenced him to a day in prison for contempt.

Taylor was at Brigham's side in the carriage as a horde of Saints braved a heavy blizzard to accompany the prophet to the penitentiary, where the warden accommodated the distinguished prisoner at his home. The following day Brigham returned to the Beehive House, escorted by a multitude.

As Taylor had predicted, if given enough rope McKean would hang himself. The national press was outraged at the calculated humiliation of Brigham Young. Five days later a dispatch from Washington announced the removal of McKean from office for what President Grant considered "fanatical and extreme conduct . . . considered ill-advised, tyrannical, and in excess of his powers as judge."[20]

Taylor had counseled the people to be quiet and hold the faith. Once more, he felt, the Lord had spared his people.

Head bowed, John Taylor felt his bosom burn as Daniel H. Wells offered the dedicatory prayer for the St. George temple. It was April 6, 1877, and after thirty years the Saints finally had completed a temple in Utah.

"We dedicate and consecrate the foundation of this building," Wells prayed, starting from the ground up.

> We dedicate and consecrate the lower and upper walls of the building and the buttresses which support the same and all the materials: the stone, the lime, and the sand which compose the mortar, and all that pertains thereunto, together with the flagging, the timbers, the joists, the floors, and the foundations upon which they rest. . . .
>
> We also present to Thee the baptismal font, with the steps, the railings around and the oxen upon which it rests, the foundations, together with the connections and apparatus for furnishing, conveying, holding, and heating the water. . . .
>
> We dedicate also to Thee the rooms of this building in the first, second, and third stories, with the pillars and supports thereof, including the siderooms, with the partition walls, for the purposes for which they may be used. . . . We also dedicate the roof and the tower with its dome, its covering and walls and the battlements around and above the roofs with the timbers and frames and supports upon which the roof and tower

---

[20] The divorce case, begun in January 1873, finally came to trial in April 1877. The judge ruled that the polygamous marriage was void, and annulled all orders for alimony.

rest, and are made permanent, and the fastenings and all that appertain thereto and the materials of which they are composed.

We dedicate also the entrances, the steps, and the circular stairs, with the railings and banisters thereunto attached. Grant, O Lord, that the roof which covers all, may shield and protect the building from the storms which may come upon it. We dedicate the pipes which convey the water from the rooms with their fastenings and the materials of which they are composed. We also dedicate the chimneys, flues, conduits, and sewers and openings for ventilation; also all the doors, windows, and glass, the hinges and nails and screws, the door locks and handles, the windows, weights, and cords and fastenings of every kind; and all the paint, putty, plaster, whitewash, and all the ornamental work within and without, everything used in the construction and completion of the entire building, from the foundations unto the top thereof that all may be holy unto the Lord our God.

Holy Father, we dedicate unto Thee the furniture and utensils used in the holy washings, anointings, and ceremonies of this Thy holy house; also the curtains and frames for partitions; together with the altars and their cushions and the tables and chairs, stools and desks that all may be sanctified for the use and purposes intended. We dedicate also the tower on the outside, containing the fountain, also the aqueduct and pipes conveying water thereunto.

We dedicate the block of land upon which this Temple is situated and the fence which encloses it, with its openings and gates, the hinges, hangings, and fastenings and the materials of which they are composed, also the roads and walks leading thereto and through the same.

We dedicate and consecrate the pulpits with the cushions thereon, and the ornamental fringe around, together with the steps, railings, and banisters and the seats, with the cushions on them; and the floors, and the foundations upon which they stand. May nothing unholy, impure ever enter here but may the same be holy unto the Lord our God. . . .

Accept, O God, of this tribute of our hearts. . . .

A truly spiritual experience. Heavenly spirits attended, as had been the case at the dedication of the first temple, at Kirtland. Wilford Woodruff told Taylor that George Washington appeared to him in the temple, together with all the signers of the Declaration of Independence, requesting endowment work be done for them. "I straightway went into the baptismal font," Woodruff said, where he was baptized by proxy "for the signers of the Declaration of Independence, and fifty other eminent men, making one hundred in all, including John Wesley, Columbus, and others." Also baptized at this time were every president of the United States "except three; and when their cause is just, somebody will do the work for them."[21]

---

[21] JD, 19:229. People apprehensive of this method of posthumously making Mormons out of the dead need have no fear. The ceremony simply gives the dead the privilege of accepting the gospel. They are free to reject it.

But there was tension mixed with the spirituality as annual conference began at St. George the day following the dedicatory services. Once again the Utah ring had tried to get the deadwood on Brigham for murder, by raking up the massacre at Mountain Meadows twenty years previously. Only the offering of John D. Lee as scapegoat had finally quieted that. But Lee had been understandably bitter, and just the month prior to the conference he had fired anti-Mormon frenzy by publishing his *Confessions.*[22]

St. George was Mountain Meadows country. When Taylor and other brethren were stricken by violent purging, he wondered if it was the alkaline water or an attempted retaliation by poison. Brigham Young, obese and failing in health, could no longer get around with his cane and crutch, and was carried about in a specially-constructed armchair.

Brigham had semi-retired some years previously, delegating various responsibilities. It was freely predicted that he intended to abdicate in favor of his sons.[23] It was expected that he would do so at conference.

Alarmed, Taylor prepared to fight to the last ditch to prevent it. Relations between himself and Brigham neared the breaking point during the ceremonies. Then when Taylor, in addressing the Saints packed into the main auditorium (there was no room for a scribe's table; the recorder made notes using the back of the man ahead), made reference to the lack of complete success of the United Order of Enoch, the communal system dearly beloved by Brigham, the prophet steamed with fury. As Taylor sat down Brigham sprang up, without his crutch and, clutching his cane like a club smacked the rostrum a resounding whack. He then "most terribly scourged" Taylor, as only Brigham could do, before the vast audience of appalled faithful.[24]

On the stand behind Brigham, Taylor's gorge rose in turn, until at the climax Brigham told him to go back to Salt Lake and make wagons. At this reference to the sugar-making failure, Taylor leaped up and broke into the prophet's discourse, demanding why Brigham didn't go back to

---

[22] T. B. H. Stenhouse and his wife Fanny also had published books detailing the seamy side of Mormonism. In the British edition of her *Tell it All* (the London edition carried the title *The Tyranny of Mormonism; or, An Englishwoman in Utah*) Fanny added a postscript claiming: "The publication of this book has probably contributed more to bring the terrible realities of Mormon life to the knowledge of the public, and to hasten their day of judgment, than has any other human agency." Actually, her shrill tone was largely self-defeating. Her husband's book had much more impact.

[23] See Salt Lake *Tribune*'s report of conference. Also Lee's *Confessions.* Stenhouse devoted considerable space to Brigham's plans to found a dynasty.

[24] See journals of Abraham H. Cannon and Wilford Woodruff. The *Tribune* called it a "merciless drubbing," and referred to "Apostate" Taylor (rather than apostle) being "whipped into Enoch."
Incidentally, the dents from the cane are still in the rostrum.

Salt Lake and dig another canal. This referred to Brigham's irrigation project which failed because the water, when turned into the canal, wouldn't run uphill.

Taylor knew that his church standing hung in the balance; but the man who had said he wouldn't be a slave to God himself was unable to take this public lashing for telling the truth. "It looked for a time as though these two great men would separate in anger," Lorenzo Snow said of the brouhaha. Taylor was in no mood to apologize until Snow, delegated peacemaker, pointed out to him that he was out of order to interrupt another man's discourse. Taylor realized that he had infringed Brigham's right to speak. He went to the prophet's house, apologized, and the two shook hands.

This was for the last time. Four months later, Brigham Young was dead.

The question of the dynasty was buried with him. If Brigham had intended to abdicate at the St. George conference, the Mountain Meadows affair had caused him to postpone matters until October conference; he died in August. In which event scapegoat John D. Lee got his revenge, by spiking Brigham's fondest dream.

17

The Ghost of
Brigham Young

His CARRIAGE WAS WAITING when John Taylor emerged from Maggie's home on Taylor Row and paused to admire the sparkling morning of early spring. The sky held no cloud. The mountains thrusting abruptly into the eastern sky glittered in whiteness. The air was wine. He came out the picket gate to the carriage and told the driver, Brother Green, that he'd walk to the office this morning. As the carriage rumbled away, Brother Green shook his head dubiously at the informality surrounding the president under the new regime. Nobody, in thirty years, had ever seen Brigham Young walk the streets of Salt Lake City unaccompanied.

Taylor liked to walk. For one thing, it kept the leg limber that still held a slug from Carthage jail. The bullet was an infallible weather barometer, and also a source of embarrassment: of late years after sitting awhile he limped the first few steps upon arising. Walking was also helpful in solving problems, of which he had many as leader of the church in troubled times. Ironically, one of the most thorny and complicated concerned Brigham Young. Though the late president had been dead six months, his hand was still heavy on church affairs. Taylor had the eerie feeling of being haunted, as if Brigham refused to stay buried. President Young had left a last will and testament that couldn't have been better designed as a legacy of discord within the church while providing aid and comfort to the Gentiles.[1]

---

[1] In his article on "The Settlement of the Brigham Young Estate, 1877-1879," *Pacific*

Brigham had bequeathed to his family a million dollars in property and assets that clearly belonged to the church. Upon assuming leadership, John Taylor had insisted on an audit of the books and an accounting. He was aware that some would ask, why rake up such facts from the past? Was money that important? Wasn't the reputation of the Mormon Moses beyond price? Yet Taylor felt that he had no choice in the matter. Aside from principle and integrity, regardless that an accounting was necessary upon a change of leadership, there was another reason that impelled and guided what he had done: he believed that the Lord had spoken. The settlement of Brigham Young's estate was directed by revelation.[2]

Taylor stepped into the drugstore of Sharp and Younger on Main near Third South for a copy of the *Tribune*. He was receiving his change when a voice at his elbow said that during Brigham's time, men were cut off for reading that paper.

He shook hands with Edwin D. Woolley, bishop of the Thirteenth ward. Short, compact, with a close-cropped beard and bulging forehead, Woolley was noted for his outspoken bluntness. He had been a friend since the Kirtland days of forty years ago, and Taylor always admired Woolley's integrity, lack of pretence, and sense of humor.

When Taylor asked what a bishop was doing in a Gentile store, Woolley said the ZCMI didn't carry the remedy he needed. With a grin the bishop indicated a counter display of "The Mormon Elder's Damiana Wafers," proclaimed to be,

> The most Powerful INVIGORANT Ever Produced.
> Permanently Restores those Weakened by Early Indiscretions. Imparts Youthful Vigor. Restores Vitality. Strengthens and Invigorates the BRAIN and NERVES. A positive cure for IMPOTENCY & Nervous Debility.[3]

Taylor glanced over the shelves, which were loaded with cures for everything from cancer to canker, and asked to see a box of Dr. Gibbon's Remedy for the evil consequences of the "solitary vice," whose victims "with unerring certainty" were afflicted with

> Sallow countenance, dark spots under the eyes, pain in the head, ringing ears, noise like rustling of leaves or rattling of chariots, uneasiness about

---

Historical Review, February 1952, Leonard J. Arrington says, "It is probable that no estate in America presented so many difficulties and complications as this one, because of the interests involved, the number of heirs, and the types of property."

[2] Taylor's objectives in the estate settlement are given in his letter to Orson Hyde: "justice, tempered with mercy," is the goal, that "no right minded person . . . will ever charge us 'with a want of generosity.'" See letter #509, *John Taylor Letter Book. Church Business Book #15*; Church Historian's Office.

[3] The brand name of this nostrum is indicative of the Gentile attitude toward plural marriage. As a source of ribald humor, the subject was mined in a thousand variations.

the loins, weakness of confidence, diffidence in approaching strangers, a dislike to form new acquaintances, a disposition to shun society, loss of memory, pimples and various eruptions about the face, hectic flushes, furred tongue, foetid breath, coughs, consumption, night sweats, mono-mania, and frequent insanity.

And this, Taylor said, evidently was intended for Gentiles.

Bishop Woolley's laugh caused the flames in the overhead gas lamps to quiver. He made his own purchase—a copy of the *Tribune*—and the two went out and turned north along Main. Taylor had to slow his pace for Woolley, whose joints were stiffening. With a pang Taylor realized that another old friend from the days of Kirtland, Far West, Nauvoo, and Winter Quarters—compatriot in the grand struggle for the Kingdom —was nearing the end of his earthly trials.

But if Woolley wasn't as spry as he'd once been, his opinions were as abrasively honest. As they paused at the corner, where the bishop would turn off toward his home on Second South Street, Woolley commented on the new feeling in Zion. Spring had come with the promise of better times. Too bad Brother John hadn't been able to attend the talk by Elias Harrison at the Liberal Institute about the new era for Utah.

Woolley declared that Harrison had pulled no punches. "Many of the evils of the Judaic form of theocracy which had existed here," Harrison said, "especially those of the most absolute period of Brigham Young's administration, have passed away." And, Woolley declared, you could hear gasps in the audience; people weren't used to hearing Brigham talked about like that.[4]

Harrison had pointed out that since Brigham's death it was no longer immoral to disagree with church leadership; a man wouldn't be cut off and his character destroyed for a difference of opinion. He reminded the audience that the church had done an about-face in other matters, too. Whereas mining had been strictly forbidden by Brigham, now the priesthood "sees the hand of God" in developing our mineral resources. The numbered ballot had been abolished.[5] Harrison said, "The last Utah legis-

---

[4] E. L. T. Harrison was a Godbeite, cut off by Brigham for advocating freedom of the press in Utah.

[5] Harrison declared that church leaders had "voluntarily stripped themselves of one of the greatest safeguards of their absolute power—the numbered ballot; marvelous, considering the harsh spirit of the past, as is the friendliness now displayed to both Gentile and Apostate. . . ."

For thirty years under Brigham Young, the numbered ballot had made democracy an empty form; every man's vote could be checked. Accused of "one man" rule, Brigham defended it as by Divine right: "Would it be democratic to get up an election in heaven and have [political] opposition?" He furthermore warned "the political world . . . that the opposition they are so anxious to promote contains the seeds of destruction of the government we live in. This is the plant or tree from

lature witnessed scenes of freedom and expressions of independent thought never manifested before." In fact, he declared, Utah today stood on the threshold of a new era; the old "reign and spirit of force" had been buried in Brigham's grave.[6]

Harrison really spoke the gospel, Woolley declared. What a different atmosphere in Zion, within a few short months!

As to that, Taylor said, he could make no comment.

No need to, Woolley said; everyone felt it. Could anyone imagine him standing on the corner of Main and Second South talking with Brigham Young? Or Brigham taking a morning walk alone? He never put a foot out of his fortress without a bodyguard.[7]

Woolley turned east toward his home. As Taylor continued up Main,

---

which schism springs; and every government lays the foundation of its own downfall when it permits what are called democratic elections." (JD, 14:93.)

The summer following Brigham's death, Taylor wrote letters to all stake presidents, advising them: "The forthcoming election being the first under the new law giving the secret ballot, it is deemed essential that extra care be taken, by all interested in maintaining the liberties of the people of this Territory, that everything connected therewith be done to the uttermost in accordance with the provisions of the law...."

[6] For complete text of Harrison's talk of March 10, 1878, see *Tullidge's Quarterly Magazine*, October 1880. He makes a penetrating analysis of Mormonism and the reasons for its phenomenal success, pointing out that it was "born an Iconoclast," a religion of joy, happiness, and eternal progress in contrast to the hellfire and damnation so prevalent with other faiths. "It abolished the ancient Devil of Horns and Hoofs.... It struck Hell and its fires out of existence thirty years before Beecher. ... It antagonized with the doctrine of the Fall, asserting that man had only 'fallen upward.' It affirmed in opposition to general orthodox views of the meanness of human origin, that man was no 'mere worm of the earth,' but a 'spark from the fire of God's eternal blaze' ... declaring that all honest men of all creeds, or no creed at all, would find a Heaven adapted to the aspirations of their souls.

"Its greatest success," Harrison said, "lay in its appeals to the human heart." The family relationship was eternal. "For man himself, its doctrines opened up an endless vista of progress; asserting that eternity would never reveal the limits of his intellectual powers and researches, the development of his spiritual perfections, or the grandeur of his destiny...."

The power and influence of the Mormon priesthood, Harrison said, was "*Obedience to an idealism*! It needs no peculiar cunning, no especial skill, no remarkable shrewdness, where this exists, as in the case of the Mormon people, for a man like Brigham Young to lift himself into power, display great ability, and manifest wonderful controlling influence."

[7] Richard F. Burton, in his *The City of the Saints*, said that Brigham lived in fear of assassination, and "seldom leaves his house except for the tabernacle; when inclined for a picnic, the day and the hour are kept secret.... He has guards at his gates, and he never appears in public unattended by friends and followers, who are of course armed." Burton reported that, "It is said that Mr. Brigham Young, despite his powerful will and high moral courage, does not show the remarkable personal intrepidity of Mr. Joseph Smith: his followers deny this, but it rests on the best and fairest Gentile evidence."

he reflected that while he had tried to liberalize the administration of church affairs, the root issue—the struggle between Mormon and Gentile for control of Utah—was getting worse, not better.

Arriving at the president's office, behind the high cobblestone wall of what had been Brigham's fortress, Taylor sat down again to the problem he'd worked on for the six months since Brigham's death, the settlement of the former president's financial affairs.

At his death, Brigham Young's estate had been estimated at $2.5 million. However, after a careful audit the value had been found to be far less.[8] The auditing committee reported that a million dollars of the wealth which Brigham had bequeathed to his heirs actually wasn't his own, but belonged to the church.[9]

Taylor had hoped to keep matters quiet while ironing things out with the disappointed Young family. But such was not to be. A family of such enormous size couldn't be expected to be unanimous about anything. While most members would accept an equitable accounting—particularly in view of the fact that the settlement was in accordance with revelation —there were a few dissidents. They resented the attempted settlement as an attack on the dead man's integrity; they also charged that, as trustee-in-trust of the church, John Taylor was transferring assets from the estate to himself and others.

Someone on the inside was leaking information. The *Tribune* hooted at Taylor's attempt to settle the estate by revelation, and began calling him "John the Revelator." The *Trib*'s comments on the will itself were caustic: "One of the Most Remarkable Documents in the World." "Millions of the People's Tithing Divided Among His Families." The twelve-page instrument had apportioned the estate among nineteen classes of wives and children, "reminding one," the *Trib* said, "of the premium lists of an agricultural fair."

Fortunately, the *Tribune* didn't have access to the sacred records, which would have revealed that some thirty additional wives were not mentioned at all in the will, nor provision made for their support.

Property in the will was referred to by legal description. On checking this against a lot map of the city, the *Tribune* was delighted to discover

---

[8] The final sum available to the heirs was finally determined at $224,242.42—less than one-tenth the expected bequest. See *Deseret News*, August 5, 1879.

[9] Arrington, op. cit., says, ". . . it was necessary to go back to the very beginnings of the accounts in 1848 and trace through all the transactions of the trustee-in-trust and Brigham Young—the countless cross-borrowings and repayments. This was a task which was difficult and time-consuming. It came as a great surprise to many— including his close associates—that the obligations of Brigham Young to the church at the time of his death totaled $999,632.90. . . . Thus, the investigation into the estate revealed that many of the enterprises which bore the name of Brigham Young as principal stockholder or officer were, in fact, enterprises of the church. . . ."

that Brigham had bequeathed as his personal assets the Social Hall, scene of many church recreational functions; the LDS Museum; the President's Office itself; the Council House, in which the pioneer legislature held sessions; the Constitution building adjoining it; and even that historic church edifice, the Salt Lake Theater. Brigham also willed to his family a one-third interest in ZCMI, valued at $118,000, and stock in the city's street railway and gas companies, worth $113,500, whose ownership was in question.

"John Taylor is now walking in the footsteps of Brigham, and John is a gobbler," the *Trib* said, who "fattens sleek on tithing." When the time came to publish Taylor's will, the paper predicted that "the brethren may find the temple willed to his numerous progeny."[10]

At the office, Taylor and his secretary, L. John Nuttall, spent an hour together, going over estate matters and the daily correspondence.[11]

Nuttall's ears pricked up as Taylor dictated a letter, directing a request for the president of the European mission to furnish traveling expenses for a lady, "now about sixty years of age," to gather in Zion. The lady would have been in her twenties when Taylor was in England on his first mission. The great Utah guessing game was matching up secret wives with husbands; but the question never could be put to those involved.[12]

Correspondence finished, Nuttall left with several property deeds to be signed by executors of Brigham's estate. Taylor decided to have tea out back in the garden, for the first time that spring. Sitting there alone, he remembered pleasant summer days when Lucy Decker brought the pot of weird composition brew. John Taylor realized that it would be difficult for many Saints to understand—and impossible for Gentiles to believe—that the intermingling of Brigham Young's personal business interests with those of the church was neither irregular nor dishonest, but was inherent in the Mormon tradition. Since early days at Kirtland, the church had largely controlled temporal affairs.

No aspect of private life or business activity was separate from the church. The block teachers made regular visits to the home of every Saint and reported any need, sickness, or unorthodox thinking. If a man

---

[10] Actually, John Taylor died in modest circumstances. "He never devoted himself to money getting," Roberts says. "He never bowed at the gilded shrine of mammon. The yellow god of this world found in him no devotee. . . . He had his eyes and heart fixed upon the better riches, those which moth and rust could not corrupt, neither mobs break through nor steal. These things filled his soul, engrossed his attention and left but a small margin of time to him in which to fall in love with the wealth of this world."—*Life of John Taylor.*

[11] Nuttall was Taylor's son-in-law.

[12] See *Letter Book of John Taylor. Church Business Book #15.* Church Historian's Office. See also John Hyde (*Mormonism, Its Leaders and Designs*), who states that Taylor was romancing a Jersey girl during his mission to France.

got into a dispute, it was settled in bishop's court. If he wanted to open a store or repair shop, he asked the church's permission. His standing in the community was related to his church office, which in turn was reflected by his social status, military rank in the Nauvoo Legion, and his material wealth.

The church was everything, and Brigham Young ran the church. Under his direction it built highways, iron works, a sugar factory, woolen mills, irrigation projects, public buildings, railroads, and other enterprises. Brigham Young as trustee-in-trust managed the "bible commonwealth" of Deseret—the Great Basin—where the Mormon colonies pooled their resources in a great cooperative effort.

Property ownership by the church was further complicated enormously by a vindictive Congress. The Anti-Bigamy Act of 1862, which dissolved the church as a legal corporation and prohibited it from owning property worth more than $50,000, forced Brigham from that time on to continue operations by legal subterfuge, deeding church property to himself and other officials.[13]

As Taylor finished his tea and went from the garden to his desk, he reflected that there was little wonder that accounts became mixed up.

An audit was necessary if the church was to be run upon a business basis from now on. There was no good reason why a change of leadership should throw everything into confusion. He remembered the situation at Nauvoo, where after the death of Joseph Smith titles of church property became so clouded that most of it was lost. The management of church funds was casual, to say the least. Men of high office dipped into the pot to finance personal projects. They paid no interest, and too often the method of repayment was by what some called the "double entry" system —money owed the tithing fund was cancelled "for services rendered."[14]

In his *Rocky Mountain Saints*, T. B. H. Stenhouse said that Brigham was prone to settle his own obligations in this fashion.

---

[13] These provisions of the law hadn't been enforced because the church had challenged the Anti-Bigamy Act in the courts, and the case was still being appealed. The threat was there, and as subsequent events proved, it was not an idle one.

[14] Arrington, op. cit., points out that "This ability to draw, almost at will, on church as well as his own funds, was a great advantage to Brigham Young and was certainly one of the reasons for his worldly success." Also, "the studied and deliberate policy of placing properties acquired by the church in the hands of the church president and other trustworthy individuals, to be administered by them on behalf of the church, but in a private capacity . . . led to a confusion between Brigham Young, trustee-in-trust, and Brigham Young, private businessman." In his business dealings "representing the church, President Young almost invariably signed for properties in his own name as if the deal were a strictly private one. . . ." This "accounts for the widespread tendency among newspapermen, writers, and historians to give Brigham Young credit for many enterprises which were in reality enterprises of the church."

He is charged with having, in 1852, balanced his account with the church to the modest sum of $200,000, by directing the clerk to place to his credit the same amount "for services rendered," and in 1867, he further discharged his obligations, amounting to the small sum of $967,000, in a similar fashion.

Taylor had hoped that by ordering an audit he wouldn't give credence to such stories by apostates. He resented the leak of confidential matters to the *Tribune*; the whole thing might have been settled quietly, with nothing to reflect on either the church or the previous administration.

The report of John Taylor, trustee-in-trust, based on the audit, listed amounts totaling $139,678.09 due from railroad construction contracts which Brigham had undertaken as church projects. Bookkeeping errors had given Brigham a credit of $52,200 in ZCMI stock that was owned by the church. Three pieces of real estate, containing the Social Hall, Museum, and Constitution building, were clearly church property. The remainder of the $999,632.90 owing the church by the estate consisted of various "errors and credits on B. Young's private account," totaling $779,106.28.[15]

In settlement, the church offered to allow the heirs generously inflated prices for property returned to church ownership (Salt Lake Theater $125,000, for example; Gardo House $100,000), and to credit President Young's estate with $300,000 in salary for thirty years at $10,000 per year. By the next afternoon everything was signed, sealed, and delivered to Probate Judge Elias Smith, who approved the settlement. "Upon which the business being fully completed, Elder G. Q. Cannon at the request of Prest Taylor offered thanks to Almighty God," Nuttall recorded with feeling. George Q. Cannon caught a train to Washington to take his seat

---

[15] Nuttall in his *Journal* detailed the claim as follows:

To amount of balance due on Railroad Contract A/–	$ 88,000.00
" amount of balance due on Utah Central Railroad A/–	51,678.09
" Zions Co-op Mertle. Inst. A/–	52,200.00
" manifest errors in Book A/–	10,404.60
" Errors in footings and extensions	9,079.41
" balance of Book A/– from June 30/73	100,755.09
" real estate "Social Hall" & lot	17,438.97
" " " "Museum" & lot	4,000.00
" " " Constitution bldg. & lot	7,209.56
" amount of errors in credits on B. Young's Private A/–	628,867.18
" amount to reimburse the Trustee-in-Trust for sum erroneously credited to private account of Prest B. Young for subsistence & Quartermasters Bills &c as per entry of August 28, 1866	30,000.00
Salt Lake City, Utah Territory	$999,632.90
April 8, 1878	

in Congress. Taylor went home with springs in his heels, having laid down a heavy burden.

Then at five next afternoon, as Taylor was preparing to leave the office, Nuttall dashed in with the news: Two of Brigham's sons, Ernest and Alfales, had filed suit in Third District Court, and secured injunctions prohibiting the executors from making settlement of the estate until the case had been heard.

Taylor went home with Brigham's burden again on his back.

The period of nice weather proved to be a false spring. Snow halted the Union Pacific in the mountains, and fell on the valley in mid-April. And, as the estate settlement also proved premature, Taylor spent much of the spring and summer holding meetings between the auditing committee, the executors, and the Young family, while the *Trib* had a field day with the case.

Cannon returned from Washington, and used his excellent powers of persuasion to bring everyone together in harmony. On returning to the capital in November, he wrote,

> In leaving home I had the satisfaction of knowing that all the legatees except one (Nabbie Young Clawson) had been settled with and they had signed releases; all the debts, excepting one or two trifling amounts, have been paid and everything closed up as far as possible.

The *Tribune*, as might be expected, was scornful of the settlement. "THAT WILL BE DONE," it headlined, charging that "an organized system of fraud and violence was adopted to secure the signatures to the release." The heirs were "forced to sign" by "threats of being cut off the church, and ostracized from society."

Let the *Tribune* rant. Taylor was glad for peace on any terms. Brigham's ghost at last was at rest.

It was almost a year after the supposedly "final" settlement of Brigham Young's estate, that Emmeline A. Young, a daughter, filed suit on behalf of the heirs against the executors of the estate and John Taylor, trustee-in-trust of the church.

"FRAUD ON THE WILL," the *Tribune* headlined. "Over a Million Dollars Stolen by Taylor & Co." "Suit of the Heirs to Recover the Money." "Full Exposure of the Robbery, Trickery, and Collusion."

This was exactly the sort of public mess Taylor had tried to avoid. But no private meetings of the family were possible, this time. Emmeline A. Young, now married to a popular stage comedian, W. C. Crosbie, was living in California, out of reach. This would be a battle between lawyers. He called a meeting of the Quorum in the Council House, and counseled that the "brethren take a straight forward course—with no equivocation or falsifying," in the pending suit.[16]

The following day W. S. McCornick, a local banker who had been appointed receiver for the estate by the court, arrived at Taylor's office to demand custody of all property of the estate as described by the will. Backing up McCornick was hulking Sam Gilson, deputy for U.S. Marshal Michael Shaughnessy, appointed co-receiver in order to supply McCornick with muscle. Taylor referred them to his attorneys. The fight was on.[17]

He and the executors were cited for contempt of court. Sam Gilson let fellow deputies take Cannon, Young, and Carrington into custody, while he personally served John Taylor with a warrant of arrest. The four were hauled into court Saturday afternoon, and released under $5,000 bond until Monday afternoon to think it over.

It was a bad weekend for John Taylor. Following a period of comparative quiet, trouble was boiling up again between the Saints and Gentiles. After seventeen years of tenacious legal warfare, the Mormons had lost the right to free exercise of religious belief: the U.S. Supreme Court upheld the Anti-Bigamy Act of 1862, confirming the test case, the conviction of George Reynolds for polygamy.

Taylor sought divine guidance over the weekend, but the heavens seemed closed; the Lord already had spoken on the subject of the estate and had no more to add. Taylor's insides tightened into a knot. He visited various families on Sunday, and each wife tried to tempt him with delicacies; but he had small appetite, and what food he did take was like a rock in his stomach. Even Maggie's saucy charm failed to relax him. By Monday morning he was so tense it seemed that something might snap. The day was blistering hot. There was no opportunity in the busy forenoon for a walk to unwind himself, what with getting ready for the court appearance. The office was sweltering, yet the conferences with lawyers and others made it necessary to wear a coat. While at lunch he suddenly became dizzy, broke into a sweat, began vomiting. He wondered if someone had poisoned him, but after lying down awhile was able to go to the U.S. District Court, now located in the Wasatch block at Main and Second South, accompanied by Erastus Snow, Franklin D. Richards, Bishop John Sharp of the Twentieth Ward, and Nuttall. A horde of Saints, outraged at the treatment of their leaders, crowded the courtroom, sullenly glowering. A spark, some small incident, might precipitate an explosion.

---

[16] Nuttall, op. cit.

[17] Two weeks later, six siblings joined Emmeline in the suit, Miranda Y. Conrad, Luisa Y. Ferguson, Elizabeth Y. Ellsworth, Vilate Y. Decker, Dora Young, and Ernest I. Young.

The courtroom was stifling. Taylor began again getting dizzy while the lawyers wrangled forty-five minutes getting a postponement. Bishop Sharp took him to Maggie's in his carriage. A slender, keen-eyed man, with bristling black eyebrows in contrast to a white Van Dyck, Sharp was a wealthy contractor who had first heard the gospel while a coal miner in Clackmannanshire, Scotland. After coming to Utah he became superintendent of the granite quarry which furnished stone for the tabernacle, for the foundations of the temple, and for the wall around Temple Square—paying his men in wheat, chickens, flour, molasses, potatoes, and other produce from the tithing account. Later, in partnership with Brigham Young, he cut the tunnels in Weber canyon and laid the stonework of bridge abutments for the Union Pacific.

As his carriage pulled up before Maggie's, Sharp said, "Brother John, we will neither of us live long enough to see this estate mess settled."

"It will be settled before the year's out!" Taylor retorted testily.

Sharp regarded Taylor a moment. "I've got a thousand dollars that says differently."

"You have a bet, Bishop Sharp!"

Later, lying on the sofa in his private room at Maggie's, Taylor felt remorse. A fine thing, leader of the church making wagers with his bishops. Particularly when he was betting on a sure thing; the Lord had told him how to settle the estate. He thought of releasing Sharp from the wager, but, no, it would teach the bishop a lesson in faith. And Sharp could well afford it.

While the contempt case was pending, Taylor and the Mormon people received another blow: A wire from a missionary in Georgia, Rudger Clawson, brought news of the death of his companion, Joseph Standing, killed by a mob near Varnell's Station.

The following Saturday Taylor and the executors again appeared in a jammed courtroom, where Judge Jacob Boreman, a pious Methodist and notorious Mormon-eater who was temporarily on the bench, decreed they would go to prison unless Taylor turned over all property conveyed to him by the executors and the executors relinquished assets of the estate amounting to $124,999.52. As the lawyers fought to secure bond, and the price for Taylor to stay out of prison rose to $200,000, he stood in wrath and declared he'd go behind bars before he'd pay extortion. The lawyers soothed him, explaining it just wouldn't do for the head of the church to go to prison; that would give the Gentiles and federal carpetbaggers too much satisfaction. Taylor grudgingly agreed to the bond for himself; but as a matter of principle the executors, George Q. Cannon, Brigham Young, Jr., and Albert Carrington, refused to furnish bond of $50,000 each (Carrington wanted to, but was overruled). Judge Boreman sentenced them to prison, giving them a day's grace to put their affairs in shape.

The series of events had brought tempers on both sides to a hair-trigger. The following morning, Sunday, some 10,000 people attended the funeral of Joseph Standing. Taylor spoke at the ceremony, and an hour later learned that his good friend, A. Milton Musser, formerly traveling bishop of the church and now assistant church historian, had been assaulted at his home with a rawhide whip.

Next afternoon Taylor shook hands with Cannon, Briggie, and Carrington and walked them out the gate of the high cobblestone wall. Deputy Marshal Sprague waited with the carriage to take them to Sugar House.[18] "Good day, brethren," Taylor said as they climbed in; "I hope for a speedy return." Then with a glance at Sprague, as the deputy climbed over the front wheel, he added, "In the meantime, we will take care of these vagabonds."

Sprague deliberately spat tobacco juice into the dust of the roadway, then cut the team with the whip, and the rig rattled east along South Temple toward Hyland Drive.

Next morning, Taylor drove down to A. Milton Musser's home on First South. It was a shock to see the patrician face of his friend, with its high-bridged nose and neat beard, swollen black and blue from the beating. Musser wasn't seriously hurt, but he was furious about the assault. The two men sat in the parlor, the whip coiled on the table beside them, while Musser told of the fracas.

The wife of General M. M. Bane, a hostile federal carpetbagger appointed to the position of Receiver of the Land Office, had been prominent in organizing the Anti-Polygamy Society. This group was composed of some 200 Gentile ladies and apostate Mormon females who had petitioned Congress, the women of the nation, and Mrs. Rutherford B. Hayes, wife of the president, "for the abolition of this great crime."[19]

In rebuttal to the pious crusaders, the Salt Lake *Herald* devoted a series of articles on the moral short-comings and shady backgrounds of some of the Anti-Polygamy Society's members. Though unsigned, the articles were attributed to Musser's pen, and Harry Bane, adopted son of the general, set out with a hulking friend, G. W. Elliott, to avenge this slur

---

[18] At Sugar House, they lived at the Warden's home as honored guests, preaching to their fellow prisoners on Sundays. They were in custody from August 4 to 28, when the Territorial Supreme Court reversed the lower court's decision.

[19] The petition not only denounced polygamy as "degrading to man and woman, a curse to children, and destructive to the sacred relations of the family," but raised the spectre of its insidious spread and the eventual Mormon takeover of the government: "An apostle [Cannon], a polygamist, with four acknowledged wives, is permitted to sit in Congress. . . . Our [territorial] legislature is composed almost entirely of polygamists and members of the Mormon priesthood. . . . The Mormons are rapidly extending their settlements in Arizona, Idaho, New Mexico, and Wyoming. They have the balance of power in two territories and are, without doubt, plotting it for others."

on Gentile womanhood. Though under arrest, dismissal of the ruffians was a foregone conclusion, Musser said, his swollen face forming a wry smile; just another incident.

Coming atop the Reynolds conviction, the Standing murder, the wrangle over the estate, and the sentencing of three apostles to prison, the attack on Musser had brought the Mormon people to a dangerous pitch of frustration. Unless something relieved the pressure, there might be an explosion of public outrage. Arising to leave, Taylor whirled the rawhide whip overhead, snapped it with the report of a gun shot. There was one language these ruffians understood, he said, repayment in their own coin. He handed the whip to Musser and went out.

The courtroom at City Hall was jammed next morning, air electric with disgruntled citizens. Everything was cut and dried. Bane and Elliott waived examination and gave bonds for appearance before the grand jury. This, everyone knew, ended the matter. U.S. Attorney Van Zile, a typical appointee, would drop the case. Wearing smug expressions, the defendants, with General Bane, friends, and lawyers, left the courtroom.

As the party entered the hallway, men suddenly sprang to the various doors, locking out police and bailiffs. Harry Bane's friend, Elliott, took in the situation with a glance and dived out the window. The others of the party began defending themselves. Musser was there, whip in hand. He singled out Harry Bane and gave the young man a thorough rawhiding before police broke down the doors and stopped the fight.

The *Tribune*, of course, was outraged. The U.S. Attorney indicted Musser and his friends for "assault with intent to kill." But nothing would come of this, Taylor knew. The incident provided a safety valve for the people, who enjoyed it as much as he did.[20]

He drove to his farm in Taylorsville after council meeting that afternoon, and got in an hour's work before dark. As he broke into a sweat

---

[20] During this period Taylor stepped in for a brief period as editor of the *Deseret News*. His hand can be seen in the editorial following the Musser incident:

"If the carpetbaggers want to inaugurate a collision, we think they can be accommodated; but the time has come when the people will not succumb to their villainies. If there are any more attacks upon peaceable citizens in their private dwellings, the thugs who attempt it will surely meet their desserts, and if there is no protection from the courts we shall not any longer counsel submission. We are not here to bow down as serfs to government appointees, nor to lick the bribe-stained hands of satraps. We are still in possession of certain inalienable rights which we do not propose to surrender; among them are 'life, liberty, and the pursuit of happiness.' We shall protect our lives as best we may from the murderous assaults of imported assassins. We shall contend for our liberties and resist the incarceration of honorable men in jails, while land-sharks, conspirators, murderers, seducers, and other vagabonds go at large; and we propose to pursue happiness in our own way without the dictation of those corrupt scoundrels, who, while heaping abuse upon us, are seeking to introduce here the foulest forms of vice."

the tension and the half-sick feeling that had ridden him suddenly was gone; he felt great, and after a hot bath slept like a baby.

The estate case dragged on another five weeks, when finally it was settled a second time, the church giving the seven litigants $75,000 to quiet title.[21]

A stream of visitors called at the office all afternoon to offer congratulations on the settlement of the case. One of them was John Sharp, who handed Taylor a check for $1,000.[22] In accepting it, Taylor reminded the bishop that it was poor policy to make wagers, and particularly to bet against the Lord. Then when Sharp went out, Taylor handed the check to Nuttall and told him to credit it to the bishop's tithing account.

---

[21] Four days after the settlement one of the litigants, Ernest I. Young, was found dead in bed. The following May he, along with the other six, were excommunicated for "going to law with a brother."

[22] Nuttall, October 4, 1879.

18

Jubilee

THE VISITOR arrived at Taylor's office with the ingratiating smile of a favor-seeker. Edward W. Tullidge was a lean man of nervous intensity, domed forehead tapering to sunken cheeks, a white Van Dyck contrasting to dark hair parted in the middle. He and Taylor had a great deal in common: both were Englishmen, converts, missionaries, scholars, and authors; both were liberals and idealists, intellectuals who had chafed under Brigham's regime. But while Taylor had survived, Tullidge had voluntarily resigned his church membership during the Godbeite brouhaha. Taylor could respect a stand on principle; however, he had reason to believe Tullidge had had ulterior motives. His reception of the man definitely was reserved.

Tullidge explained that while working as a missionary in the Liverpool office of the *Millennial Star* twenty years ago, he had been called by the Lord to write the life story of Joseph Smith. Now at last the project was finished, and he would like President Taylor's blessing and sponsorship. "President Young requested me to write this book," Tullidge said, while Joseph's cousin, Apostle George A. Smith "on his death bed charged me concerning it." Joseph's nephew, Apostle Joseph F. Smith, and one of the prophet's wives, Eliza R. Snow, had both "kindly read and revised the manuscript."[1]

Taylor pointed out that Tullidge in his *Life of Brigham Young* had

---

[1] John Taylor reported the affair in the *Deseret News*, October 30, 1878. See also J. Cecil Alter, *Early Utah Journalism*; William Frank Lye, "Edward Wheelock Tullidge, the Mormons' Rebel Historian," *Utah Historical Quarterly*, April 1960; *Tullidge's Quarterly Magazine*. Tullidge's *Life of Joseph Smith* was published in Salt Lake, 1878, and the revised edition at Plano, Illinois, 1880.

proclaimed himself an apostate for many years, and thus "cannot be justly charged with the spirit of Mormon propagandism."

"That is not my doing," Tullidge protested; it was put in by the publisher, "with the expectation that it would make the book sell better in the East." And he wasn't an apostate, he said; in fact, he'd been re-baptized.

Nothing infuriated Taylor like lack of integrity. "Then, in the East, you are an apostate, because it is expected your book will sell better," he said scathingly; "and here you are a Saint, because to be a Saint pays better."

Tullidge flushed. "It was taken out of the last edition," he said. "I do contradict it."

"Yes, privately; but you allow it publicly to go uncontradicted," Taylor pointed out. "If, as you say, you have been baptized, how is it that you will permit so foul a stigma on your character. Where is your manhood?"

Tullidge lost his temper. "I repudiate your remarks!" he cried.

"We cannot look upon you as a fit person to write the history of the prophet," Taylor retorted. "I forbid you having access to the Historian's Office."

Despite Taylor's disapproval, Tullidge published his *Life of Joseph Smith* a few months later. The book itself bore evidence that the author was actually in spirit a Josephite. Taylor knew that, while east with his stage play, Tullidge had been strongly influenced by a visit to the prophet's first wife, Emma Smith, and her oldest son, Young Joseph, who recently had accepted leadership of the Reorganized LDS Church.

Investigating, Taylor found that both Joseph F. Smith and Eliza R. Snow denied having approved or revised the manuscript. "How far the alleged statements of President Brigham Young and George A. Smith are correct, we are not prepared to say," he said wryly in his account of the affair in the *Deseret News*, "and they are not here to speak for themselves."

Soon afterwards, Taylor's suspicions were confirmed when Tullidge defected again and joined the Josephites. The second edition of the book was revised into a Reorganized tract.

This experience brought home to Taylor the pressing need for an honest and objective history of the Mormons that would be read with respect both within Zion and in the outside world. None existed. While the archives of the Historian's Office bulged with a vast storehouse of material, nothing came out of it except missionary tracts. Gentiles were refused access to the material. As a result, the world knew almost nothing of Mormonism except from unfriendly authors. The faith-promoting literature published in Utah was unreadable outside.[2]

---

[2] Unfortunately, this is still true. The veritable flood of material issued by the man-

To get things underway, Taylor issued an epistle calling upon the Saints "to gather up and preserve a history of all the facts pertaining to" the Mormons, copies of documents, journals, personal histories, stories of persecution. "We are desirous that a truthful record may be had, in convenient form."[3]

Shortly thereafter, the prestigious historian, Hubert H. Bancroft, who was engaged in compiling his monumental *History of the Pacific States*, wrote the church asking for material for his projected *History of Utah*. Orson Pratt, church historian, offered to supply the history if Bancroft would guarantee to publish it "without mutilation." "This only showed," Bancroft commented, "that they were wholly mistaken in the character of my work." He realized that

> Utah was not the easiest of problems with which to deal historically. . . .
> Prejudice against the Mormons was so strong and universal, and of such
> long standing, that . . . I well knew that strict impartiality would bring
> upon me the condemnation of both Mormons and Gentiles. If this, then,
> was the test of truth and fair dealing, I must subject myself to the censure
> of both sides; . . . I would not write for the approbation of one side or
> the other.[4]

Writing to James Dwyer, in charge of territorial school books, Bancroft outlined his aims and methods of writing "after a careful weighing of all gathered testimony, . . . in a word, exact history."

> Hence the extract of what Mr. Pratt should so kindly furnish me
> would be added to the extracts of all other material within my reach. . . .
> Its presence would be felt in proportion as it presented new truths and
> disclosed unknown facts.[5]

Bancroft asked for every type of material, both religious and temporal, "the seeming trivia as well as the more apparently important," and in particular the personal stories of living people "whose adventures, counsels, and acts," shaped the course of events.

> There are men yet living who helped to make our history. . . . A score
> of years hence few of them will remain. Twenty years ago many parts
> of our territory were not old enough to have a history; twenty years
> hence much will be lost. . . .

---

aged press of Utah is strictly for internal consumption. For example, of hundreds of titles published in Utah about Joseph Smith, not a single one has passed through the Zion Curtain. Only one biography of the prophet is known to the Gentile world, Fawn M. Brodie's definitive *No man knows my history*, published in New York and, of course, anathema to the Saints.

[3] March 8, 1879.

[4] *Works*, XXXIX, *Literary Industries*.

[5] January 12, 1880.

Orson Pratt was reluctant to open the archives to a Gentile, and understandably was nettled at the rebuff of his own offer. However, when Dwyer took Bancroft's letter to Taylor, he reported that the church leader was "very much pleased by your ideas."

Taylor particularly endorsed Bancroft's aims:

> If I succeed in my efforts my work will constitute the foundation upon which future histories of western North America must forever be built. . . . I do not hope to satisfy the people of Utah or their opponents, because I cannot espouse the cause of either. But I can promise to give, I think, as fully as lies in the power of most men, a simple, truthful statement of facts. . . . Every truthful writer of history must hold himself absolutely free to be led wherever the facts carry him. The moment he becomes partisan his work is worthless.

Taylor held a council with members of the Twelve, who endorsed the suggestion that Bancroft should be given all cooperation and furnished with complete information. Taylor then wrote Bancroft, "pleased to place myself in direct communication with you on this subject." Orson Pratt, his nose evidently out of joint, found himself unable to supply his manuscript because "of the very feeble state" of his health. "I, however," Taylor wrote,

> take great pleasure in informing you that the Hon. Franklin D. Richards . . . is one of our leading and respected citizens, and a gentleman who is fully conversant in literary and legal matters. . . . He is now nearly prepared to start for San Francisco, and will take with him the historical data.

In addition to published work, Richards supplied Bancroft with many manuscripts—community histories, autobiographies, journals, reports on Mormon institutions and culture. As the work progressed, Bancroft came to Salt Lake, where he met with Taylor, George Q. Cannon, Wilford Woodruff, and Franklin D. Richards to discuss the project and read portions of the manuscript. All were delighted. Taylor and Cannon wrote an official letter to stake presidents and bishops urging "support and patronage" of the work.

> It will, no doubt, find its way into all the chief libraries of the civilized world, and . . . will be authentic and calculated to extend a knowledge of the true condition of our affairs.[6]

---

[6] Bancroft was the first outsider to receive full church cooperation—and the last. It is difficult to overestimate the importance of his *History of Utah* as a framework for subsequent scholars and historians. Considering the iron censorship of the controlled press of Utah, both prior to and following Taylor's liberal administration, plus severe restrictions on access to church archives and the encrustations of dearly-beloved mythology, Mormon history would be in an appalling state of distortion, except for Bancroft. His collection of materials, housed in the Bancroft Library, University of

Taylor meanwhile was working nights in his book-lined study at Margaret's on a book, *The Mediation and Atonement of Our Lord and Savior Jesus Christ*. This was of great significance doctrinally, because it marked the rejection of the Adam-God concept which had permeated Mormonism for three decades. In effect, the *Mediation* restored Christianity to the church. It, together with Taylor's sermons, reemphasized principles which old-timers welcomed as a return to the gospel of Joseph Smith's time.[7]

Tullidge returned from his Josephite excursion and made his peace with Taylor. The author saw Mormonism as falling into three periods. Joseph first created the spiritual kingdom. Brigham then built the temporal kingdom. John Taylor "wonderfully blends in himself the spiritual and the temporal," Tullidge said. "He is at once what Joseph was and what Brigham was—the two halves in one whole."[8]

The spring and summer of 1879 were hot and dry. Crops burned. Grasshoppers devastated what little was left. Then came the most severe winter since the Saints had arrived. Thousands of cattle and sheep turned tail in the blizzards and froze to death.

Next spring on April 6, 1880 the church was fifty years old, and the Saints met for the Jubilee Conference. In ancient Israel on the jubilee year

---

California at Berkeley, is still being mined by researchers. While some historians, such as Linn, have criticized Bancroft for being too sympathetic, because the book was designed to sell widely in Utah, its value in blazing the trail simply cannot be questioned.

See also, "Hubert Howe Bancroft and the History of Utah," by George Ellsworth, *Utah Historical Quarterly*, April 1954.

[7] Today, Brigham's Adam-God doctrine has been so thoroughly abandoned that apologists deny that he ever preached it. Contrary evidence abounds in the *Journal of Discourses*. During Brigham's time the Hebraic values were emphasized to the extent that Tullidge could write, without disapproval:

"All America, the New Jerusalem of the last days! All America for the God of Israel! . . . All America, then, is Zion! . . . Mark this august wonder of the age; the Mormons build not temples to the name of Jesus, but to the name of Jehovah—not to the Son, but to the Father. . . .

"Mormonism is no Christian sect, but an Israelitish nationality. . . . The Hebrew symbol is not the cross. It is the symbol of heathenism, whence Rome perceived her signs and her worship. Rome adopted the cross and she has borne it as her mark. . . .

"The reign of Messiah! Temples to the Most High God! The sceptre, not the cross!"

See Tullidge, *The Women of Mormondom*, Chapter XI.

[8] *Tullidge's Magazine*, p. 392. Upon returning to Utah, Tullidge joined the literary renaissance of the Taylor regime, beginning work on his *History of Salt Lake City*, subsidized by the city yet objective. Incidentally, Tullidge found himself given respect as a Josephite, where he had been scorned while posing as an apostate outside and a faithful Saint within Zion.

the poor debtor had his account cancelled; those in bondage were set free; an inheritance lost through misfortune was restored. "It occurred to me," Taylor told the assembled Saints, "that we ought to do something, as they did in former times, to relieve those that are oppressed with debt, to assist those that are needy, to break off the yoke of those that may feel themselves crowded upon, and to make it a time of general rejoicing."

Thousands of members were indebted to the Perpetual Emigration Fund, which had advanced credit for passage to Zion; church books showed an outstanding debt of $1,604,000. Taylor cancelled half of this, writing off entirely debts of the poor. "The rich can always take care of themselves," he commented, "—that is, so far as this world is concerned." Worry about the next world caused a considerable number of them to pony up what they owed.

Taylor also cancelled half the tithing indebtedness on the books, forgiving the poor entirely. Next, he said, "We propose to raise 1,000 head of cows—not old cows which do not give any milk, nor any one-teated cows, but good milk cows—and have them distributed among those who might be destitute." Five thousand sheep would be distributed to the poor in the same manner. The church would furnish 300 cows and 2,000 sheep from the tithing herds, while the local stakes would donate the remainder.

For years Brigham and other brethren had been exhorting the people to store up "seven years of bread" for a day of famine. Despite the strongest urging, Brigham felt ashamed to admit that not one man in a hundred had his wheat stored ahead. Finally after the men had failed, Brigham in the last months of his life turned to the women. He called in Emmeline B. Wells, editor of the *Women's Exponent* and an officer of the Relief Society. "I want to give you a mission," he told her, "and it is to save grain."

Though the women were laughed at—"ridiculed more over this than over any other thing" undertaken by the Relief Society, Emmeline related —they began buying grain, storing it in her husband's barn. The following year, after Brigham's death, Taylor met with the grain committees of the wards and stakes, where he complimented the women and urged them to further efforts. Women exchanged housework for wheat; midwives delivered babies for wheat; mothers and daughters gleaned wheat fields after harvest; women raised orphan calves and lambs to trade for wheat. Relief Societies overseas and in the nation outside Utah contributed funds for wheat. When Squire Wells' barn overflowed, men pitched in to build granaries.

And now in the jubilee year the time of need had come. The Relief Society had 34,761 bushels of wheat, to be "loaned out to some of our poor brethren," Taylor said. With a grin he added: "We do not want any more harsh talk about the women question after this."

He then urged the people to forgive one another their debts, promising that God would relieve them in turn when they were in difficulties. In a circular to all stake presidents and ward bishops he extended "to all our brethren and sisters the privilege of aiding in this good work of compassion and love," counseling the people to cancel notes of the poor, tear up mortgages, "extend to them a jubilee," to forgive them their debts "as you might desire them to forgive you, were their and your circumstances reversed," to live the golden rule, "for upon this hangs the law of the prophets."

He urged ZCMI and other cooperatives, and businessmen engaged in railroad, banking, mercantile, manufacturing, or other enterprises "to extend a helping hand. Free the worthy debt-bound brother if you can. Let there be no rich among us from whose tables fall only crumbs to feed a wounded Lazarus."

The Jubilee year saw a great spiritual awakening among the Society, flowering in the climate of freedom and good will. The gospel became not a Sunday ceremony, but a way of life. In letters to bishops and stake presidents Taylor counseled them to settle disputes among themselves, to avoid "going to law against a brother," because "we have a superior source for achieving justice."

He was outraged on learning that the giving of patriarchal blessings had degenerated to a competition for fees, patriarchs going from door to door, "underbidding each other in the price of blessings," degrading the office "to a mere means of obtaining a livelihood."[9] He immediately put a stop to the practice of taking fees.

Taylor instituted weekly priesthood meetings for the male membership in the wards, monthly in the stakes, and the practice of holding quarterly stake conferences. He personally attended local conferences when possible, but saw to it that one of the general authorities was on hand if he wasn't. And he pushed forward with increased zeal work on the three temples under construction, at Salt Lake, Logan, and Manti.

He revitalized the missionary system, calling a greater number into the field than ever before. Some of these were harassed polygamists, "taking a mission" to avoid persecution; but most were young single men, sent out without purse or scrip, to trust in the Lord for food, raiment, transportation, and lodging while traveling throughout the world.

Taylor called his own son, John W. (of Sophia's family), to a mission in the southern states, and John's good friend, Matthias F. Cowley, as his companion: When Cowley reported to the president's office Taylor said, "Well, I understand you're going on a mission."

"I am if that is the Lord's will."

"Oh, the Lord's willing if you are." Taylor told the young man to go over to the Historian's Office to be set apart for the calling.

---

9 Letter to George Q. Cannon, November 7, 1877.

"I suppose that's where I'll get my instructions."

"Oh, no. You don't need any instructions," Taylor said. "Put your trust in the Lord and he will carry you through."[10]

Taylor had complained that the turtle-shaped tabernacle built by Brigham was "too large and too cold," so he'd built "a fine, new, substantial tabernacle in place of the old [adobe] one, for holding meetings in the winter."[11] However, for October conference the large tabernacle was jammed with 13,000 people, so closely packed that heating was no problem. John Taylor, who for three years had led the church as president of the Quorum of the Twelve, was to be officially ordained president of the church. He selected two of the most capable and well-liked men in the church to be his counselors in the presidency, his nephew, George Q. Cannon, Utah's delegate to Congress, and Joseph F. Smith, the martyred Hyrum's son.

Taylor's enlightened and liberal administration had made him enormously popular. Where the people had paid great respect to Brigham, the old-timers had loved Joseph; and now the Saints loved John Taylor.[12]

The Utah ring and the Washington coterie, however, cared nothing for the renaissance in Utah, the enlightened administration, the increase of spirituality, and the era of good feeling during the jubilee year. In fact, the previous January the U.S. Supreme Court had finally, after a legal struggle, affirmed the anti-polygamy law of 1862, and now Congress was busy with numerous bills to put teeth into it.

The man and three young ladies arrived at Taylor's office by appointment. Listening to their tangled tale of romance, John Taylor had no idea of the far-reaching results of John Miles' marital affairs.[13]

---

[10] Cowley, "Reminiscences of Prest John Taylor."

Modern policy is to prepare the missionary thoroughly by an orientation program before he leaves, and by an intensive course of study while in the field. He is furnished transportation and entirely supported by money from home. However, the great days of the early missions, when elders went out without purse or scrip and with no guidance except the spirit, have never been equalled.

[11] It is now known as the assembly hall.

[12] Even the Salt Lake *Tribune*, though calling Taylor "The Ruffian," for his combative temperament, "The Foreigner" because he was born in England, and "John the Revelator" for his spirituality, showed him a respect never accorded Brigham.

An apostate, Josiah F. Gibbs, said, "John Taylor was an exceptionally able man, and well educated. Mild in his government of the Saints, and 'approachable' in his intercourse with them." (*Lights and Shadows of Mormonism*, p. 261.)

[13] Whitney says, "The Miles case takes its place in history as the incipient cause of a general anti-polygamy agitation. . . . It was the spark which kindled the conflagration that swept over all Mormondom . . . and ended with the issuance . . . of the famous 'Manifesto' suspending the practice of plural marriage."

With Miles were Emily and Julia Spencer of St. George, and Caroline Owen, recently arrived from London. Some years previously, in their native England, John Miles and Caroline fell in love. He went to sea, and when she didn't hear from him she concluded in time that he was dead. However, after landing in Australia Miles met Mormon missionaries, embraced the faith and came to Utah, from where he wrote Caroline an offer of marriage. She accepted, but the letter never reached him. Subsequently he became interested in the Spencer sisters, Emily and Julia. He proposed; they accepted. Then he was called on a mission to England, where he looked up Caroline, and found her single. He again proposed; she accepted again. Upon his release, she accompanied him to Utah to be married for time and all eternity. When the train arrived in Salt Lake, Emily and Julia Spencer were there to greet Miles and Caroline. Emily and Julia had been faithfully awaiting their intended.

Such was the situation. The problem was that while Caroline Owen was perfectly willing for Miles to marry the Spencer sisters, she insisted that because of his prior proposal to her she was entitled to be first wife. Emily, however, pointed out that she and Julia actually had become engaged to Miles before Caroline, so that, since Emily was the oldest, shouldn't she be the first wife?

Taylor considered, then delivered his counsel: as with baptism, the principle of seniority should prevail in plural marriages. Emily as the oldest should precede the other two to the altar. If this wasn't satisfactory, Taylor advised all four to call off the whole thing. Caroline, however, still insisted on being number one. Miles agreed.

Soon afterwards, Miles and Caroline entered the Endowment House to be sealed in marriage. But the happy occasion was blighted for Caroline when she met Emily Spencer there. She suspected that Miles, contrary to her understanding with him, had previously married Emily that very day. This was confirmed when Daniel H. Wells, performing the ceremony, told Miles, "Your first wife ought to be present."

Caroline was steaming that evening at the wedding reception held in the home of Angus M. Cannon. Taylor put in only a brief appearance, and missed the excitement: the hot-headed Caroline, incensed by Emily's presence and overhearing her addressed as "Mrs. Miles," flew into a rage and assaulted Emily, then fled the house. Miles chased out after her and coaxed her to return, but next morning Caroline went before the U.S. Marshal and swore out a complaint. This was a boon to the surprised official, who promptly arrested Miles.

Taylor was called as witness when the case came to trial in federal court. His testimony was brief, that he'd had no direct connection with the alleged polygamous marriage. As one Mormon witness after another was noncommittal, the case rested upon the unsupported testimony of Caroline that she knew Emily had been married that day because of the temple clothing worn. On other details of the ceremony Caroline was vague, because, the prosecution claimed, the "Endowment House oath," was "ringing in her ears."

Taylor, seated in the courtroom, nodded approval of Caroline's reluctance to reveal the endowment ceremony. While he had freely furnished such information to H. H. Bancroft for publication in the *History of Utah*, it was not something for publicity in open court.[14]

Former mayor and counselor in the presidency, Daniel H. Wells, lean and craggy, took the stand. Asked to describe the temple robes, Wells said, "I decline to answer."

The judge fined him $100 and sentenced him to prison two days for contempt of court. This caused a sensation second only to the arrest of Brigham Young.[15]

Wells was given the hospitality of the warden's quarters at Sugar House over the weekend. A line of carriages containing President Taylor and various church and civic officials—including the mayors and city councils of eleven municipalities—arrived to greet the hero on his release. Wells entered Taylor's carriage and the cortege returned to the city. At the foot of Main Street eight bands and ten thousand paraders waited. With bands playing, banners waving, flags flying, the various church and civic organizations marched up Main between a throng of cheering citizens. Only at the corner of Second South was glowering silence, where frozen faces watched from windows and balconies of the federal building. The procession continued to the tabernacle, where, with every seat taken and thousands outside, eight bands playing in the choir seats, the reception took place.

Taylor opened the *Tribune* next day:

> Never has such a crowd thronged the streets, nor such a cavalcade of human beings and brutes in point of numbers, promiscuous and motley confusion, been witnessed before. . . . Hundreds of poor dupes were forwarded by all the trains centering in this city, to participate in a celebration which in spirit and substance was designed as a public defiance of the national judicial authorities.

Taylor chuckled. The *Trib* was always good for a laugh.

---

[14] Many Mormons firmly believe today that the temple ceremony is secret, despite the fact that it has been published repeatedly since Nauvoo days. When William J. Whalen printed it again in 1964 in his *The Latter-day Saints in the Modern Day World*, a good member of the author's ward stole the book from the local library to preserve the secrets.

[15] Whitney, in his *History of Utah*, says, "The imprisonment of the gray-haired veteran, a man universally beloved by the Mormon people, and highly esteemed of the Gentiles, caused a great sensation. Mormondom was stirred to its center," and "like a blaze from an electric battery" came "indignation toward the judge and admiration for the aged prisoner."

No political hack rewarded with the governorship of Utah could have been more fitted for the role of carpetbagger than Eli H. Murray. On meeting him, Taylor was impressed, but not favorably. While Taylor was a man of striking appearance, compared to Murray he was a veritable hayseed. General Murray was vain of his reputation as the "handsomest man in Kentucky"—though ashamed that, as U.S. Marshal there, he had been involved in petty graft.[16] His eyes were clear and large, the broad brow of alabaster, cheeks peaches-and-cream, lips full, while the symmetry of the features was strikingly framed with dark curls; the almost feminine beauty was given manly virility by a handsome moustache and luxuriant beard. He dressed well, but with flashy taste. However, vain as he was, a weakness for high living had undermined his appearance. No expensively tailored suit could conceal the corpulent body, nor his beard the jowls. The governor reminded Taylor of a rubber doll that had been inflated to twice its size.

The meeting between the new governor and the church leader was brief and formal, for Murray was careful not to sully himself by fraternizing with polygamists. He took charge of the Fourth of July celebration on the jubilee year, deliberately snubbing the Saints by making it an all-Gentile celebration. No Mormon marched in the parade, played in the band, took part in the program, or sat on the stand at Washington Square as the foppish governor delivered the official oration. Though uninvited, Taylor thought it would be unwise to absent himself from the observance of Independence Day, and from his carriage heard Murray declare,

> The tree of liberty planted in 1776 has grown . . . broad enough to shelter all patriots; . . . and rich enough in timber to construct scaffolds and coffins for all those who may treasonably conspire to break down our constitution and to violate its written laws. . . .
>
> No new state will be formed, no new star placed upon the folds of the flag, until the people it represents come with the badge of freedom upon their breasts. Free to think for themselves. Free to act for themselves. Free from all kingly and priestly dictation. . . . Utah shall be free, and then, and not till then, a state.

Taylor nodded to the driver, and Brother Greene drove on as the tirade continued. Brother Greene's cheeks were puffed and flushed with anger. When a block away he started in amazement as Taylor burst into hearty laughter. *Pompous ass!*

July 24, Pioneer Day, was a Mormon holiday, and Taylor approved plans for a celebration to show the Gentiles how it was done. Heaping coals onto the fire, invitations to participate were sent to all federal appointees. Murray and his cohorts accepted with polite thanks but re-

---

[16] Charges in Congress that Murray pocketed illegal fees were quashed on a whitewashing technicality. CHC, 6:64.

mained conspicuous by their absence; however, the governor issued an order forbidding the Nauvoo Legion from bearing arms in the parade. The absence of muskets and swords was hardly noticed in a procession more than three miles long that wound through the streets to the tabernacle.

The nation's president, Rutherford B. Hayes, visited Utah soon afterwards, and again the Mormons were snubbed. When Mayor Feramorz Little wired Washington that a committee would meet the president at Ogden and escort him to Salt Lake, there was no answer. A second wire, intercepting the presidential party at Chicago, brought the curt reply, "By prior arrangement I am to be the guest of the governor and hope you are acting in concert."

Suppressing the impulse to ignore the president's visit, Taylor boarded a special train for Ogden together with several church officials, a wife apiece, and a number of their pretty daughters. Governor Murray, however, had stolen a march on the church greeters by going beyond Ogden in his own special train to meet the presidential party at Weber station. The Ogden brass band played a lusty welcome as the presidential train pulled in, but when Hayes was called on to speak he excused himself owing to it being the Sabbath. Mormons accustomed to hearing orations from morning to night on Sunday exchanged glances.

The two church coaches were joined to the presidential train for the trip to Salt Lake, which made the meeting of dignitaries obligatory. George Q. Cannon performed introductions, and presently the leader of the Saints and the chief executive of the nation were deep in discussion of the Mormon problem.

"We are not generally understood by the people of the world—by outsiders," Taylor admitted. For this reason, he could be lenient with legislators and others who "expressed strong indignation" regarding plural marriage. When he himself learned of this commandment of God from Joseph Smith, "It made my flesh crawl."[17]

"From your viewpoint, you think we are a corrupt people," Taylor said, that the Saints were encouraging licentiousness and trying to legalize "the thing you call the social evil."

Hayes nodded, admitting that this was his concept.

Taylor explained that when practiced as a religious ordinance, living the Principle had quite the opposite result. Sexual relations were only for procreation; there was no birth control, no prostitution, no abortion. The Principle was "only for honorable men and women, virtuous men and women, honest men and women," Taylor said. "It is only such people as these that can be admitted to participate." It was not for the world. Among the Saints it was considered celestial marriage, for time and eter-

---

[17] JD, 23:64.

nity; it couldn't be practiced by Gentiles, nor even by most Mormons.

By the time the train arrived at Salt Lake, Taylor had had time to present the church concept, and he was gratified at the president's show of understanding. However, it was quite obvious that Mrs. Hayes hadn't changed her mind. Her relationship with the Mormon ladies was that of a vice crusader conversing with the soiled doves of a brothel.

That evening the presidential party attended the Methodist church where the minister, Dr. Fisher, preached on the text, "Seven women shall take hold of one man, saying . . . let us be called by thy name. . . ."

Though the president stayed only until noon the following day, his wife found time to assure the Gentile ladies of her "cordial cooperation with the Anti-Polygamy movement."[18]

Three months later, reading the president's annual message to Congress in the *Deseret News*, Taylor let out a roar of rage. Remembering his attitude during the train trip, he couldn't understand the president now telling congress

> The political power of the Mormon sect is increasing. It now controls one of our wealthiest and most populous territories, and is extending steadily into other territories. Wherever it goes it establishes polygamy and sectarian political power. . . .
>
> To the reestablishment of the interests and principles which polygamy and Mormonism have imperiled . . . I recommend that the right to vote, hold office, and sit as jurors . . . be confined to those who neither practice nor uphold polygamy.

"He's either a hypocrite or a coward!" Taylor exploded. When L. John Nuttall hurried into the office to see what was wrong, Taylor dictated a letter to George Q. Cannon in Washington, indignant about politicians who talked out of both sides of their mouths.[19]

Meanwhile, the Gentile ladies of Salt Lake issued a monthly magazine, the *Anti-Polygamy Standard*, which enlisted the support of Harriet Beecher Stowe and other notables. The author of *Uncle Tom's Cabin* urged every wife and mother to "give her sympathy, prayers, and efforts to free her sisters from this degrading bondage."[20]

Taylor was amused to learn that plural wives of Godbeites were active in the Anti-Polygamy Society. At meetings Godbeite wives vied with each other in lurid tales of the horrors of polygamy, while authors such as Mrs. B. A. M. Froiseth and Mrs. A. G. Paddock took notes and gave speeches.

---

[18] *Tribune*, September 8, 1880.

[19] Taylor to Cannon, December 30, 1880, Archives, Church Historical Department.

[20] "Here, indeed, was a challenge to the Christian womanhood of America," says Robert Joseph Dwyer in *The Gentile Comes to Utah*.

"Witty, scornful, and sarcastic by turns," he read in the October issue of the *Anti-Polygamy Standard*, "Mrs. Paddock held the audience by an almost magnetic power. She aimed some telling shafts at those whose policy is to remain neutral."

Mrs. Paddock was a thorn in the flesh of Zion. Her purple prose and sentimental bathos had made her novel, *In the Toils—America's Valley of Death*, a best-seller, and she was at work on another, *The Fate of Madame La Tour, a Tale of Salt Lake City*.[21] Mrs. B. A. M. Froiseth was also mining this rich vein with her *Women of Mormonism*, an exposé of polygamy from the mouths of its victims.

The Caroline Miles affair had become a rolling snowball, helped along by thousands of meetings in church parlors by Christian ladies determined to save their Mormon sisters from bondage, flooding Congress with memorials and petitions to abate the remaining relic of barbarism.[22]

To counter the furor, Taylor sent the apostles out among the Saints. He himself toured the stakes and wards, to bolster and sustain the people at the grass-roots level. "We are not serfs, and have not learned to lick the feet of our oppressors," he told the congregation at the Provo tabernacle. "Shall we give up our religion and our God and be governed by practices that exist in the nation which are contrary to the laws of God?"

The answer echoed from the organ pipes, and the hanging lamps shivered. "They have passed a law for political effect which is really intended as a trap for us," he warned; but stand fast, for "The God who rules in the heavens is watching over their movements as well as ours. . . . He will put a hook in their jaws."

He called upon the nation to repent of

> . . . infamies which have been the overthrow and ruin of many mighty cities, nations, and empires, and which now are the loathsome, unnatural, disgusting, damning sins of Christendom. . . . But it is for us to cleave to God and observe his laws and keep his commandments; and then we need fear no evil. . . . And God will bless and protect Israel . . . and roll forth his work and build up his kingdom and establish Zion, and bring to pass all the things spoken of by the holy prophets since the world began.

---

[21] Dwyer (op. cit.) comments that *In the Toils*, "a masterpiece of bathos, drew from the aged Whittier words of praise"; while the second edition of *Madame La Tour* "ran to one hundred thousand copies, indicating, if not the refinement of American literary taste of the period, at least the prevailing interest in Mormonism."

[22] "What the Mormon women themselves thought of all this was hardly the question," Dwyer points out. "The Christian women . . . realized that the votaries of error have a way of clinging to their fleshpots. And if plural wives insisted upon signing petitions to congress asking . . . that they be permitted to continue their immoral way of life, it could be ascribed to the nefarious influence of the Mormon priesthood rather than to the inner corruption of their souls."

Shortly afterwards, the nation's press shouted "Treason!" at the *Trib*'s report of Taylor's defiant counsel to the Saints at the Assembly Hall in Temple Square. "The people of the rest of the country are our enemies," the pugnacious prophet declared frankly.

> They do not understand us. We do not understand them. We should pray for them, but we must not yield to them. They think we are foolish, and we think they are foolish. They think we are a pack of rascals; but we have the best of them, for we know that they are a pack of rascals.
>
> We believe in honesty, morality, and purity, in freedom and loyalty to our country. But when they enact tyrannical laws, forbidding us the free exercise of our religion, we cannot submit. God is greater than the United States; and when the government conflicts with Heaven, we will be ranged under the banner of Heaven against the government. . . . We want to be friendly with the United States, if the government will let us; but not one jot nor tittle of our rights will we give up to purchase it. . . . When adulterers and libertines pass a law forbidding polygamy, the Saints cannot obey it. . . . I defy the United States. I will obey the will of God. These are my sentiments, and all of you who sympathize with me in this position raise your right hand.[23]

Surveying the forest of hands, Taylor was sure the Lord would take care of his people if they stood steadfast.

Next day the *Deseret News* reported the Washington reaction to Taylor's fire-eating counsel:

> Mr. Hayes is reported to have decided to recommend to congress a very vigorous and radical scheme for the solution of the Mormon question. He proposed to break up Mormonism . . . by disfranchisement of the Mormons and the transfer of the government of Utah to Gentile hands. . . . Under such a system, all Mormon inhabitants of the Territory would be completely disfranchised, and the few Gentiles made the only qualified voters. The first Gentile legislature chosen under this scheme would pass severe laws against polygamy, the effect of which would be to extirpate polygamy and break the power of the church.

While President Hayes' scheme died in Congress because of its obvious constitutional problems, it put a bug in the ear of Sen. George F. Edmunds of Vermont. Taylor learned that Edmunds was working month after month on a bill which would incorporate Hayes' recommendations and still hold up in court.

When Hayes' term of office ended two months later, Taylor hoped for saner times; but in his inaugural address James A. Garfield declared, "The Mormon church not only offends the moral sense of mankind by sanctioning polygamy, but it prevents the administration of justice." He called upon Congress to stop the rebellion.

---

23 January 6, 1880.

On July 1, four months after taking office, Garfield was shot by a disappointed office seeker named Charles J. Guiteau. Taylor immediately notified all Utah communities to cancel plans for celebrating the Fourth while the president's life hung in the balance. Then to his amazement the *Anti-Polygamy Standard* and other papers claimed that Guiteau was actually a Mormon Danite acting under orders from Salt Lake.

Following Garfield's death, the Chicago *News* reported:

> The Mormons of Colorado, Texas, and New Mexico are greatly elated over the success of Guiteau, or Utah, as they call him. . . . The Josephite who murdered the late president acted under advices from headquarters at Salt Lake City, and more deaths will follow if Guiteau is hanged.
>
> In 1874, Guiteau joined the Mormons. He was presented with five wives, who now live in Ivingston, Utah, and his name is Utah, not Guiteau.
>
> When the Mormons saw that the late president in his inaugural address stated that he meant to put his foot on polygamy, the leaders at Salt Lake were heard to say, "Yes, if we do not put our foot on you first."

This dispatch was shot through with absurdities. Guiteau was never a Mormon; there was no town of Ivingston in Utah; a Josephite with five wives would be something to see, inasmuch as the Reorganized sect was passionately opposed to polygamy. Taylor passed the item around the church office; in times like these it was good to enjoy a laugh.

As one anti-Mormon bill after another was introduced in Congress, Taylor looked at the silver lining of the cloud. "There is one thing very evident," he wrote Cannon in Washington,

> The excitement with regard to the work of God is drawing the attention of thousands to us and to the principles in which we believe, who could never have been reached in any other way.
>
> In this, certainly, the design of the Lord is apparent. He is executing his purposes by methods beyond the reach of his servants clothed in mortality. The world is being warned if not converted, and the present manifestations of intense and bitter feeling may end only in their condemnation—whilst it may also prove,
>
> > *The clouds we so much dread*
> > *Are big with mercy and will break*
> > *In blessings on our heads;*
>
> and all the threatened evils be averted by the matchless love and care of our divine Father.

Or, in more succinct terms, publicity was good even when it was bad; just spell the name right.

19

The Gardo House

As HE DID twice each year, John Taylor dismantled the brass bedsteads of his homes on Taylor Row; then after the families had poured boiling water through the tubes assembled them again. This was part of the regular spring and fall housecleaning; it was the never-ending fight against bedbugs.[1] He also went over the bedsprings with a rag dipped in coal oil, as well as the seams and tufts of the mattresses.

On this occasion it was more than just periodic housecleaning. Taylor and his seven acknowledged families were moving into the ostentatious mansion known as the Gardo House. Built by Brigham for his favorite wife, and known as Amelia's Palace, this largest and finest mansion in all of Utah was now officially designated the residence of the church president.

Month after month Taylor had kept postponing the move for one reason or another. In truth, his tastes ran to simplicity; ostentation repelled him. The great pile was a masterpiece of rococo architecture, with four elaborately ornamented stories and a cupola, surmounted by wrought-iron grillwork. The arched windows featured protruding frames and

---

[1] L. John Nuttall's *Journal* mentions bedbugs encountered in the very best homes while Taylor traveled among stakes and wards. Earlier, a Forty-Niner named Stuart declared, "Great Salt Lake could beat the world for bedbugs and skunks." Stuart was guest at the home of John Taylor's "wife No. 1" for a month. Leonora "was a most amiable woman, a good cook, and a good housekeeper. She kept everything nice and clean but the confounded bedbugs ran us out of the beds in the house and we all slept in the yard. Luckily it never rained. Mrs. Taylor felt greatly mortified about the bedbugs and said that she just couldn't keep them out although she fought them all the time." (Archer Butler, *Forty-Niners*, Boston, Hulbert: 1931.)

lintels, both single and double, of various baroque designs. There were balconies, balustrades, colonnaded porches, railings, ornamented cornices, and bay windows. No expense had been spared; no gewgaw of design rejected. The interior was furnished to match, soft carpets, elaborate furniture, statuary in nooks and oil paintings on the walls. The Gardo House sat on spacious grounds at the corner of South Temple and First East streets among velvet lawns and manicured shrubbery, the whole enclosed by a low masonry wall topped by a fancy picket fence of ornamented wrought-iron matching the design of the roof railing.

"It was some time before I could make up my mind to accept a proposition of this kind," Taylor admitted. This was something of an understatement. The Gardo House was designated his official residence at the conference in April 1879, yet he kept postponing the move for twenty months until late December 1881. While he appreciated "the feelings and views of my brethren," he added that "personally, I care nothing about the outside show, the glitter and appearance of men."

His homes on Taylor Row were of adobe brick which he'd helped make and lay; he had crafted much of the furniture. As his financial situation improved after the eight years in the mission field, he'd made no plans for moving; the modest adobe houses were snug and tight, adequate for his families—why change?

Also, he was reluctant to display ostentation at a time of austerity and hardship among the Saints. Under the relentless hectoring of Congress and the carpetbaggers, Zion was being bled white. As men "took a mission" or went underground to avoid arrest, their affairs were left to women and children, who tried to manage businesses and run farms and ranches.[2] The "gathering" compounded hard times. In a steady stream, thousands of converts poured into Zion, all needing employment.

The early colonization of the pioneer period had largely blanketed Utah's severely limited agricultural land. (Only 4 percent of the Territory could be cultivated; the remainder was rugged mountain, alkali desert, and barren slickrock, good for little except spectacular scenery.) To meet the situation, Taylor revived the colonization program, calling families to establish settlements outside Utah, in Idaho, Arizona, Colorado, Wyoming, New Mexico, and Nevada. He sent scouts to locate future colonies in Mexico and Canada. In Utah he spurred dam-building and irrigation development to get more water from the canyons to reclaim more desert.[3]

In addition to temporal affairs, Taylor developed the spiritual and

---

[2] Samuel Woolley, the author's grandfather, lost heavily after being driven underground; his three wives and young children were unable to attend properly to the ranch and livestock.

[3] Arrington (*Great Basin Kingdom*) says, "With the exception of the initial colonization movement in 1847–51, it was the greatest single colonization movement in Mormon history."

artistic renaissance both at home and abroad. He extended the awakening to the outside world, sending missionaries out with the exuberance of the early days, crying the good news of the gospel to all nations. A blooming of freedom in thought and spirit permeated Zion, as the Saints enjoyed a liberalized regime which reminded the old-timers of the golden days under Joseph.[4]

Ironically, at exactly the same time that the renaissance in Zion came to full flower, Senator Edmunds in Washington was completing the final draft of legislation designed to demolish the Mormon Church once and for all, in an entirely constitutional manner.

A storm was blowing in as John Taylor's party gathered at the railway station. It was the afternoon of October 27, 1881; the president was embarking on a tour of southern stakes and settlements that would occupy nearly six weeks and involve sixty-eight public addresses in addition to many council meetings with stake presidents, bishops, and other office holders. Taylor boarded the Utah Southern with his wife Sophia; his daughter Ida (whose mother was Mary Ann); his secretary, L. John Nuttall (whose second wife was John and Harriett Taylor's daughter, Sophia); three apostles, George Q. Cannon, Wilford Woodruff, and Franklin D. Richards; and a scribe, George F. Gibbs. The total party, including families of the men, numbered just fourteen. Each member of the entourage, and every Saint who attended the meetings for the next six weeks of the tour, couldn't help but compare Taylor's mode of travel with Brigham's caravan of some seventy-five carriages, hundreds of people, outriders on the flanks, fifty armed horsemen fore and aft, and a band of Lamanites for color. The elaborate preparations for feeding and housing the royal caravan en route had placed on small settlements a strain that was remembered after the inspired counsel from the pulpit was forgotten.

President Taylor's tour wasn't a royal caravan, but a party of friends. He was a man of the people, with a deep respect for individual dignity that brought respect and love in return. His counsel on the tour, Roberts records,

> dealt very largely with the duties of the Saints in all relations of life; as
> husbands and wives, parents and children, neighbors and citizens; unity,

---

[4] In contrast, Meyer (*The Origin and History of the Mormons*) says that under Brigham's regime every Mormon "was under continuous control. No actions, no words remained unnoticed. . . . The individual found himself surrounded by spies and informers, and the refractory member or even the apostate saw himself in the position of the non-believer, on the other side of a wall through which he could never break."

It might be added that this situation has been reestablished, in varying degree, subsequent to Taylor's regime.

honor, integrity, honesty, purity in thought and act were his themes—in one word he preached righteousness as essential to the favor of God, and with the favor of God he assured the Saints they need not fear what man or nations could do. "God will be on the side of Israel, if Israel will be on the side of right," was his oft-repeated assertion.

It was raining at Nephi on the first day's stop. After a meeting that night, the party went next morning to Juab, the end of track, and from there continued by teams and carriages, which had been shipped ahead. Huddled against the storm, the group slogged through deep mud to Scipio. After a midday meeting there, the carriages headed for Fillmore, stopping on the way for an afternoon meeting at Holden Lake. After public and officer meetings that night at Fillmore, the party was off again at dawn, as the day broke clear but cold.

En route, Taylor inspected dams and irrigation projects. He checked the accounts of cooperatives, looked at tithing herds, examined granaries to check on local wheat-storage programs. The condition of farms and livestock, of business and commerce, were inseparable from things of the spirit; the welfare of the Saints was all part of the Kingdom of God.

Up early and late, on the go, speaking, counseling on affairs both spiritual and temporal week after week—this might have been considered rigorous for a man who, during the trip, turned seventy-three. Yet Taylor thrived on it. There was no stoop to his shoulders; his step was elastic, eyes bright, the deep voice with the timbre and power of a young man. He never tired in work for the Kingdom of God, though sometimes he tired others. Like Joseph, he enjoyed thinking and talking during long walks; legends grew of John Taylor giving counsel mile after mile, stride lengthening as his mind quickened, while his companion gasped to keep up on blistered feet.

He was touched by the dedication of destitute colonists in the broken San Juan country. After years of fighting the desert on one hand and the silt-laden floods of the river on the other, they were at the end of their tether. He advised them to go where opportunity beckoned. While they had been called as a mission, they were not required to stay and starve.[5]

At St. George, Aaron Nelson showed Taylor a vein of coal, two feet thick, discovered nearby on the Virgin River. The local Saints wanted it put under church supervision. Taylor agreed to accept title as trustee-in-trust, to have it surveyed, and to finance development of the mine by the church. Nelson would remain as supervisor.

The Saints at Kanab had raised $1,000 toward buying a farm at Moccasin Spring for the Indians. Taylor donated the remaining $500 from church funds, and advised the purchase of farm implements and tools.

---

[5] They moved to Blanding, where it was discovered that the climate was ideal for dry-land beans; most everyone became rich.

That evening a number of Lamanites attended meeting, and stayed to shake Taylor's hand in thanks. He invited the chief to visit him in Salt Lake, promising a new suit of store clothes from ZCMI.

Taylor appropriated tithing produce for the poor in several areas, and had flour in the bishop's storehouse delivered to the Indians. He gave counsel on many domestic and spiritual matters, and on leaving for Salt Lake warmly thanked Brother Pugh for donating a gallon of Dixie wine to cheer the return trip.[6]

On returning to Salt Lake in December, Taylor finally agreed to occupy the presidential mansion. On January 2, 1882 two thousand friends attended the official opening of Gardo House. Since the die was cast, Taylor made it an occasion: Croxall's band, Professor C. J. Thomas' orchestra, and the Tabernacle Choir serenaded the throng. Taylor's right arm ached to the shoulder from shaking two thousand hands. The guests attacked mountains of food and drink, constantly replenished on two huge tables in the dining hall, until finally the Choir concluded the affair with "Auld Lang Syne."[7]

The capacious Gardo House provided each of his seven families with its own quarters, with accommodations for the housekeeper and caretaker. However, Taylor didn't particularly relish the patriarchal clan aspect, as Brigham had. He missed the intimacy of the individual homes of Taylor Row. As he entered each, it was as husband and father in a family world, with the others respecting its privacy. On the Row, he had been a special individual to each family, sharing experiences and love; but at the mansion he must treat each wife not as a husband but as patriarch. Here there must be order and delegated authority, each wife ranking according to seniority.

Except for holiday outings, birthdays, and other special occasions, the clan at Taylor Row had not really been the great patriarchal family; instead it was seven separate households, each with its own leadership, its special character, its problems and triumphs.

The easy informality of relaxing for an evening with suspenders down and stockinged feet on the oven door, reading the paper with a cup of tea or glass of wine at hand, was no more. He was now President John Taylor day and night, on formal display and in formal dress not only in Zion but within his own home.

---

[6] See Roberts (*Life of John Taylor*) and Nuttall for details of this trip.

[7] Several factors influenced Taylor's decision to make the move. The people really wanted their president installed in style, particularly since the mansion was built with church funds. Also, growth of the organization had made the former church offices inadequate. The Gardo House would be used, in part, for official business. Roberts adds the faith-promoting story that when Taylor's "circumstances were the poorest," Heber C. Kimball "boldly prophesied that he would yet live in the largest and best house in Salt Lake City." Taylor possibly agreed to fulfill prophecy.

With one kitchen, he couldn't decide to have breakfast with Maggie's family, lunch with Sophia, supper with Jane, or pull taffy with Harriett in an evening. During waking hours it was impossible to drop in for a chat with Mary Ann or Elizabeth. The wives shared the same parlor. This was the Lord's plan; but things would be better in the hereafter, with each wife queen of her separate world.

How had Brigham managed it so well? Belatedly, Taylor was forced to admit that he'd never given Brigham proper credit for handling his enormous menage.

Fortunately, there were no young children in Gardo House, except for Margaret's brood, or it would have been a madhouse.

He missed in particular the book-lined study at Maggie's, where he had spent so many evenings in creative work. While he did have a study at Gardo House, it also was an office where he received callers. There was privacy only late at night, with the household asleep. Here he worked into the small hours, finishing *The Mediation and Atonement*.

One night as the clock struck three, he put down his pen and picked up the lamp. In the hallway, on impulse, he turned downstairs to the basement. In a far corner was his workshop: the bench, his old turning lathe and chisels, his planes and glue clamps, saws, rasps, draw-knife, brace and bits, squares, sandpaper, varnish, and wax. He loved to work with his hands. He'd made most of the equipment here. Nothing relieved the tension of a hard day like turning a salad bowl or making mortise and tenon joints for a piece of furniture. Everything was dusty now, his tools rusting. Stacked in a corner was an unfinished settee, bits and pieces of several uncompleted projects. He put the lamp on the bench, turned up his cuffs, and while sanding and oiling the metal remembered that he'd used some of these same tools in constructing the carriage during a stop en route from Kirtland to Missouri. He'd built one of the first sawmills in the Salt Lake valley, designing and helping make and install much of the machinery. Before church duties absorbed his time, he was noted for mechanical ingenuity. He'd still kept his hand in at Taylor Row. Some husbands of the neighborhood resented having their wives point out that the Taylor homes never had sticking doors, loose windows, sagging hinges, faulty latches, or wobbly chairs.

No chance, these days, to spend an evening in the workshop. He missed this more than anything else.

The job done, he wiped his hands, took the lamp and went upstairs. As he moved along the hallway he realized that the situation was much harder on the wives than on him. It was the Lord's test for the worthy, and they certainly were earning the glory.

In the same month that he moved into Gardo House, Taylor read a vitriolic article in *Harper's Magazine* by Sen. George F. Edmunds, who had briefly visited Utah and received all his alarming information from carpetbaggers and the Gentile ring. In "Political Aspects of Mormonism," the senator warned that the Saints aimed at "exclusive political domination," and that if they obtained statehood, "polygamy and every revolting practice they might choose to set up, would be absolutely beyond the legal reach" of the United States government. Within days he introduced the Edmunds Bill, on which he had worked so long, designed to settle the Mormon problem once and for all.

Taylor met in council with the presidency and the Twelve at the Gardo House to discuss the impending legislation. They donned temple robes, partook of sacramental bread and wine, then sought the Lord's guidance.[8] Though there would be opposition, particularly in the Senate, public hysteria about the Mormon menace made the bill almost certain of passage. Senator Edmunds had most carefully contrived to emasculate the Mormons politically, imprison their leaders, and deliver Utah over to carpetbag government. Polygamy was declared a felony meriting five years imprisonment and a $500 fine. If polygamy was impossible to prove, unlawful cohabitation with a suspected wife would draw six months in prison with a $300 fine—which could be imposed for each and every visit to the woman's house. All polygamists were disfranchised, as well as anyone who *believed in* plural marriage, and were disqualified for jury service. No polygamist could hold public office, which meant that George Q. Cannon would lose his seat in Congress. Utah would be without voice in Washington. Governor Murray had attempted to unseat Cannon previously. Though Cannon had received 18,458 votes against 1,357 for Allen G. Campbell, the governor declared Cannon disqualified because of polygamy, and issued a certificate of election to Campbell. Congress was forced to rule that Cannon was legally elected; but the Edmunds Bill got rid of him. Not only Cannon, but every elected office holder in Utah was cast out by the bill—from legislators and judges to sheriffs, mayors, city councilmen, justices of the peace, school boards, and town clerks—all offices to be filled by an election under control of the Utah Commission, five carpetbaggers appointed by the president, who would also supervise the observance of every measure of the Edmunds Bill.

In short, the bill would apply similar humiliating and repressive measures to Utah as had been imposed on the South during Reconstruction days. In addition to depriving Utah of local self-government, this law made virtually the entire leadership of the Territory criminals.

The *Tribune*, of course, hailed its impending passage. It declared the

---

[8] The use of wine at the sacrament in council meeting is mentioned in Abraham H. Cannon's *Journal*. He speaks also of eating "the Lord's supper" in the manner "as Joseph and the brethren did occasionally at Nauvoo; we had several loaves of bread and bottles of wine. The former was broken and we ate and drank till we were fully satisfied." (Entry April 9, 1890.)

legislature "is an instrument in the hands of John Taylor. It has not dared to pass a law without his approval."

In alarm, the Utah Assembly sent a memorial to Congress, protesting "baseless rumors and monstrous exaggerations," by "persons whose aim is to gain control of this now wealthy and prosperous Territory." These "have succeeded in arousing the ire of the clergy, and through them the anger of many," until Utah was "now threatened with the deprivation of the right of local self-government."

"For thirty years Utah has been ruled by an absolute despotism," the *Trib* retorted, and quoted Smiler Colfax, speaking in Chicago:

> For a quarter of a century Asiatic polygamy has grown, strengthened, and fortified itself in the heart of our domain. This American cancer has grown and spread till it has filled all Utah with its poison. What can be done? There should be enacted laws whose supreme object should be the utter and complete extirpation of this un-American institution which defies our national law, denounces our national judiciary, mocks our national authority, and reviles all who dare lift their finger against it.

The "one effective way to solve the Mormon problem," declared the New York *Graphic*, was "to resort to force." Either be prepared "to kill thousands of people in Utah," or quit talking about "suppression of the twin relic of barbarism." There was no middle course. And the Brooklyn *Eagle* declared that polygamists "must go to jail or betake themselves to Turkey."

Opposition in the Senate came primarily from the South, where the memory of Reconstruction was still vivid. John T. Morgan of Alabama pointed out there was no law against polygamist Indians, so why discriminate against Mormons? Sen. Wilkinson Call of Florida declared that the bill "deliberately provides that the person charged with crime does not have an impartial trial. It imposes a religious test upon the jurors, which is a violation of the cardinal provisions of the constitution."

> Sir, this is worse than open, flagrant war. . . . This is assertion by the Congress of the United States that there may be a trial by a packed and prejudiced court, by partial jurors, by a man's enemies and not his friends; that a government shall be constructed in which the vast majority —nine-tenths of the people—[shall be ruled by] . . . a minority.

"If there is one single clause in our Constitution or Bill of Rights dear to the American heart, it is that no citizen shall be deprived of life, liberty, or property without the judgment of his peers or of a competent tribunal," stated Sen. George Graham Vest of Missouri.

> This bill takes away from a citizen the right to vote or hold office before conviction by his peers of any crime. . . . Never in any of the darkest days of despotism, was there ever enacted a statute more exactly within the meaning of a bill of attainder.

"If we commence striking down any sect, however despised or however unpopular, on account of opinion's sake," warned Joseph Emerson Brown of Georgia, "we do not know how soon the fires of Smithfield may be rekindled or the gallows of New England for witches again be erected, or when another Catholic convent shall be burned down."

> I, for one, shall not be a party to the enactment or enforcement of unconstitutional, tyrannical, and oppressive legislation for the purpose of crushing the Mormons or any other sect for the gratification of New England or any other section. . . . If the Mormons will conform to its requirements . . . the practice of prostitution in Utah need not in the slightest degree be diminished. The clamor is not against the Mormon for having more than one woman, but for calling more than one his wife.

Christian churches sent missionaries to India and China where five hundred million people accepted polygamy, the Senator said; so instead of trying to crush the Mormons because 12,000 practiced it, why not send missionaries? "It may be easier to cry 'crucify them' than it is to try to help convert them. But can the churches reconcile [their] conscience? . . ."

With fine irony, Senator House of Tennessee said scathingly:

> Let the carpetbagger, expelled finally from every State in the American Union with the brand of disgrace stamped upon his brow, lift up his head once more and turn his face toward the setting sun. Utah beckons him to a new field of pillage and fresh pastures of pilfering. Let him pack his grip sack and start. The Mormons have no friends, and no one will come forward to protect their rights. A returning board, from whose decision there is no appeal, sent out from the American Congress baptized with the spirit of persecution and intolerance, will enter Utah to trample beneath their feet the rights of the people of that far-off and ill-fated land. Mr. Speaker, I would not place a dog under the domination of a set of carpetbaggers, reinforced by a returning board, unless I meant to have him robbed of his bone. A more grinding tyranny, or more absolute despotism, was never established over any people.

Despite opposition of the South, determination of the North made passage of the bill virtually certain. Taylor authorized the employment of the former U.S. Attorney General, Jeremiah S. Black, to represent the Saints in Washington, now that Cannon would be ousted; and on his knees he sought counsel from the highest authority. Should he compromise? Should he risk destruction of the church by refusing to bend to man-made law? Would it not be possible to set aside the Principle, at least temporarily, or until statehood was achieved? Should he continue to subject the entire body of the Saints to unrelenting persecution by clinging to a commandment which the great majority of them didn't obey anyway?

But the heavens were as brass when he prayed in such manner.

And then Brigham visited him. "He came to me in the silence of the night, clothed in brightness and with a face beaming with love and confidence told me many things of great importance."[9] Reassured by this, Taylor stood firm, and waited for the Lord to speak.[10]

"We will worship the Lord our God," Taylor told the Saints in the Provo Tabernacle as debate on the Edmunds Bill continued in the Senate,

and if we are faithful, live our religion, and keep his commandments, the God whom we worship will deliver us out of the hands of our enemies, and we shall triumph over our foes.

There have been men . . . who could meet the inquisition with its fagot, rack, and thumbscrew, and in the midst of their suffering could commit themselves in all serenity and calmness into the hands of God. And we can surely do the same.

One of the first things I ever heard preached by the elders of this church was that the world would grow worse and worse, deceiving and being deceived. Should we be surprised at its coming to pass? Another thing I have heard from the beginning is that people would persecute us. . . . We have got about fifty millions of people on our backs now—and it is a pretty heavy load to carry, too—but the Lord will see us through. . . . And inasmuch as this people are found faithful to God and true to themselves and their fellowmen, I will risk the results of what our enemies may do to injure us.

The test was soon to come. A self-righteous Senate passed the Edmunds Bill. Then it was rammed through the House, debate being limited to five minutes for each member. On March 22, 1882, it was signed by the president and became the law of the land.

Two weeks later there was storm and cold in Utah, typical "conference weather," and Taylor hurried through driving sleet to Temple Square for April conference. From the rostrum he referred to the new legislation, warning that a storm was coming. "Let us treat it the same as we did this morning in coming through the snowstorm—put up our coat collars." He turned up his own collar, and his lips curled up at the corners. Wait till the storm subsides, he counseled. "After the storm comes sunshine. While the storm lasts it is useless to reason with the world. When it subsides we can talk to them."

On the final day of conference, Taylor talked for two hours, counseling the people at a time of dire trouble.[11] In the audience was the inevi-

---

[9] Zina Young Williams, Brigham's daughter, was told this by Taylor. See "Short Reminiscent Sketches of Karl G. Maeser," typescript, BYU.

[10] Taylor's son, John W., during a meeting of the Twelve related that his father asked permission of the Lord to compromise on the Principle; but in answer received two revelations that "the law" must be obeyed. See Abraham H. Cannon *Journal*.

[11] Of this talk, Roberts says, "President Taylor preached one of the most remarkable and powerful sermons of his life." (*Life of John Taylor*, p. 361.)

table sneering reporter from the *Tribune*, but also a correspondent of entirely different stripe, the celebrated journalist and author, Phil Robinson of the New York *World*.[12]

Taylor traced the rise of the church from the beginning, in its trials and tribulations. He promised the people "that there is nothing of which you have been despoiled by oppressive acts or mobocratic rules, but that you will again possess."

> The Lord has a way of his own in regulating such matters. We are told the wicked shall slay the wicked. He has a way of his own of "emptying the earth of the inhabitants thereof." A terrible day of reckoning is approaching the nations of the earth. . . .
> Congress will soon have something else to do than to proscribe and persecute an innocent, law-abiding, and patriotic people. Of all bodies in the world, they can least afford to remove the bulwarks that bind society together in this nation, to recklessly trample upon human freedom and rights.

"And I tell you now from the tops of these mountains," Taylor thundered, his powerful voice filling the tabernacle, "that unless these crimes are stopped, this nation will be overthrown."

The *Tribune* called the speech "treasonable," and broadcast it to the world as evidence that the Mormons were in "open rebellion." The alarmed Anti-Polygamy Society petitioned Congress for stiffer legislation; and the attitude of the world press was typified by the Syracuse *Standard*:

> Mormon insolence increases. In the face of a national effort to crush polygamy, the proud hierarchy sent out 300 additional proselyting hellhounds to make perverts. Let the law just framed for dealing with them be fairly tried, then if it fail, let the Territory be placed under military law, until rebellion against the United States is terminated.

Still there was one Gentile newspaper, the New York *World*, which carried an objective account. Phil Robinson wrote:

> Of the advice given at this Conference it is easy to speak briefly, for all counseled alike. In his opening address, President Taylor said,—
> "The antagonism we now experience here has always existed, but we have also come out of our troubles strengthened. I say to you, be calm, for the Lord God Omnipotent reigneth, and He will take care of us."

---

12 Phil Robinson remained in Utah three months, sending dispatches to the *World* which were compiled into a book, *Sinners and Saints*. Roberts says of him, "Mr. Robinson is one of the few writers who have endeavored to tell the truth about the Mormons." (Ibid, p. 366.) Yet his book, and also Richard F. Burton's *City of the Saints*, have never been reprinted by the Utah press; while favorable and sympathetic —extremely rare qualities in Gentile books of the nineteenth century—they also are objective. Robinson, for example, criticized Taylor for not being more like Brigham. He considered Taylor's restoration of rights to the people as weakness.

Each succeeding speaker repeated the same advice, and the outcome of the five days' conference may therefore be said to have been an exhortation to the Saints "to pay no attention whatever to outside matters, but to live their religion, leave the direction of affairs to their priesthood, and the result in the hands of God."

As Taylor called for affirmation, Robinson reported, "Here, like the sound of a great sea-wave breaking in a cave, a vast *Amen* arose from the concourse."

> The great tabernacle was filled with waves of sound as the "Amens" of the congregation burst out. The shout of men going into battle was not more stirring than the closing words of this memorable conference spoken as if by one vast voice: "Hosannah! for the Lord God Omnipotent reigneth; He is with us now and will be for ever. Amen!"

Summing up his impressions, Robinson said,

> Acquainted though I am with displays of Oriental fanaticism and western revivalism, I set this Mormon enthusiasm on one side, as being altogether of a different character; for it not only astonishes by its fervor, but commands respect by its sincere sobriety. The congregation of the Saints assembled in the tabernacle, numbering . . . eleven thousand odd . . . reminded me of the Puritan gatherings of the past as I had imagined them, and of my personal experiences of the Transvaal Boers as I knew them. There was no rant, no affectation, no straining after theatrical effect. The very simplicity of this great gathering of country-folk was striking in the extreme, and significant from first to last of a power that should hardly be trifled with by sentimental legislation.

Preparing for the storm, Taylor sent a personal "Epistle on Marriage" to stake presidents and bishops. In it, he took the first step toward taking plural marriage underground, as the practice had been during most of the church's existence. The "Epistle" carefully defined the New and Everlasting Covenant of Celestial Marriage—polygamy—as a privilege reserved for a select few. But what of young people

> who, while they are desirous to marry and fulfill the great law of nature and be fruitful and multiply, are not justly and consistently entitled to those blessings which the fulness of the Gospel covenant provides?

In the event such couples could not qualify for a temple marriage, Taylor advised bishops to perform the marriage ceremony, by authority of the priesthood but outside the temple, "rather than to have them go . . . to justices of the peace and others."

This authorization of church marriage outside the temples was a significant departure from established practice. While ostensibly pertaining only to those unprepared for the "fulness," it would be only one short step from this to the situation existing before the official endorsement of polygamy thirty years previously. At that time, the church furiously denounced polygamy, while the priesthood within the church most vigorously sponsored it as essential to the highest exaltation.[13]

John Taylor dismantled the brass bedsteads of the seven family apartments of the Gardo House, and after boiling water was poured through the tubes, assembled them again. It was more than just spring housecleaning: after less than six months in the mansion, the families were moving out. With the passage of the Edmunds Bill, the old order was gone forever. No longer could a Mormon maintain two or more wives under one roof. U.S. Deputy Sam Gilson would dearly love to arrest John Taylor and haul the church president into court on a charge of u.c.

The wives and families moved back to Taylor Row, leaving Taylor in the great mansion, alone except for his sister, Agnes Schwartz, who was housekeeper, and Samuel Sudbury, custodian.

Taylor found that the privacy he had wanted could be echoing. The seclusion was loneliness. His study was not a retreat at night but a prison, when no one was beyond the door. Now that he had time to tinker in the basement workshop, it held no appeal without someone to see his handicraft. During the day, affairs of his office kept him occupied, but at night he'd lay down his pen, his book, or his chisel, and, as in the old days at Nauvoo, slip through side streets and over back fences to the rear doors of those he loved.

---

[13] The "Epistle on Marriage" was published in the *Deseret News*, 1882, and reprinted in *Truth*, 9:129.

20

"In the Marriage Relation"

GUSTS OF RAIN shattered against the coach windows as the Utah Central rumbled north through the storm. The pot-bellied stove at the front of the car was cherry red, yet Taylor tucked his greatcoat around his knees against the chill wind worming through the cracks. From the train window he saw pools standing in sodden fields that couldn't be harvested. Apples torn loose by the screaming wind lay thick in the orchards. Livestock huddled in the lee of barns and haystacks, tail to the gale. The long period of storm and raw cold during late September and early October was a disaster to farmers—"conference weather" with a vengeance.

At Ogden, a white-top awaited, with a grim-faced stake president at the reins. The local church organization was rent with dissension, and John Taylor had arrived with two members of the Twelve to settle the difficulty. During luncheon at the stake president's home, the man suggested that it would be well to review the situation before the meeting. Taylor, however, told him he'd rather wait until both sides were represented.

The meeting was at two o'clock. Taylor sat on the stand, facing angry men on both sides of the dispute. The stake presidency and high council were divided against themselves; bishops and their counselors of the various wards, leaders of the high priests, seventies, and elders quorums, were gathered for a confrontation, each side of the dispute determined to vanquish and humble the other. After the meeting was opened with prayer, Taylor arose and advised the gathering that he hadn't come to hear bickering, nor was he going to arbitrate an argument. He then organized prayer circles for the purpose of seeking reciprocity, forgiveness, and a more complete reliance upon the Lord. When they obtained the spirit of God, he counseled, they could settle their own problems.

He adjourned the meeting, and took the next train back to Salt Lake.[1]

The grossly-handsome Governor Murray had returned from Washington, where he had performed valiant duty helping to frame and lobby for the Edmunds Bill. The five carpetbaggers of the Utah Commission arrived to oversee the replacement of every elected official of the Territory, and at this time of foul weather and dire forboding, the heavens opened and the Lord spoke to John Taylor:

> Thus saith the Lord to the Twelve, and to the priesthood and people of my church: . . .

George Teasdale and Heber J. Grant were appointed to vacancies in the Quorum of the Twelve. Seymour B. Young was to be appointed to the presiding quorum of the seventies, "if he will conform to my law; for it is not meet that men who will not abide my law shall preside over my priesthood. . . ." The various church officials from top to bottom were to "purify themselves," and organize "according to my law." The unworthy were to be removed; for only those who "shall honor me and obey my laws" could hold office.

> I call upon my priesthood, and upon all of my people, to repent of all their sins and shortcomings . . . and to seek with all humility to fulfill my law. . . . And I will bless and be with you, saith the Lord, . . . and I will hear your prayers, and my Spirit and power shall be with you, and my blessings shall rest upon you . . . and your enemies shall not have dominion over you, for I will preserve you and confound them. . . .

The weather broke. The storm cleared away and the late fall season became beautiful. John Taylor was at peace. There was no remnant of nagging doubt as to what his course as leader of the Saints would be.

The first act of the Utah Commission was to require a test oath of everyone registering to vote, a man to swear that he had never lived simultaneously with more than one woman "in the marriage relation," the woman to swear that she never had entered into such relation. Taylor

---

[1] Such incidents were typical of his method of handling local disputes. See Taylor to Cannon, December 30, 1880. "The condition of their entering these circles being that they should first be at peace and in full fellowship with each other and with their bishop and the members of their several wards; that the bishop and his counselors should be in fellowship with one another and with the presidency of the stake and with the presidency of the church and the general authorities, and that all should be in strict harmony and good fellowship with one another."

bitterly denounced the oath, which gave the vote to the roué, the libertine, the strumpet, the brothel-keeper, but excluded those who lived the Principle. He told of the venerable Feramorz Little, early mayor of Salt Lake City, whose two wives had died years previously.

> He had a son who was appointed registrar, . . . and this son had the mortification of being compelled . . . to refuse his father permission to register. . . . Soon after, ... a well-known keeper of a bagnio and her associates presented themselves, and the son had the humiliation of having to permit them to register. These courtesans afterward voted.
>
> Another case: A man came to the place of registration and remarked to the officer that he supposed he could not register, as he had a wife and also kept a mistress. . . . But the officer knew what was in the oath better than this man, and . . . [he] was at once sworn and registered.[2]

The unseating of George Q. Cannon, the casting out of polygamists in the territorial legislature and prohibiting them from jury service, was supposed to break church power in Utah. However, John T. Caine, a Mormon candidate to succeed Cannon, received 23,039 votes to 4,884 for his Gentile opponent, Judge P. T. Van Zile. Monogamous Mormons in the local legislature showed identical attitudes to the polygamists they had replaced, as did non-polygamous juries.[3] Frustrated, the Utah Commission reported that though the Edmunds Bill was designed to break the power of the Mormon church,

> we are in truth compelled to say that in its practical operation it has not effected and will not effect the desired reforms. The local government is still composed of the Mormon church as fully as before. The disfranchised portion dictates the course of those who are not disfranchised as completely and absolutely as before.

---

[2] *North American Review*, January 1884.

[3] During debate on the Edmunds Bill, Taylor took action to circumvent its provisions. He mentioned one example in a letter to George Q. Cannon March 9, 1882: "In view of the threatened legislation against those in polygamy, it has been deemed wise to make a change in the *personnel* of the Board of Regents of the University [of Deseret], so that if those in plural wedlock be ousted, a majority of monogamists would remain to carry on business, whoever else might be appointed." After passage of the Edmunds Law March 22, 1882, Taylor issued an epistle "On Marriage," authorizing church marriages outside the temple or Endowment House. This was the first step toward taking polygamy underground again, as in Nauvoo days. He also sent Erastus Snow and Moses Thatcher to Mexico to scout colonization sites for refuges. (See letter to Snow, November 15, 1882.) By the end of the year, the *Tribune* called the Edmunds Law a failure: "We assert, without the slightest egotism, that as yet not one scratch has been made upon the imperious armor of church rule which this Territory wears," the *Trib* declared December 21. "We assert that the disposition to never surrender polygamy was never more pronounced in Utah than at this time, and that the Edmunds law is simply what we said it was when it was framed, soothing syrum for a tiger."

The laws already enacted have served only as a gentle irritant, having united the people, strengthened the control of the Mormon priests, and failed to diminish the celebration of polygamous marriages.

The Commission advocated as the "most feasible and effective plan" the appointment of a legislative council, "with power to legislate for the Territory in place of the present legislature."

On receiving this report, Sen. George F. Edmunds began drafting new and stronger measures to settle the "Utah question."

Failure of the Edmunds Bill to bring the church to its knees touched off a crusade against the "unholy hierarchy" in Utah. Missionaries were mobbed, particularly by southern rednecks. "The time is coming swiftly when there is going to be surrender," the *Trib* fumed (February 18, 1883).

The political portions of the Mormon creed, together with polygamy, are going to surrender to the Republic, or the Republic is going to surrender to them.

But a few newspapers maintained a level head. The Omaha *Bee* said,

To disfranchise a Mormon today, because he is a Mormon, would simply mean that tomorrow you disfranchise a Roman Catholic because he is a Catholic.

Denouncing the Commission plan "that shall virtually abolish self-government in Utah, and the minority put in control," the St. Paul *Pioneer Press* said,

Unfortunately for the hopes of those who desire the suppression, Congress will not waste time in discussing the demands of the Utah delegation of Gentiles.

Taylor, however, knew that the furor was only gathering momentum. New legislation in preparation at Washington would make it legal for wives to testify against husbands, and small children against parents.

"The days for the peaceful solution of this question are past," thundered the Rev. DeWitt Talmage.

Mormonism is gathering momentum. A few batteries on the hill east of Salt Lake might once have put a quietus on this great outrage, but not now. God only knows by what national exhaustion the curse is to be extirpated. But go it must.

Meanwhile another petition for Utah statehood was denied by Congress. In the Senate there was furious debate over the new Edmunds Bill.

"This bill proposes to disfranchise a whole people," Senator Call charged.

Why? Because it says they entertain opinions different from those which the Senator from Vermont entertains upon the subject of polygamy—without trial, without conviction, without hearing, and without evidence.

In reply, Senator Logan said, "Why not strike suffrage down completely in Utah? I am willing to go to any length within the constitution for the suppression of this crime."

Call pointed out,

What is there in the constitution in regard to marriage, polygamy or monogamy, to authorize Congress to declare what shall be the domestic relations of the people of the several territories? No reason can be given for a proposition that congress has authority, exclusive and absolute, without limitation in regard to the subject of marriage in the territories.

The *Deseret News* thundered,

The truth is that the whole territorial system, which has grown up outside of constitutional powers, is not only unrepublican, but is antirepublican, despotic, tyrannical and oppressive; and, as exercised over Utah, is more than anything attempted by the British Government over the colonies which repudiated its authority.

There was jubilation in Utah when the newest Edmunds Bill was defeated in Congress. But this, Taylor knew, was premature. Smarting, the obsessed senator from Vermont began working on yet another measure. That he had full administration support was indicated by President Arthur's message to Congress, December 1883:

I am convinced . . . that polygamy has become so strongly entrenched in the Territory of Utah, that it is profitless to attack it with any but the stoutest of weapons which constitutional legislation can make. I favor, therefore, the repeal of the act upon which the existing government depends, and the resumption by the National Legislature of the entire political control of the Territory. . . .

A crowd was gathered at the Federal Building on Main Street, Friday afternoon, October 17, 1884, as John Taylor alighted from his carriage, together with his secretary, L. John Nuttall. The president of the LDS Church had been subpoenaed as a witness.

The courtroom was stifling, every seat taken, people standing tightly packed around the walls. The trial of Rudger Clawson, accused of polygamy, was the first major case to be tried under the Edmunds Law. Clawson, now twenty-seven, had as a young missionary been mobbed in the south, and his companion, Joseph Standing, murdered. Clawson had received a hero's welcome on bringing the body home for burial.

Rudger Clawson had married Florence Ann Dinwoodey, and the indictment charged that two years later he also had married Lydia Spencer. Preliminary testimony was entirely hearsay.

"I could not help thinking as I looked upon the scene," Taylor reflected, "that there was no necessity for all this."[4]

"Here was a young man blessed with more than ordinary intelligence, bearing amongst all who know him a most enviable reputation for virtue, honesty, sobriety, and all other desirable characteristics that we are in the habit of supposing go to make a man respected and beloved the civilized world over." Rudger Clawson had shown his devotion to the gospel "by going forth without purse or scrip to preach in the midst of the unbelieving the doctrines of a most unpopular faith." When his companion fell victim to mob violence, Clawson rescued the mangled body and brought it home.

> This heroic young man is the one now arraigned before the courts of his country, for an alleged offense against the morality of the age. He from his earliest recollection had been taught to reverence the Bible as the word of God, to revere the lives and examples of the ancient worthies whom Jehovah honored by making them His confidents; . . . yet all these men—the friends, associates, and confidents of the great Creator of heaven and earth—were men with more than one wife, some with many wives, yet they still possessed and rejoiced in the love and honor of the great judge of all the world, whose judgments are just, and whose words are all righteousness.
>
> This young man is charged with following these worthy examples. It is asserted that he has taken to wife a beautiful and virtuous young lady, belonging, like himself, to one of our most respected families, and who also believes in the Bible, and in the example set her by those holy women of old, such as Rachel, Ruth, Hannah, and others, who honored God's law, and became mothers of prophets, priests, and kings.

Taylor thought: "What need had these two to follow such examples of a by-gone age? Why not walk in the way of the world today, unite with our modern Christian civilization, and if passion guide their actions why call each other husband and wife? Why hallow their association by any sacred ceremony? Was there any need of such?"

> Why not do as tens of thousands of others do, live in the condition of illicit love? And then if any child should be feared from this unsanctified union, why not still follow our Christian examplars, remove the foetal incumbrance, call in some . . . abortionist, male or female, that polute our land? That would have been, *sub-rosa*, genteel, fashionable, respectable, Christian-like, as Christianity goes in this generation. . . .
>
> Or, again, these two, in the event of a child being born, might consign it to the care of some degraded hag, some "baby farmer," where grad-

---

4 Related two days afterwards. JD, 25:356.

ually and quietly its innocent life would ebb out, and bye and bye the grief-stricken parents would receive the anticipated notice that their dear little offspring, notwithstanding every care, was dead and buried.

"This young man and woman could have done all this and no marshals with ready feet would have dogged their steps. No packed grand juries with unanimous alacrity would do the bidding of over-zealous prosecuting attorneys. No federal judge would overturn precedent, ignore law, disregard justice on purpose to convict. No, they might have been the friends, associates, companions of judge and prosecutor, governor and commissioner." Instead, Rudger Clawson "stands in the felon's dock,"

with every person who might possibly be his friend excluded from the jury, without the possibility of a fair trial by his peers; . . . by such people this unfortunate young gentleman has to be tried, judged, prosecuted, proscribed, and condemned because of his firm and unswerving faith in the God of Abraham, Isaac, and Jacob. . . .

The placing of John Taylor on the witness stand provided the sensation of the day. The prosecution's purpose was to establish the fact of Lydia Spencer's marriage to Clawson, to prove it had taken place in the Endowment House, and to discover who had authorized the marriage and what record had been made of the ceremony. In turn, Taylor was determined not to give aid and comfort to the enemy.[5]

It quickly became apparent that Taylor was a reluctant witness. When the government prosecutor, William H. Dickson, asked how long he had been president of the church, Taylor replied, "Well, I cannot say precisely. The records will show."

When Dickson attempted to question Taylor about marriages in the Endowment House, church lawyers immediately raised a cloud of objections. The judge, Chief Justice Charles S. Zane, overruled. Dickson pursued the subject, to establish "that plural marriages are required by the laws of the church to be celebrated in the Endowment House."

Yet when Dickson asked Taylor where marriages took place, "in the Endowment House or elsewhere?" Taylor frankly admitted that sometimes they were performed there, "and sometimes elsewhere."

Dickson was not prepared for such an answer. "Where else, if not in the Endowment House?"

"I do not know that I can say. There is no specific place appointed in which marriages occur."

Dickson pursued the question, over many objections by church lawyers. "Are not the plural marriages entered into by the members of the church, so far as you know, performed in the Endowment House?"

---

[5] Full transcript of John Taylor's testimony was published the following day in the *Deseret News*, October 18, 1884. It is significant in revealing that plural marriage had gone underground, very much as in Nauvoo days.

"No, sir," Taylor said.

"Where are they performed?"

"I cannot say."

"Do you know of any plural marriages," Dickson persisted, "ever having been performed and entered into outside of any one of the Endowment Houses [i.e., the one at Salt Lake, and the temples at St. George and Logan] within the past three years?"

Taylor, under oath, either had to tell the truth or refuse to answer. He said, "I have recollections of many such."

Dickson was unprepared for such an answer. He rephrased the question. Taylor replied, "There is no specific place set apart for the celebration of marriages."[6]

Dickson asked who authorized plural marriages.

"I give that authority," Taylor said.

"Have you conferred upon any person that authority within the past three years?"

"Yes, sir." Taylor identified his counselors, Joseph F. Smith and George Q. Cannon. When Dickson pressed for other names, Taylor evaded the question, by giving a most astounding and unexpected reply: "There are," he said flatly, "hundreds of people who have that authority."

The air was electric in the courtroom. Both Saints and Gentiles were surprised at this sworn testimony by the one person who knew the full extent of hitherto secret practices. President John Taylor had taken the Principle underground again, and had appointed the organization for its continuance.[7]

Dickson next tried to find out about the records of marriages. "I am not acquainted with the records," Taylor replied, though he did admit he could find out.

"Will you be good enough to do so?"

"Well, I am not good enough to do so," Taylor replied, and the packed courtroom exploded in laughter.

With order restored, Dickson asked, "Who is the custodian of the records?"

"I cannot tell you."

"Did you ever know who the custodian of the records was?"

---

6 The plural marriage of the author's mother and father took place during a carriage ride in Liberty Park at Salt Lake City.

7 The significance of this testimony regarding the underground organization for continuing the Principle has been either ignored or suppressed by internal historians. Whitney, in his *History of Utah*, gives the most complete account, but concludes with the identification of Smith and Cannon being authorized to perform plural marriages, thus indicating that they were the only two so authorized. Roberts makes the astounding statement that "President Taylor was subpoenaed in his [Clawson's] case, but the testimony he gave was not material." (*Life of John Taylor*, p. 371.)

"I do not know that I ever did."

"Do you know that you don't?"

"Yes; I know that I don't."

When Dickson tried to elicit details of the ceremony of plural marriage, Taylor refused to answer, and the question was withdrawn.

Franklin S. Richards, church attorney, cross-examined: "President Taylor, in your direct examination you spoke of having appointed or authorized persons to celebrate plural marriages. State whether or not such authorization or appointments extended only to the plural marriages, or whether the appointees had the authority to celebrate first marriages also. In other words, was the authorization general as to marriage, or confined to plural marriage only?"

"It was general in all these matters, and things performed in the [Endowment] House," Taylor said, whether first or plural marriages.

When Taylor left the witness stand, air in the stuffy courtroom became easier to breathe, for most of the jam-packed crowd followed him out.

Two days later at Ogden, Taylor told the congregation:

> I was lately called upon as a witness . . . and I want to make some explanation: . . . I was required to divulge certain things. I did not know them to divulge. Perhaps some of you have had people come to you with their confidences. I have. But I don't want to be a confidant. Why? Because if they made a confidant of me and I was called before a tribunal, I could not, as an honorable man, reveal their confidences, yet it would be said I was a transgressor of the law. . . . Therefore I tell them to keep their own secrets, and remember what is called the Mormon creed: "Mind your own business." . . . I have studiously avoided knowing any more than I could possibly help about such matters.

Regarding marriages outside the temples and Endowment House, he reiterated:

> It is the authority of the Priesthood, not the place, that validates and sanctions the ordinance. I was asked if people could be sealed outside. Yes. I could have told them I was sealed outside, and lots of others.[8]

As Rudger Clawson's trial continued, Lydia Spencer was placed on the witness stand. Accused of the crime of being Clawson's wife, she still could be compelled to testify against him because the marriage was illegal. In this situation, other plural wives would, in effect, brand themselves loose women by swearing that they didn't know the father of their children, or that they were never married. Lydia couldn't do this. She

---

[8] JD, 25:355. Taylor had prepared for this policy with his "Epistle on Marriage" two years previously, which authorized marriages outside the temples or Endowment House.

simply refused to testify. Judge Zane cited her for contempt of court, and had her imprisoned until she would cooperate. Previous cases had shown the determination of the Utah courts to force testimony from plural wives. Annie Gallifant was released only to avoid giving birth to a baby in prison. Belle Harris, niece of the Book of Mormon witness, Martin Harris, was imprisoned more than two months. The most recent case was Nellie White, who was in the penitentiary from May 22 to July 7 of that year for refusing to testify.

After a night in prison Lydia Spencer, pale from lack of sleep, testified as her husband had requested: yes; she was married to Rudger Clawson.

Clawson was sentenced to four years imprisonment and a fine of $800, on the charges of polygamy and unlawful cohabitation.[9]

After a council meeting of the First Presidency and Quorum of the Twelve, Taylor was alone in the office. Alice Schwartz brought afternoon tea on a tray. He was pouring a cup when L. John Nuttall came in with accumulated mail. He went through the letters as he sipped a steaming cup, making marginal notations regarding replies. He approved sending a handkerchief to a sick man in Brigham City who had faith it would cure him. Another letter wanted him to arbitrate a bitter feud over water rights. Irrigation was the lifeblood of the desert; the man at the end of the ditch might take his rifle along as well as shovel if the canal was dry when his water turn came. Taylor referred the case to the local ward bishop's court, suggesting appeal to the stake high council if necessary. As a policy, he wanted people to settle their own problems, and do it "without going to law against a brother." However, he did intercede in the case of land-jumping on the Portage Indian Farm, advising jumpers that they must decide if the land was worth more than membership in the church, for he couldn't countenance defrauding the Lamanite brethren.

A long letter from a man in Soledad, California, told of receiving a vision commanding him to seek out John Taylor, the Lord's prophet, and could Taylor advance him train fare to Utah? Taylor scrawled the notation, "Make our usual answer." This, given to all who asked what Mormonism offered them, was that the church could promise nothing except persecution at the hands of the enemies of Christ.

This answer also went to the man who wanted the church to sponsor his invention of a secret cipher, and share the profits.

Sensitive to the need of sympathetic representation in the world press,

---

9 Clawson served more than three years of the sentence, before his mother went to Washington and secured a presidential pardon. At first Rudger was repelled by association with criminals at the prison. As the crusade continued, however, the best men of Utah became his companions there. Among others, his own father became an inmate, as did Lorenzo Snow, who was to become president of the church.

Taylor approved the sending of contributions—generally of less than $100—for printing and distribution of articles by hardy Gentiles with courage to stand up for a highly unpopular minority.[10]

Plural marriage brought a host of complications. A widow with two children was to become a plural wife. Since she had been sealed for time and eternity as the only wife of her former husband, a good man, should she marry her new husband only "for time," and thus sacrifice the special blessings given plural wives in the hereafter? And should her children be sealed to their father or step-father?

Taylor advised her, and the children, to make their own decision.

Not all who entered the Principle were prepared to meet its requirements. One man obediently took a second wife, but after eighteen months she complained to the bishop's court that he had never "treated her as a wife." Taylor approved the court's decision that the husband give her a piece of land, a house, and a divorce so that she could marry someone willing to accept his marital responsibilities.

A man wrote asking permission to have his wife's "aged mother," sixty-two, sealed to him for time and eternity. She had had two previous husbands, but they were Gentiles who couldn't give her glory in the hereafter. "We do not expect," he wrote, "to cohabit as husband and wife."

Nevertheless, Taylor advised against the appearance of evil.

A woman wrote of her worshipful love for a polygamist. She didn't ask for his support, nor even his love; she just wanted to be his wife, if in name only. Taylor suggested that she talk with the man and see how he felt.

A widow of John D. Lee, mother of a dozen children, wanted to be sealed to another husband, not for support nor for love, but because Lee, having been excommunicated, "would not be able to save her" in the hereafter. Taylor advised that things might be adjusted in the realms beyond the grave.[11]

A woman with an abusive husband wanted to be rebaptized, but had been accused of "taking medicine to avoid having children" by him. Was she worthy? Taylor approved the baptism, noting that while "these things are unpleasant" they were beyond his control. It was her own business.

He canceled the amount due from a missionary's family who had been unable to pay rent on the house—which Taylor owned—while the man was in the Lord's vineyard. Another mission problem came from a widow in Philadelphia, who wrote that although her faith was firm, she simply

[10] For originals of Taylor's mail, see "John Taylor Letterbook," Church Historical Department.

[11] After a century it was finally admitted that Lee was merely a scapegoat for Mountain Meadows, and he was reinstated to church membership.

was unable to keep on feeding, clothing, and housing the missionary who had stayed at her home for nine months. Taylor instructed the elder to go elsewhere.

Taylor had called the bishop at Montpelier, Idaho, to take a mission. Eighty-one members of the ward signed a request that he stay at home. Arrival of the railroad had brought a rough class of men; the ward needed the bishop's counsel. Taylor canceled the mission call.

Reports from Lamanite missions indicated that some converts were Indians first and Mormons second. A missionary at Blackfoot, Idaho, took sick and asked an Indian elder to administer by the laying on of hands. The Lamanite refused, saying he wasn't a medicine man.

When a man's wife was seduced while he was away on a mission, the guilty man offered to let the husband kill him. But the husband wasn't vindictive. He just wanted to know if the wife could be forgiven. Yes; and sin no more, Taylor advised.

A bishop's counselor in Ogden created a scandal by going to an astrologer when sick, who gave him medicine that cured what the laying on of hands hadn't. What to do? Smiling, Taylor made the notation to Nuttall: "A letter to his bishop should be sufficient."

Lot Smith, leader of the colony at Sunset, Arizona, was at once one of the most capable and faithful men in the church, while possessed of a wild temper which constantly embroiled him in squabbles. A stream of complaints from Sunset reached Taylor's desk. The situation was complicated by personal friendship; Lot Smith and John Taylor had worked together harassing Johnston's Army during the Utah War; they shared mutual trust and respect from long association. And, Taylor realized, the complication of living the United Order at Sunset would have tried the patience of Job.

Brother Pipkin complained of the settlement received on leaving the Order at Sunset.

> I had taken two good yoke of Oxen one good wagon & one horse beside many other things to numerous to mention for which he gave me three young steers & one little old ox not worth $20 the steers unbroke & so wild that I could not manage them. . . . & for the horse I never got anything at all and for a good wagon which could not have been bought anywhere in this country for less than $125 it was apprised in at $55 for which I got a wagon which is of no use only for the Old Iron & this is in keeping with the whole Settlement if it can be called a Settlement.

When Lot heard that Pipkin refused to sign a receipt before leaving, he

> run in before my horses with an Iron wagon Rod in his hand swinging around saying that I would sign it before I left I told him if force was his game to pop his whip.

After a wrangle Pipkin did sign, though "I do not consider I had anything like a fair Settlement," he said, adding "but that has nothing to do with the Gospel."

Taylor valued the faith of souls like Pipkin; he also appreciated Lot's problems, colonizing virgin land, bringing water onto the desert, and at the same time living the communal ownership of the Order. He counseled Lot to give liberty and justice to all, and to keep accurate accounts to prevent misunderstandings and possible lawsuits.

Refuting charges of an unfair settlement, Lot charged, "He's got that ass-end to." Was the Order to be run for the benefit of malcontents who pulled out, or for those with the gumption and faith to stay and make it a success?

While Taylor loved Lot Smith, handling the wrangles at Sunset demanded too much of his time, so he assigned Lot's problems to gentle Wilford Woodruff. Lot didn't like dealing with a subordinate. He found it hard to believe, he wrote Woodruff, that Taylor was "too busy to read a letter."[12]

The mail showed that a surprising number of intellectuals and liberals believed the Mormons should be allowed to practice their religion. Taylor was amused that the Edmunds Law even made converts. Ira C. Hillock wrote from Michigan that ever since the Edmunds Bill started through Congress,

> I have been alarmed by a voice sounding in my ears seeming as the loudest thunder (Ira you *must be a Mormon*) Sometimes in the field—sometimes in the dead of night I leap out of my sleep at this cry (Ira you *must be a Mormon*) . . . at last I cried out like Samuel of old (What shall I do to be a Mormon) the answer came at once (Ask President Taylor).

John Whitaker of Ogden asked a difficult question: "In what year will the son of man make his appearance on the Earth to Reign?"

Taylor's notation in reply was "Matt 24:36."[13]

From out of the past came a letter from John Goodson:

> It is now about forty-five years since you and I, Isaac Russell, Joseph Fielding, and several others, were baptized into the church by the late P. P. Pratt at Charlton's settlement near Toronto. . . .

Goodson had been a member of that great first mission to England, which had saved the infant church. Taylor remembered that after a quarrel with Heber C. Kimball, Goodson not only quit the mission and

---

[12] Lot Smith's temper brought him to a violent end. He was shot at Tuba City, Arizona, June 21, 1892, in a squabble with Indians over grazing rights.

[13] "But of that day and hour knoweth no man. . . ."

sailed home, but burned his entire stock of the badly-needed Book of Mormon.

> Since that day, the divine providence has connected us by diverse roads, to bring to pass his strange acts. You have become president of the church, and I have become a classical organist and pianoforte teacher. . . .

Having heard of the prosperity and culture of the Saints, Goodson asked "if there would be a reasonable chance of obtaining moderate employment in my profession" in Utah. Taylor welcomed the repentance of an old friend, but could offer him nothing but persecution by the enemies of Christ.

The final letter was from William Gustaveson, a bewildered convert newly arrived from Sweden. A man who owed him money gave him a ZCMI order in payment.[14] However, the value of the order had been altered, and when Gustaveson tried to cash it he found himself arrested and cast into the county jail. Inasmuch as Gustaveson had a very sketchy command of English, a fellow inmate who admitted to being "a horse thief with a little bit of honest feeling for a fellow man," explained the situation.

> I have written this for Gustaveson (I am a Gentile myself) and I think it is a sin and a shame to have this man down here. . . . If ever there was an innocent man he is innocent, and fretting himself to death, and we rough characters do not make him feel any better by jeering and scoffing. . . . I would not keep my brother's dog in a hole like this.

Agnes came in for the tea tray. Taylor asked her to have Brother Greene get his carriage ready. He wanted to go to the county jail.

Taylor was working on an article, "Ecclesiastical Control in Utah," at the request of the *North American Review*, when the traveling correspondent of the London *Daily News* arrived on the Overland Stage. Taylor readily granted his fellow Englishman an interview, and gave him what essentially was a preview of the manuscript in preparation. Some reporters twisted his words beyond recognition, but the Londoner was accurate, perceptive, and objective.[15]

> Mr. John Taylor, president of the Mormon church and state, lives in a fine house within a few minutes walk of the tabernacle. . . . It is a building of somewhat florid style, but is roomy and convenient. The drawing room where the president received me is . . . very comfortable with a large coal fire burning in an open grate. . . .
> The president is about seventy years of age,[16] but his tall powerful

---

[14] ZCMI scrip circulated as money.

[15] Interview October 8, 1883; published November 2.

[16] Taylor was in his seventy-sixth year.

figure shows little sign of advancing years. His hair, snow white, sets off a strong, kindly, and still ruddy face. Like all officers of the church, the president has earned his living by the sweat of his brow. Since he was elected to the presidency he has, of course, given up his farm. . . .

Taylor "never used the word 'polygamy,' except with the rider, 'as the world calls it,' insisting that it was 'the order of celestial marriage,' " the *News* reported. As for being married for time and all eternity, "It did not seem to occur to him that this was not a prospect that would recommend itself in all households."

The intent of the Edmunds Act was, Taylor said,

> to disfranchise Mormons and get the whole machinery of office in the Territory in the hands of the small minority of the Gentiles. After this Mormonism might be harried out of Utah as it was thirty-seven years ago hounded out of Illinois. . . .
>
> "Their Edmunds Act," the president said, "is *ex post facto*. . . . Here there are tens of thousands of men who entered into the state of celestial marriage years before this Act was passed. You can't . . . find them guilty of doing what was not declared illegal at the time of the Act. The Commissioners have gone even farther. They have imposed an oath as a preliminary to . . . voting. But it is against the constitution . . . to impose a test oath in respect of the exercise of the franchise. Thus you have the Commissioners performing an illegal act under unconstitutional law. That's a double plea we shall submit, if necessary, to the Supreme Court of the United States."

Despite the power and determination of the opposition, Taylor took a philosophical view as he talked "with quiet assurance and tone of simple confidence" of the future:

> "But," the president says, "we have always had trouble with the world, and things are not nearly so bad now as they were when the blood of Joseph Smith cried freshly from the ground, and we, driven out by Christians, went forth beyond the bounds of civilization to found a home and a nation.
>
> "When I used to go out as a missionary and, tramping through some remote, unfriendly country, did not know where I should get a crust of bread for my supper or a covered corner in which to lay my head, I used to pray to God, and I always had enough to eat. That is what we do now in this time of trial. The world is against us, but we trust in God—and keep our powder dry."

In his article for the *North American Review*, published January 1884, Taylor added material not contained in the London *Daily News* interview. He appreciated the plight of the Utah Commission, arriving in Utah "as the executors of the Edmunds Law, the passage of which had been procured by the influence of religious fanatics and political demagogues," who were surprised to find conditions so different from what they had anticipated, that it was impossible for them to meet the exorbitant demands of the country and at the same time comply with the requirements of the law. As one of their number expresses it, . . . they "stretched the legal tether to its utmost tension." Yet, on the other hand, as honorable men and representatives of the government, it was incumbent on them to comply with the plain provisions of the law.

The church had been denounced for opposing a law, which by taking the vote from the Mormons and giving it to "the most depraved, the vilest of mankind," meant that the Territory was "actually threatened with being governed by such an element."

Yet we are charged with being a menace to the United States, with being inimical to the constitution and government, simply because we have undertaken to legitimately and legally test in the courts, as we have the most perfect right to do, the legality and constitutionality of the law and the commissioners' rulings.

"Should we be worthy of the name of men, much less of freemen," the Champion of Rights demanded, "if we permitted these grave encroachments on our rights without one effort in their defense?"

For if radicalism, imperialism, oligarchy, and despotism are to bear rule, and the rights of the franchise to be refused to citizens by the dictum of commissioners, without a hearing, without proof, and without trial; if test oaths are to take the place of courts and legal testimony, and one principle of liberty after another nullified; if our constitution, our laws, and the fundamental principles of our government are to be trampled underfoot, it would seem to be high time that all honorable men should stand up in defense of liberty and the rights of man.

He pointed out that a common misconception concerned "the illegality of plural marriage."

Many persons suppose that there is some provision in the United States Constitution touching this subject. This is an error. The constitution leaves all matters relating to marriages to be regulated by the people of the various states; and hence it is that so many diversified marriage and divorce codes exist throughout the country. Congress claims the power to regulate these matters in the territories. We do not admit that this right belongs to the general government, but claim that in matters of local concern the territorial legislative assemblies are manifestly the proper parties to act.

Taylor excoriated those who "ignorantly or maliciously asserted that Mormonism is not a religion," but actually was a gigantic conspiracy to dominate the world.

What presumption for one set of men to declare that the faith and religious tenets of others are not a religion! Farewell to religious liberty when this is admitted. Soon the dominant sects in the land would secure religious uniformity by declaring all other bodies of worshipers non-religionists. When one man is permitted to decide what another's religion shall be, and to set metes and bounds beyond which he may not travel, then religious liberty is simply a misleading name, a delusion, and a snare.

The Gentile ring, scrutinizing the fine print of the first anti-polygamy law enacted twenty-two years previously, had complained that the LDS Church violated it by owning property in excess of $50,000. Taylor admitted that the half-finished Salt Lake temple alone "has already cost probably $2,500,000";

> but it would be going back to barbarism indeed to forbid by Act of Congress the erection of all but the most primitive structures in which to worship God or perform acts of charity. And again, the Latter-day Saints are not the only religious body that owns more than the prescribed $50,000 in the territories; others would be affected equally with us if this ill-considered law was enforced.

In conclusion, Taylor said:

> The Mormon question today really resolves itself into the query whether a small and unscrupulous minority, for private ends and personal aggrandisement, shall prevail upon the government of this nation to destroy every vestige of republican liberty in Utah, or whether the grand and glorious principles upon which this great government is founded shall be extended to all people alike.

When the *North American Review* published the article, Taylor was surprised to find a rebuttal to it by Governor Murray, who obviously had been given access to Taylor's manuscript. The governor took full advantage of the privilege.

The missionaries, traveling without purse or scrip to proclaim the gospel of Christ, became, in Murray's eyes, evidence of the gigantic Mormon conspiracy to overwhelm the world: church leaders had kept "the country in ignorance of their designs and actions through the machinations of adroit and unscrupulous agents throughout the country."

Far from being persecuted, Murray asserted, the Saints remained entirely untouched by legal restraints. He said

> that there has been no remedial legislation ever passed by congress. The "Edmunds Bill" contained much that was effective, but does not provide the remedy.

What was needed was tougher laws, laws with teeth, to curb the "political power vested in its adherents," and prevent the perpetuation of "an illegal and unrepublican government."

Polygamous Mormonism "has made Utah a deformed child."

The surgeon who takes in hand the case of a deformed child . . . must not be deterred from performing the necessary operation because of the protests and cries of the patient. To allow it to grow into manhood, helpless and a burden to its kindred, would be criminal. In this, congress is the surgeon, and must perform the operation.

Taylor was astounded to read that Mormonism was "a monster," which "means mischief," and to find the embattled Saints—virtually voiceless—described as

the most adroit and successful lobbyists our national capital has ever known. Besides, they readily spend thousands of dollars to mislead the country and to prolong their power from Congress to Congress.

The impoverished church, bled white by the long war, was in Murray's words a wealthy conspiracy led by

scheming traders, who handle the vast revenues of their corporation from year to year . . . at the expense of their creditor—the country. The day of settlement must come.

The Perpetual Emigration Fund—perpetually in debt—became a wealthy octopus which "gathers the poor and deluded from all parts of the world."

Designing men control ignorance which is joined with fanaticism, rob the poor of the results of honest toil, womanhood of its chief adornment, and inspire the souls of a confiding people in Utah with hate toward the people of the United States. These same men employ as counsel "wise men of the East," fill newspapers with interviews which in the light of facts are laughable, deceive amiable people, and pose as martyrs about the lobbies of Washington.

Indeed this was, in light of the facts, laughable, and Taylor's guffaw echoed throughout the Gardo House. The entire basis for Murray's allegations regarding the great and sinister Mormon lobby in Washington rested on the employment of one man, the venerable Judge Black. Being old and infirm, however, Black had proved a disappointment.[17]

Although Murray claimed the Mormons monopolized natural resources through "exclusive grants of timber, water, canyons, etc." granted church officials, he unblushingly admitted in the next paragraph that the Gentile minority possessed "to a great degree the wealth" of Utah.

They largely pay the taxes to carry on the government, both territorial and municipal, in which they have no voice.

"The remedy" to the Mormon question, Murray said, "is as follows":

---

[17] Black died a few months after being employed as Washington counsel for the Saints.

Abolish the legislature, and substitute in lieu of it a legislative council of not more than thirteen "of the most fit and discreet men of the Territory"; . . . they to be appointed by the president and confirmed by the Senate.

All this meant, of course, Taylor commented as he handed the magazine to L. John Nuttall for filing, was absolute and complete carpetbag government.

21

Skunks and Cohabs

At SEVEN O'CLOCK Thursday evening, John Taylor stepped from his carriage and, looking straight through U.S. Deputy Marshal Sam Gilson and another skunk lurking at the doorway of the Valley House, entered the hotel for the demonstration of the Swan Incandescent Electric Lamp. This night in March 1883, was reserved for the president's party. He found his various wives and families, both known and secret, on hand, together with a considerable number of church officials with their families. By sheer weight of numbers, the audience would baffle the deputies.

The hall was well lit by gas fixtures. The prime question: should there be conversion to incandescent lights, with the gas company already in operation? This and other questions were answered by the affable manager of the Rocky Mountain Electric Light Company, G.S. Erb: electric lights were superior in brightness, one single bulb giving off the light of twenty-five candles; it would eliminate the necessity for lamplighters, a single switch turning on the street lights of the city; there was less danger of fire; for home illumination it was more convenient; and the generators could be run by water power from the nearby canyons, eliminating the necessity of manufacturing gas from coal. Erb explained the operation of the new brush system of generating electricity, the machine for this demonstration to be operated by a small steam engine.

On signal, men turned off the gas lights, leaving the hall in pitch blackness. Then Erb's voice called, "Let there be light!" The place sprang into brightness approaching the light of day from the carbon-filament bulbs festooned from the ceiling, amid the ooh's and ah's of the audience.

On the return trip to the Gardo House, Taylor was glad he'd spiked the previous attempt to involve the city and church in an abortive electrical promotion three years previously. "Why should there be such haste in trying a thing that is only an experiment?" he'd asked in a memorandum to the city council, October 18, 1880.

> We are now being well supplied with gas. . . . The Gas Company would be prepared to furnish an Electric Machine at as low rates as this stranger can, if it is proven a success. If it is not a success we don't want it. . . .
> The city is interested in the Gas Works to the amount of $78,700—the church to the amount of $82,200, and private citizens to the amount of $89,100, making in all a sum of $250,000. Are we to allow this large and successful enterprise to be interrupted, injured, and perhaps destroyed on the bare word of a stranger?

The promoter's sole interest was selling the generators. "The Gas Company can buy them as well as he," Taylor pointed out; "they are in the market for sale."
As yet, no system had proved itself.

> Edison claims his is very good and a success; this man calls him a fraud. Edison if not more polite might retort in the same elegant manner. There are numerous other projectors, each claiming superior improvements for their machines. What has this man done that he should have five years' franchise, when, perhaps, in a few weeks or a month or two something superior shall be developed?

In the three years since then, electric lighting had indeed made rapid progress. The Swan system, he believed, merited serious consideration. However, there was a problem: the *Tribune* was highly enthusiastic about electric lighting, so there must be *something wrong with* it.

At the time the Edmunds Law was under debate in Congress, Taylor had written George Q. Cannon in Washington, advising him "let not your heart fail nor your knees falter, for the Lord will sustain you."

> If a crisis has got to come, we might as well meet it now as at any other time. Standing on the rock of eternal truth with God for our guide and protection, what have we to fear?

He had been asked to request the United States president to allow two non-polygamist Mormons on the Utah Commission, but had scorned the idea, saying "that we had no compromise to make with such men."

> In times like these, when the whole nation is combined against us and the power of the adversary is brought into requisition, it behooves us not only to trust in God but to exhibit an unswerving, unflinching front to the fiendish attacks which are now being made upon us.

Far from fearing the overwhelming might of fifty million Gentiles arrayed against 160,000 Saints, Taylor welcomed the conflict.

It is a glorious thing to be on the side of right; it is a glorious thing to battle for truth, virtue, purity, liberty and the rights of man; it is a glorious thing to feel that God is our friend and that we are the friends of God. All is well in Zion, all is peace and tranquility.[1]

In preparation for the storm, Taylor had a shelter made, as Saints all over the Territory were doing. For several days a faithful brother arrived at the Gardo House each morning with a manuscript for an appointment with Taylor. After arriving, he went to the third floor, put on a carpenter's bib, and worked diligently, fashioning a secret closet. Taylor supervised the work, designed on the pattern of Joseph Smith's hideaway at the Mansion House in Nauvoo.

As pressure from the government, the carpetbaggers, and the Utah ring increased, the Saints discussed new interpretations of the Principle. Taylor had no patience with this; it was for him the Kingdom or nothing. A typical letter was from Mrs. Malinda J. Merrill of Fremont, Utah, dated January 19, 1883. "According to my understanding," she wrote, concerning Joseph's revelation on plural marriage, "I thought it was the sealing [i.e., marriage endowments], but some say it is plurality."

"Permit me to say it is both," Taylor replied.

Mrs. Merrill asked,

If a man and woman go to the House of the Lord and get their Endowments and are sealed for time and all eternity, and they two live together quietly and peaceably and teach their children the principles of life and salvation, and bring them up in the fear of the Lord, will they gain an exaltation in the Celestial Kingdom with a continuation of their seed or not?

"The question is: What is the Law?" Taylor said.

You seem desirous to take part of the Law and reject the other part, but it is plainly stated . . . that they were "to do the works of Abraham." . . . It is evident therefore . . . that other wives were included in this Law.

Mrs. Merrill then asked about a practice that would, some said, satisfy the requirements of the Principle and at the same time conform to U.S. law:

What is the difference in a man having dead wives sealed to him than living women, so that he has one living wife? . . .

"This Law," Taylor replied, "pertains more particularly to the living."

You seem to be desirous of having dead women sealed to your husband instead of living ones, whereas the Law pertaining to these matters does not put things in that shape. . . .
Circumstances do not always place it in the power of man to enter

---

[1] Taylor to Cannon, February 27, 1882.

into this Covenant, and these matters are left with the Lord to adjust; but no man or woman has authority to point out any other way than that which the Lord has appointed.

Taylor had previously emphasized this in council with the first presidency and the Twelve. Wilford Woodruff recorded in his journal, October 13, 1882:

> Concerning the Patriarchal Order of Marriage, President Taylor said: "If we do not embrace that principle soon, the keys will be turned against us."[2]

The successful prosecution of Rudger Clawson touched off the u.c. crusade. Washington appropriated funds for more deputies—called skunks by the Saints—who descended on villages in gangs, hunting for cohabs. They broke down doors at midnight for evidence that a man lived with his wife; they grilled children about parents; they arrested pregnant girls, for this was evidence—not of adultery, but of marriage. The skunks didn't bother about arrest warrants. They raided from hearsay information, gossip, tips from spotters; and spotters, traitors within the ranks, were even lower on the scale than skunks.

Under Taylor's supervision, the Saints formed an underground, to protect wanted men and to harbor pregnant plurals until, as time of delivery neared, the girls were spirited outside the Territory to bear babies.[3]

Since skunks were held in such contempt, the ranks were recruited largely from carpetbaggers, apostates, loafers, and malcontents, bitter men who took great glee in hounding men of position and authority. Officials of the church were almost to a man classed as criminals, fair game for the skunks. The prison began filling with the most distinguished citizens of the Territory, until it became known as the most exclusive social club of Utah.[4]

Taylor never tired of pointing out that the entire frenzy of the crusade was based upon violation of a legal misdemeanor. Unlawful cohabitation wasn't a felony.

Governor Murray and the territorial legislature became deadlocked. Murray insisted on a bill outlawing polygamy in Utah; when the legislature refused to enact it, Murray vetoed other bills, then called upon Washington to abolish local government entirely and appoint a carpetbag commission to rule the Territory.

---

[2] This is the same counsel Joseph Smith had given at Nauvoo.

[3] The large adobe home at Grantsville of Samuel Woolley, the author's grandfather, was a way station on the underground. The author's mother, a plural wife, became so well known by her underground name that she used it the remainder of her life.

[4] Pictures exist of groups of prominent men, dressed in stripes, during prison terms.

"They want to kill this incipient commonwealth," the *Deseret News* accused, February 13, 1884.

> They want to establish an oligarchy here. The chief agitators here do not care a cent about polygamy. Political chicanery is at the bottom of the whole movement.

In a memorial to Congress, the Utah Legislature pointed out that it had passed an act required by the Edmunds Law concerning election officials and registration of voters, but that this and "other bills needful to the progress of this Territory have been nullified by the governor."

> We appeal to you not to condemn us unheard, not to take from us the few political privileges that distinguish us from conquered slaves; not to deliver our fair and flourishing Territory into the hands of men irresponsible to the people; not to reverse for us the established rules of civilized jurisdiction; not to disfranchise the innocent for the alleged offenses of the presumably guilty; not to encroach upon our rights to property; not to apply to us a religious test for political purposes, nor to pass any such rash and revolutionary measures as have been proposed, but to postpone any further action toward Utah until a committee of your own number shall have impartially investigated the whole subject of the situation in Utah.

The vindictive Edmunds, in cooperation with Senators Hoar and Cullom, again prepared a bill to smash Mormonism. The *Tribune* hailed it as a cure for treason:

> The Mormon Church is essentially in all its teachings and practices an anti-republican hierarchy; it is a union of church and state, antagonistic to our republican form of government; it is a foreign government planted on American soil. John Taylor, president and autocrat of Utah; Cannon, the prophet and leader, are, as has heretofore been shown, foreigners by birth, and hate the government under which they live.

Major points of the new legislation would compel a first—or "legal"— wife to testify against her husband, dissolve the Mormon Church as a legal corporation, abolish the Perpetual Emigration Fund, eliminate election districts, put schools under administration of the federal courts, and provide more stringent punishment for unlawful cohabitation.

When the bill passed the Senate June 19, the *Trib* hailed it as "notice served upon the hierarchy that rules us here to . . . haul down their treasonable flag and come under the laws of the United States."

As a reward for his valiant work, Murray was appointed to a second term as governor. The *Deseret News* called this "an inexcusable abuse of the appointive power."

> A party that would frame such a measure as the Hoar-Edmunds bill for political ends, wants just such tools as ex-Marshal Murray. If the gov-

ernment can stand an officer who was "vindicated" from grave charges by a successful attempt to stifle inquiry into them, the people of Utah will have to endure it.

Taylor was elated when the new Edmunds measure failed passage in the House. However, when Grover Cleveland was elected president, the lame-duck Arthur in his final message to Congress called for "the most radical legislation consistent with the restraints of the constitution," to suppress "that abominable practice."

> I again recommend, therefore, that Congress assume absolute political control of the Territory. . . .

As the frenzy of the u.c. crusade became hysteria, Taylor wondered if it was wisdom to stand and fight in this unequal war of attrition. When in the east, the Saints had left New York, Ohio, and Missouri in the face of overwhelming opposition; then, in abandoning Nauvoo, they had left the United States itself. Would it be necessary to abandon Utah for foreign soil? Writing to stake presidents in the Arizona colonies, December 16, 1884, Taylor counseled them to explore lands in Mexico as "a place of refuge under a foreign government to which our people can flee." He also was considering propositions from the Sandwich and Samoan islands as possible refuges for the Saints. Of one thing he was sure: if he led his people out of the Great Basin, they would scorch the earth behind them, leaving it as they'd found it, a desert.

"A general attack is being made upon our liberties throughout all the territories where our people reside," he wrote the Arizona officials.

> There can be no question that there is apparently a concert of action . . . to push our people to the wall and to destroy our religious liberty and with it our religion itself. . . .
> Our brethren are like sheep surrounded by ravening wolves, and you as shepherds of the flock . . . must take steps to protect them.
> Our counsel . . . is to obtain a place of refuge under a foreign government to which our people can flee . . . and you should adopt such measures as shall be necessary to preserve your people being entrapped.

At present, the exodus would be primarily for the victims of the u.c. crusade. Future events would dictate whether the entire society of the Saints would follow.

Taylor didn't entrust such a letter to the mails, but sent it "by the hand of Elder Seymour B. Young, who will also be able to state to you our feelings more in detail."

Upon getting the message at Sunset, Lot Smith hurried to Salt Lake to confer with Taylor about conditions in Arizona. Shortly thereafter, on January 3, 1885, Taylor left on the Union Pacific in a private car, with a party of church officials, to visit Arizona and Mexico in order to get the program underway.[5]

Five years previously Moses Thatcher, while president of the Mexican mission, had proposed the first colonization in that country, after being approached by a Belgian land agent, Emelio Biebuyck. The promoter offered settlers free public land, together with a subsidy of $80 per adult and $40 per child; they also would be exempted from taxes and military duty for twenty years, and could bring in free of duty implements, materials, and supplies to establish colonies. At that time, Taylor decided that Mexican colonization was "premature." But the Edmunds Law had changed the picture.

The projected move presented some serious problems. Indians were powerful in Mexico, and two of the most feared tribes, the Apaches and Yaquis, could resist encroachment on their lands. The Mexican government, though lenient regarding polygamy, was in other respects a dictatorship. Under the iron rule of Porfirio Diaz the rights of the common man had virtually disappeared. He had ruthlessly suppressed the press, abolishing opposition newspapers, imprisoning or executing editors and writers who voiced the slightest criticism. Under pretense of ridding the country of bandits, thousands of political dissidents were arrested and by the notorious *ley de fuga* were shot "while attempting to escape." Diaz had consolidated his power by dealing out lands, concessions, monopolies, and offices to his supporters while eliminating all opposition. He appointed all members of congress, hand-picked the judiciary; in fact the entire machinery of government, from the 27 governors of states to the 4,574 justices of the peace, held office at his will. While his favorites amassed great wealth, the people existed in grinding poverty, using wooden ploughs, harvesting with sickles, treading out grain with oxen. Smallpox, malaria, and typhoid were epidemic. Though theoretically free, the peonage system kept the worker in debt to his master and in bondage throughout his lifetime.

To John Taylor, Champion of Liberty, these were things to ponder before establishing colonies in Mexico.

Traveling among the Arizona colonies, he found a "slackness" due to the crusade. The leaders were gone—driven underground, taking missions, or sent to the American Siberia of the federal prison at Detroit. Although there was a territorial penitentiary, men convicted of u.c. were sent

---

[5] In addition to Lot Smith, Taylor was accompanied by Joseph F. Smith; Brigham Young, Jr.; Moses Thatcher; Francis M. Lyman; Charles W. Penrose; John Q. Cannon; George Reynolds; Charles Barrell; John Sharp; and Brigham Randall. Erastus Snow, apostle of Utah's Dixie, met the party en route. Despite painful prostrate and bladder trouble, Snow had recently made a 450-mile trip by wagon into Mexico during bitter weather, accompanied by Moses Thatcher, to investigate various colonization sites.

2,000 miles away, making visits by family and friends impossible. By pyramiding indictments, judges levied sentences of three and a half years imprisonment, plus a $500 fine, for a misdemeanor.

At St. David, near the Mexican border southeast of Tucson, Taylor met with presidents of the four Arizona stakes, Jesse N. Smith, Christopher Layton, Alexander F. McDonald, and Lot Smith. After discussing the situation, he sent two parties again into Mexico to scout locations, with instructions to find places close to the border. Meanwhile, he authorized the organization of a colony which would be ready to emigrate the following month.

Taylor's party then went into Mexico as far as Guaymas, on the Gulf of California in southwestern Sonora. This was a fertile district of sugarcane fields, bamboo, and subtropical vegetation near the mouth of the Yaqui River. Taylor had recently sent an exploring party here, who reported that both Gov. Luis E. Torres and the Yaqui chiefs were sympathetic and friendly.

Returning to Guaymas in late afternoon from a tour of potential colonization sites, Taylor found an urchin waiting at the hotel with a note scrawled in a quavering hand. It was from Samuel Brannan, who had sailed through the Golden Gate in the *Brooklyn* with the first colony of Mormons to settle the west. Sam asked for an audience to discuss colonization in Sonora, the reply to be returned by messenger. Taylor hadn't had his daily walk, so he followed the boy through narrow streets to see what was on Brannan's mind. The previous year, he recalled, two missionaries had found Sam Brannan at Guaymas, living in "squalid penury and wretchedness," and the *Deseret News* had recalled the malediction by Parley Pratt.

At the height of Brannan's success, he had owned one-fifth of booming San Francisco, including most of Market Street. He had founded the city of Sacramento. He had personally kept the lid on the discovery of gold at Sutter's Mill while he fitted out four stores to cash in on the boom, and he raked in so much gold from them that it was dumped into chamberpots under the counters.

Sam Brannan had an income of a thousand dollars a day when Parley Pratt arrived in San Francisco to pick up the pieces of the Mormon colony which Brannan had shattered with neglect and sharp dealings. Parley and two wives lived in a shack on Pacific Street, where he preached twice each Sunday at the Adelphi theater. But San Francisco was stony soil for the gospel; Parley and his wives often went hungry. When Sam's mother-in-law urged Brannan to contribute to the cause, he told her that if Parley needed money he could come ask for it.

"I don't need to ask Sam Brannan for money," Parley retorted on hearing the message. "The Lord is my shepherd; I shall not want." Then he added, "Tell Sam Brannan that he may be a Midas now, but he will live to see the day when he will want for a dime to buy a loaf of bread."[6]

The boy went through a low doorway of a mud hut. Taylor ducked under the lintel and straightened cautiously to avoid brushing the wattles of the ceiling. The hut was a single room, with a mud fireplace for cooking. Two chickens scratched at the earthen floor; a pig nuzzled at a heap of straw in a corner. The room was bare of furniture except for a small chest, a couple of packing boxes, and a hammock where Sam Brannan reclined, puffing at a black cigar with a bottle of tequila at his elbow.

Surprised at Taylor's arrival, Brannan got out of the hammock with difficulty. He told the boy to go, then advanced stiffly with the aid of a cane. For a few moments it was difficult to recognize in this physical wreck the vital young man at Nauvoo whom Brigham had commissioned to take a party of Saints around the Horn and prepare a place in California for those who would follow from Illinois. Drink had taken its toll of Brannan, and he never had recovered from wounds received in a shooting scrape. Though eleven years younger than Taylor, at sixty-five Sam Brannan was an old, old man.

But though in bad health and dire circumstances, Sam Brannan still had the qualities that had made him California's first millionaire. He graciously ushered Taylor to a seat on a box, offering him a cigar and recommending the tequila, which his guest declined. Sam was temporarily out of funds; but he wasn't poor, just pressed for cash at the moment.

Getting down to business, Brannan said the Mormons were looking for a place of refuge. Well, he just happened to have exactly what they wanted. The Mexican government had given him a grant of 1,687,585 acres in Sonora. It had rich agricultural land, with plenty of water, that would produce two crops a year. Oranges were superior to those of Florida. There were splendid stands of virgin timber, grazing lands, and, in the Sahuaripa district the country was underlaid with an immense bed of anthracite coal.[7]

Listening to Brannan's eloquent presentation, Taylor was almost caught up in the spell. The entire LDS population could emigrate onto Brannan's grant, and forget the Edmunds Law. However, he'd heard

---

[6] Reva Scott, *Samuel Brannan and the Golden Fleece.*

[7] See Reva Scott for Brannan's last promotion. There is a legend that Sam cashed in on it, and ended his days wealthy again. Not so. He died in poverty at San Diego May 14, 1889, a pauper and so friendless that his body lay unburied several months until a nephew supplied funds to have it interred. Ironically, Samuel Brannan's name has been saved from oblivion by members of the church he rejected. Mormon historians have dredged up his story, not because of his financial triumphs or the scandal of his personal life, but because Elder Samuel Brannan was once a man of responsible church office.

there was a hitch in the title of the grant; he knew that Sam's New York associates had sold stock in the enterprise to many of the former millionaire's San Franciscan friends and associates, then vanished with the funds. Taylor decided against getting entangled in such an enterprise and, after advancing Brannan a small loan, walked back to the hotel for supper.

On the return trip, Taylor's party stopped at Hermosillo, beautifully situated among orange groves, where Governor Torres said he was receptive to Mormon colonization. When he reminded them of adverse press reports regarding the previous exploring expedition to Guaymas—newspapers accusing the Mormons of joining with the Yaquis to make war on the United States—Taylor burst into laughter. He explained to the puzzled governor that this hoary tale was shopworn: it had been used in Missouri, then at Nauvoo, and again in Utah.

In parting, Torres presented Taylor with a sample of local produce, a branch of a lemon tree bearing enormous fruit. One of the lemons measured 16½ inches around. Yes, it was rich country; but considering Brannan's conflicting claims, and the fierce reputation of the Yaquis, Taylor decided against colonization so far inland, at least for the present.

Returning to Arizona, Taylor learned that the Supreme Court had ruled in the Clawson case that bail was not a right for a man accused of polygamy, "but distinctly a matter for the discretion of the court to judge." This meant that anyone arrested for u.c. could be jailed indefinitely while awaiting trial and pending appeal.

Taylor immediately authorized colonization of Mexican tracts near the American border, along the Casas Grandes River in Chihuahua and in the Corrales Basin at Sonora.[8]

After visiting settlements in the Phoenix area, the Taylor party went west, passing through the former LDS outposts of Las Vegas and San Bernardino to Los Angeles, then up the coast to San Francisco. It was here, less than forty years ago, that Sam Brannan landed the *Brooklyn* at what was then the tiny hamlet of Yerba Buena, and preached the first non-Catholic sermon in California. Soon he was publishing the first newspaper, the *California Star*, had started the first school, performed the first marriage under the American flag, settled his colonists on the first farm in the San Joaquin valley, and, charged with misappropriation of colony funds, was defendant in California's first jury trial.[9]

In San Francisco, Taylor and his party had an audience with Gov. Leland Stanford; they attended the theater; they saw Chinatown; they visited Golden Gate park to see the acacia in bloom; they lunched at

---

[8] Within six weeks, some 350 colonists were in Mexico. Eight Mormon colonies eventually were established, six in Chihuahua and two in Sonora.

[9] *A Vineyard by the Bay*; the section concerning the history of Mormonism in the bay area was written by this author.

the Cliff House overlooking Seal Rocks. But Taylor liked to get away from official functions and tours to prowl about the city. Was this the shack where Parley Pratt lived on Pacific Street? Was this the headquarters for George Q. Cannon, Joseph Bull, and M. F. Wilkie who, at the time Taylor was issuing *The Mormon* in New York almost twenty years ago, had published the Book of Mormon in the Hawaiian language and founded the *Western Standard?* In the industrial section Taylor walked along Brannan Street, the only remaining recognition of the man who had been its most wealthy and prominent citizen.

Mormons were remembered now primarily through place names. There was Mormon Island on the American River, where one of the richest gold strikes was made by three members of the Mormon Battalion; Mormon Gulch, site of Tuttletown; Mormon Corral, in El Dorado County. And even these names were disappearing. Colonists of Brannan's ship gave the name Brooklyn to the city across the bay that now was Oakland. The settlement of New Hope, where the colony grew the first wheat, now was Stanislaus. Mormon Road in Toulumne County had become Slumgullion Road (hardly an improvement); and Mt. Joseph Smith was now Mt. Palomar.

Taylor recalled his own prediction that temples would rise on the Pacific shore. When?[10]

The January weather at San Francisco was sparkling bright. Having seen the citrus groves, the fruit orchards coming into bloom, the fields of winter crops growing in the rich soil of the immense valleys, Taylor couldn't help speculate on what might have been, had Brigham followed the original plan of bringing the Saints from Nauvoo to New Hope on the Stanislaus.

He walked down Valencia Street on a brisk afternoon, the wind blowing off the Pacific, and visited the historian, H. H. Bancroft, who took him through his library of 60,000 volumes and 100,000 manuscripts. Taylor saw the busy staff at work, compiling the volumes of his immense *Works*, of which the *History of Utah* was one. He shook hands with Alfred Bates and Edward P. Newkirk, the two writers assigned to prepare the history of the Saints for Bancroft's final draft and polish.

Bancroft had visited Salt Lake for several weeks the previous summer, at which time Taylor had read proof sheets of several chapters approvingly, noting only a few minor errors of fact. At that time the historian had added about fifty additional Mormon manuscripts and journals to the almost 2,000 he already had; but with his passion for knowing everything

---

10 There are now two, Los Angeles and Oakland. Taylor's prediction was made during the exodus from Nauvoo.

he was still collecting. His agents, out taking orders for the *Works*, were also researchers, collecting diaries and taking verbatim notes of interviews.

It now had been exactly five years since Taylor had endorsed Bancroft's project, and at last the end was in sight. The historian estimated that the Utah volume would be completed by the end of the year, 1885.[11]

In talking with Bancroft, Taylor mentioned seeing Sam Brannan at Guaymas. Bancroft immediately was interested. How could he obtain Brannan's story? Taylor suggested that a little cash might work wonders.[12]

Returning to the hotel, Taylor found the others of the party anxiously awaiting him. George Q. Cannon had telegraphed that a messenger was en route from Salt Lake with important news. Obviously this pertained to some crisis which Cannon couldn't entrust to the wires.

The courier, Samuel Hill, arrived next day with the message: Deputy Sam Gilson had arrested Cannon for u.c.; he was out on bail. Gilson had warrants in his pocket for the remainder of the first presidency, Joseph F. Smith and Taylor. The U.S. government was determined to put the leaders of the faith behind bars. Smith already had been on the underground several months, before joining the expedition to Arizona and Mexico, reason being that he'd recently taken two wives, one the daughter of Heber C. Kimball, the other Taylor's niece.

Hill reported that Cannon was in hiding at Salt Lake, together with L. John Nuttall, living in the new barn behind the tithing office.

Despite the warrants, Taylor decided to return to Utah and preach a last sermon to the Saints. However, he advised Smith to take a mission to the Sandwich Islands for awhile. Taylor slipped into Salt Lake Tuesday, January 27. Two bodyguards, Sam Bateman and Charles Wilcken, escorted him to the barn where he joined Cannon and Nuttall. At a night session with members of the Twelve, Taylor decided to go underground, as Joseph had done during cloak-and-dagger days at Nauvoo.[13]

Inasmuch as it might well be his last chance to see them, Taylor visited his wives and families at guarded hideouts during the remainder of the week, while Sam Gilson and his deputies scoured the valley for him.

On Sunday afternoon, February 1, the great tabernacle was filled to overflowing as Taylor entered the rear door. An electric gasp greeted his appearance when he walked onto the stand and took his seat. He saw

---

[11] It was finished late in 1885, edited for printing the following year, and published 1889.

[12] Bancroft subsequently engaged Brannan to write his autobiography.

[13] "There is a determination among the brethren not to allow President Taylor to get into the hands of our enemies," Abraham H. Cannon recorded in his journal.

heads turn, eyes going to the exits, where guards stood sentinel. Yet as he arose to address his people, they didn't know that this was farewell. It would be John Taylor's last official public appearance.

He reviewed his recent trip, comparing the Siberia of the Detroit prison to "the example of Russia."

> It may suit others to violate the law, to trample upon human rights and desecrate the sacred term of liberty . . . in the name of justice. But we profess to be governed by higher, by nobler, and more exalted principles; . . and if Jesus could afford to endure the attacks of sinners . . . we ought to be able to endure a little. . . .
>
> God has revealed to us . . . certain principles pertaining to the perpetuity of man and woman . . . He has told us to obey those laws. The nation tells us, "If you do we will persecute and proscribe you." Which shall I obey?

Surveying the sea of faces, he asked, "Shall I be recreant to all these noble principles that ought to guide and govern men?" He answered firmly, "No, never!" His deep voice rose. "NO, NEVER!" Then his roar filled the great hall, "NO, NEVER!" and he smacked the Bible on the rostrum. The audience responded with a fervent "Amen."

He told of being visited at the Gardo House by U.S. Attorney General Edwards Pierrepont. "Mr. Pierrepont, permit me to introduce to you my sister, who is my housekeeper," he said to his guest. "It is not lawful for us to have wives now."

A ripple of sardonic laughter greeted this story.

"No man's liberties are safe under such administration," he declared. "The result will be that those who sow the wind will reap the whirlwind."

> When men begin to tear down the barriers and tamper with the fundamental principles and institutions of our country, they are playing a very dangerous game, and are severing the bonds which hold society together.

Referring to past violence, of his brethren "shot to pieces in cold blood," he asked: "I want to know if anybody can tell me . . . of any individual that was ever punished according to law for killing a Mormon? Speak it out, if you know it."

No voice came from the vast congregation. On the stand behind Taylor, Erastus Snow said there was no such instance on record.

> Well, what would you do? I would do as I said some time ago: if you were out in a storm, pull up the collar of your coat and button yourselves up . . . until the storm blows past.

When the storm was over, the miserable sneaks crawling about would crawl back into their holes. Meanwhile,

Would you resent these outrages and break the heads of men engaged in them, and spill their blood? No. Avoid them . . . as you would wolves, or hyenas, or crocodiles, or snakes.

"Avoid them," he counseled, "and take care they do not bite you." Laughter swept the hall, and again when he continued: "What?—won't you submit to the dignity of the law? Well, I would if the law would only be a little dignified."

Under oppression, "When such a condition of affairs exists," he said, "it is no longer a land of liberty, and it is certainly no longer a land of equal rights." He reminded the people that "we must take care of ourselves as best we may, and avoid being caught in any of their snares.

"But," he counseled, "no breaking of heads, no bloodshed, no rendering evil for evil."[14]

Taylor had spoken almost two hours, but the timbre of his deep voice gained strength as he reached the peroration. "I will tell you what you will see by and by," he told his people.

You will see trouble, TROUBLE, TROUBLE enough in these United States. And as I have said before I say today: I tell you in the name of God, *woe!* to them that fight against Zion, for God will fight against them.

He slipped out before conclusion of the services. Escorted by Sam Bateman and Charles Wilcken, he joined Cannon and Nuttall at their quarters in the barn. Wilcken, a giant of a man who had served in the Prussian Army and been decorated with the Iron Cross for bravery, stood guard. That night Wilcken harnessed up a buggy. After Taylor, Cannon, and Nuttall climbed in, Wilcken slapped the team with the reins and drove south out of town.

The president of the church had gone underground.

Wilcken continued south about six miles, then in the vicinity of Little Cottonwood creek turned west, crossing the Jordan and continuing to Taylorsville. Near Taylor's former farm Bishop Samuel Bennion received the fugitives warmly. They stayed with him nine days before moving ahead of the deputies to another refuge.

[14] It is remarkable, considering the arrogance of many skunks, and the violence done by some of them, that no U.S. deputy was ever injured by the Saints.

22

The DO

As HE STEPPED OUTSIDE the Hansen home into the bitter night, the wind cut through Taylor's greatcoat. He'd had a cold the past few days, and the raw air brought on a spasm of coughing. Sam Bateman steadied his arm as the two men crossed the rear yard toward the harnessed rig, stepping carefully. The snow had melted to slush this afternoon, and now was frozen solid.

A bad night to travel, but a good time to move. Skunks would be less apt to prowl in weather like this.

Charles Wilcken was waiting with the rig, team ready and luggage stowed. Taylor got in between the two massive guards, and felt small between them, though he himself was pushing six feet. As the buggy rattled down the lane he waved good-bye to Peter Hansen and his wife, who watched from the door apprehensively. These good people didn't have much, but their hospitality had been royal during his stay. Then this evening had come word that United States deputies had smelled out the DO. Taylor was leaving his fourth hideout in two months.[1]

Presently the rig left Sugar House, heading northwest on Hyland Drive toward the city. More than an hour later, they rolled along South Temple Street past the Gardo House. Behind those lighted windows

---

[1] He had stayed near his farm in Taylorsville at two places, Bishop Bennion's and at the bishop's sister-in-law's home; then he'd moved to Big Cottonwood, at Charles Bagley's, before going to Peter Hansen's place at Sugar House.

Underground headquarters for the church was variously called "Safe Retreat," "Halfway House," and, most generally, the "DO." Undergrounders were "on the dodge," thus, "DO" in the "cohab code."

were Taylor's loved ones. It was impossible, of course, to pay them a call.[2]

Despite the lap robe, Taylor was chilled to the bone when the buggy finally entered the lane at Brother Will's big mansion in the fashionable district on the west side. At times like this, it was good to have dear friends such as Brother Will and his charming wife, Sister Cathy.

No light showed at the windows, as Wilcken drove around to the back. Brother Will would, of course, give the appearance of having retired. Sam Bateman climbed down stiffly and, blowing on his hands, went onto the back porch, where he gave the secret rap on the kitchen door. Presently it opened a crack. After a few low words a man slipped out with a shawl clutched over his nightshirt and hurried to the rig. It was Brother Will. Speaking hurriedly, he warned that they'd been tipped off. The feds would raid the house in the night. Under the circumstances, President Taylor . . .

Taylor said he understood, and as Brother Will kept talking suggested he go inside so as not to arouse suspicions. The man hurried onto the porch, the raw wind whipping the shawl and nightshirt, and slipped through the kitchen door. Bateman climbed into the rig. Wilcken wheeled the team around. As the carriage passed out of the lane Bateman spoke, saying that Brother Will couldn't look them in the eye.

Not a single rich person had offered refuge to the church president, Wilcken pointed out. Money had cankered their souls.

With a wry grin Taylor said it was good to find out who your true friends were.

Wilcken asked, where to? The two guards pondered. Couldn't return to one of the places they'd stayed previously; skunks would be watching. Bateman said that David James had invited them, any time they needed a place.

That's too far, Taylor said; they'd go to the Gardo House.

The bodyguards regarded him incredulously. That was the one place the feds would watch; they'd already raided it several times.

Taylor told them he needed some papers that only he could get. But this was not the reason. He was hard hit by Brother Will's shallow friendship; right then he had to be with people he loved. At the moment he didn't give a hoot about the skunks. If they raided, they'd never take him alive.

The moment of slipping into the living room—seeing the family gathered, some reading, some doing needlework, two of Margaret's older children playing checkers, while she got the younger ones ready for bed; then the frozen moment, the dawning joy, the rush to embrace

---

[2] His families had moved back into the mansion.

him—made it all worthwhile. These were his families, through time and all eternity. He had paid a great price for them, but certainly it was a bargain.

Presently, despite his protests, his wives had his feet in a pan of hot water, a mustard plaster on his chest, camphor ointment in his nostrils. They fussed about him like hens over a lone chick. A bad cold; was he sleeping warm at night? Was he getting the right kind of food? Dodging the feds, fleeing in the night; should be in bed—a wonder he didn't have pneumonia.

Taylor growled that it was nothing, just a little cough; he didn't want to be babied. But he loved every moment of it.

His sister Alice brought in tea, black and steaming hot, with a plate of oatmeal cookies and a bottle of valley tan on the tray. Taylor laced a cup of tea with valley tan, took a sip, and sighed. Ah! That hit the spot! Hadn't had a real cup of tea since he went on the dodge. He didn't really mind tension, pursuit, and escape—that was excitement, not hardship. What really wore on a man was monotony, being cooped up, strange beds, being president of the church at all times, no chance to relax, to sit around in shirtsleeves with his boots off and his feet on the oven door. And that dishwater they called tea—weak as a baby, never a spike in it, and even so, the silent disapproval. People just wouldn't believe, any more, that the prophet Joseph also liked his tea and coffee, and a glass of wine.

He was finishing his second cup when an owl hoot sounded, followed by the wail of a coyote. Taylor sprang up, splashing water from the foot bath. Deputies were coming.

He waited in the blackness of the secret closet on the third floor, listening to the sounds of skunks searching the mansion: strident voices; slamming doors; women asking them to be careful as they banged about. And why, Alice demanded, did they have to rip up the carpet? Nobody could be hiding under it. Looking for the trap door, lady, came the reply; there was a hideout here somewhere, and they'd find it.

From outside came the rumble of angry voices as the Saints gathered in the street. Someone called on them to disperse, do nothing to invite violence. A voice yelled back that they'd never stand by and see President Taylor dragged off to jail. The crowd roared approval.

Taylor realized his mistake. His capture could touch off an armed uprising. He shouldn't have given way to temper.

Heavy boots thumped along the third floor hallway; the bedroom doorknob rattled. The voice of his son, John W., spoke just beyond the thin false wall, saying this was just an unoccupied bedroom, used for storage. The authoritative voice of U.S. Deputy Marshal Sam Gilson boomed that they'd have a look anyhow. He had a warrant for John the Revelator in his pocket, and he'd serve it tonight. He told a fellow deputy to take a look in that closet. Steps thudded close; the closet door latch rattled; the deputy's voice came loudly just beyond the false panel, saying nothing here except some boxes of junk.

And at that moment Taylor struggled with an almost overwhelming urge to cough. He fought it back. From the bedroom John W.'s voice suggested that he'd show them the tower. Never mind, Gilson replied; they knew the way. Boots of the two deputies thumped out the door.

Taylor suddenly coughed. Strangling to suppress it, he heard the footsteps pause, return. And then even though his life might depend upon it, he was racked by a coughing spell.

When it was over, he heard coughing beyond the false wall, a veritable spasm. As it subsided, Gilson said that that was a bad cold there, young fellow. John W. in a strangled tone said the bug was going around, everybody had it. Take coal oil and sugar to cut the phlegm, Gilson suggested. Boots thumped into the hallway and away.

It was past midnight when the rig with Taylor and his two guards rumbled over the planks bridging the Jordan. At the farm of David James they found a warm welcome.

Three days later his wives began leaving the Gardo House to avoid prosecution.[3]

Idaho had passed a Test Oath law, disfranchizing all Mormons who *believed in* plural marriage, on the ground that this made them unpatriotic citizens. The Test Oath resulted in denial of the vote, and the holding of public office, to some 2,000 church members of the Territory. The U.S. Marshal of Idaho was a rabid Mormon-eater, Fred T. Dubois, who relentlessly secured convictions for polygamy and u.c., boasting that he could empanel a jury which "could convict Jesus Christ."[4]

Taylor heard that the governor of Idaho, William Bunn, a man with a strict sense of justice, had refused to sign the Test Oath bill; whereupon H. W. ("Kentucky") Smith, who had sponsored the measure, together with another member of the legislature, George Gorton, and Marshal Dubois, called at the governor's office and demanded that Bunn do so. When Bunn said he'd made up his mind to veto it, Kentucky Smith pulled a pistol from his pocket, and said, "Governor, you will not leave this room alive unless you sign that bill."[5]

---

[3] Upon learning that "subpoenas were being issued for witnesses to appear before the grand jury," Taylor's son, Thomas E., wrote his father that "I have had mother [Elizabeth Kaighin] leave home for the present."

[4] As reward for his untiring efforts, Dubois subsequently became Idaho's delegate to Congress, and the state's first senator. He was prominent in the Smoot Investigation of 1904–7, which was the final attempt of the U.S. government to smash the Mormon Church.

[5] *Idaho Statesman*, January 25, 1931, confirms the story. "Now It Can Be Told: Gun

Fighting fire with fire, Taylor passed the word for Idaho Mormons to "apostatize" from the church, in order to meet voting and office-holding requirements, while the Test Oath was being tried in the courts.[6]

Taylor strongly disapproved of men who cooperated with oppressive laws. Instead of capitulating, they were supposed to take a mission, go underground, join the Mexican colonies—never voluntarily surrender nor plead guilty.

There was some justification in the cases of Charles L. White and John W. Snell, who sought counsel from Taylor. Their plural wives, Elizabeth Ann Starkey White and Eliza Shafer Snell, had been cast into prison for refusing to answer questions of the grand jury which would have convicted themselves and their husbands. The wives remained imprisoned nearly four months, and had recently been indicted again. It was the obvious intent of the feds to keep them in custody indefinitely to force confessions. Meanwhile, their children were motherless. Outraged by this vindictive punishment against women whose only offense was to stand upon their right to avoid self-incrimination and being witnesses against their husbands, Taylor conceded that the best course for White and Snell was to free their wives by confessing to u.c.

It was an entirely different matter when the editor of the *Deseret News*, John Nicholson, made a bargain with the court to plead guilty in return for immunity for his families. At his trial, he waived his rights as defendant, and became a witness for the prosecution. He admitted that he was married both to Susannah Keep and Miranda Cutler, and lived with both as wives. Testimony was short, and the jury returned a guilty verdict within five minutes.

While Nicholson awaited sentence, Taylor summoned him to the DO. The editor arrived at night, a slender man, almost frail, dark, with a full beard, walking with a limp he'd had ever since a saddle horse fell on him years previously while crossing ice. Taylor reminded him that he'd initiated a precedent that could result in great damage to the Saints. What made it worse, his plea-bargain was looked upon as having quasi-official sanction because of his position as editor of the *Deseret News*, the voice of the church.[7]

Nicholson admitted his mistake; he should have sought counsel before-

---

Point Forces Bunn to Sign Test Oath Bill." Related by S. H. Hays of Boise, former attorney general of Idaho. Incidentally, after fifteen years the U.S. Supreme Court in 1890 upheld the legality of the Idaho Test Oath.

6 In one instance, a Mormon refused his bishop's call to employ this subterfuge, and he was un-churched for not being willing to apostatize.

7 While the name of Charles W. Penrose remained on the paper's masthead as editor, Penrose had taken a mission to England to avoid prosecution. Nicholson was editor in charge.

hand. It was done now, Taylor told him; but, "John," he reminded the editor, "never surrender."[8]

Stiffened by Taylor's counsel, Nicholson printed an impassioned defense of the Principle in the *Deseret News:*

> What would be necessary to bring about the result nearest the hearts of the opponents of "Mormonism?" . . . Simply to renounce, abrogate, or apostatize from the new and everlasting covenant of marriage in its fullness. Were the Saints to do that as an entirety, God would reject the church as a body. The authority of the priesthood would be withdrawn, with its gifts and powers, and there would be no more heavenly recognition. . . . Therefore the Saints have no alternative but to stand by the truth and sustain what the heavens have established and propose to perpetuate. This they will do, come life or death, freedom or imprisonment.[9]

When Nicholson appeared in court for sentencing, he gave such a stout testimony upholding plural marriage that an angered Judge Zane, despite the plea-bargain, sentenced him to six months in prison and $300 fine.

In the case of John Sharp, bishop of the Twentieth Ward, Taylor took wrathful action. Instead of disappearing when indicted, Sharp voluntarily surrendered and entered a plea of guilty. "I am the husband of more than one living wife, and the father of a number of children by each of them," he admitted. Although he considered the law harsh, he agreed to abide by it.

Chief Justice Zane was delighted. John Sharp, in addition to his office as bishop, was one of the richest and most influential men of Zion. He was known as the railroad king of Utah, being a director of the Union Pacific, and also was a director of ZCMI and Deseret National Bank.

"It is gratifying, of course, to the court and to all law-abiding citizens," Judge Zane said with a satisfied smile, "that a man of as much influence in the community and the church to which he belongs as you have, should take this stand. . . . Your example today, I think, will have a better effect on society than any imprisonment the court could impose. . . . I will simply impose a fine of three hundred dollars and costs."

John Sharp paid the fine and walked out of court a free man. However, the Mormon press and people deplored his action, and Taylor ordered his release from the office of bishop.[10]

---

[8] Whitney, *History of Utah*, 4:339, says Taylor repeated this exhortation three times in saying farewell.

[9] April 23, 1885.

[10] Whitney, 3:420, says, "it was because of the possible effect of that example upon the Mormon cause that many found difficult to excuse him. . . . In these cases . . . where 'promises to obey' were given, it was the examples set, the effect of which was to weaken the cause of the church and strengthen the hands of the crusaders, that were mostly criticized and condemned."

Traveling at night and in disguise by "underground railroad," Taylor toured outlying settlements to get grass-roots sentiments of his people and bolster their courage. The arrival of the church president at a remote meeting house electrified the congregation, and at such times Taylor preached some of his most fiery sermons.

As the rig rattled across the moonlit sage flat at Grantsville, the strains of music came from the meeting house. The yard was filled with carriages, nosebags on the horses. As Taylor's carriage approached, two men emerged from the shadows, one blocking the way, the other greeting the strangers and asking their business. Though the man questioning them was a good friend, Samuel Woolley, son of Taylor's former associate, Edwin D. Woolley, he didn't recognize them. Bateman had dyed his hair and beard; Wilcken had grown whiskers; Taylor, known for fastidious dress, was attired like a laboring man, had shaved his beard, and covered his distinctive mane of white hair with a brown wig.

The guards burst into laughter, Taylor took off his wig, and Samuel Woolley gave them a warm welcome.

The men changed clothing at the stable out back. As the church president entered the hall, the bishop hurried up, explaining that although a waltz was in progress, only two round dances were allowed during the evening, all others being square. Taylor nodded approval, and the waltz continued.

As the couples circled the crowded hall, he was surprised to see two members of the apostles' Quorum present, his son John W., and Heber J. Grant, each with a pretty girl. Taylor touched Grant on the shoulder, and whirled away with the tall and willowy Nellie Eva Todd.

During the break, John W. joined his father at the punch bowl. Taylor asked, casually and indirectly, if John was interested in the girl he'd brought to the shindig. With a grin, John W. shook his head, then asked what his father thought of Nellie Todd. A most beautiful and charming young lady, Taylor admitted. Well, John W. said, the deputies thought he was seeing the girl he'd brought to the dance, and that Heber J. Grant was interested in Nellie Todd—but it actually was the other way about.[11]

The dance concluded with a talk by Taylor, after which he went to Samuel Woolley's ranch for the night, and stayed in the big adobe house of Woolley's first wife, Marie—his other two wives, Rachel and Polly, each had a separate residence on the place.[12] The ranch was a way station on the underground, and before retiring Taylor went upstairs to visit

---

[11] Nellie Eva Todd became the second wife of the author's father, John W. Taylor.

[12] Samuel Woolley's second wife, Rachel Cahoon, was the author's grandmother.

the pregnant plurals, girls en route to destinations outside Utah to have their babies. He gave each brave and dedicated girl his blessing.

A shattering crash woke Taylor. It was dawn. He sprang out of bed and to the window. Armed deputies were outside. An axe was chopping at the front door. Sam Woolley slipped into the bedroom, his shanks bare below the nightshirt. It was Gilson and his skunks, he whispered; they'd broken down the door. No chance to get to the secret hideout. He opened the tall wardrobe, pulled back the clothing hanging from the bar. Taylor crowded in behind them. Woolley shut the door and the bed screaked as he slipped into it.

Crouching there, Taylor heard the door open and slam back against the wall. A voice asked, where is he? Woolley asked to see the search warrant. The deputy said Sam Gilson had the indictment in his pocket, and his orders were to find John Taylor if they had to tear the house down brick by brick.

As the wardrobe door swung open, Woolley cautioned not to disturb anything there or his wife would give the fellow a wooling, deputy or no; those were Sunday best clothes.

Hooks of the hangers screeched against the bar as a big hand swept back the rack of clothing. Taylor was eye to eye with the deputy, a muscular young fellow named Mayfield, whom Taylor recognized as a former Saint—the man would have turned bitter and apostatized to have joined the feds. And now before Mayfield's startled eyes was the plum, the sought-after prize that would bring him recognition and fame.

But not yet. Though the deputy held a rifle, Taylor gripped the handle of a pistol in his waistband; Mayfield would know that John Taylor had declared he never would be taken into custody alive. It was kill or be killed.

From the doorway Sam Gilson's heavy voice asked if everything was all right in here. Nobody in here who ought to rot in prison, Mayfield said. Gilson walked on, and the young deputy extended a hand. Taylor gripped it.

After a few minutes the deputies galloped away. Samuel Woolley climbed out of bed and opened the wardrobe door. A spotter had betrayed the church president, he said; but, thank goodness, the Saints had infiltrated the ranks of the feds.

During breakfast, Sam Bateman regaled the table with a story of deputies searching his own home. Three came in a buggy, two stood guard outside, the third searched the house. Sam's wife, Miranda, watched as the deputy looked in the cupboard, opened a small sugar can, investigated the flour bin. "Do you realize the size of the man you're looking for?" Miranda asked.

"Mrs. Bateman, I do know his size," the deputy said. "And I also know the character of the man. He and I were friends before this mess began. I trust it will never be my lot to arrest him."[13]

That night Taylor headed south, on a trip that would take several weeks, to keep in touch with his people. Sam Bateman was driving, and presently Charles Wilcken's head dropped and he began to snore. Bateman glanced sidewise at Taylor, seemed about to speak, then turned away. Taylor asked if there was something he wanted to say.

Yes; it was about his father, Bateman said. His mother was now seventy-five, without much time left here, and she wondered if things could be straightened out? Did President Taylor remember his father?

Very well, Taylor said. Tom and Mary Bateman had arrived at Nauvoo with a party of English converts, when Sam was a lad of seven. Tom ran a brickyard, and found his product much in demand in the booming city. Later, when Taylor was going on his mission to France, the Bateman family was at Winter Quarters, and Tom had driven the missionaries in his wagon from Council Bluffs to St. Louis.

A few months after arriving in Utah the following year, Sam Bateman said, his father had an argument with church authorities, and was cut off in public meeting. The shock was more than he could stand; he was never the same after that. Tom Bateman went to England to dispose of property there. During the return voyage, the strain of his excommunication preyed on him until he had a nervous breakdown, and had to be restrained for several days. He seemingly recovered, but shortly after being released a storm blew up and he leaped overboard. A boat was put out, but the body was never found.

Taylor said that Thomas Bateman shouldn't be judged harshly; he wasn't in his right mind. Sam nodded, and slapped a line on the rumps of the team. Brother Brigham had said the same thing, that his father wasn't responsible, and the time would come when things would be righted. But now his mother was seventy-five. Five of her children had been born outside the covenant. Could her husband be restored to his priesthood and blessings, and his children sealed to him?

Yes, indeed, Taylor said; he'd see to it.[14]

Bateman's face bloomed with joy. He'd been relieved of a heavy load that he'd carried for many years.

During the trip south, traveling on the underground, generally at night, Taylor's rest was broken for weeks at a time. The cold he'd had clung on, getting worse instead of better. It was settling in his lungs by the time he returned to Salt Lake. He arrived at the home of John Carlisle, near the junction of Big Cottonwood Creek and the Jordan

---

[13] Juliaetta Bateman Jensen, *Little Gold Pieces.*

[14] See letters concerning Thomas Bateman, August 11 and September 12, 1885. John Taylor Letter File.

River, a sick man. He refused supper, and was lying on a couch in the front room when Dan Bateman, Sam's son, arrived with Margaret. Taylor's youngest wife fussed over him like a mother hen, dosing him with Brigham tea, putting a mustard plaster on his chest. She scolded him for making the trip when he wasn't well, declaring he'd be lucky if it didn't develop into pneumonia. Taylor growled that he'd be all right; just a little tired from the trip. But when he tried to go upstairs to bed, he was unable to walk. Sam and Dan Bateman carried him up. Maggie tucked him into bed, then went down and told the people waiting below that the president was sicker than he realized.

Margaret slept on the front room couch. Early in the morning she quietly went upstairs. Her husband was sleeping. She went downstairs and was helping Mrs. Carlisle fix breakfast when heavy steps thumped downstairs and John Taylor bounced into the kitchen with the spring of youth, his color restored, radiant in health, the cold gone. He declared that he was hungry as a wolf.

Maggie poured him a strong cup of tea. Mrs. Carlisle served ham and eggs. As he ate with gusto, Taylor told of being visited in the night by Joseph Smith, who had blessed him in his work and endowed him with strength.[15]

From various "safe retreats," Taylor and George Q. Cannon issued counsel to the Saints through "Epistles of the First Presidency" and the columns of the *Deseret News*.[16]

> Well-meaning friends of ours have said that our refusal to renounce the principle of celestial marriage invites destruction. They warn us and implore us to yield. . . . They say it is madness to resist the will of so overwhelming a majority. . . . But they perceive not the hand of that Being who controls all storms, whose voice the tempest obeys, at whose fiat thrones and empires are thrown down—the Almighty God, Lord of heaven and earth, who has made promises to us, and who has never failed to fulfill all His words.
>
> We did not reveal celestial marriage. We cannot withdraw or renounce it. God revealed it, and He has promised to maintain it, and to bless those who obey it. Whatever fate, then, may threaten us, there is but one course for men of God to take: that is, to keep inviolate the holy covenants they have made in the presence of God and angels. For the remainder, whether it be life or death, freedom or imprisonment, prosperity or adversity, we must trust in God. We may say, however, if any man or woman expects to enter into the celestial kingdom of our God without being tested to the very uttermost, they have not understood the gospel. If there is a weak spot in our nature, or if there is a fibre that can be made to quiver or to shrink, we may rest assured that it will be tested.

---

[15] See article, "Daniel R. Bateman," *Truth*, June 1942.

[16] Quotations are for the year 1885.

Far from bewailing their plight, the first presidency declared that

> Never at any time in our lives have we had more joy and satisfaction in the Gospel, and in the labors thereof. . . . [The] knowledge that God is near to us, and hears and answers our prayers, is an unceasing cause of thankfulness and praise.

Regarding the ultimate outrage, the first presidency driven into hiding, Joseph F. Smith having taken a mission to Hawaii, Taylor and Cannon on the underground, "The question has been asked us, how long we intend to pursue this course," an Epistle stated.

> In answer we say, that at no time during our existence have we ever shrunk from the investigation of our conduct, our utterances or our lives, by any fair tribunal. . . . But if there are laws made to entrap us, because of our belief in and practice of the revelations which God has given His Church . . . we desire at least that it shall be upon what all the world calls good evidence and substantial proof, and not upon religious prejudice and through a determination to convict and punish, evidence or no evidence. We ought, at least, to have the same rights that burglars, thieves, and murderers are accorded under the law. In that case, should conviction follow, we should submit to it as martyrs have submitted in every age . . . as persecution inflicted upon us for our adherence to His laws.

At present there was little to do except seek shelter from the storm.

> For a few months past we have seen in these valleys an exhibition of deadly hostility against the Latter-day Saints. . . . The best men in the community . . . have been selected as victims of a vile persecution, and been assailed and denounced as criminals of the lowest grade. Juries have been selected for the express purpose of convicting men who are prominent in the church; and their partisan bias [is such] . . . that an accusation in the courts, as now constituted, is equivalent to a conviction. . . . The result has been that a reign of terror has prevailed. . . . Seeing no prospect of fair trial, men have deemed it better to avoid arrest for a season, or until there was a prospect of receiving impartial treatment by the courts and juries. Prosecution has degenerated into persecution. A law which is in and of itself, as we believe, unconstitutional, and aimed at the practice of religion—and so viewed by a number of our leading statesmen in congress—is taken advantage of and carried to lengths probably never dreamed of by many of the men who voted for it. We have sometimes thought that it was impossible for men to indulge in such vindictive feelings as have been manifested here; but in searching for a cause we have been forced to the conclusion that these violent prosecutions were only intended to provoke the people to commit some overt act.

Despite Taylor's exhortations to endure, to avoid retaliation, there were sporadic instances where oppression and frustration goaded individuals to violence. Hoodlums in the night bombarded the homes of U.S. Commissioner William McKay, U.S. District Attorney William H. Dickson, and his assistant, Charles S. Varian, with a barrage of "filth pots"—two-quart glass jars filled with human excrement—lobbing them through windows and transoms to shatter within. The perpetrators remained undetected, amid Gentile charges that the Salt Lake City police didn't want to solve the case. There were unsolved beatings and shootings, some victims Mormon and some Gentile, with no arrests made, accusations on both sides. As the tension increased, Taylor counseled endurance, warning that the oppression was deliberate provocation to illegal violence.

Discrimination in administration of the Edmunds Law was particularly galling to Taylor. "Thus far no criminal, however guilty, who has not been a Mormon, has been punished under it," he declared.

> Acts of the most sickening depravity have been committed by non-Mormons within easy reach of its arm, but have scarcely had a passing notice. While it is also worthy of note that . . . out of all who have been accused and brought before the district court, only one Mormon has been acquitted. (The man acquitted, we understand, was charged with being the husband of a woman, on the ground that he had camped his wagon in a ten-acre lot in which her residence stood, and had carried chickens for her to market.) . . .
>
> The rulings of the court in several instances have been made to secure convictions where the evidence was open to question. The extraordinary ruling concerning "holding out" is one in point: notwithstanding the Edmunds Law specifies that the penalty for unlawful cohabitation shall not be more than six months' imprisonment, and three hundred dollars fine, the notorious ruling from the same bench concerning the number of indictments which can be found against a person accused of unlawful cohabitation, states that he not only can be indicted once for the whole period since the passage of the law, but an indictment can be found for every week of that time; so that, if found guilty in this manner, a man's punishment would aggregate an imprisonment of 92 years, and fines to the amount of $55,200.
>
> Still more extraordinary is the ruling of another judge, who, not to be outdone in his zeal, says that an indictment can be found for this charge against a man for every day, or other distinct interval of time, since the enactment of the law. As about 1,292 days have passed since then, a man found guilty can be incarcerated in prison for 646 years, and made to pay fines to the amount of $387,600.

The discrimination in application of laws against sexual misconduct was demonstrated in the case of Brigham Y. Hampton, chief of Salt Lake City's detectives and a prominent Mormon, who set out to gain evidence of vice activities among the Gentile carpetbaggers and the Utah ring.

Hampton made arrangements with the madame of a bordello on West

Temple Street, who allowed the police to bore peepholes in the walls of various rooms. From these vantage points, detectives observed the frolics of the Gentiles with the soiled doves of the establishment, gaining eyewitness evidence against more than a hundred federal appointees—judges, members of the Utah Commission, prosecuting attorneys, marshals, and others—together with members of the Gentile ring who had been most zealous in prosecuting the Mormons for sexual irregularities.

The trap snapped shut with the arrest of U.S. Deputy Marshal Oscar C. Vandercook on the charge of lewd and lascivious cohabitation and resorting to houses of ill-fame. Vandercook had been relentless in hounding prominent Mormons for u.c., and his arrest delighted the Saints. Next day, Hampton bagged bigger game, arresting Assistant U.S. Prosecuting Attorney Samuel H. Lewis, together with a former member of the Utah Commission, C. E. Pearson.

At the DO, Taylor learned that news of the arrests was a bomb-shell to the Gentile camp, particularly when Hampton let it be known that he was preparing indictments from a list of a hundred more names—men who had served warrants, sat on juries, and had been most self-righteous in prosecuting the Saints for their marriage customs. Men on "the list" of course knew their guilt, and were terror stricken. They were citizens of substance and position, most of them married. This scandal threatened a wholesale debacle of wrecked careers, broken families, and disgrace.

Taylor roared with laughter on learning that men on the list were going underground to avoid scandal. Leaders of both sides of the conflict were now on the dodge.

However, carpetbaggers controlled the courts. The full weight of the anti-Mormon combine swung behind protection of the establishment. Judge Zane quashed the prosecution by granting a motion by Assistant U.S. Attorney C. S. Varian to dismiss the cases on grounds that evidence was gained by entrapment. "I would not believe such scoundrels on oath," Varian declared of eyewitnesses to the bordello high jinks, "even in the high court of heaven itself."

Judge Zane concurred.

Next came a twist that, to Taylor, was incredible. Brigham Y. Hampton, who had prepared the case, was arrested on a charge of conspiracy, tried in the carpetbag court before the customary Gentile jury, and sentenced to a year in prison.[17]

"Notwithstanding all that we are now passing through, our hearts are filled with joy and peace," Taylor assured the Saints. Zion would emerge from the present trials "stronger and purer."

---

[17] For both sides of the Hampton case, see Whitney's *History of Utah* (3:443-47); R. N. Baskin's *Reminiscences of Early Utah*; and Joseph Fielding Smith's *Life of President Joseph F. Smith*.

Our trust is not in numbers, but in the strength and protection of Israel's God, who controls all the millions of the world, and puts down one and sets up another according to the counsel of His own will.

If we can only manage to observe His law and keep His commandments, He will protect us "while grass grows or water runs," while sun, moon, and stars exist, or the earth and the heavens endure, and when there shall be a "new heaven and a new earth whereupon dwelleth righteousness." . . . Every promise concerning Zion by the Almighty will be fulfilled.

Taylor chafed at the restraints of the underground when the Rev. M. T. Lamb, assistant pastor of the First Baptist Church at Salt Lake, gave a series of four lectures aimed at destroying the credibility of the Book of Mormon. A discussion—yes, Taylor would have welcomed that. He remembered the debate between Orson Pratt and the Rev. Dr. J. P. Newman, as well as his own three-night discussion with Gentile ministers at Boulogne. But the Rev. Lamb had the cheek to denounce the Book of Mormon from his pulpit in Salt Lake City, with no opportunity for reply.

Most certainly, times had changed.

Reading reports of the lectures in the *Deseret News* and *Tribune*, Taylor denounced Lamb's tirades as of the Devil. He predicted that the Book of Mormon would be known throughout the world long after Lamb and his attack was forgotten.[18]

In his correspondence, interviews, and epistles from the underground, Taylor drew a distinct line between his official attitude toward human frailty and his private counsel. Inasmuch as the Saints were under attack for sexual practices, Taylor never could condone adultery, a transgression he condemned as second only to murder. Yet in cases which did not come to public attention he showed compassion for weakness of the flesh. A young couple arrived at the DO with their baby. They'd been outcasts in their ward, for the child was born just two months after their marriage. After seeing the love of the parents for the child and for each other, and hearing the reasons why marriage was impossible sooner, he gave them forgiveness and his blessing.

Yet when it became public knowledge that a member of the Quorum of the Twelve had disgraced his position, Taylor was forced to have him

---

[18] At the urging of Gov. Eli H. Murray and others of the Utah ring, the minister made a book of his lectures: Rev. M. T. Lamb, *The Golden Bible; or, the Book of Mormon, Is it From God?*

Some half million copies of the Book of Mormon are published now each year. Lamb's book was long forgotten until reprinted by photocopy in 1965 by Jerald and Sandra Tanner in a limited edition for scholars and historians.

cut off for "lewd and lascivious conduct and adultery." "We hear that the excommunication of Albert Carrington has created a great sensation in the community," he wrote to Erastus Snow. "If it will only have the effect to arouse the Saints to purify themselves and to live lives more strictly in accordance with the principles of their religion, the case will not be one of unmixed evil."[19]

Having himself been a gadfly to Brigham Young for forty years, Taylor had a soft spot for individualists who got into trouble. One man, his bishop reported,

> was cut off for no criminal offense; his wrong consisted in correcting Bishops, Stake Presidents, and even Apostles, when he thought their teachings and counsels were not according to the written word. His dogged persistence finally led to the above result. After six years and a genuine repentance, he is baptized and confirmed, and now on the verge of the grave.

Taylor wrote on the bottom of the letter, "Let Bro Broadhurst be ordained an Elder."

Sometimes it was a question of what was bothering a man. A fellow named Williams, of Malad, Idaho, wrote long tirades to Taylor, calling on Zion to repent. When Taylor asked the man's bishop to report on his standing, the bishop took this for an order to cut him off. Williams protested at length to Taylor, and it became apparent that all that ailed the man was that he wanted to go on a mission. Taylor had him restored to membership, then shipped him to belabor the Gentiles at St. Johns, Arizona. Everybody was happy.

Joseph E. Taylor (no relation) acted as liaison between the Saints and the DO. On September 7, 1885 he presented a delicate problem. A girl in the Eighteenth Ward was engaged, and wanted a temple marriage. Problem was that her father "was a very light mulatto."

> She now desires to press her claim to privileges that others who are tainted with that blood have received. For example, the Meads family in the Eleventh Ward. . . . I am cognizant of all these having received their endowments here. Brother Meads is a white man. He married his wife many years ago; she was a quadroon and died some three years ago. . . .
>
> The question I desire to ask is: Can you give this girl any privileges of a like character? The girl is very pretty and quite white, and would not be suspected as having tainted blood in her veins unless her parentage was known.

Not all correspondence was of a serious or sensitive nature. Sam Bateman, hearing guffaws in the DO, stepped inside to find Cannon, L. John

---

[19] Carrington was subsequently baptized again into the church, but wasn't restored to the Quorum.

Nuttall, and Taylor howling with mirth. Nuttall handed Bateman a letter from a man named Walter Williams, of Boonville, Missouri, who showed his grasp of national affairs by asking, "Will you kindly tell me if polygamy is commanded by the doctrines of the Mormon church?"

With the future of the Saints hanging in the balance, Taylor entertained a proposition from Edward Lycan, a land developer of Honolulu,

> to have your people migrate here. In the valley where I live, four miles from Honolulu, there are several thousand acres of splendid land that needs no irrigation for any kind of crops, and almost every valley on the island is the same. . . . Should you conclude to try colonizing here there is not a doubt but that your people could in five or six years have control of political powers and so adjust laws as to suit the requirements of your church. The wonderful energy and skill displayed in Utah would here make a veritable Garden of Eden.

To Taylor, moving the DO to its fifteenth hideout of the year, the prospect of peace and prosperity in the Pacific islands was a heady lure.

He also was investigating more Mexican tracts. In response to a letter came a wire:

> WOULD YOU ENTERTAIN PROPOSITION TO BUY ONE MILLION AND HALF ACRES LAND OR MOVE INTO SOUTHERN PART OF OLD MEXICO. TITLE PERFECT. SOIL VERY BEST. WELL TIMBERED. PART MINERAL WELL WATERED. CLIMATE BEST IN WORLD. SUBSIDIES FROM GOVERNMENT MORE THAN ENOUGH TO PAY FOR PROPERTY WITH OTHER CONCESSIONS. IF SO TELEGRAPH ME WHEN AND WHERE I CAN SEE YOU QUICK.
>
> S. E. HESS

As 1885 neared its end, Taylor had been underground a year. His example of defiance and refusal to compromise sustained many Saints; but still there was a rising clamor among others for peace at any price. A Mormon named Benedict had served on the grand jury which had indicted Taylor, Cannon, and other church leaders for u.c. Benedict's bishop had labored with him and his wife, and reported they didn't accept polygamy "as any part of the faith." The wife was in full sympathy with her husband, and said that if all were cut off who didn't believe in polygamy, "there would be a great slaughter."

Taylor could remain unmoved by the opposition of the world, but this open defiance from within, by an otherwise devout couple who had belonged to the faith forty-five years, shook him.

He was convinced that the Saints could never be defeated by outside oppression. But he remembered Kirtland, Missouri, and Nauvoo, where defeats had followed inner dissention. Would this happen in Utah?

Late in December he took another trip, visiting outlying wards and stakes to bolster the faith. At Parowan, in southern Utah, he stayed with the local bishop, Charles Adams. Deputies had arrived, alerted that Taylor was in town, and had put up in the local hotel a block away. A corner of the bishop's living room was railed off as the telegraph office, and the deputies would come to send messages. The bishop's youngster, Joe, together with his five-year-old cousin, Eleanor Ward, played before the front window, on watch for the deputies' white-top. If the rig stopped in front, Taylor slipped into the secret room. In the evening, Taylor would put the children on his knees, tell them stories, and sing them asleep.

On Christmas morning he came out as the children were opening their presents, and was delighted to find that the bishop's wife had knitted him a pair of socks, made from wool she had washed, carded, and spun.

"See! I have the best present of all!" he cried, stripping off shoes and socks. "A pair of nice warm stockings to keep my tootsie wootsies warm!"

Staring at his long, bony feet, the children giggled. Tootsie wootsies, they said, were baby feet. Well, Taylor said with a grin, he was being babied here, wasn't he?[20]

In early January Taylor was again in Salt Lake, once more at the John Carlisle home near the junction of Big Cottonwood Creek and the Jordan River. His health had been restored during his previous stay here; but this time he faced the new year with the realization that the forced confinement was undermining his constitution. His vitality was dwindling. The cast-iron stomach was becoming delicate. He needed naps now after meals.

John Taylor was aware that his days were numbered. And with growing dissention within his people, he was haunted by the possibilities of what compromises or capitulations might occur under new leadership.

The *Deseret News* had reiterated his stand:

> The principle of plural marriage, against which the main force of the opposition is being hurled, has been a divine institution from before the foundation of the world.
>
> There has been some talk about President Taylor issuing a revelation abolishing that system of marriage. When a revelation of that kind is given, it will be when the Lord has no use for the Latter-day Saints; and this will never transpire, for He has promised to give them the Kingdom and to sustain them.[21]

Was it too much to expect the people at large to endure martyrdom for heavenly blessings—when those blessings would come only to a select few? The great majority of the Saints didn't practice plural marriage;

---

[20] Related seventy-five years later by Eleanor Ward Ogden.

[21] April 6, 1885.

was it reasonable to ask them to accept persecution to benefit the few who did?

Taylor went to the Lord for answer, but the heavens seemed closed. There was no sanction for appeasement.

23

The Thousand Cuts

IN THE CONFINEMENT of the DO, each day was like a leech applied to his vitality. Every day John Taylor needed just a little more rest. Compromise with his principles undoubtedly would restore his health, allowing him the physical activity essential to maintain vitality. To appease the world by setting aside the practice of plural marriage would enable him to extend his life span another ten years, or even more. His ancestors were long-lived; he had an iron constitution; and there was nothing wrong with him, really, except the creeping onset of debility. There was nothing wrong that brisk daily walks, working in the garden, keeping his homes in repair, making projects in the basement shop, and having the stimulation of family association and social events wouldn't cure.

Ten more years. With that much time he could see this through. He was absolutely convinced his course was correct. He and his people would tough it out. The Kingdom of God would prevail.

But he didn't have ten years, not in confinement. And for him it was the Kingdom or nothing. No compromise. No weaseling. No arbitration. No appeasement. No surrender.

He didn't know how much time he had. But he did know that each day at the DO drained a little of his life's blood. It was literally the death of the thousand cuts.

George Q. Cannon was packing up when Lorin C. Woolley arrived at the DO with the mail, together with a handbill he'd torn from a telegraph pole offering a reward of $500 "for information leading to the arrest of George Q. Cannon."

John Taylor burst into laughter as Lorin Woolley displayed a mock poster in the *Deseret News*:

WANTED: A CHEAP JUDAS.

Lorin reported that the reward had stimulated the spotters and deputies to eager activity. Skunks had raided the Cannon farm and served subpoenas on members of the family; a force of twenty feds also raided the Gardo House, the president's office, the tithing and the historian's offices, while another force raided the church farm south of the city, ransacking houses, barns, sheds, and stockyards.

With a grin on his round face, Cannon said it looked like he was leaving just in time.

Taylor would sorely miss Cannon—which was precisely why Marshal Edwin Ireland had put a price on the counselor's head. Cannon, almost twenty years younger than Taylor, was in the prime of his vigor. Moreover, as a former congressman, he had a practical grasp of politics and national affairs. With him away, and Joseph F. Smith in Hawaii, Taylor would be without counselors in the presidency.

Ranks of the hierarchy were thinning. Wilford Woodruff, president of the Twelve, had gone underground. Lorenzo Snow, next in rank, had recently been convicted on three counts of u.c. Though Snow was seventy-two, and had separated from six of his seven wives upon passage of the Edmunds Law, he was convicted on evidence that (1) he rode in a carriage with a plural wife to the scene of an accident, where her daughter's skull was fractured; (2) in company with his sister he rode in a carriage with another plural wife; and (3) that all seven of his wives were present, among hundreds of others, at an anniversary dinner at Brigham City on his seventieth birthday. This constituted legal evidence of unlawful cohabitation, even though the defense proved he hadn't seen any of his plural wives on other occasions. Snow was tried for u.c. committed in 1883, 1884, and 1885, convicted three times, and sentenced to a combined total of $900 in fines and imprisonment for eighteen months.[1]

Taylor didn't expect Cannon to be gone long. His trip to Mexico was to wind up final business details there for acquisition of property for colonies.[2] The church president also had sent Charles O. Card to Canada to pioneer LDS settlements there. It was now possible for a Mormon to have a wife in the U.S., another in Canada, and several more in Mexico, without breaking a law of any country.

---

[1] *Have Mormons Any Rights?* "Brief in re Senate Bill No. 10," by A. M. Gibson, Attorney for the Mormon People.

[2] However, District Attorney W. H. Dickson alerted U.S. Attorney General A. H. Garland that both Taylor and Cannon "intend leaving the United States and going to Mexico." Letter, March 28, 1885. (N. A., D. J. File, Utah.)

That night Lorin drove Cannon and his party—Erastus Snow, Samuel H. Hill, and Orson F. Arnold—into the switch yards, where they boarded a freight car for Ogden. From there another team took them north to the flag stop of Willard, where a curious brakeman wondered why men boarding the Central Pacific at this jerkwater had a drawing room reserved. By the light of his lantern he recognized Cannon, and with dollars in his eyes slipped into the station to wire Marshal Ireland. When the train reached Winnemucca at eleven next morning, Sheriff Fellows of Humboldt County stepped aboard to arrest Cannon. Marshal Ireland and a deputy went to Winnemucca for the prisoner.

On the return trip Cannon either fell or jumped at dawn from the train near Promontory Point, and this became a highly controversial issue. Cannon claimed that he had a severe cold, affecting his kidneys and forcing him to arise several times in the night; that the heat of the stateroom caused him to step out onto the rear platform for a breath of air, when a lurch of the train flung him over the railing.

Skeptical Gentiles pointed out that despite the severe injuries supposedly received in the fall, Cannon was agile enough to elude pursuit for an hour's chase across the bleak desert. Also, if he'd just stepped onto the platform for some air, he had been remarkably well prepared, for when captured he carried a loaded revolver, a flask of water, and two loaves of bread.

Taylor was outraged that in court the judge set bail of $45,000 for Cannon, charged with the misdemeanor of u.c. However, Cannon was worth more to the presidency than the bail; when the case came to trial, Cannon didn't appear.[3]

In Washington, Senator Edmunds had devoted another year of his life to framing a stiffer bill to meet President Cleveland's call for "such further discreet legislation as will rid the country of this blot upon its fair name."[4] The new Edmunds Bill provided that a first wife (legally married) could be compelled to testify against her husband. Female suffrage, given Utah women in expectation that they would throw off the yoke of bondage, would be taken from them again because they had voted their religious convictions just like the men. The property of the church would be confiscated by the government. The Perpetual Emigration Fund would be abolished, and election districts done away with.

---

[3] Enormous stress is placed by Roberts (CHC, 6:127–32) and Whitney (History of Utah, 3:478–90) on the proposition that Cannon was law-abiding, and accidently fell from the train. Just why the point is belabored, when he subsequently jumped bail to evade the law, is baffling.

[4] Message to Congress, December 8, 1885.

The bill passed the Senate, and under sponsorship of Representative Tucker began heading toward ratification in the House.

In Utah, Governor Murray had vetoed bills to end discrimination—such as the exclusion of Mormons from juries because of belief in polygamy and the setting of excessive bail for u.c.—as well as the key bill of the session, the appropriations measure, which meant no money was available to keep the territorial government functioning.

With Taylor's blessing, the Legislative Assembly fired off a memorial to Congress:

> Eli H. Murray, governor of Utah, has openly advocated the disruption of the Territory by depriving its citizens of every vestige of local self-government . . . and has persistently abused, insulted, and maligned [them]. By the most atrocious falsehoods, by attempted usurpations, by insolent messages, he has sought to provoke a conflict between the people and the federal authority. . . .
>
> During the present session he has vetoed twenty bills and contemptuously ignored thirteen others. . . . The power of absolute veto which is vested in the governor . . . stands as an anomaly and a solecism in this great Republic. It is a menace to freedom and a relic of monarchial absolutism.

Murray had at last gone too far. President Cleveland replaced him. "His veto of the appropriations bill was the last straw," the *Deseret News* reported, also saying that twice Murray had deceived the president with false alarms of a "Mormon uprising."

The case of Lorenzo Snow went to the Supreme Court, which made the curious ruling that it had no jurisdiction in the case of a man convicted three times for the same offense. Caleb W. West, the new governor of Utah, visited the prison and offered pardons to Snow and others "upon a promise, in good faith, that you will obey and respect the laws, and that you will continue no longer to live in violation of them."

"I am not here because of disobedience of any law," Snow retorted. "I am here wrongfully convicted and wrongfully sentenced."

When the other inmates convicted of u.c. were offered the same proposition, they made written reply:

> . . . the forty-nine Elders of the Church of Jesus Christ of Latter-day Saints now imprisoned in the Penitentiary for alleged violation of the Edmunds Law . . . were united to our wives for time and all eternity by the most sacred covenants, and in many instances numerous children have been born as a result of our union, who are endeared to us by the strongest paternal ties. . . .
>
> So far as compliance with your proposition requires the sacrifice of honor and manhood, the repudiation of our wives and children, the vio-

lation of sacred covenants, heaven forbid that we should be guilty of such perfidy. Perpetual imprisonment, with which we are threatened, or even death itself, would be preferable.

Taylor was pleased to learn that some benefit was resulting from the crusade: there were now enough polygamist inmates to give a spiritual tone to the entire penitentiary. They held Sunday School and other services, and labored as missionaries to bring the gospel to fellow prisoners incarcerated for other crimes.

As for Governor West, the rebuff caused him to abandon all hope of rehabilitating the Saints. In reporting to the Secretary of the Interior, he urged the passage of the Edmunds-Tucker Bill to bring the church to its knees.

With Taylor's sponsorship a mass meeting of women convened at the Salt Lake Theater to protest mistreatment in federal courts. They authorized a memorial to Congress:

> In order to fasten the semblance of guilt upon men accused of this offense [u.c.] women are arrested and forcibly taken before sixteen men and plied with questions that no decent woman can hear without a blush. . . . If they decline to answer, they are imprisoned in the Penitentiary as though they were criminals. . . .
>
> But this is not all. In defiance of law and the usages of courts for ages, the legal wife is now compelled to submit to the same indignities. . . .
>
> We also direct your attention to the outrages perpetrated by rough and brutal deputy marshals, who watch around our dooryards, peer into our bedroom windows, ply little children with questions about their parents, and, when hunting their prey, burst into people's domiciles and terrorize the innocent.

After listing examples of outrages by raiding deputies, the women said:

> We ask for justice. . . . We ask that the laws may be fairly and impartially executed. . . . We see the wretched creatures who pander to men's basest passions left free to ply their horrible trade—and they may vote at the polls—while legal wives of men with plural families are disenfranchised. . . . And now we are threatened with entire deprivation of every right and privilege of citizenship. . . .
>
> We respectfully ask for a full investigation of Utah affairs.

Emmeline B. Wells and Ellen B. Ferguson found little sympathy when they carried the memorial to Washington. "Probably no American women ever engaged in a more degrading occupation than that of lobbying Congress for defeat of measures calculated to break up polygamy in Utah," the Chicago *Herald* said of "these shameless lobbyists."

> They are not the tearful sufferers and helpless victims which the sentimentalists would have us believe. They are fanatical supporters of the odious system of plural marriage, and they rejoice in their degradation.

At the DO, Taylor and Cannon worked long hours on an Epistle that was read to the Saints at annual conference; it filled thirteen columns of the *Deseret News.* "Persecution has raged, and hideous wrongs have been . . . perpetrated against us," the presidency said. Yet things had been worse during previous troubles in Missouri and Illinois.

> However grievous the wrongs under which we suffer today, there is much to be thankful for. Our land is filled with plenty. . . . And with these blessings . . . we have the inestimable blessing of the peace of God. . . . Let your hearts, therefore, brethren and sisters, be filled with thanksgiving and praise to our God for His goodness and mercy unto us as a people. He has made promises concerning Zion; be assured He will not forget them. . . .

"Persecution develops character," the presidency declared. "It has strengthened and infused new zeal, courage and determination," and had driven home the Savior's words: "If ye were of the world, the world would love his own; but because ye are not of the world . . . therefore the world hateth you."

> Our enemies have designed to destroy the work of God. For this they plot and toil and descend to the depths of infamy. . . . Instead of crushing the truth, they are advertising it; instead of showing the world how unworthy and contemptible we are, they are unwittingly furnishing us with opportunities to exhibit the heroic qualities we possess; instead of weakening or unsettling the minds of true Latter-day Saints, they are stimulating their faith and supplying them with additional proofs of the divinity of their religion.

"They would have the world believe that we are low, sensual, ignorant, and degraded, that our religion is a system of lust," the Epistle said of the popular straw-man; "but thinking people of the world know that there is no necessity to endure that which the Latter-day Saints are now enduring, to gratify lustful appetites or desires. . . .

"The scenes which we are now witnessing in this Territory are the results of a deep-laid and carefully planned conspiracy which has been in process of formation for years," the presidency declared flatly.

The determination of the small Gentile minority to rule the Territory was the real issue.

> So that, being as voiceless in the affairs of government as the Indians or Chinese, we could be taxed and plundered with impunity, and be lorded over by a set of political harpies who would revel and fatten at our expense.
>
> This has been . . . the object of all the outcry raised against us, of the innumerable falsehoods with which the public journals have teemed, of the constant appeals to congress to legislate against us, and of all the outrages in the name of law inflicted upon us by the courts.

The presidency minced no words regarding the federal appointees.

> Instead of seeking to insure domestic tranquility, these officers have fomented strife, they have fostered religious hate, they have embittered class against class, they have sought in every possible way to destroy that charity which should exist in every community composed of citizens of different religions and politics.

Considering that "some of the principal officers sent here to govern and maintain law, are the people's greatest enemies," the Epistle said,

> Is it any wonder . . . that prejudice upon all questions affecting us and our Territory should prevail? Or that Congress should be induced, under the pressure brought to bear upon it by the incessant clamors and misrepresentations of this class, to enact measures that would reach such a people as we are described to be?
>
> The Edmunds Law was begotten by prejudice, conceived in ignorance, and brought forth in hate. But its enforcement in these territories is in the spirit of merciless severity and undiluted malice, and those who prosecute under it have not the excuse which a deceived and blinded Congress might plead for its enactment. . . .

"Against the brutalities, usurpations, and falsehoods of men dressed in a little brief authority," the presidency declared, they had "appealed in vain."

> Our request has been a very modest one: it was simply that the wrongs under which we were suffering might be investigated. But investigation was the last thing that the foes of our liberties desired.

In Idaho, things had gone from bad to worse. All Mormon school teachers had had their certificates revoked.

> which means the placing of our children, by the help of our taxes, under the tuition of those who would gladly eradicate from their minds all love and respect for the faith of their fathers.

"It is alleged that we are in danger of perverting the nation's morals," the Epistle stated, and again refuted this with criminal statistics. In the previous year, even though the Saints had been hounded for u.c., more than 90 percent of the arrests in Salt Lake City had been of Gentiles, who comprised only one-fifth of the population.

> There are now in the city some six Brothels, forty Tap Rooms, a number of Gambling Houses, Pool Tables, and other disreputable concerns—*all* run by non-Mormons.

As for the "Mormon menace," the Epistle stated,

> It is a remarkable fact that in all these years since the introduction of polygamy among us, not one Gentile has ever entered it through our

agency. Those who are corrupt have easier methods which are furnished and approved by the professed Christian world. . . .

If in thirty-four years not one Gentile has adopted polygamy, how many years will it take to demoralize the fifty-five millions of the United States?

The presidency listed six violations of the constitution "sanctioned, approved, or winked at by those who have sworn to sustain that charter of liberty"; (1) Religious test oaths; (2) *ex post facto* legislation; (3) laws prohibiting "the free exercise of religion"; (4) a "law impairing the obligation of [marriage] contracts"; (5) disregard of the fourth amendment, guaranteeing protection against unreasonable search and seizure; and (6) violation of article eight, providing "Excessive bail shall not be required, nor excessive fines imposed, nor cruel and unusual punishments inflicted."

With withering scorn the presidency rejected the proposition of their oppressors to "become like them."

What does it mean, to be like them? It means that *E pluribus unum* is a fiction; it means that we tamper with and violate that grand palladium of human liberty, the Constitution of the United States, and substitute expediency, anarchy, fanaticism, intolerance, and religious bigotry for those glorious fundamental principles of liberty, equality, brotherhood, human freedom, and the rights of man. . . .

We cannot do it.

The *Tribune* sneered that the Saints should be "ashamed" of "the malignity, untruthfulness, weakness, and ignorance embodied in this latest Epistle." However, Taylor was showered with praise, the Epistle hailed as a masterpiece by his people.

While pleased at the reception of the message, Taylor was fully aware of the hard core of opposition, led by influential men, pressing for appeasement, compromise, peace at any price. Even his counselor, Cannon, was involved, dealing with men who negotiated with federal officials on an acceptable arbitration to end the conflict.[5]

The horrors of Mormonism meanwhile was a topic mined by hacks to supply the nation's literary market with its hottest subject. Kate Field, a career Mormon-eater, published an inflamatory article in the *North American Review*, "Mormon Blood Atonement," as debate on the

---

[5] It is sometimes assumed that during this period, with Taylor's health declining, he was merely a figurehead, and that Cannon ran the show. The fact that Taylor and Cannon had opposite viewpoints on compromise, and that no hint of Cannon's convictions appeared in official Epistles, indicates that Taylor was in full control. At this time his handwriting was firm and without tremor. The Epistle just quoted is not only Taylor's philosophy, but written in Taylor's literary style, which was distinctly different from Cannon's.

Edmunds-Tucker Bill continued in Congress. Her piece, even if true, was a rehash of hearsay horror stories of blood-letting during the Reformation, some three decades past.

The belligerent Robert N. Baskin hurried to Washington to testify before Congress in support of the bill. Baskin claimed that the Gentile minority were political slaves to Mormon rule; that the church controlled all political affairs; that church officials taught violation of the law and shielded criminals; that law was disregarded, civilization retarded, and republican institutions ignored; that the minority demanded redress of grievances; and that Utah was not a democracy but a theocracy, Mormon power coming from God and being superior to all earthly law.

The *North American Review* wasn't interested in an answer to Kate Field's article, nor Congress in a refutation of Baskin's charges.

If it were not enough that the whole world was against him, Taylor wondered if family ties were disintegrating during his enforced absence. Opening a letter from his pretty daughter, Ida, he let out a roar of rage. Ida wrote that she was engaged—to some whippersnapper entirely unknown to her father. Well! Taylor didn't particularly blame the girl—women were of the weaker sex, whose heads could be turned by designing roués—but he had a low opinion of a man insinuating himself into her affections without asking the father's permission nor stating his intentions.

"You inform me that the gentleman's name," Taylor replied, "is Whitaker. As I do not happen to know him, I therefore beg leave to make the following enquiries":

> Who are [his] Father & Mother? Where do they reside? Are they good faithful Latter-day Saints? upright honorable & above reproach? Is his father an Elder, High Priest or Seventy? Or does he hold any official position in the Church & where? Has he been on a mission or otherwise distinguished himself? Is his son who desires to pay his addresses to you a good, faithful, honorable Latter-day Saint; sincere in his religion & true to God & to his cause? Has he been on missions & where? To what quorum does he belong? Is he connected with Sunday Schools, Mutual Improvement Associations, or otherwise engaged in the cause & service of God? And does he exhibit that faith in God which is necessary to promote true happiness? And then again, what are his prospects for a living, or making you & family comfortable?

When Ida showed the letter from the church president to twenty-two-year-old John M. Whitaker, he gulped, sat down, dipped his pen and for ten agonized pages scratched gravel. He was "born of goodly parents"; his father had served on missions to the Society Islands and the Sandwich Islands, being a High Priest and "some fifteen years ago, entered the Patriarchal Order of marriage and has a family (which is an honor to him) of some twenty-two.".

Taylor was pleased to learn that Whitaker's mother was from the Isle of Man, where two of his own wives had lived.

Whitaker admitted that he didn't have much, because of helping support the family. "My trade is that of carpenter; my profession that of a reporter." Meanwhile he was working in the Church Historian's Office, "type-writing, ect."

> The teachings of my early training still speak as a monitor with me, prompting me to keep inviolate the principles of the gospel. Wherever I have labored, I have sought the associations of the good, the just, and the noble; but my truest and best companions have I found in reading good books.

Hmm. Taylor wondered if Ida had coached him on what to say.

Whitaker was an Elder, secretary of the YMMIA of the Fourteenth Ward, a member of the Theological Class, and Sunday School teacher.

> Character, to me, is esteemed more than all the luxuries and allurements of this world. It is above price—the noblest possession, the richest gem—and something on which I can proudly look back upon with satisfaction. Without it, my life would be like this earth without the sun; but with it, the genial rays of truth and hope are shed around me and I feel a consciousness of right which brightens my hopes, and kindles anew the glorious anticipation of the future.

A bit flowery; but Taylor couldn't fault the sentiment.

The boon of character "has taught me self-denial, and self-control," Whitaker said.

> Spiritous liquors have never calloused and clogged my brain; tea and coffee have never scorched and burned my mouth. Tobacco has never defiled and poisoned my system; and bad associations have I shunned, as a serpent.

Perhaps a bit stuffy; but devout. And it was Ida who had to live with him. (And he *was* writing for presidential approval.)

Whitaker had found the "one suited to my condition and one for whom I have great respect," in Ida.

> Since my first visit I have acted honorable and just. . . . I spoke to Miss Ida's mother, as well as to Ida, and both were agreeable. I wrote to you the same day, but have never received any answer; and I was led to deeply regret, when Ida showed me your letter to her in which you think I have acted unwisely, that I have tried to keep it covered.

Taylor realized that Whitaker's original letter had gone astray, what with cloak-and-dagger times of the underground. He gave the union his blessing.

> Ida is a good girl, a dutiful child, an honorable lady and a faithful Latter-day Saint; and in resigning her to your hands I place therein an

inestimable treasure. Treat her justly, generously, & tenderly; so may the Lord deal with you. Together may you fear God, observe His laws, & do the works of righteousness. May your name be honored & your habitation known in Israel, for true integrity, honor, and virtue. May your pathway in life be pleasant & your children rise up and call you blessed; & then may you be crowned with eternal exaltation, in the Celestial kingdom of God.

One of Lorin C. Woolley's assets with affairs at the DO was his unprepossessive appearance; he was of slight build, mild of manner, with a scraggly beard—not a man to attract notice. But he carried two guns and knew how to use them, and his loyalty to John Taylor was absolute.

As a bodyguard and personal friend of the church president, Lorin was worried about "the Boss" during the spring and summer. As it became certain that the stringent and vindictive Edmunds-Tucker Bill would become the law of the land, the Boss wasn't eating the way he used to, nor sleeping well. Every mail that Lorin brought to the DO contained letters from prominent men, urging John Taylor to make some compromise, to issue a manifesto that would appease Congress and head off impending legislation.[6] George Q. Cannon, while supporting the official position, was as a practical politician trying to avoid a confrontation. Church officials not on the underground were discussing compromise with federal representatives.

While the Boss remained adamant, Lorin knew he felt cornered and forsaken. He was spooky. In the night, the Boss would have the sudden impression that deputies were coming. Then Lorin and the other bodyguards would hitch up in frantic haste, throw on the luggage and drive to another hideout. During July, the DO changed location six times. In early September, the DO was again at the John Carlisle home in Murray; then at three A.M. everyone fled to George Stringfellow's at Draper. But before dawn the Boss dreamed once more of pursuit, and the DO moved to William White's home in the Sixteenth Ward. Nine days later the DO went north to Centerville and located at the farm of Lorin's father, John W. Woolley. Here, the Boss had a feeling of security for awhile. He began pitching quoits again with the guards, and in the evening would play a game of checkers.[7]

---

[6] "These letters not only came from those who were living in the Plural Marriage relation, but also from prominent men . . . of the church who were not," Lorin stated. "They all urged that something be done to satisfy the Gentiles." (From Lorin's statement, quoted later in this chapter.)

[7] The journal of a DO guard, Samuel Bateman, contains almost nothing except such trivia during this stirring period of suspense. It has been suggested that it was written in a "cohab code," and that in reality it is a dramatic account. If so, no one has broken the code. More likely, Bateman purposely restricted the journal to trivia, avoiding making a record of secret matters.

Lorin knew by another sign that the Boss was more relaxed: he wasn't twiddling thumbs and forefingers, a nervous habit when agitated. He was comfortable and secure at the Woolley farm, and Lorin took time off from guard duty to attend to his own place nearby, do the fall plowing and get ready for winter.

Lorin was doing his chores on the morning of September 23 when Little Charlie arrived with news the Boss wanted to see him in a hurry.[8] Lorin went to his father's house, where he found the Boss worrying his thumbs. The Boss told him a messenger had brought bad news. Deputies had surrounded the house of Brigham Young, Jr., and while they hadn't found him yet, they knew he was hidden somewhere inside. They were going to keep the place covered until they found him.

Lorin's job was to get Young Briggie out of the house, past the deputies, and on the underground railway to a safe retreat in the canyons. He didn't ask the Boss how he was to do it, but after receiving a blessing for the mission Lorin rode away with full confidence that with the Lord's help he'd find a way.

Three days later he returned home, mission accomplished, and went to bed, exhausted. He'd been in the saddle night and day. But he got little sleep; two hours later Sam Bateman shook him awake. The Boss wanted him at the DO, where an important meeting was in progress.

> Brother Bateman . . . asked me to be at my Father's home where a Manifesto was to be discussed. I went there and found there were congregated Samuel Bateman, Charles H. Wilckens, L. John Nuttall, Charlie Barrell, George Q. Cannon, Franklin S. Richards, and Hyrum B. Clawson. We discussed the proposed manifesto at length, and we were unable to become united in the discussion. Finally George Q. Cannon suggested that President Taylor take the matter up with the Lord and decide the same the next day.[9]

Richards and Clawson returned to Salt Lake in the early evening. Lorin planned on going home and getting some sleep, but the Boss, twitching forefingers on thumbs, after congratulating him on his recent mission said that while he realized Lorin was very tired, he felt the need to have him and Little Charlie on guard duty the first shift.

---

[8] To distinguish between the two guards at the DO named Henry Charles Barrell and Charles Henry Wilcken, Barrell was called Little Charlie and Wilcken Big Charlie.

[9] Jesse Burke Stone, *An Event of Underground Days.* The events of September 26–27, 1886 have been published many times, particularly by J. W. Musser in *Truth* magazine. See also B. Harvey Allred, *A Leaf in Review;* and *The Keys of the Priesthood Illustrated,* by Lynn L. Bishop and Steven L. Bishop.

Inasmuch as events related in Lorin C. Woolley's statement have become the cornerstone on which the Fundamentalists (who today practice polygamy to the extreme embarrassment of the church) base their faith, the subject is highly controversial. Evidence pro and con can be found in the "Addendum" of this chapter.

It was a tense evening; no checker games. The Boss paced the living room. Lorin and Little Charlie took particular care in checking the house inside and out, making sure the heavy window screens were fastened and doors locked. The Boss used the south bedroom, opening off the living room. Lorin double-checked it before the Boss retired. By nine o'clock everyone except the guard was in bed. Little Charlie curled up on the living room sofa, leaving Lorin by the president's door reading the *Doctrine and Covenants* in the quiet of the night. Except for the lamp on the nearby table, the house was in darkness.

Presently a light of intense brilliance appeared under the door of the president's room. Lorin "was at once startled to hear the voices of men talking there." He distinguished "three distinct voices."

> I was bewildered because it was my duty to keep people out of that room, and evidently someone had entered without my knowing it.

On trying the bedroom door, he found it "bolted as usual." He awakened Little Charlie, who stood guard while Lorin went outside to check window screens.

> While examining the last window, and feeling greatly agitated, a voice spoke to me, saying, "Can't you feel the spirit? Why should you worry?"

At peace, Lorin went inside. He and Little Charlie sat wide-eyed, filled with awesome wonder, while the conversation continued beyond the door. Though words were inaudible, the voices were so distinct that

> although I did not see the parties I could place their positions in the room. . . . The three voices continued until about midnight, when one of them left, and the other two continued.

One voice was that of the Boss, the other two were strangers.

Lorin's father, an early riser, joined the two guards about five o'clock, to witness the voices and the light. Other members of the household joined the hushed group, until at dawn the voices ceased and the light went out. No one thought of breakfast. The group waited in awed silence at the living room until the president's door opened.

> When John Taylor came out of his room about eight o'clock . . . we could scarcely look at him on account of the brightness of his personage.
> He stated, "Brethren, I have had a very pleasant conversation all night with Brother Joseph [Smith]."
> I said, "Boss, who is the man that was there until midnight?"
> He asked, "What do you know about it, Lorin?"
> I told him about my experience.
> He said, "Brother Lorin, that was your Lord."

The family and staff at the DO consisted of thirteen people on that day, who fasted during a meeting that continued "from about nine o'clock in the morning until five in the afternoon without intermission."

President Taylor called the meeting to order. He had the Manifesto, that had been prepared under the direction of George Q. Cannon, read over again. Then he put each person under covenant that he or she would defend the principle of Celestial or Plural Marriage, and that they would consecrate their lives, liberty, and property to this end, and that they would personally sustain and uphold that principle.

By that time we were all filled with the Holy Ghost. President Taylor . . . placed his finger on the document, his person rising from the floor about a foot or eighteen inches, and with countenance animated by the Spirit of the Lord . . . said, "Sign that document? Never! I would suffer my right hand to be severed from my body first. Sanction it? Never! I would suffer my tongue to be torn from the roof of my mouth before I would sanction it."[10]

President Taylor then announced that he had received a revelation during the night, which he now wrote:

My son John: You have asked me concerning the New & everlasting Covenant, how far it is binding upon my people. Thus saith the Lord: All commandments that I give must be obeyed by those calling themselves by my name. . . . Have I not given my word in great plainness on this subject? . . . I have not revoked this law, nor will I, for it is everlasting, & those who will enter unto my glory must obey the conditions thereof; even so, Amen.

But the president now knew that despite all he could do, there would be inevitable compromise, after his death.

President Taylor said that the time would come when many of the Saints would apostatize because of this principle. . . . Rising from the floor while making this statement, he also said the day will come when a document similar to that [manifesto] then under consideration would be adopted by the church. . . .

To meet this contingency, at the close of the meeting he held a private session with five of the men, to whom he gave "authority to perform marriage ceremonies," Lorin said,

and placed them under covenant that, while they lived, they would see to it that no year passed by without children being born in the principle of plural marriage. They were given authority to ordain others when necessary. . . .

During these proceedings, a most remarkable event occurred. The door of Taylor's bedroom opened and Joseph Smith entered the living room, a resurrected being. The prophet

---

[10] Up to this point, Lorin Woolley's statement evidently isn't controversial. He filed a "Statement of Facts" with the Church Historian's Office October 6, 1912, that essentially agrees with a subsequent statement made September 22, 1929. His original statement ended at this point. His later statement recounted details of the meeting that have been sharply challenged.

stood by directing the proceedings. Two of us had not met the Prophet Joseph Smith in his mortal life, and we ... were introduced to him and shook hands with him.

In setting men apart with authority to perform plural marriages after the church would have suspended the practice, Taylor was reverting to the situation at Nauvoo during the days of the prophet. During that period, the church officially denounced polygamy in the strongest terms; meanwhile the priesthood authority within the church fostered it as a secret practice and as essential to attainment of celestial glory.

The Principle once more had gone underground. The world would be appeased, but John Taylor had done all he could to make sure the law of God would continue. He slept that night in dreamless peace.[11]

ADDENDUM

On June 17, 1933, two years after Lorin C. Woolley published his account of the meeting, the church issued an "Official Statement from the First Presidency":

> It is alleged that on September 26–27, 1886, President John Taylor received a revelation from the Lord. . . .
> As to this pretended revelation it should be said that the archives of the church contain no such revelation; the archives contain no record of any such revelation, nor any evidence justifying a belief that any such revelation was ever given. . . . From the absence in the church archives of any evidence whatsoever justifying any belief that such a revelation was given, we are justified in affirming that no such revelation exists.

The key word seems to be "revelation." The church does not accept any message as the word of the Lord until it is presented to the church membership and accepted as a revelation. With this definition in mind, there is little conflict between the official statement and certain facts; it is a matter of definition of terms.

We will, therefore, use the term "alleged revelation."

This alleged revelation of John Taylor's, which unquestionably is in his handwriting, has been widely circulated in photocopy. After President Taylor's death his son, John W. Taylor, found the original among his father's papers,[12] and made a copy in his own handwriting. This also

---

11 In 1890, three years after Taylor's death, the church issued the Manifesto, officially setting aside the practice of plural marriage.

12 Corroborated by the *Journal* of Abraham H. Cannon, March 29, 1892. See also the pamphlet, "1886 Revelation; A Revelation of the Lord to John Taylor."

has been widely distributed in photocopy. The original of the alleged revelation was delivered by the Taylor family to the church. It has not surfaced since.

However, there is evidence that it is safely preserved. On April 21, 1972, Raymond W. Taylor found copies of this alleged revelation among the John Taylor papers in the Church Historian's Office. He located a total of eleven reproductions, bearing the notation that they had been copied from the original. A number of these were personally copied by the church historian.

This brings up the definition of the word "archives." The Webster definition is: a place for keeping public records. The CHO has always been a repository, never a library; its records are not public. Access is carefully restricted, authorization for research limited to certain records and not others.

In his research, Raymond W. Taylor got so far inside the CHO that, in effect, he went out the other side into orbit. In outer space was the "Special Documents Department," which is not officially part of the "archives"; and it was here that he found the eleven copies of the alleged revelation. There are also various safes at the CHO, to which he did not have access; these also are not part of the "archives."

Thus in perfect truth the alleged revelation of 1886 could be said not to be in the archives, nor would the archives contain any record of any such alleged revelation, nor any evidence whatsoever justifying a belief that any such alleged revelation was ever given.

The same sort of denials concerned Joseph Smith's original revelation on plural marriage at Nauvoo. Later, when the Principle was officially endorsed, these repudiations were characterized as "seeming" denials, which denounced not the "true coin," but the "counterfeit" of unauthorized practice.

Daniel R. Bateman corroborated Lorin C. Woolley's statement as "correct in every detail." He was present at the meeting, and copied the alleged revelation in his journal at that time.

It is significant that despite official suppression, none of the twelve witnesses at the meeting ever denied it, except for a carefully worded statement by George Earl, the fifteen-year-old chore boy, who admitted being "in and out" during the day while attending to his farm duties.

Some of the most impressive evidence is the blanket suppression of material relating to events of September 27, 1886. L. John Nuttall's detailed journal is unavailable for this period. The underground journals of John Taylor are deep in some recess of the official records. It is said that B. H. Roberts wrote an account of the 1886 meeting in his *Life of John Taylor*, but that this and "many other wonderful events" were censored. Roberts "was heartsick and went to John and Lorin Woolley for advice." They counseled obedience.[13] The original manuscript has also vanished.

However, in recent years church scholars have been forced to admit the existence of the alleged revelation. Brigham Young University actually approved a study of the controversy by Dean C. Jesse.[14] Kenneth W. Godfrey, director of LDS institutes and seminaries for Arizona and New Mexico, quoted from the alleged revelation in *Dialogue* (Autumn, 1970), and said that "Dean Jesse concluded in his study that it is highly probable that such a revelation does exist."

Two church authorities have admitted its existence, but denied its authenticity because it was unsigned. In this respect it resembles revelations given Joseph Smith. In fact, Joseph's original revelation on plural marriage was unsigned, and, since it had been dictated, wasn't in his handwriting.

The vital issue of the controversy is not the existence of the alleged revelation, but whether or not it is accepted as church doctrine. The statement of the first presidency says on this point:

> Furthermore, so far as the authorities of the church are concerned and so far as the members of the church are concerned, since this pretended revelation, if ever given, was never presented to and adopted by the church or by any council of the church, and since to the contrary, an inspired rule of action, the Manifesto, was (subsequently to the pretended revelation) presented to and adopted by the church, which . . . was directly opposite to the interpretation given to the pretended revelation, the pretended revelation could have no validity . . . and action under it would be unauthorized, illegal, and void.

In this respect, the alleged revelation of 1886 has exactly the same status as more than half of Joseph Smith's own revelations. For reasons best known to the keepers of the records, the majority of the prophet's instructions from the Lord were "never presented to and adopted by the church or by any council of the church," and therefore "could have no validity."

---

13 Bishop and Bishop, p. 143.

14 Dean C. Jesse, "A Comparative Study and Evaluation of the Latter-day Saint and the Fundamentalist Views Pertaining to the Practice of Plural Marriage."

24

The Last Pioneer

AFTER LUNCH, John Taylor retired to his room to write a letter. There was to be a reception for family and friends at the Gardo House on his seventy-eighth birthday, and for the second time since going underground he would be there only in spirit.

> I desire to send you my benediction and blessing, and to say unto you: May grace, mercy, and peace be extended to you.

He reminded them that while "some people suppose that persecutions and trials are afflictions," they were "in accordance, however, with the design of our Heavenly Father," and "may truly be said to be blessings in disguise." The Savior said,

> Blessed are ye when men shall revile you, and persecute you, and shall say all manner of evil against you falsely, for my sake. Rejoice and be exceeding glad, for great is your reward in heaven, for so persecuted they the prophets which were before you.

He was sorry to hear "of the sickness of my wives Jane and Sophia." Jane was recovering, but Sophia had suffered a severe stroke. After "making careful inquiry," he had "learned that it is no uncommon thing for people to be healed."

> A lady of about her age that I conversed with quite recently said she had had two strokes of that kind, and she is now quite well, hale, and hearty. . . .
>
> I am pleased to be informed that the health of the family is generally good, and that the disposition and feeling of both wives and children is to fear God, to work in righteousness, and to yield obedience to His laws. . . .

We expect, and have faith, that this earth will yet be renovated and purified, the wicked will be rooted out of it, and the righteous inherit it; and we further look forward to the time when there will be a new heaven and a new earth, wherein dwelleth righteousness; and a new Jerusalem, wherein the Lord God and the Lamb will be the light thereof, and you, my wives and children . . . will have the privilege, if faithful to your covenants, of entering into and partaking of the most exalted, glorious, and eternal blessings which any men or women on earth have enjoyed in this world or in the world to come; and will eventually be associated with the Gods in the eternal worlds.

Although at the DO Taylor belligerently refused to admit his health was failing and scorned suggestions that he allow a doctor to examine him, his letter became a farewell and final counsel.

We should be strictly honest, one with another, and with all men; let our word always be as good as our bond; avoid all ostentation of pride and vanity; and be meek, lowly, and humble; be full of integrity and honor; and deal justly and righteously with all men; and have the fear and love of God continually before us, and seek for the comforting influence of the Holy Ghost to dwell with us.

"The protecting care of the Lord over me and my brethren has been very manifest" at the DO, he reported.

I am happy to inform you that we now are, and always have been during our exile, supplied with everything that is necessary to our comfort and convenience. Go where we will, we have good accommodations, plenty of good food and the necessaries of life, kind and sympathetic friends, and the best of treatment.

"Some of you have written that you 'would like to have a peep' at me," he concluded. "I heartily reciprocate that feeling, and would like to have a 'peep' at you on this occasion; but in my bodily absence my spirit and peace shall be with you."

His eyes were brimming as he sealed the letter. He went to the commode, dashed water in his face and combed his hair while regaining composure. Through the curtain he saw that a covered wagon had arrived, no doubt for another meeting with those tenaciously wanting concession and appeasement. The wagon was well disguised with a bundle of hay, plow handles sticking out of the wagon cover, and even a chicken coop lashed to the tailgate; it could pass right under the noses of the deputies without arousing suspicion.

As he left his room with the envelope, he stopped in surprise. Then there was a happy bedlam of greetings. Three of his wives were there, Elizabeth Kaighin, Mary Ann Oakley, and Margaret Young, along with his sons, George J. and John W., and Margaret's two little boys, Abraham and Samuel. With the Woolley family and the DO staff, the room was filled. A chocolate birthday cake stood on the table with a blazing forest of candles. After everyone had tendered greetings, Maggie struck up "Now Let Us Rejoice" on the parlor organ, and the two little boys struggled forward with the surprise, bearing between them in a heavy gilt frame a large photograph of John Taylor's seventeen living sons.

After dark the family left in the covered wagon. Waving good-bye, John Taylor was sure that this birthday celebration, though premature, was the best of his lifetime.

Turning back inside, he wondered if he'd have another.

Deputies were particularly active, determined to capture the big prize, the church presidency. They raided the Gardo House and other official buildings several times. The DO guards noted that the Boss was twitching forefingers and thumbs. On November 3, just two days after his birthday, Taylor moved back to Salt Lake to the home of William White in the Sixteenth Ward. Within a week he went to John Carlisle's place in Murray and then returned to Centerville at the John W. Woolley farm. But his fingers twitched here, and on November 22 he went north during a snowstorm to the farm of Thomas F. Roueche at Kaysville, on the flatlands bordering Great Salt Lake.

Here at last he felt secure and at ease. The guards winked at one another, commenting that maybe it was the isolation of the farm and the solidarity of the people hereabouts; but again, was it Josephine Elizabeth Roueche? The Boss hadn't lost his eye for a pretty girl.

Of course, nothing would *happen*. Impossible—the Boss was fifty-one years older than Josephine, and with one foot in the grave. But still . . . she was tall and slender, high-waisted, with dark hair and eyes, a serene and gentle temperament. And the Boss was lonely. . . .

The two-story Roueche home was the best house that had been used as the DO, sturdily built of adobe with four rooms on the ground floor and three upstairs. Thomas Roueche also was the most prominent man to offer shelter to the president, having served six terms as mayor of Kaysville. He moved his family into the pioneer log cabin behind the house, which he'd occupied on settling there thirty years previously, allowing the DO full use of the main house.

From his upstairs window Taylor could look east across the farmlands to the little town a mile away, with the Wasatch mountains rising abruptly beyond. He was careful about appearing in the front yard during daylight, for Bluff Road, the main route from Salt Lake to Ogden, was only a short distance away. Twice a day the Utah Central, paralleling the road, whistled past. Kay's Creek ran between the road and the house, and where it angled across the farm toward Great Salt Lake Roueche had made a reservoir for irrigation. It was frozen over now, but Taylor looked forward to fishing and swimming there, come summer.

Behind the house, a mile to the west, marshes edging the lake teemed with waterfowl. Sam Bateman liked to take a shotgun and bring back ducks and an occasional goose for the DO table. Taylor resisted the urge to go along; the marshes would provide concealment for deputies.

The DO was now twenty-six miles from Salt Lake City. It was impossible to make the trip daily by team for official mail, as formerly, so one courier brought it from the city to "Halfway House"—John W. Woolley's at Centerville—where another picked it up for the DO. Visitors took the train to Centerville, and from there came by covered wagon.

Taylor found both his spirits and his health improved at the Roueche farm. He attributed it to divine blessings, but Sam Bateman, Lorin Woolley, and the two Charlies exchanged knowing looks. They noted that with Josephine helping with office work at the DO, the Boss was frisky as a colt; and while he was too old for romance, he was getting younger every day. Wasn't it true that when a man began showing his age there was nothing like a young girl to restore his youth? The Boss, always a fastidious dresser, really duded himself up these days; always well-mannered, he became downright courtly.

Not only the guards, but Josephine's brothers noticed it. There were five of them, Jacob and Will Henry still at home, Joseph, Thomas, and John married and living in the vicinity. Josephine either was at the DO of an evening, or President Taylor was visiting at the log cabin. It wasn't right, the brothers growled, him an old man ready to die, and Neen with her life before her.

In a private ceremony on December 19, 1887, John Taylor and Josephine Elizabeth Roueche were joined for time and all eternity in the New and Everlasting Covenant.[1] Her father performed the ceremony, with George Q. Cannon witness. Taylor had been at the Roueche home slightly less than a month.[2]

The brothers suspected what had happened, and were bitter. The youngest, Will Henry, while on guard saw deputies slip across Bluff Road and creep toward the farm. Looking toward the house, he saw the church president taking the afternoon breeze at an upstairs window. "Tell the old son-of-a-bitch to pull in his head before he gets it shot off!" Will Henry yelled.[3]

---

[1] Herb Barnes, an old resident of Kaysville, told the author that the reason for the marriage was that John Taylor needed a nurse, and it was embarrassing to be attended by a young girl.

[2] "Lesser Known Wives of President John Taylor," Brigham Young University. Details of this marriage also related to the author by Josephine's nephew, Leonard Roueche.

[3] Told by Will Henry's son, Leonard. He remembered Josephine as "Aunt Neen."

As Taylor turned from the window, flushing, Josephine slipped into the room with a dress and sunbonnet in her arms. She helped him put them on, saying that Will Henry was really only a boy; he didn't understand. She'd see to it that he apologized. Never mind, Taylor said, as he rolled up the legs of his trousers; he didn't want to make an issue of it. An entire generation of Saints didn't understand. They were willing to sacrifice the eternal Kingdom for friendship with the Gentile world.

Not altogether; not an entire generation, she reminded him. She had dedicated herself to the Principle. As she tied the sunbonnet under his chin she quoted part of the verse that had accompanied his proposal, the dazzling reward to "gain a seat among the Gods."

> *In robes of bright seraphic light; and*
> *With thy God, eternal—onward goest, a*
> *Priestess and a queen—reigning and ruling in*
> *The realm of light. Unlike the imbeciles*
> *Who dared not brook the scorn of men, and knew not*
> *How to prize eternal life.*
>
> *Josephine, the cup's within thy reach; drink thou*
> *The vital balm and live!*

They went downstairs and out the back way as the two deputies came to the front door. If another man was lurking at the rear, what he would see was a young woman helping a bent old crone carry a swill bucket out to the pigpen. Then they got some shorts in the bucket from the granary and fed the chickens. A deputy would have no eyes for the old woman in the sunbonnet, when a beautiful girl with willowy figure tossed shorts from the bucket.

"Here, chick-chick-chick-chick!"

Taylor was still brooding, after the deputies had searched the place and gone. He told Josephine that the pressure was growing intolerable for concession and appeasement. John W. Young was in New York, and the church attorney, F. S. Richards, in Washington, both negotiating with influential men regarding what would have to be done to achieve statehood. Telegrams in cipher flew back and forth. Cannon directed negotiations, both with the local ringites and in the east. Though President John Taylor had said time and again he never would compromise, that didn't stop negotiations.

And what was the price of statehood for Utah?

First and foremost, polygamy must be abandoned. Now they wanted him to agree to have delegates meet to draft a proposed constitution that would make polygamy forever illegal. Never!

But regardless of man-made law, Josephine pointed out, the Principle would continue, practiced quietly and in secret, as it had been at Nauvoo, as it was now being done under persecution. The Principle was so difficult to live, it required such dedication, that it never could be for the masses anyway. What difference whether or not it was declared illegal? With statehood, Utah would have control of its own law enforcement. Each state regulated its own marriage customs. It was not a matter of legality, but of how the law was administered.

Yes; that is the argument—concede anything now, pay the Devil in his own coin, he retorted scathingly. But deceit and insincerity would boomerang, he predicted. Once the first step was taken, Gentile pressure would force others until, in time, concessions made for expediency and appeasement would become official policy. One backward step now, he declared, and the time would come when the greatest enemy of the Principle would be the church itself. Unless he could hold the line, Josephine would live to see this come to pass.[4]

If only he had ten more years.

Preparing for the anticipated passage of the Edmunds-Tucker Bill, Taylor called on stake presidents, and presidents of temples, to form local associations to acquire title of assets now held in the name of the church. The earlier Edmunds Law had prohibited the church from holding more than $50,000 in property, but had lacked provision for enforcement. The new law had teeth: the church no longer would exist legally, while the government would confiscate all property in excess of the legal limit, sell it and keep the money.

By transferring title of local assets to the various stakes, wards, and temples, each would possess less than $50,000 in assets. Taylor cautioned them to make sure the value was within the legal limit.[5]

Though the *Tribune* howled over this method of circumventing the law, it showed a renewed respect for Taylor; in fact, it had done so since the impact of the powerful Epistle in April. Prior to that time, the paper had claimed that the hardships of the underground had so weakened the president that he was incompetent, and that Cannon was running the church.[6] But the Epistle was undoubtedly written in his distinctive style, and, moreover, though co-signed by Cannon, was directly opposed to Cannon's well-known negotiations for appeasement.

---

[4] She did. Josephine lived until 1943, and died at San Jose, California.

[5] Isaac M. Waddell was principal agent for transfer of property deeds. See his letters to Taylor, March 22, 1886 to April 2, 1887; also the seven-page letter of attorney LeGrand Young, January 13, 1887, discussing legal aspects of this method of circumventing escheatment.

[6] Taylor's son, John W., wrote that the April Epistle had been hailed a masterpiece that filled the Saints with renewed strength and perseverance. He added, "I have not seen any more reference in the anti-Mormon newspapers (since the publishing of the Epistle) that the trouble and care that the raid has brought you had weakened your mind, and totally disqualified you for active service."

The opening of the Gentile home for plural wives at this time provided Taylor vast amusement. For six years Mrs. Angie F. Newman, a woman with a horror of polygamy and a flair for publicity, had been beating the drum to establish a house of refuge for abandoned or repentant plural wives.[7]

Enlisting the support of Kate Field, Fanny Stenhouse, Governor Murray, and others of the ring, Mrs. Newman got the ball rolling, and went to Washington with a memorial endorsed by the Woman's Christian Temperance Union, the Woman's Home Missionary Society, and the Presbyterian Missionary Society, claiming to represent 300,000 members who were outraged by her tales of hordes of abandoned plurals skulking the streets of Salt Lake City, living in chicken coops and eating from garbage cans. Mrs. Newman gave Congress "an argument remarkable for its eloquence and power," causing it to appropriate $40,000 to open the home and an annual sum for maintenance.

The crusader was accorded a triumphal reception by her supporters on returning to Salt Lake. "Our sister has enshrined herself by her faith, courage, and genius," declared the Rev. S. J. Carroll of the local Methodist church, keynoting the reception, "and has inaugurated a grand philanthropic movement for the disenthrallment of the women of Utah."

Taylor was amused on hearing that after the home was opened with much fanfare, only one woman sought refuge, and she proved to be not a plural wife but a prostitute.[8]

At the DO, covered wagons came and went, carrying prominent Mormons talking compromise. Cannon kept negotiating; Taylor wouldn't yield an inch. On an early evening when another meeting was scheduled, Taylor sighed as another covered wagon turned off Bluff Road into Roueche Lane. He'd listen, but his mind was made up.

A yell from outside. A guard fired into the air. The driver of the wagon cut the team with the whip as the guard tried to grab a bridle. "Deputies!"

Taylor followed Lorin Woolley out back and into the granary. They climbed to the upper story by the big wheat bins. Sam Gilson's heavy voice shouted orders as the wagonload of deputies searched the house, log cabin, and outbuildings. When Gilson and a deputy climbed the outside wall ladder to the bins, Taylor was under the wheat, a sack pulled

---

[7] Jeanette H. Ferry, *Industrial Home of Utah*. Also Dwyer, *The Gentile Comes to Utah*, who says, "This lady, filled with enthusiasm for the advancement of Methodism and the abolition of polygamy, conceived a project to the fulfillment of which she bent her considerable and restless energies, as well as her flair for political action, during the entire decade" of 1880–90.

[8] After a year of operation, the home had acquired a total of eleven women. The number steadily declined until after seven years Washington cut off the annual appropriation and the home closed.

Evidently the Mormon women liked their bondage.

over his head and his hands holding an air space for breathing. From below a deputy called that there was nobody downstairs. And nobody up here, either, Gilson replied. Then, "Wait a minute!" he said. "Hey, bring up a pitchfork!"

Taylor wondered if this was the end, if he would be captured in the wheat bin, as John D. Lee had been found hiding in a pigpen. But it wouldn't be alive. If—

Sudden yell from the barn, whoop, crack of whip, clatter of hoofbeats, rattle of carriage wheels. "Stop 'em!" Gilson yelled. "Stop 'em!"[9]

Later that night, Taylor thanked Lorin and Little Charlie for creating the diversion. Shortly afterwards, the frustrated Gilson issued a reward notice:

$800 REWARD!
To be Paid for the Arrest of John Taylor
and George Q. Cannon.

———————————

The above Reward will be paid for the delivery to me,
or for information that will lead to the arrest of
JOHN TAYLOR
President of the Mormon Church, and
GEORGE Q. CANNON
His Counselor; or
$500 will be paid for Cannon alone, and
$300 for Taylor

———————————

All Conferences or Letters kept strictly secret.
S. H. GILSON
22 and 23 Wasatch Building, Salt Lake City.
Salt Lake City, Jan. 31, 1887.

The Saints were indignant at the petty attempt to humiliate the president by offering a lesser reward for him than for his counselor. Taylor chuckled, however, on seeing the notice. He pointed out that Cannon had committed the greater crime by jumping bail.

Taylor fancied the storm clouds of persecution were at last breaking. A shaft of sunlight had come in December with the pardon of the man who had provided the government's test case, Rudger Clawson.[10] Then in early February the Supreme Court reviewed the Lorenzo Snow case a second time and knocked down the segregation device by which he had been convicted three times for the same offense. The Saints celebrated the release of Snow and all others serving segregating sentences. Taylor

———————————

[9] Told by Leonard Roueche.

[10] Clawson's homecoming was marred by the fact that while he was in prison his first wife divorced him—on the charge of "adultery" with his plurals—and married a local hotelkeeper. She sacrificed church membership by doing so.

warmly welcomed his old friend when Snow visited the DO, congratulated him on his stand, and sent personal blessings to the others who had refused to knuckle under to oppression.

Two things, however, preyed on his mind. One was the condition of Sophia, who was sinking after her stroke. He tried to arrange a visit before the end, but Sam Gilson was using the sick wife as a decoy, deputies watching her quarters day and night. Taylor was enraged at learning that the skunks actually raided the bedroom of the dying woman in the night, trying to apprehend her husband.[11]

The other matter was the snowballing sentiment within the church for compromise. F. S. Richards had returned from talking to people in Washington; the church attorney had a plan designed to satisfy the government, head off passage of the Edmunds-Tucker Law, and at long last obtain statehood for Utah. This was a heady prospect, and Cannon made secret trips almost daily to parley with Richards and Charles W. Penrose, who had returned from England to resume editorship of the *Deseret News.*

After a stormy session at the DO, at which Taylor again rejected appeasement, Cannon prevailed upon him to allow Richards and Penrose to write up the proposition, for prayerful study. Their letter suggested that, inasmuch as polygamists already were disfranchised, monogamist Saints should take the test oath, in order to maintain voting control of the Territory. Taylor made no objection to this. Then came the proposal to make another appeal for statehood based on a proposed constitution that would prohibit polygamy forever in Utah. This provision, they maintained, was absolutely obligatory to the achievement of statehood. However, the church would continue to control the state.[12] The framing of the constitution would be strictly a political issue, having nothing to do with religious practice. With statehood, the church would have to contend only with the law of Utah, not of the United States.

"You have made a very able, clear, and comprehensive presentation of the case from your standpoint," Taylor replied February 19.[13]

---

[11] *Millennial Star*, 49:525.

[12] While the church ostensibly refrained from politics, it actually controlled everything not under supervision of the carpetbaggers. Gentiles considered it a victory when they succeeded in electing one lone member to the legislature. A letter to Taylor says, "The enclosed document contains the sentiment of the majority of the members of a caucus held by the members of both houses of the legislature. They have not signed the same, fearing that the document might be miscarried. . . . Whatever way or policy you recommend will be adopted as the unanimous sense of all members of the legislature (except McLaughlin)." (Letter March 1, 1886 from John W. Taylor and Elias A. Smith to the church president.) McLaughlin was the Gentile.

[13] This was an official letter of the first presidency, signed by both Taylor and Cannon. However, it expresses Taylor's own convictions, for Cannon was actively working for compromise.

In most forceful language you describe the evils with which we are menaced . . . under the operation of the [Edmunds-] Tucker bill should it become law . . . unless we adopt this plan . . . of framing and voting for a constitution which shall forever prohibit the practice of bigamy and polygamy in the new state.

Though admitting that the arguments "are very plausible," Taylor asked,

What good grounds are there for supposing that if we were to adopt such a constitution . . . our request [for statehood] would be favorably considered? Nothing that we have heard from President Cleveland gives us warrant to believe that he would be satisfied upon this point by such an instrument.

John W. Young had recently interviewed the president on the matter, and had reported that such a concession would not be all that would be required for statehood. Furthermore, Taylor had just received a report of interviews with nearly all members of the House, and "nineteen out of twenty" had no confidence in the sincerity of such a provision.

They would not consent to the admission of the Territory as a State on any such terms; that nothing short of the complete extirpation of polygamy by harsh measures, such as the Tucker bill, would satisfy them.

"It appears clear, therefore," Taylor wrote, that the provision "would not satisfy Congress and the country at large, and its adoption by us would only result in humiliation to us without any corresponding benefit."

If we were to make such a proposal, we should . . . have the mortification of proposing a concession that would be spurned and thrown back at us with contempt. We should, thereby, not only lose our own self-respect, but our own people would be weakened, and the world would say that we offered to barter away principle for the name of expediency.

Whatever the evils and terrors of the Tucker bill may be, personally we prefer to endure them than to take this other course. We have put our trust in God in the past, and we must trust Him in this as in all other things in the future. In doing this we are not troubled with even the shadow of a doubt as to what the result will be.

That, Taylor felt, settled the matter. But the appeasers worked tenaciously, gathering strength among church authorities and the lay membership, until Taylor felt that he, and he alone, stood in the gap, holding back the flood of capitulation.

Early on Sunday morning a courier arrived at the DO with news that Sophia had died. Since he couldn't attend her funeral, Taylor conducted memorial services for this wife who had raised eight children, seven of her own and an adopted daughter. After the meeting, he retired to his room.

Four days later, March 3, 1887, the dreaded Edmunds-Tucker measure became the law of the land. The test oath was obligatory to voting, while carpetbaggers took steps to confiscate and escheat all church property above $50,000.

Meeting fire with fire, Taylor recommended that all monogamists take the oath to keep control at the polls. Most church property had been deeded to local associations, and payment of tithing had ceased. "But Bishops are authorized to accept voluntary donations or offerings from the people," he wrote to Erastus Snow, "and to hold them subject to the order of the president of the church."

The *Tribune* was outraged as Mormons by the thousands took the test oath. Taylor chuckled at the *Deseret News* response:

> The professed object was to force the "Mormons" to agree to obey the law. Now that the majority . . . are responding to the demand, those who demanded it accuse the "Mormons" of "monstrous depravity" for complying. . . . If they had refused they would have been denounced as rebels and disloyal ingrates for spurning the offer of political salvation. And now that they submit, their compliance is proclaimed as "moral rottenness."

The *News* further pointed out that despite all the hullabaloo, the last thing the Gentile ring wanted was to see plural marriage set aside.

> It has often been said that the abandonment of polygamy by the "Mormons" would be the worst misfortune that could happen to their maligners. Nothing would be so disastrous to the . . . ambitious wire-pullers and their pious and profane toadies and tools, than the abolition of the theory and practice which they pretend to be anxious to suppress. Everybody who understands the situation knows that the local plotters care nothing whatever for polygamy, except as a popular cry in their interest.
>
> What they want and all they are after is possession of the Territory, its offices and its treasury.[14]

But Taylor realized that the *News* circulated only among the Saints. The *Tribune* went on the wires to the outside world.

Again in May, two months after passage of the Edmunds-Tucker Law, Taylor once more repudiated efforts at appeasement. Writing to F. S. Richards and to John Sharp, who had been negotiating with the Utah Commission, he declared, "It is all very well to talk glibly about compromising and arranging for dispensing with polygamy," but this was a subject on which the commissioners were "blindly ignorant."

---

14 March 15, 1887.

They cannot measure its tremendous consequences . . . if we offended our God by repudiating the commands He has given us . . . and their suggestions and recommendations . . . would only have the effect to destroy us.[15]

George Q. Cannon didn't co-sign these two letters. Cannon frankly was now in opposition to the church president on the matter of compromise. He was at Salt Lake more than he was at the DO. At long last, the *Tribune*'s conviction that Cannon was running the church had a basis of fact.

Reason was that John Taylor was a dying man.

His iron constitution had collapsed. The physical clock had stopped, reversed itself, and was running backwards. The foods he'd loved all his life now nauseated him. His stomach would hold nothing except liquids, a little milk, ice cream, cider or carrot juice; but primarily he sustained his dwindling vitality with stimulants, tea with a pony of rum, a cup of grog, glass of beer.

Each day while shaving he saw the change in the mirror. Each day he looked more and more like his father and grandfathers. He was returning to his ancestors.

Ironically, the clock had reversed itself coincidental with passage of the Edmunds-Tucker Bill. At the very time he needed strength, it was taken away. Edema puffed ankles, wrists, and abdomen. It was difficult to grasp a pen; the signature quavered. Joints seemed to be rusty hinges. His strength was gone; moving a chair took all the effort he had. Exercise,

---

[15] Regarding this capitulation, the prestigious German scholar, Eduard Meyer, said, "with the act of submission of 1890 [setting aside the practice of polygamy], the history of the Mormon Church reached its end; the further destiny of the church can, therefore, demand no more deep interest. . . . The religion which sought to overcome America and to achieve mastery of the world," he said, became just another sect. *Ursprung und Geschichte der Mormonen.* Certainly this conclusion would be most emphatically challenged by the modern church. We must bear in mind that belief in continual revelation is basic doctrine, and such guidance means there will be change; if there was no need of change, there would be no necessity for divine guidance.

However, internal historians have corroborated Meyer's appraisal of the overwhelming importance of the pioneer period. Whitney's *History of Utah* devotes 3,061 pages to events up to the Manifesto, and concludes, "It is not the author's purpose to here portray the wonderous changes that have taken place since the issuance of that notable declaration." The seven-volume *History of the Church* (known as the *Documentary History*) has more than 4,000 pages regarding events before the migration to Utah, and ends at Winter Quarters. The six-volume *Comprehensive History of the Church* devotes more than 3,000 pages to events prior to the Manifesto, and only 382 pages to the modern era from 1890 to the date of its publication in 1930. Success, peace, booming membership, great wealth, and friendship with the world obviously isn't as interesting to historians as the great pioneer fight for a dazzling ideal.

that marvelous cure-all, now tore him apart; a game of quoits made ankles and wrists throb and swell. He had to have help getting dressed. He wore house slippers; his feet no longer would go into his shoes.

But he wouldn't go to bed. He had never bowed to an enemy, and he wouldn't to death. He refused to see a doctor.

Mary Ann and Maggie came to the DO to attend their husband. They treated Josephine politely, but it was difficult for them, and for her.

When finally L. John Nuttall brought Dr. William F. Anderson of the Deseret Hospital to the DO, Taylor grudgingly submitted to examination. Then he asked the doctor for his frank opinion. Dr. Anderson said that he really could do nothing to help, but the symptoms could be relieved with proper diet and medication.

Taylor thanked him, and bid him good-bye. *Fathead. He'd show them. He'd get well despite what they thought.*

He refused to eat the diet or take the medicine.[16]

He rejected the suggestion to make a will. Plenty of time for that. Right now, there were more important things to attend to. He was fighting a battle against the Edmunds-Tucker Law, and against the coterie of appeasers within the church leadership.

Let them plot and scheme. He was prophet, seer, and revelator. He had taken a stand, and they couldn't counter it without his approval.

In mid-June he revived. He could eat again—sparingly, but solid food. He could enjoy a game of quoits with the guards, checkers at night. "Our own health is moderately good, better than it was some time ago," he wrote George Teasdale, president of the British mission, on the fifteenth, for which he was "sincerely grateful to the Father of all mercies for His blessings." He was on the mend.

The enemies of the church, he reported, had been defeated.

> It is evident that they are by this time entirely satisfied that they have signally failed in the scheme they devised against us and sought to give effect to by the . . . passage of the Edmunds-Tucker Bill. For this deliverance we give God the glory . . . because nothing but His power could have thwarted the extreme measures that were concocted for our hurt.

The revival was brief, and Taylor retired to his room; but he sat in an armchair, refusing to go to bed.

"It becomes my painful duty to advise you concerning President Taylor's health," Cannon wrote to Wilford Woodruff.

> For a number of weeks past his health has been seriously impaired, and he has steadily declined in vigor, though he, himself, has constantly asserted that he would recover. . . . But now I am forced to the conclusion

---

[16] For Taylor's defiance of approaching death, see journals of L. John Nuttall and Samuel Bateman, also letters of George Q. Cannon during this period.

that his condition is dangerous, and . . . he cannot last for any great period.

On the last day of June Taylor bowed to the inevitable, and signed his will. It was witnessed by two guards at the DO. Cannon was in Salt Lake, for on this day delegates convened to write a constitution for the proposed state of Utah that would forever prohibit polygamy. It finished the task within a week.

At 10:30 on the morning of July 7, Cannon met with Lorenzo Snow, Franklin D. Richards, Moses Thatcher, Heber J. Grant, and John W. Taylor of the Quorum of the Twelve[17] at the old adobe president's office, between the Lion and Beehive houses, as guards patroled the high cobblestone wall. Nuttall recorded:

> Prest Cannon suggested that the Presidents of Stakes, their Counselors, and Bishops and their Counselors be seen and be told that the First Presidency and Twelve see no reason why the Latter-day Saints who are eligible to vote should not vote for this State constitution, and in doing so they would not offend God nor violate His laws.

However, this abrupt reversal of long-held policy would be a shock to many. Inasmuch as it couldn't be explained, the least said about it the better.

> He thought that the giving of reasons and the indulging in argument should be avoided. That our newspapers should say but little, and that our public speakers should be exceedingly careful in their utterances, lest our enemies should take advantage of what might be said.

Cannon delegated those present to be responsible for visiting every stake and ward in the church with the message.

At the DO, Taylor surprised everyone by appearing, shaved, combed, and dressed, for breakfast, striding from his room with eyes bright and hungry as a wolf. He sat down and in a voice with its old timbre called for ham and eggs. Watching the women bustling about, exchanging awed looks of ecstasy as they prepared the meal, he said what a blessing it was to feel good again, and to have three beautiful wives here with him.

After breakfast, Josephine read the accumulated mail to him, and he indicated replies. A six-page letter from Joseph A. West concerned a haven in Mexico. West and David Eccles had bought a small ranch near the Mormon settlement of Colonia Diaz, and he proposed that Taylor move the DO there.

> I am satisfied . . . that your own personal condition demands that you have a rest & enjoy that freedom of air, exercise, &c, that you cannot get

---

17 The other seven members of the Twelve were on the dodge.

there. Again, the rigors of another winter will soon be upon us when your condition . . . will doubtless be very much worse than at present. Mexico possesses a delightful and balmy winter climate, and . . . would be a place of absolute freedom & safety to you.

He proposed installing a telegraph line the 90 miles to Deming, New Mexico. "The cost would not exceed 2,000 dollars." Business could be conducted in cipher, using West's name. He outlined methods of traveling to Mexico in secret, either by sleeper stateroom or "A freight car could be fitted up & well supplied with all the necessities . . . under the supervision of Bro Sharp, and be Way Billed Via the U P"; or "If you could not go thus, a dozen other plans could be devised for your safety."

Mary Ann, Margaret, and Josephine waited expectantly for their husband's reply. He considered a few moments, then with a smile said to thank Brother West, but to inform him that the president had other plans. He quoted the great promise that had ruled his life, as he lived without compromise or concession to gain the Kingdom of God or nothing.

> Ye shall come forth in the first resurrection . . . and shall inherit thrones, kingdoms, principalities, and powers, dominions, all heights and depths . . . [and be with those] who shall pass by the angels, and . . . be gods, because they have no end. . . . Then shall they be gods, because they have all power, and the angels are subject unto them.
>
> Verily, verily, I say unto you, except ye abide by my law ye cannot attain to this glory. . . . But if ye receive me in the world, then shall ye know me, and shall receive your exaltation; then where I am ye shall be also. . . .
>
> For I am the Lord thy God, and will be with thee even unto the end of the world, and through all eternity; for verily I seal upon you your exaltation, and prepare a throne for you in the kingdom of my Father. . . .[18]

Tell Brother West, he said, that he expected to go to another place soon, a destination even better than Mexico.

He began the journey a few days later, on the evening of July 25, 1887.

---

[18] D&C, 132.

Bibliography

ABBREVIATIONS

CHC   *A Comprehensive History of the Church of Jesus Christ of Latter-day Saints. Century I* (B. H. Roberts)

D&C   *Doctrine and Covenants of the Church of Jesus Christ of Latter-day Saints*

DHC   Smith, Joseph. *History of the Church of Jesus Christ of Latter-day Saints. Period I. History of Joseph Smith, the Prophet, by Himself* (Joseph Smith) This work is known as the "Documentary History of the Church."

JD   *Journal of Discourses*

JH   *Journal History of the Church*

UHQ   *Utah Historical Quarterly*

SOURCE MATERIALS

During the fifty-one years of John Taylor's affiliation with the church, the Mormons were continually at war with the "world"—local, state, or national government. It is vital to remember this in assessing source materials.

In their record of events, the purpose was to defend the faith, not write history. They did so with passion in the heat of battle, and their account bears every earmark of war propaganda, including the customary atrocity stories. Ordinarily, when passions cool and time gives perspective, the history of a war is rewritten with dispassionate objectivity. This has been impossible with the Mormon story, because the original writers were prophets of God, whose account cannot be altered without reflecting on their veracity.

In order to gain an objective viewpoint, therefore, it is necessary to look at the other side of the coin, the account of events as seen by participants on the "enemy" side. To paste the label "anti-Mormon" on all such material, and reject it, can satisfy only apologists.

What would be the public impression of the Watergate scandal in Washington, if the only acceptable explanation was President Nixon's original statement of the affair? If we ignored court records, newspaper accounts, testimony of those who turned state's evidence, and the results of the congressional investigation, we would have a limited and distorted version of Watergate. And yet, regarding the Mormon troubles in Missouri, to use one example, official history ignores Gentile newspaper accounts, statements of defectors from the faith, the report of the governor to the state legislature, the testimony before the court of Judge Austin King, and the evidence of a Senate investigation (*Senate Document 189*).

Small wonder that care must be taken to pick a way through the jungle.

My brother Raymond, collaborator on this work, was a most perceptive student of Mormon history and culture. Sam Weller, the big independent book dealer of Utah, called Raymond "the Walter Winchell of Salt Lake," who "knew more about what was going on than the *Tribune*." Raymond had a remarkably open mind regarding research. He also had a method of evaluation. "Read Mormon apologists for facts, and ignore their conclusions," he said. This advice can produce surprising results. Even the most abject apologists, who write for approval rather than from truth, try to shoehorn in facts by hook or crook.

Juanita Brooks, the historian's historian of Mormonism, made a cogent appraisal of the outpourings of the captive press of Utah in commenting on one of its star contributors. "He's not a historian at all," she said. "He's a lawyer, proving a case."

There is an identical problem with the opposite side of the coin. Much "anti-Mormon" material is written with venom. From John C. Bennett's *History of the Saints* in 1842 to the dedicated work of Jerald and Sandra Tanner of the modern day, it shows the fervent desire to demolish Mormonism. However, Bennett and the Tanners unearth truth which apologists carefully ignore or conceal. Again, we should read for facts and ignore conclusions.

THE WORKS OF JOHN TAYLOR

Paul Anthon Nielson's "An Annotated Bibliography of the Works of President John Taylor," is an important reference listing 308 writings and speeches. It is at Brigham Young University.

John Taylor was a prolific letter writer. Much of his correspondence survives. While in the mission field, he and other elders saved letters received from each other, and mailed them back for preservation. All of Taylor's later correspondence, while he was leader of the church, has been preserved. Raymond copied at least a thousand letters in the church archives (by typewriter; xerox not allowed). The result of this heroic research is on deposit at the University of Utah.

While the 26 volumes of the *Journal of Discourses* contain many of John Taylor's talks over a period of thirty-two years, we must remember that they were carefully edited before publication. A comparison with the unexpurgated version published by the Salt Lake *Tribune* can show surprising differences. The *Deseret News* published speeches not included in the *Journal of Discourses*, such as his fire-eating Fourth of July oration of 1861, and the *Tribune* published unvarnished accounts of "The Ruffian's" talks too strong for the *Deseret News*.

Some of the more important works of John Taylor are listed individually in this bibliography.

NEWSPAPERS QUOTED

Specific dates are indicated in the text.
Arkansas Intelligence.
Alton (Illinois) *Telegraph.*
Boston *Watchman.*
Chicago *News.*
—— *Tribune.*
Deseret News (Salt Lake), 1850–87.
The Evening and the Morning Star (Independence, Missouri), 1832–34; this was the first Mormon newspaper.
Idaho Statesman.
Interpreter Anglais et Francais (Boulogne, France), 1850.
Indianapolis *Sentinel.*
London *Daily News.*
—— *Dispatch.*
Manx Liberal (Douglas, Isle of Man), 1840.
Manx Sun (Douglas, Isle of Man), 1840.
The Mormon (New York), edited by John Taylor, 1856–57.
Mormon Tribune (Salt Lake), 1870.
Nauvoo (Illinois) *Expositor*; one issue, 1844.
—— *Neighbor*, edited by John Taylor, 1843–45.
—— *Wasp*, edited by John Taylor, 1842–43.
New York *Graphic.*
—— *Herald.*
—— *Independent.*
—— *Mirror.*
—— *Post.*
—— *Sun.*
—— *Tribune.*
—— *World.*
Omaha *Bee.*
—— *Herald.*
—— *Republican.*
Quincy (Illinois) *Argus.*
St. Louis *Gazette.*
St. Paul *Pioneer Press.*
Salt Lake *Herald*, 1870–87.
—— *Telegraph*, 1864–70.
—— *Tribune*, 1871–87.
Sangamo (Illinois) *Journal.*
San Francisco *Chronicle.*
—— *Examiner.*
San Jose (California) *Mercury.*

Springfield (Massachusetts) *Republican.*
Syracuse *Standard.*
Times and Seasons (Nauvoo), edited by John Taylor, 1839–46.
Union Vedette (Salt Lake).
Valley Tan (Salt Lake).
Woman's Advocate (New York), 1856.
Warsaw (Illinois) *Signal,* 1839–46.

PERIODICALS

Anti-Polygamy Standard, monthly (Salt Lake), 1880–83. On file, Salt Lake City Library.

Congressional Globe.

Dialogue, a Journal of Mormon Thought. Quarterly, 1956 to present. A most excellent magazine, particularly considering that it is the first objective periodical published within the Mormon culture since the short-lived *Utah Magazine* a century previously.

Edmunds, Senator George F., "Political Aspects of Mormonism," *Harper's Magazine,* January 1882.

Ellsworth, George, "Hubert Howe Bancroft and the History of Utah," *Utah Historical Quarterly,* April 1954.

Etoile du Deseret, edited by John Taylor (Paris), 1851.

Field, Kate, "Mormon Blood Atonement," *North American Review,* 1886.

Latter-day Saints Messenger and Advocate, monthly, Kirtland, Ohio. October 1834–September 1837.

Lye, William Frank, "Edward Wheelock Tullidge, the Mormons' Rebel Historian," *Utah Historical Quarterly,* April 1960.

The Latter-day Saints Millennial Star (Liverpool), 1840–87.

Miller, George, "Correspondence of Bishop George Miller with the *Northern Islander,* from his first Acquaintance with Mormonism up to near the close of his Life," 1855. Published as pamphlet by Wingate Watson, Burlington, Wisconsin, 1916. Parallel material published by H. W. Mills, "De Tal Palo Tal Astrilla." *Publications* of the Historical Society of Southern California, 1915–17. The two accounts differ in significant detail.

Morgan, Dale L., "The State of Deseret," *Utah Historical Quarterly;* April, July, October 1940.

Nebeker, John, "Early Utah Justice," *Utah Historical Quarterly,* July 1930.

Newsletter, "Friends of the Brigham Young University Library," March 1971. Significant as documentation that Joseph Smith married a woman with a living husband.

Taylor, John, "Ecclesiastical Control in Utah," with reply by Governor Eli H. Murray, *North American Review,* January 1884.

Truth, monthly (Salt Lake), 1935–56. This periodical is invaluable in reflecting the pioneer attitude toward plural marriage.

Tullidge, Edward W., *Tullidge's Quarterly Magazine,* Salt Lake, 1880–81.

Utah Genealogical Magazine, 21:88.

Utah Magazine (Salt Lake), 1868–70.
Woman's Exponent (Salt Lake), 1872–87.
Zion's Panier, edited by John Taylor (Germany), 1851.

BOOKS, DOCUMENTS, AND JOURNALS

Allred, B. Harvey. *A Leaf in Review.* Caldwell, Idaho: Caxton, 1933.

Alter, J. Cecil. *Early Utah Journalism.* Salt Lake: Utah Historical Society, 1938. Reprint. Westport, Conn.: Greenwood Press.

Anderson, Nels. *Desert Saints; The Mormon Frontier in Utah.* Chicago: University of Chicago Press, 1942. Filled with pioneer anecdotes.

Arrington, Leonard J. "The Settlement of the Brigham Young Estate, 1877–1879," *Pacific Historical Review*, February 1952. Excellent account from the establishment viewpoint.

———. *Great Basin Kingdom, an Economic History of the Latter-day Saints, 1830–1900.* Cambridge, Mass.: Harvard University Press, 1958.

Ashton, Wendell J. *Voice of the West.* New York: Duell, Sloan & Pearce, 1950. The story of the *Deseret News.*

Bancroft, Hubert Howe. *History of Utah.* San Francisco: The History Co., 1890.

———. *Works, XXXIX, Literary Industries,* San Francisco: The History Co., 1890.

Baskin, Robert N. *Reminiscences of Early Utah.* Salt Lake: Published by author, 1914. Of value as viewpoint of Gentile judge and mayor of Salt Lake.

The Beet Sugar Story. Washington, D.C.: U.S. Beet Sugar Association, 1959.

Beadle, J. H. *Life in Utah.* Philadelphia: National Publishing Co., 1870.

Bennett, John C. *The History of the Saints; or An Exposé of Joe Smith and Mormonism.* Boston: Leland & Whiting, 1842.

Berrett, William E. and Burton, Alma P. *Readings in LDS Church History, from Original Manuscripts,* Vol. II. Salt Lake: Deseret Book, 1967.

The Bible & Polygamy. Salt Lake: 1870. Pamphlet, containing "Discussion between Professor Orson Pratt, Sen. and Dr. J. P. Newman, Chaplain of the U.S. Senate, in the New Tabernacle, Salt Lake City, August 12, 13, and 14, 1870."

Bishop, Lynn L. and Steven L. *The Keys of the Priesthood Illustrated.* Draper, Utah: Preview & Review Publishers, 1971. An extended treatment of the political Kingdom of God, the Council of Fifty, and plural marriage. A total of seventy-two pages deals with the John Taylor revelation of 1886.

Bolton, Curtis E. *Diary of Curtis E. Bolton.* Collection of Mormon Diaries, BYU.

A Book of Commandments for the Government of the Church of Christ, organized according to law, on the 6th of April, 1830. First compilation of Joseph Smith's revelations. Zion [Independence], 1833.

Bowles, Samuel. *Across the Continent: A Summer's Journey to the Rocky Mountains, the Mormons and the Pacific States.* New York: Hurd & Houghton, 1865.

Brodie, Fawn M. *No man knows my history; The Life of Joseph Smith, the Mormon Prophet.* New York: Knopf, 1945, 1971. Despite an unrelenting attack on this book for more than a quarter century, it remains the only definitive biography of the prophet. Mrs. Brodie reported that when "minor errors" were called to her attention, she corrected them during seven printings and a revised edition (1971). Thus Mormon scholars have inadvertently performed a most helpful service in buttressing the documentation of the book. Mrs. Brodie was un-churched for writing it, and it is a commentary on the managed media in Zion that with all the denunciation of the Brodie book, no Mormon had the courage to defend the prophet by publishing a more acceptable biography for the outside world.

Brooks, Juanita. *The History of the Jews in Utah and Idaho.* Salt Lake: Western Epics, 1973.

——. *John Doyle Lee—Pioneer—Builder—Scapegoat.* Glendale, Calif.: Arthur H. Clark, 1962.

——. *The Mountain Meadows Massacre.* Stanford University, 1950. Also Norman, Okla.: University of Oklahoma Press, 1970.

Burton, Richard F. *The City of the Saints, and Across The Rocky Mountains to California.* London: Longman, Green, Longman & Roberts, 1861.

Cannon, Abraham H. *Journal.* Archives, Church Historical Department.

Carmer, Carl. *The Farm Boy and the Angel.* New York: Doubleday, 1970. The church went outside to find a man qualified to do a definitive biography of Joseph Smith, to be published throughout the world. Certainly there couldn't be a more qualified scholar and historian than Carl Carmer. But then he began finding out what the kind offer of reading his manuscript for "accuracy" really meant, as apologists rejected everything except the missionary story. Carmer struggled for almost two decades, trying to do the impossible, maintain his integrity and at the same time satisfy apologists. When the book finally appeared, it was not the definitive work he had intended, but a small and rather superficial book. Gentile reviewers were surprised that he had accepted the story of Joseph Smith so uncritically. As a culminating irony, the book was banned by the church, because he had not followed niggling "suggestions" in the final draft.

Caswall, Rev. Henry. *The City of the Mormons, or Three Days at Nauvoo.* London: J. Rivington, 1842.

Chandless, William. *A Visit to Salt Lake.* London: Smith, Elder & Co., 1857. Reprinted, New York: AMS Press, 1971.

"Correspondence, Orders, etc., in relation to the disturbances with the Mormons; and the evidence given before the Hon. Austin A. King, Judge of the Fifth Judicial Circuit of the State of Missouri, at the Court-house in Richmond, in a criminal court of inquiry, begun November 12, 1838, on the trial of Joseph Smith, Jr., and others, for high treason and other crimes against the State." Published by order of the General Assembly, Fayette, Missouri, 1841. Also published, in part, as *Senate Document 189.*

Corrill, John. *A Brief History of the Church of Christ of Latter Day Saints (Commonly Called Mormons), Including an Account of Their Doctrine and Discipline, with the Reasons of the Author for Leaving the Church.* St. Louis, 1839. Published by the author.

Cowley, Matthias. "Reminiscences of Prest John Taylor." Typescript of talk, October 4, 1925. BYU.

DeVoto, Bernard. *The Year of Decision, 1846.* 6th ed. Boston: Houghton Mifflin, 1961.

Doctrine and Covenants of the Church of Jesus Christ of Latter-day Saints. Kirtland, Ohio: 1835, and subsequent editions.

Durham, Reed C., and Heath, Steven H. *Succession in the Church Presidency.* Salt Lake: Bookcraft, 1970.

Drummond, W. W. Letter to U.S. Attorney General Jeremiah S. Black, March 30, 1857.

Dwyer, Robert Joseph. *The Gentile Comes to Utah.* Washington: The Catholic University of America Press, 1941.

Eagan, Howard. *Pioneering the West, 1846 to 1878.* Richmond, Utah: Howard R. Eagan Estate, 1917.

Evans, John Henry. *Charles Coulson Rich, Pioneer Builder of the West.* New York: Macmillan, 1936.

————. *Joseph Smith, an American Prophet.* New York: Macmillan 1933.

Ferry, Jeanette H. *Industrial Home of Utah.* Salt Lake: Salt Lake Lithographing Co., 1893.

Furniss, Norman F. *The Mormon Conflict, 1850–1859.* New Haven: Yale University Press, 1960.

Gibbs, Josiah. *Lights and Shadows of Mormonism.* Salt Lake: Salt Lake *Tribune* Publishing Co., 1909.

Gibson, A. M. *Have Mormons Any Rights?* "Brief in re Senate Bill No. 1c." Pamphlet, February 18, 1886.

Goodman, Louis S., and Gilman, Alfred. *The Pharmacological Basis of Therapeutics.* 2nd. ed. New York: Macmillan, 1955.

Hafen, LeRoy R. and Ann W. *Handcarts to Zion.* Glendale, California: Arthur H. Clark Co., 1960.

Hansen, Harold I. *A History and Influence of the Mormon Theater from 1839–1869.* Provo: Brigham Young University Press, 1967.

Hansen, Klaus J. *Quest for Empire: The Political Kingdom of God and the Council of Fifty in Mormon History.* East Lansing: Michigan State University Press, 1967.

Hatch, Nelle Spilsbury. *Colonia Juarez, an Intimate Account of a Mormon Village.* Salt Lake: Deseret Book Co., 1954.

Hickman, Bill (Written by J. H. Beadle). *Brigham's Destroying Angel: Being the Life, Confession, and Startling Disclosures of the Notorious Bill Hickman, the Danite Chief of Utah.* Salt Lake City: Shepard Publishing Co., 1904.

Hirshson, Stanley P. *The Lion of the Lord: A Biography of Brigham Young.* New York: Knopf, 1969.

Howe, Eber D. *Mormonism Unvailed, or a Faithful Account of that Singular Imposition and Delusion, from its Rise to the Present Time.* Painesville, Ohio: 1834.

Hulbert, Archer Butler. *Forty-Niners.* Boston: Little, Brown, 1931.

Hyde, John. *Mormonism, Its Leaders and Designs.* New York: W. P. Fetridge & Co., 1857.

"Isles of Man—Wight—Jersey." Pamphlet, Daughters of Utah Pioneers, 1973.

Jensen, Juliaetta Bateman. *Little Gold Pieces.* Salt Lake City: Stanway Printing Co., 1948.

Jenson, Andrew. *Autobiography.* Salt Lake: Deseret News, 1938.

——. *Biographical Encyclopedia.* Salt Lake: Andrew Jenson History Co., Vol. 1, 1901.

——. *Church Chronology.* Salt Lake: Deseret News, 1899.

Jesse, Dean C. "A Comparative Study and Evaluation of the Latter-day Saints and the Fundamentalist Views Pertaining to the Practice of Plural Marriage." Master's thesis, Brigham Young University, 1959.

Journal of Discourses. 26 volumes. Liverpool, Published by various presidents of the British Mission. 1854–86.

Journal History of the Church, 1830–87. Church Historical Department.

Kane, Thomas L. *The Mormons.* Philadelphia: King & Baird, 1850.

Kort, D. L. *History of Daviess County.* Reprinted in Roberts, B. H., *The Missouri Persecutions,* Salt Lake, 1890.

Kraut, Ogden. *Seer Stones.* Dugway, Utah: Pioneer Press, n.d.

Lamb, Rev. M. T. *The Golden Bible; or, the Book of Mormon, Is it from God?* New York: Ward & Drummond, 1887.

Larson, Andrew Karl. *I Was Called to Dixie.* Salt Lake: Deseret News Press, 1961.

Larson, Gustiv O. *The "Americanization" of Utah for Statehood.* San Marino, California: Huntington Library Pubns., 1971.

Lee, John D. *Mormonism Unveiled; or the Life and Confessions of the Late Mormon Bishop, John D. Lee.* St. Louis: 1877.

Linn, William Alexander. *The Story of the Mormons.* New York, 1902. Reissued, New York: Russell & Russell, 1963.

Lundwall, N. B. *Assorted Gems of Priceless Value.* Salt Lake: Bookcraft, 1944.

——. *The Fate of the Persecutors of the Prophet Joseph Smith.* Salt Lake: Bookcraft, 1952.

——. *Temples of the Most High.* Salt Lake: Bookcraft, 1968.

McBride, William. Letter from Captain McBride of the Mormon militia from "Head Qrs., Tooele Expedition No. 3, Third Pasture Creek, June 24, 1851," during Indian troubles, requisitioning arsenic and strychnine to poison the wells and meat of the Lamanites. Utah Historical Society.

Malmquist, O. N. *The First 100 Years; a History of the Salt Lake Tribune, 1871–1971.* Salt Lake: Utah State Historical Society, 1971.

Messages of the First Presidency, compiled by James R. Clark; Volumes I, II, and III. Salt Lake: Bookcraft, 1965 and 1966. A valuable collection of "Epistles" and official statements. The first volume in particular is marred by uncritical use of secondary sources.

Meyer, Eduard. *Ursprung und Geschichte der Mormonen.* Halle: Max Niemeyer, 1912. English translation, "The Origin and History of the Mormons." Salt Lake: University of Utah, 1961.

Morgan, Dale L. *The Great Salt Lake.* New York: Bobbs-Merrill Co., 1947.

The Most Holy Principle, volumes 1 and 2. Murray, Utah: Gems Publishing Co., 1970. A collection of source materials on plural marriage.

Nelson, Lowry. *The Mormon Settlements in Alberta*. Toronto, n.d.

Nibley, Preston. *Brigham Young, The Man and His Work*. Independence: Zion's Printing & Publishing Co., 1936.

Nuttall, L. John. *Journal*. John Taylor's personal secretary kept a detailed diary. Unfortunately, it has been heavily censored. BYU, Special Collections.

Parkin, Max H. *Conflict at Kirtland*. Master's thesis, Salt Lake: 1966.

Patton, Annaleone D. *California Mormons by Sail and Trail*. Salt Lake: Deseret Book Co., 1961.

Peterson, LaMar. *Hearts Made Glad*. Unpublished monograph regarding drinking habits of Joseph Smith and other pioneers.

Polk, James K. *Diary*. Vol. I, pp. 443–46. June 2, 3, 5, 1846.

Pratt, Orson. *Works*. Liverpool: R. James, 1851.

Pratt, Parley P. *Autobiography*. Salt Lake: Russell Brothers, 1874.

Provo, Pioneer Mormon City. American Guide Series. Portland: Binfords & Mort, 1942.

Pyper, George D. *The Romance of an Old Playhouse*. Salt Lake: Seagull Press, 1928.

————. *Stories of Latter-day Saint Hymns*. Salt Lake: Deseret News Press, 1939.

"Report to the Honorable Legislature of the State of Missouri," Caldwell County, Missouri, 1838.

Richards, Ralph T. *Of Medicine, Hospitals, and Doctors*. Salt Lake: University of Utah, 1953. Pioneer Utah medical practice.

Richardson, Albert D. *Beyond the Mississippi*. Hartford, Conn.: American Publishing Co., 1867.

Richardson, Arthur M. *The Life and Ministry of John Morgan*. Salt Lake: Nicholas G. Morgan, Sr., 1965.

Roberts, B. H. *A Comprehensive History of the Church of Jesus Christ of Latter-day Saints. Century I.* 6 volumes. Salt Lake: Deseret News Press, 1930.

————. *The Life of John Taylor, Third President of the Church of Jesus Christ of Latter-day Saints*. Salt Lake: George Q. Cannon & Sons, 1892.

————. *The Missouri Persecutions*. Salt Lake: George Q. Cannon & Sons, 1900.

————. *The Rise and Fall of Nauvoo*. Salt Lake: Deseret News, 1900.

Robinson, Phil. *Sinners and Saints*. Boston: Roberts Brothers, 1883. Reprint, New York: AMS Press, 1972.

Romney, Thomas Cottam, *The Mormon Colonies in Mexico*. Salt Lake: Deseret Book Co., 1938.

Scott, Reva (Stanley), *Samuel Brannan and the Golden Fleece*. New York: Macmillan, 1946.

Senate Document 189. February 15, 1841.

Smith, Joseph. *History of the Church of Jesus Christ of Latter-day Saints. Period I. History of Joseph Smith, the Prophet, by Himself.* 7 volumes. Introduction and notes by B. H. Roberts. Salt Lake: "Published by the Church," 1902–12. Known as "Documentary History of the Church."

————. *The Pearl of Great Price*. Liverpool: F. D. Richards, 1851.

Smith, Joseph Fielding. *Life of President Joseph F. Smith*. Salt Lake: Deseret Books, 1938.

Smith, Joseph III. *Joseph Smith III and the Restoration*. Independence: Herald House, 1952. Memoirs of the prophet's son.

Smith, Lucy Mack. *Biographical Sketches of Joseph Smith the Prophet and his Progenitors for Many Generations*. Liverpool: Orson Pratt, 1853. Reprinted, New York: Arno Press, 1969.

Spencer, Clarissa Young, and Harmer, Mabel. *Brigham Young at Home*. Salt Lake: Deseret Bk, 1963.

Stanley, Reva. *The Archer of Paradise*. Caldwell, Idaho: Caxton Printers, 1937.

Stenhouse, Fanny. *"Tell It All"*: *The Story of a Life's Experience in Mormonism*. Hartford: A. D. Worthington & Co., 1875.

Stenhouse, T. B. H. *The Rocky Mountain Saints*. New York: D. Appleton & Co., 1873.

Stewart, John J. *The Glory of Mormonism*. Salt Lake: Mercury Publishing Co., 1963.

Stone, Jesse Burke. *An Event of Underground Days*. Pamphlet, Salt Lake, 1931.

Stout, Wayne. *History of Utah*, Volume I, 1870–1896. Salt Lake: published by the author, 1967. This work is almost completely ignored by historians. However, it is valuable by reason of copious quotations from newspapers on events of the times.

Sugar company meeting *Minutes*. March 17, 1853. Copy at University of Utah.

Tanner, Jerald and Sandra. *Joseph Smith and Polygamy*. Salt Lake: Modern Microfilm, 1966.

———. *Mormonism—Shadow or Reality?* Enlarged edition, Salt Lake: Modern Microfilm, 1972.

Taylor, Fred G. *A Saga of Sugar*. Salt Lake: Utah-Idaho Sugar Co., 1944.

Taylor–Colfax Discussion. Pamphlet, "The Mormon Question. Being a Speech of Vice-President Schuyler Colfax, at Salt Lake City, a Reply thereto by Elder John Taylor; and a Letter of Vice-President Colfax Published in the *New York Independent*, with Elder Taylor's Reply." Salt Lake: Deseret News, 1870.

Taylor, John. *The Government of God*. Liverpool: S. W. Richards, 1852.

———. *Journal*. Church Historical Department.

———. "Notes" on "the lesser-known wives of President John Taylor," Brigham Young University, Special Collections.

———. *The Mediation and Atonement of Our Lord and Savior Jesus Christ*. Salt Lake: Deseret News, 1882.

———. "1886 Revelation; A Revelation of the Lord to John Taylor." Pamphlet, 1963. n.p.

———. Nine revelations of John Taylor, dated June 25 and 26, 1882; June 27, 1882; late June or early July 1882; October 13, 1882; April 14, 1883; April 28, 1883; May 1884; December 25, 1884; September 27, 1886. Church Historical Department. Typescript in possession of author. Some of these revelations were published in various foreign editions of the *Doctrine and Covenants*.

————. "A short account of the MURDERS, ROBBERIES, BURNINGS, THEFTS, and other outrages committed by the MOB and MILITIA of the State of Missouri, upon the LATTER-DAY SAINTS. The Persecutions they have endured for their Religion, and their Banishment from that State by the Authorities thereof." Springfield, Illinois: published by author, 1839.

Townsend, George Alfred. *The Mormon Trials in Salt Lake City*. New York: American News Co., 1871.

Tullidge, Edward W. *History of Salt Lake City and Its Founders*. Salt Lake: Star Printing Co., 1886. Reprinted, New York: AMS Press.

————. *Life of Joseph Smith*. Salt Lake, 1878. Revised edition, Plano, Illinois, 1880. Reprinted of 1880 edition, New York: AMS Press.

————. *The Women of Mormondom*. New York: Tullidge & Crandall, 1877.

Turner, J. B. *Mormonism in All Ages; or the Rise, Progress, and Causes of Mormonism*. New York: Platt & Peters, 1842.

Twain, Mark. *Roughing It*. Hartford: American Publishing Co., 1872.

A Vineyard By the Bay. San Mateo: San Mateo Stake, 1968.

Waite, Mrs. C. V. *The Mormon Prophet and His Harem*. Cambridge: Riverside Press, 1866.

Wallace, Irving. *The Twenty-Seventh Wife*. New York: Simon and Schuster, 1961.

Werner, M. R. *Brigham Young*. New York: Harcourt, Brace, Jovanovich, 1925. The only definitive biography of the pioneer leader.

West, Franklin L. *Life of Franklin D. Richards*. Salt Lake: Deseret News Press, 1924.

Whitney, Orson F. *History of Utah*. 4 volumes, Salt Lake: George Q. Cannon & Sons, 1892–1904.

————. *Life of Heber C. Kimball*. Salt Lake: Kimball Family, 1888.

Williams, Zina Young. "Short Reminiscent Sketches of Karl G. Maeser." Typescript, Brigham Young University, n.d.

Woodruff, Wilford. *Journal*. Church Historical Department.

Wyl, Dr. W. (Wilhelm Ritter von Wymetal). *Mormon Portraits*. Salt Lake: Tribune Printing & Publishing Co., 1886.

Young, Anna Eliza. *Wife No. 19, or the Story of a Life in Bondage*. Hartford: Dustin, Gilman & Co., 1876.

"Last Moments of President Brigham Young." Report of doctors attending his terminal illness. *Deseret News*, August 31, 1877. Also included in pamphlet, "Particulars of the Death of Prest Brigham Young and Account of the Funeral Ceremonies." Salt Lake, 1877.

Young, Kimball. *Isn't One Wife Enough?* New York: Henry Holt, 1954. Reprinted, Westport, Conn.: Greenwood Press.

Index